MARY WEIT̶̶̶̶̶GIBBONS

The Genealogy of Women

Studies in the Humanities
Literature—Politics—Society

Guy Mermier
General Editor

Vol. 62

PETER LANG
New York • Washington, D.C./Baltimore • Bern
Frankfurt am Main • Berlin • Brussels • Vienna • Oxford

Stephen D. Kolsky

The Genealogy of Women

Studies in Boccaccio's
De mulieribus claris

PETER LANG
New York • Washington, D.C./Baltimore • Bern
Frankfurt am Main • Berlin • Brussels • Vienna • Oxford

Library of Congress Cataloging-in-Publication Data

Kolsky, Stephen.
The genealogy of women: studies in Boccaccio's
De mulieribus claris / Stephen D. Kolsky.
p. cm. — (Studies in the humanities; vol. 62)
Includes bibliographical references and index.
1. Boccaccio, Giovanni, 1313–1375. De mulieribus claris.
2. Women in literature. I. Title. II. Series: Studies
in the humanities (New York, N.Y.); v. 62.
PQ4274.D6K65   851'.1—dc21   2002010685
ISBN 0-8204-6183-0
ISSN 0742-6712

Die Deutsche Bibliothek-CIP-Einheitsaufnahme

Kolsky, Stephen D.:
The genealogy of women: studies in Boccaccio's
De mulieribus claris / Stephen D. Kolsky.
–New York; Washington, D.C./Baltimore; Bern;
Frankfurt am Main; Berlin; Brussels; Vienna; Oxford: Lang.
(Studies in the humanities; Vol. 62)
ISBN 0-8204-6183-0

The paper in this book meets the guidelines for permanence and durability
of the Committee on Production Guidelines for Book Longevity
of the Council of Library Resources.

© 2003 Peter Lang Publishing, Inc., New York
275 Seventh Avenue, 28th Floor, New York, NY 10001
www.peterlangusa.com

Printed in Germany

To my wife
helen

and to my son
daniel

Contents

𝔄𝔠𝔨𝔫𝔬𝔴𝔩𝔢𝔡𝔤𝔪𝔢𝔫𝔱𝔰

𝕿he distant origins of this project can be found in my work on Mario Equicola, which made me think about the uses of illustrious women in Boccaccio and later writers. More recently, a Fellowship at the Harvard University Center for Italian Renaissance Studies at Villa I Tatti allowed me, in the most congenial surroundings, to commence work on Boccaccio's *De mulieribus claris*. The presence of the other Fellows at Villa I Tatti was always never less than stimulating.

The book would not have progressed to its final stage without the assistance of the Australian Research Council which awarded me Small Grants in 1996, 1997 and a Large Grant that involved me in reassessing the influence of Boccaccio's Latin work. I wish to express my gratitude to Tony Stephens for his advice in the arduous process of applying for these grants. I wish to record the invaluable help provided by my research assistants, first in time to Sonya Solowko, and then to Carolyn James who read through the manuscript weeding out stylistic infelicities and other blemishes in the text. Most recently, Cynthia Troup provided me with first-rate assistance in preparing the manuscript for publication. The staff at the following libraries were particularly helpful in overcoming practical difficulties caused either by distance or other impediments: Bodleian Library, Oxford; British Library, London; Biblioteca Estense e Universitaria, Modena; Biblioteca Laurenziana, Florence; Biblioteca Nazionale Centrale, Florence; Biblioteca Riccardiana, Florence; Sächsische Landesbibliothek, Dresden; Warburg Institute, University of London, Biblioteca Apostolica Vaticana. The Inter-Library Loans Section of the Baillieu Library, University of Melbourne, enabled me to obtain essential material while remaining in Australia. Helen Hassard edited an earlier version of the first part of the book and made possible the undertaking of the entire project through her good spirits, determination and love. My son Daniel has been part of the book's history from the start, often coming along on research trips, he contributed his perspective and experiences to our travels. I am grateful to the following individuals who have helped and encouraged me in creating this book: the late Peter Armour, Victoria Kirkham, Kate Lowe, Thomas Mayer, Ian Robertson, Massimiliano Rossi, Deborah Parker, Letizia Panizza, Jan Zilkowski. My errors are all my own.

Grateful acknowledgment is made to the following for permission to reprint copyrighted material:

Stephen Kolsky
The University of Melbourne

Abbreviations

Chronicon	Eusebius, St. Jerome. *Die Chronik des Hieronymus. Hieronymi Chronicon.* ed. Rudolf Helm (Berlin: Akademie-Verlag, 1984).
De casibus	*De casibus virorum illustrium.* Vol. IX. *Tutte le opere di Giovanni Boccaccio,* ed. Pier Giorgio Ricci and Vittorio Zaccaria (Milan: Mondadori, 1983).
DMC	*De mulieribus claris.* Vol. X. *Tutte le opere di Giovanni Boccaccio,* ed. Vittorio Zaccaria (Milan: Mondadori, 1970)
DBI	*Dizionario Biografico degli Italiani*
FW	Giovanni Boccaccio. *Famous Women.* Translated by Virginia Brown (Cambridge, Mass. and London: Harvard University Press, 2001).
The Fates	Giovanni Boccaccio, *The Fates of Illustrious Men.* Translated and abridged by Louis Brewer Hall (New York, 1965).
para./paras.	paragraph(s)

Introduction

occaccio's *De mulieribus claris* [*Famous Women*], composed in the early 1360s, is the foundation text of a genre that will endure for over three centuries. The printed edition was available throughout the sixteenth century both in Latin and in the vernacular. The text itself will become the obligatory reference-point for all those writings on women that look to the past for confirmation of their particular ideological stance. Its durability is due in no small measure to the form of the work: a series of biographies of predominantly classical women placed in chronological order. In most cases, the biographies concentrate on one major 'event' or a series of connected 'events' which can usually be described as 'extraordinary'. Some biographies would have aroused the curiosity of the readership while others offered varying degrees of reliable information on the women. The narratives seem to present the essential 'facts' of the subject's life in an attractive and concentrated form. The text uses biographies of famous women as a vehicle for discussing the role of women in society and as a means of offering models of exemplary female behaviour.[1] The large scale of the undertaking combined with the depth of the research carried out by Boccaccio render the *De mulieribus claris* a compelling focus for competing discourses on women in the later Middle Ages.

Boccaccio's secularized presentation of women in the *De mulieribus claris* is one of the foundational—and richly complex and enigmatic—texts for our modern discourse on women, inaugurating a literary genre that flourished in the early modern period. Contemporary feminist criticism, however, has over-simply categorized the work's discursive heterogeneity as 'misogynistic'. This one-dimensional critique has been virtually institutionalized and aggravated by comparing Boccaccio's *De mulieribus claris* to the recently 're-discovered' Christine de Pizan's *Livre de la Cité des Dames* [*Book of the City of Women*] (1405). The work of this opening chapter will be to unpick the feminist straitjacket into which Boccaccio's text has been confined and release its signifying impact upon its own time.

Boccaccio positions women as active subjects, according to the criterion of an outstanding action whether negative or positive. The suggestive remodelling of biographical narrative designates women as worthy of humanistic concern. The biographies remodel the meaning of women's lives as part of the emerging humanist movement. They are employed to 'carry' key messages: about the possibilities of classical philology and the contribution that humanism can make to civil society. The biographical subjects point to an 'elsewhere' that furthers the new humanist agenda. The writer strives to ease the tensions between the individuality of his chosen women and their function as models and stereotypes.

Ultimately, Boccaccio transformed the 'model' woman by refusing to make reference to Christian narratives of saints' or martyrs' lives.[2] He hesitantly proposed a more secular form of stereotyping to enhance the prestige and influence of the new humanist enterprise, placing women on its agenda. He incorporates female biographies into the development of humanism which, by virtue of this singular text, acknowledges that the nascent movement needs to negotiate traditional conceptions of women and begin to formulate its own response in humanistic terms. Therefore, Boccaccio is rewriting his previous discourses on women: an effacement of his authorship of the *Decameron* and a reinvention of his authorial *persona*. It is not a linear process, and one certainly not without contradictions and impasses. He emphasizes a commitment to the new classical studies, mediated by his adhesion to fundamental Christian values. The women of the *De mulieribus claris* contribute to a rethinking of their social role by their being placed in situations alien, or even forbidden, to most contemporary women.

Yet, the model women are not all positive and so, the collection contributes to the persistence and confirmation of traditional, negative views of female behaviour in a more secular setting. In this sense, one can assert that the *De mulieribus claris* exerts a pernicious power because it institutes the notion of negative stereotyping in proto-humanistic Latin, perhaps stifling the potential of the new movement to challenge old systems of thought. The balance between positive and negative women is precarious, with a tendency to lean towards the latter. The women of the *De mulieribus claris* are all too frequently caught up in a 'double bind' in the first major work of modern times in Western civilization that was wholly concerned with woman as an active subject.[3] Their actions can be condemned from a moral stance alien to the women themselves (Christianity) or because they have trespassed on to male territory and therefore have failed to adhere to 'feminine' values. It is certainly true that a number of Boccaccio's women are placed in a no-win situation. These women have been selected for an outstanding achievement, but that very achievement is their undoing. The biography of Manto can serve as an illustration. Her magical powers are the main reason for her inclusion. However, the exercise of such powers is denigrated in the text, as they are referred to as "wicked arts" (FW 123). The no-win situation is further exacerbated by the reference to "the true God" (FW 123) to whom Manto's virginity should have been consecrated. No matter that Christianity had not yet entered the world. This is a typical procedure, but one has to be careful to note that it does not extend to all women in the text, some of whom are delivered from the double bind.

Boccaccio's De mulieribus claris needs to be seen as the inspiration for a new kind of mainly secular text—the collection of biographies of famous women. The adjective 'famous' indicates an attempt to re-evaluate the female presence in history: to grant space to the intervention of women in the public domain and allow them to share in the glory of the humanists' hall of fame, hitherto exclusively the domain of men. Obviously, the writer picks and chooses the women who will grace the pages of his text. These women are privileged in more than one sense, having been 'rescued' from oblivion through the act of humanist recognition that separates them from their sisters. They are considered by Boccaccio to be in some way exceptional.

This procedure has received widespread condemnation from contemporary feminists. For example, Carolyn G. Heilbrun writes: "Exceptional women are the chief imprisoners of nonexceptional women, simultaneously proving that any woman could do it and assuring, in their uniqueness among men, that no other woman will."[4] Natalie Zemon Davis allows the possibility that representations of exceptional women could act as agents of limited change in other women, arguing that, within precise limitations, they "had the potential to inspire a few females to exceptional action and feminists to reflection about the capacities of women."[5] The basic question is whether these exceptional women can be imitated or not. And if so, does this mean that new fields of experience can be opened up to the female readers of the text or is the imitation intended to be much more circumscribed?

From a twentieth-century perspective, the use of self-contained biographies may seem to emphasize the abnormality of the female behaviour inscribed therein: to set these women apart from standard preconceptions, even to stigmatize them as bizarre. In this interpretation, exceptional women are placed in isolation to prevent their 'contagion' from becoming too general. Their isolation emphasizes their exceptionality. To group them together or to make the links obvious between the biographical subjects would mean that Boccaccio had a vision that encompassed *all* women. Potential for action would not just be restricted to a few exceptional women.

Nevertheless, there is another aspect to the question: that of exceptional women acting as models for other women. Their otherness is often normalized through either commentary or some form of narrative closure.[6] Exceptional women are sometimes considered a danger: if their outstanding qualities could be found in other women, even to a lesser degree, it would imply that the traditional picture of women would have to be re-defined and societal norms reconsidered. This is especially the case with Boccaccio. His desire to maintain male hegemony creates a paradoxical interplay between the ordinary and the extraordinary, whereby the humanist imagination lends its authority to an ambiguously conservative position on women. Exceptional women are exceptional in Boccaccio's view because they behave more like men than women. Such a standpoint has been regarded as another example of Boccaccio's misogyny, a reflection of the Aristotelian substratum in the text. That is, if women are imperfect from most points of view, while men are regarded as perfect, then *naturally* women can only aspire to male perfection—female perfection is an impossibility in this system of thought. Boccaccio appears to accept this position, but fissures appear in his discourse to the extent that he posits female potential *beyond* the Aristotelian biological underpinnings.

In recent times, Boccaccio's *De mulieribus claris* has received bad press. It has been seen as a cleverly written work which ultimately reinforces a backward-looking view of women, through systematic use of ambiguity and irony.[7] Ambiguity is perhaps the kindest word that has been used with regard to the *De mulieribus claris*. One of the most thorough-going negative interpretations is provided by Constance Jordan. The critic can interpret nothing that Boccaccio says positively.[8] It appears that Jordan locates irony at every turn and reads the text as an anti-epideictic work that systematically undermines the praise it is supposed to be bestowing on its women.

Certain narratives have been singled out as being particularly 'misogynist' and either explicitly or implicitly become emblematic of Boccaccio's negative attitude towards women. It is a disconcerting aspect of scholarship on the *De mulieribus claris* in the English-speaking world that based on the evidence of a single biography, Boccaccio is labelled misogynous and consistently misogynous throughout the text. In her abbreviated reading of Boccaccio's chapter on Medea, Carol

Meale concludes that the compilation is "a deeply misogynistic work" and that "Medea's actions, though extreme, are thus in some sense interpreted as representative."[9] The "in some sense" pinpoints a crucial interpretative blind-spot which belies the sweeping nature of the earlier judgement. How exactly is Medea "representative" of all the other women in the *De mulieribus claris*? Is there not something vital lost in such a blanket interpretation? This is the space that the present study intends to open up.

Contemporary criticism of the *De mulieribus claris* has demonstrated a tendency to be dismissive of the text as a whole, putting forward generalizations about it that cannot be fully substantiated. Diana Robin maintains that Boccaccio's picture of women is totally black-and-white: "the good woman is pure in body...the bad, impure (that is, sexual). There is no middle ground."[10] The last statement seems to me reflective of a certain kind of criticism which refuses to see any trace of nuance or sophistication in the Boccaccio of the *De mulieribus claris*. The biography of Leaena, the prostitute who maintained her silence under torture so as not to reveal the names of those in a conspiracy to which she was privy, would appear to suggest that the rigid parameters that are seen by some critics to define Boccaccio's view of women are *sometimes* more flexible and subject to re-evaluation. The 'straightforward' interpretation of Leaena's silence as repression can be subtly challenged by a different version that valorizes her silence as bravery and resistance.[11] Robin, echoing Valerie Wayne, affirms that "each of Boccaccio's portraits of women constitute a negative example," is guilty of an exaggeration that attempts to place the text into a straitjacket, failing to consider medieval thought patterns and dominant discourses.[12]

Judgements of the *De mulieribus claris* can be less harsh. Laura Torretta's study is one of the first, most extensive treatments belonging to the early twentieth-century. It is notable for its refusal to flatten out and discount the contradictory elements of Boccaccio's Latin text: "mentre da un lato ne traspare il desiderio o il proposito dell'autore di ispirarsi a nuovi ideali, vi si rinvengono dall'altro le traccie evidenti di opinioni, di giudizî, di principî, che sono retaggio del passato."[13] Torretta sees the work as marking the transition from the Middle Ages to the Renaissance. She recognizes that the contradictions in the text "non possono che generare nel lettore un curioso senso di perplessità."[14] Torretta does grant that the *De mulieribus claris* is innovative in some respects, especially in its encouragement of women's education, something that many modern critics have been loath to recognize.[15] An exception is Thomas G. Bergin who speaks of an "almost feminist thesis," but he also notes that "this attitude is far from consistent" to the point that he individuates a "persistent misogynistic current."[16] Bergin's recognition of an "ambivalent feminism" may seem overstated, at least to some critics, but it does have the merit of identifying conflicting streams of thought that should not be covered by a single blanket interpretation.[17]

Earlier times had seen the ascendancy of a different kind of criticism, dominated by men, that was almost entirely concerned with the reconstruction of the manuscript tradition to establish a philologically reliable text and the discovery of sources.[18] This pioneering criticism also mapped out the areas into which it would not stray by its positivistic insistence on the textual parameters of the *De mulieribus claris*.[19] The culmination of this trend can be seen in the work of Vittorio Zaccaria, the editor of the critical edition of the *De mulieribus claris*.[20] The main weakness of this school is that the interpretation of the text takes a back seat. The question of the representation of women does not generally come in for extensive investigation. Unlike recent Anglo-Saxon feminist criticism, Italian scholars have not generally viewed the text as ripe for an analysis of its sexual politics. Many do not view it as political in any meaningful sense.[21] Anna Cerbo, who has authored many diligent critical investigations of the *De mulieribus claris* dating from the eighties, does not appear to have been aware that issues of gender and sex-roles could be of crucial significance for her understanding of the text. Indeed, she puts forward the claim that the *De mulieribus claris* is not so much interested in women as in presenting a work predominantly inspired by Christian principles.[22]

However, it must be said that reading the text as sexual politics can have its pitfalls. Writing on the biography of Dido in the *De mulieribus claris*, Marilynn Desmond makes certain claims about the text, firstly, that it is a "misogynist construct" and secondly that there is "no room to recuperate this text to a feminist point of view."[23] As used by Desmond, the term misogynist appears to transcend historical epochs, imposing on the text a negative categorization which does not take into account predominant medieval systems of thought. It becomes a feminist badge of honour to pigeonhole and denigrate one of the major writers of the European literary canon. Connected to the over-use of the term misogynist is the validity of the idea that *De mulieribus claris needs* to be recuperated "to a feminist point of view." The implications of such a methodology subdue any effort at historical reconstruction in favour of the overt ideological colonization of the text from a contemporary perspective. Boccaccio is placed in a no-win situation, a reversal of the double standard from which women have so long suffered. A more rigorous interpretation of the *De mulieribus claris* should render its complexities and blind-spots without yielding to an ahistorical formula that too neatly closes off the text from its multi-dimensionality.

The Discursive Pairing of Boccaccio and Christine de Pizan

Τhe above tendency has been accentuated by the phenomenon of the 'rediscovery' of Christine de Pizan's *Book of the City of Women* (written in 1405). In recent years, this text has begun to receive extensive attention from scholars, particularly feminist ones.[24] Paradoxically, the upturn in Christine de Pizan's critical fortunes has meant that Boccaccio's *De mulieribus claris* has come under the critical spotlight. For *The City of Women* could not have been written without the *De mulieribus claris*. De Pizan takes up numerous exemplary figures from Boccaccio's text, but it is not merely a matter of acknowledging a debt.[25] The female writer reconstructs the male text in order to provide a disambiguated reading of female achievement and potential. *The City of Women* is an assertion of the female necessity to rewrite male versions of history. If Boccaccio's attempt is paradoxical and does not present a wholly positive reading, Christine de Pizan corrects his perspective.[26] It is from this point of view that the renewed interest in the *De mulieribus* has been formulated: in order to measure just how radical was de Pizan's rewriting, scholars have had to return to one of her most important sources. This has resulted in the emergence of a dichotomy wherein Boccaccio's collection of biographies is generally viewed in negative terms,[27] whilst de Pizan's work is seen as a feminist text that undermines male hierarchies and systems. This definition of conflictual opposition is very occasionally developed into a more complex relationship, bringing into play the dominant ideological structures of medieval society that placed a man uppermost in the gender hierarchy. Within this ideological straitjacket, both male and female writers had to struggle with reformulating their social identities and roles against the powerful cultural investments of the period's great institutions.[28]

I am going to examine this 'confrontation' in some detail because of its implications for the reading of Boccaccio's Latin text. It will be necessary to indicate some of the basic strategies involved in Christine de Pizan's re-reading of the *De mulieribus claris*. My purpose is to give a sense of Boccaccio's text through the interventions made by Christine de Pizan. Obviously, there are strong grounds for such a comparison. However, it should be noted that the comparative approach usually works to the disadvantage of Boccaccio's text, favouring de Pizan's work as 'feminist'. Criticism of these two writers tends to reinforce the stereotype of the male-authored text as re-inscribing gender hierarchies and the female-authored text subverting them.[29] There may be valid grounds to argue for such a distinction between the two works, but it definitely simplifies a more complex situation. The contemporary pairing of these two works has led to some exaggeration on both 'sides', with 'Boccaccio' depicted simply as a misogynist and 'Christine' as a feminist. Yet it is of the utmost importance, I believe, to emphasize the complexities of a male writer in the later fourteenth century attempting to work through contradictory impulses in the representation of women.

Although just over forty years separated the two writers, Boccaccio's world was one that comprised both the court *and* the commune whereas Christine de Pizan was exclusively anchored in the French royal court. In the *De mulieribus,* it is probable that he was attempting to rewrite the *Decameron,* his own vernacular text which was at odds with his role as a humanist *in fieri.* It is this context that is all too often ignored. What follows is not an apology by a twenty-first-century male critic for a medieval writer based on a perceived bond of gender solidarity. It is rather an attempt to examine the problems which arise from Boccaccio's representation of women, whilst not necessarily viewing these problems as 'shortcomings' from the perspective of twentieth-century feminism.

It is true that the *Book of the City of Women* represents a critical re-reading of the *De mulieribus claris,* ironing out some of its more obvious contradictions and cleaning up some of Boccaccio's perceived misogynist swipes. However, de Pizan introduces problems of her own which, in my view, are of two orders (and, it should be added, are inherent to the genre). The first is one of reach: from a feminist perspective, the process of setting up exceptional women as models serves only to differentiate even further between women, and always leaves ambiguous or unspoken how or if the biographical episodes are to be translated into social change and public action. Secondly, the exceptional women are famous for a variety of skills and qualities: while the women fall into clearly defined groups (for example, warriors, scholars, saints), this does not render their diverse qualities any less inconsistent or contradictory. It remains extremely difficult to move from a collection of disparate female lives to a synthesis that clearly points to suitable models for women in contemporary society.

There is ample evidence to suggest that some of the details of Boccaccio's exemplary figures were neither positive nor acceptable to de Pizan's re-writing of history. A case in point is her treatment of Semiramis who, in Boccaccio's reconstruction, is a woman split in two by her rampant sexuality; a peerless queen destroyed by her unrestrained sexual proclivities.[30] Christine de Pizan confronts this problem in the last paragraph of the queen's biography by criticizing the approach of other writers, implicitly including Boccaccio in her criticism. She introduces the concept of historical relativity to explain Semiramis' behaviour in marrying her own son. At the same time, she suppresses other details deployed by Boccaccio to suggest Semiramis' lack of control over her sexuality: the invention of chastity belts, the queen's uncontrollable lust, and so on. Such 'details' do not rate a mention in de Pizan, one of the reasons being that they are not so easy to explain away as the queen's marriage. These omissions indicate the writer's decision to depict her leading female character as one in control of her destiny. Hence she ignores the comments of male historiographers and spends three-quarters of the biography on Semiramis' political achievements. Her biography is a challenge to male ways of viewing female history. Whereas Boccaccio devotes approximately half his account to railing against Semiramis' loose sexual mores, de Pizan ignores them as being irrelevant to a history in which women are required to act on the public stage. The private is suppressed here so that it does not cast any doubts on Semiramis' public achievements—de Pizan makes the point that the queen is to be judged by political and military criteria, not by the morals of her private life.

This is not the only instance in which de Pizan employs this technique: for example, she exploits it in the biography of Medea by omitting any mention of the queen's murder of her children. Jason is unequivocally regarded as the 'villain' who "left Medea for another woman" (p.190). One myth is replaced by another. The very process of writing history is demonstrated to be an ideological battleground. From this perspective, de Pizan's text assumes a critical stance towards the Boccaccian model: playing a game with its complex historical discourse; remodelling and redrawing its boundaries.[31] The episodes above provide an example of history being re-written; demonstrating along the way that all history is reconstruction. The basic historical materials may be organized in completely different ways subject to various ideological pressures. They are utilized in a manner which demonstrates that women can create their own histories just as men have always done. Boccaccio's text is rent by ambiguities and contradictions with only intermittent efforts to resolve them, whereas de Pizan ensured that she wrote a positive exemplary history of women that left no space for possible negative interpretations.

Between the two texts, there are major structural differences which have been the subject of much commentary.[32] The most obvious is the lack of an external framing device in Boccaccio's *De mulieribus claris,* and its reintroduction by de Pizan as an essential part of her message. She provided *The Book of the City of Women* with a compelling and rigorous structure that utilizes the vision motif to create a female utopia. Ironically, this is the only time that the Italian writer dropped the *cornice* as a structural device in the composition of his texts, perhaps because he was attempting to produce a serious, humanist text, far from the pleasurable antics of the *Decameron* (though he could never quite shake off the vernacular work).

From de Pizan's point of view, Boccaccio's text, which she probably read in a French translation, was a truncated piece of writing which lacked a clear ideological decisiveness and did not lead to any (positive) conclusions about women. Christine de Pizan's role as interpreter was to ensure a re-reading of Boccaccio's message; to provide a clearer sense of direction than was apparent in the Latin work; and to complete the text by providing information about a greater range of women. Thus, in de Pizan's text, when Justice finishes her description of the city, it is the sense of closure, or completeness/wholeness, which predominates: "So I turn it over to you, finished perfectly and well enclosed" (p.254). By contrast, the earlier writer portrays women as individually isolated: there is no city or community for them; they do not constitute a readable whole. Boccaccio's work is infinitely open: additions can be made to it without disturbing its structure.

The last chapter of de Pizan's text (from which the above quotation was taken) contains material which Boccaccio purposely excluded from his Latin work: biographies and references to the heroines of the Christian tradition, particularly female martyrs. By placing these exemplars in her final chapter, de Pizan was actively polemicizing against Boccaccio's choice. Boccaccio's omission simplifies his schema so that the presence of Christian women does not clash with classical ideals and representations of womanhood. Christine de Pizan ensures that there is a culmination to her text by assigning the highest point of the city to the Virgin Mary; a figure conspicuous by her absence from the *De mulieribus*.

De Pizan concludes her radical treatise on what appears to be a conventional note, dedicating the last book of *The City of Women* to Christian women. In the last book, the Virgin Mary, "the head of the feminine sex" (p.218), is associated explicitly only with humility. This points to the conservative conclusion of *The City of Women*. However, there are some indications in the text that de Pizan is attempting to use traditional Christian female figures in a way which underlines a new appreciation of the Christian woman. The other women in the chapter do not inevitably underscore a passive acceptance of life and death as the destiny of all Christian women through the category of martyrdom. Images of passivity are dissipated by an injection of heroic female endurance: "the constancy and *strength* to suffer horrible martyrdom for His holy law" (p.219; my emphasis).

The story of Saint Christine illustrates the programmatic nature of *The City of Women*.[33] It can be read as an allegory of female determination to be heard and, as such, is seen to refer to the writer's own circumstances; placing her at the centre of the text to suggest her uniqueness through a semiosis of the saintly *persona*. The longest account in the chapter, it uses Christian hagiography to reinforce the secular messages of the text, not the least being the need for women to speak out. The underlying message here is that only exceptional women will be able to do this, and that for Christine the most exceptional women in a Christian society are its saints and martyrs. Patriarchal society attempts to silence both Christines (the writer and the martyr), but to no avail: "...he had her tongue cut out, but then she spoke even better and more clearly than before of divine things and of the one blessed God" (p.239). The traditional *topos* of the silent woman is thus overturned. When Saint Christine spits out the remaining part of her tongue and blinds the tyrant in one eye, she is turning her oppression against its originator; using her suffering to rebel against authority and, allegorically, to highlight the blindness of her oppressor's behaviour, especially his refusal to see the worth of Christine.[34] The creation of a myth about herself allows de Pizan to stress the importance of female speech/discourse and the necessity to seek out suitable metaphors and language through which to express impatience or dissatisfaction with the patriarchal system.

The narration of Saint Christine marks a turning-point in the chapter. Following this highpoint there is a change in tone and emphasis in the martyriological narratives. The later groupings of female martyrs confirm women in more stereotyped roles through the representation of their ultimate sacrifices to God. The pathos of these accounts contributes to the confirmation of the importance of the nurturing function for women: "What in the world is dearer to a mother than her child, and what greater grief than that which her heart suffers seeing her child in pain?" (p.240). In contrast to these 'natural' values, de Pizan juxtaposes female saints who disguised themselves as men for religious purposes.[35] Although the stories of Marina and Euphrosyna were well known throughout the Middle Ages, in *The City of Women* they mark a return to the concept of men providing the measure of female behaviour—female achievement is thus seen in terms of a transfer of the concept of virility to women whose identity becomes lost through a change of clothes.

The theme which tends to predominate in the second part of the last chapter is that of female saints serving holy men, with the last section concentrating on women who served the physical needs of the apostles. Saint Anastasia, for example, is seen to incarnate those Christian virtues closely associated with the 'feminine': "This lady felt amazing compassion for the blessed Christian martyrs whom she saw daily afflicted with tortures" (p.245). Christine de Pizan's arrangement of the women in the last chapter highlights the way in which structure and order affect the reading of the text. At the centre we find the figure of Saint Christine who is placed between the contrasting possibilities of the 'holy' as she perceives it: rebellion against the patriarchal order versus subservience to the male.

It is the latter possibility which is developed in the final address to the reader, emphasizing the woman as wife (all the Christian women mentioned in the last chapter were virgins—a choice, as is made clear in the text, which is not open to all women). This final emphasis leads the text back to a conventional conclusion which will not upset the social order. Christine de Pizan's advice to women who have 'bad' husbands is that they "should strive to endure them while trying to overcome their vices and lead them back, if they can, to a reasonable and seemly life" (p.255). She recommends that wives should exhibit the virtue of patience in all circumstances.

De Pizan's exemplary tales thus contain quite radical messages which became diluted in other types of discourse. She can be seen as having chosen to cut off the radical implications of the *exempla* in a final plea to women to accept their situation. This certainly does not mean that her earlier messages are simply dismissed. Rather, they are relegated 'underground' in relation to a more conservative social 'program', co-existing in an uneasy equilibrium with her final address to women. Re-reading the past does not necessarily lead to a radical revaluation of the present. The 'politically correct' ending does not tell the whole story.[36] The creation of another level to the text protects it from accusations of fostering social disorder by disturbing the established gender relations in society. At the same time, in the contradiction between the *exempla* and epilogue, it allows for a subversive message to the female reader. *The City of Women*, I would argue, seems to be generally clear in its theoretical implications but the actuation of change in society is deferred. The exemplary female figures of *The City of Women*, indicative of a rich heritage of positive women, represent a complex potentiality. The problem is their insertion into patriarchal society in order to bring about radical change.

If the final image of woman in *The City of Women* is as wife, then the emphasis falls on legal relations, in other words, the social subordination of the wife to the husband. The question thus becomes one of relating the other exemplary, 'fictional' images to that of the wife and, perhaps, to other possible roles such as widow or nun. The critical problem is one of infusing the role of the wife with historical exemplarity. It is one thing to alert the reader (male or female) to the existence of various types of exemplary women—it is quite another to inform the behaviour of a wife with the qualities and possibilities given in the body of the text; it effects a kind of symbolic separation of the daughter from her putative and illustrious mothers.

De Pizan rewrites *De mulieribus claris* from a definite viewpoint—that of a woman who has experienced some of the roles that are marked out for women in society.[37] *The City of Women* suggests the need for intellectual rigour on the part of gifted women to critique male ideology and, more particularly, the literary constructs of that ideology. Yet, finally, it is unclear about how to tackle the problem of patriarchy itself in contemporary society.

Christine de Pizan's systematic rewriting of the *De mulieribus claris* has generally ensured that the intricacies of Boccaccio's text, if not exactly ignored, have been played down and have not been the subject of extensive investigation. The most positive reading of the *De mulieribus claris*, at least in the English language, is the work of Pamela Benson. She stands in acute contrast to most of her feminist colleagues, particularly Jordan and Christine de Pizan scholars. Benson strongly argues the case that "a persuasive and sensitive profeminist voice emerges from the text, a voice that admires female political, moral, and physical strength although it does not endorse a change in the contemporary political status of women."[38] Boccaccio seems to have been aware that certain ways of reading could lead to a logical case for societal change. However, the commentaries appended to a number of the biographies reject any notion of the radical transformation of society. The implication is that implementing even the slightest modifications to views about women would challenge male-dominated society. Therefore, Boccaccio has no desire to theorize a more gender equitable society. Perhaps twentieth-century feminism has expected too much from Boccaccio's hesitant introduction of women into the humanistic canon. Benson is critical of this, considering it the major gap in Boccaccio's text. But apart from this serious criticism, she reads the *De mulieribus claris* positively, arguing that Boccaccio supports the idea that the natural talents of women are able to raise them above the norm, given particular circumstances. Benson, therefore, challenges all those readings that automatically categorize Boccaccio as 'misogynous'.

However, in common with other feminist-inspired criticism, Benson does not consider the historico-philological elements of the text, such as the compositional process, which would have aided her interpretation and sharpened her argument. In my view, this separation has been quite harmful to the development of a 'balanced' interpretation of the *De mulieribus claris*. The present study aims to bring together seemingly 'old-fashioned' critical processes, such as the examination of sources and the manner of composition to clarify Boccaccio's humanism, especially with respect to Petrarch. It will be demonstrated that the dates of composition are vital in assessing Boccaccio's work: because of the writer's Neapolitan ambitions, the *De mulieribus claris* underwent a partial metamorphosis, changed at a certain point into a courtly gift. Essential to understanding the mechanisms by which the compilation operates is an analysis of the choice and range of the famous women selected by Boccaccio as well as their eventual ordering.

Furthermore, the relations between Boccaccio and Petrarch are played out in the *De mulieribus claris*, contributing to the uncertainties of interpretation. On the one hand, Boccaccio acknowledges a profound debt to the master, and, on the other, the text is a declaration of his own propensities and choices. Thus, in a fundamental way, the disciple redefines aspects of Petrarch's teaching. Boccaccio, as humanist scholar, inevitably draws comparison with his own writings, particularly the *Decameron*. A diachronic mapping of Boccaccio's discourses on women leads us to reach some conclusions about the ways in which his Latin humanism operates on vernacular constructions of woman. The virtual exclusion of love from the *De mulieribus claris* signals an obvious change of direction, a commitment to serious, humanistic male ideals of friendship and perhaps more importantly, the realization that women can be more than objects of sexual love. This effective exclusion can be seen as a questioning of his earlier work and amounts to an almost complete rejection of love as the main force in human society. Humanist social values are expressed in the text mainly as a series of negatives about contemporary society and so, they are inadequate to offer a completely renewed social vision. The *De mulieribus claris* gropes towards a tentative renewal of values, but there is resistance in the text from the ideological constraints that limit Boccaccio's reconceptualization of women.

Neither the originality of Boccaccio's project nor its difficulties should be underestimated. The *De mulieribus claris* placed humanism at the cutting edge of culture. It attempted to replace or supplement cultural forms, re-presenting age-old motifs about women in new narrative guises. The new humanism sought to position itself as a resource at the disposal of society to push for its renewal and to make itself indispensable to the organization of power. There would seem no better way towards such a renewal than a re-evaluation of the role of women. The *De mulieribus claris* puts this new learning on show. The text adds value to the author who demonstrates his possession of a formidable array of knowledge about women. He thus confirms his virility in subordinating facts about women to a body of knowledge organized by the male mind. If the new humanism could see value in forming a kind of alliance with women, however, one in which the humanist could still maintain a sense of his superiority, it ironically reflected his uncertain place in the hierarchy of power.

The *De mulieribus claris* itself is not open to straightforward interpretation. In part, this is due to the fact that unlike all of Boccaccio's writings there is no framing device. Further, Boccaccio does not make his agenda explicit and sows the seeds of contradictory analyses of the work, while rooting it in conservative notions of femineity. The chronological ordering of the text leads to a loss of cohesion and creates ambiguity because the ideological tissue is partially obscured by the overriding concern with historical chronology. Boccaccio makes the reader work extremely hard to reach any solid conclusions about the theoretical construction of the collection of biographies. The reader may even question whether there is a coherent 'philosophy' to be gleaned from the text at all, aside from the visible comments and commentary that give credence to a view of women anchored in Aristotelian thought. *De mulieribus claris* refuses to be pigeonholed. It provided readers with an encyclopaedic range of women and, at the same time encouraged them to rewrite the text in a more systematic and coherent way. An invitation that was taken up almost as soon as it began to circulate (these later variations will be the subject of a companion volume). Boccaccio's collection of biographies remained visible throughout the Renaissance as a monument to early humanist research and a reminder that women's history would not always remain buried and forgotten.

· · · · · ·

I

𝔖haping the Text

FORMATION OF THE *DE MULIERIBUS CLARIS*

Pier Giorgio Ricci and Vittorio Zaccaria have convincingly established the stages of composition of the *De mulieribus claris*.[1] Although Boccaccio wrote the bulk of the work in the early summer of 1361, it emerges that the text was the result of a number of compositional stages (seven for Ricci and nine for Zaccaria).[2] This first stage has been broken down into three closely related phases, producing three successive groups of women: (i) Eve to Gualdrada (74 biographies); (ii) Opis to Constance (21 biographies); and (iii) Sabina Poppaea to Thisbe (6 biographies).[3] Such a massive output represents by far the greatest part of the biographies as they appear in the critical edition: 102 out of a total of 106 women plus the prologue.

The second stage (4–6 in Zaccaria's classification) is marked by an external event which is crucial for Boccaccio's biography and the final appearance of the text: his summons to Naples by the powerful Niccolò Acciaiuoli, datable to the early summer of 1362.[4] At first sight, the effect of this invitation may appear to have had little impact on the text. It generated a relatively small amount of new material—the dedication to Niccolò Acciaiuoli's sister, Andrea, and two new chapters: one on Giovanna I, Queen of Naples; the other on Camiola, a Sienese woman who settled in Messina, whose life offers a parallel situation to Andrea's. At the same time, Boccaccio added some new commentaries to chapters already written and transformed the last chapter ("De feminis nostri temporis") into the "Conclusio."[5]

This small amount of new material transforms the text from a work of scholarly investigation into a courtly gift. *De mulieribus claris* gains a new purpose: Boccaccio used his Florentine connections in Naples as a conduit to a life of greater ease. Thus, he drew the work into a society associated with court literature, making a bid for an audience within that ambience. It would not be true to state that Boccaccio sacrificed his intellectual integrity on the glittering stage of courtly fame—his additions are quite restrained. However, he seems to have been acutely aware of the possibilities his collection of illustrious women might have in court circles—a lesson that was to be well, if not better, learnt by Renaissance compilers of such treatises.

In this way, the intellectual project becomes more fully integrated into the social world of the court, where women may play a more autonomous role or are, at least, more visible. The catalogue of famous women lends itself to courtly encomium by flattering the sensibilities of the dedicatee. The introduction of the biography of Queen Giovanna is a sure sign of the greater visible access of women to power in the court system. The integration of Boccaccio's humanist approach and his social interests (or ambition) was achieved with surprisingly little difficulty. It seems that he did not start out with the desire to mould his text for a court audience. He overlaid the first stage of the *De mulieribus* with the encomiastic material in such a way that it did not destroy the textual mechanisms put in place earlier. Therefore, Boccaccio brought about a tentative marriage between the new humanism in one of its more original forms and his desire to enter Neapolitan court society. Boccaccio hoped to take advantage of the Florentine Niccolò Acciaiuoli's position as dominant political power in the Kingdom.

Following his invitation to Naples (Zaccaria's stage 6), Boccaccio added a third new chapter, on Cornificia [LXXXVI], a woman poet of the Roman Empire. Unlike the other two new chapters introduced at this stage, the subject had nothing to do with Naples. Yet the insertion of Cornificia was far from accidental. Boccaccio had dedicated the book to Andrea Acciaiuoli at the time of his invitation to Naples. It is instructive to view these two women together. The text implies a contrast between them or, to put it another way, Cornificia upheld a different set of values from those which saw him dedicate the book to Andrea Acciaiuoli. Cornificia stands as testimony to the power of the written word which rises above convention and tradition.[6] The chapter interlocks with other biographies of the *De mulieribus* in which writers and painters overcome the traditional structure of women's lives by dedicating themselves to art. Cornificia's talents were not constrained by the demands of domestic life which she rejected in order to write poetry. Boccaccio's quarrel is with those women who act: "as if they were born for idleness and for the marriage bed" (*FW* 355). Boccaccio exalts the word in the new chapter, claiming that Cornificia worked under the direct inspiration of the muses ("I think that the sacred Muses inspired her to use her learned pen" [*FW* 353]). The chapter represents an assertion of the value of writing in the face of other demands made on women, and by extension on the writer. Thus, these additions should be analysed together otherwise their significance is likely to be skewed, blurring the dialectic between patronage pressures and intellectual integrity.

It is necessary to comment on two other sets of additions, one of which slightly precedes those discussed above (stage 5 in Zaccaria's classification), but both of which appear to fall into the same basic period of revision (post-summer 1362).[7] The slightly earlier stage, individuated by Zaccaria, consists of two sets of additions: (i) two new chapters on the wives of the Menii [XXXI] and the wives of the Cimbrians [LXXX]; (ii) commentaries in the following chapters: XXVI on the necessity of industry, particularly to men, in order to achieve; XXVII on the importance of Latin culture, especially the transmission of its written tradition; LI against violent means to obtain power; and LXXVII on the superiority of the Christian over pagan religion.

A similarity of themes can be noted in (i). Each of the new chapters deals with a closely knit group of women, rather than with a single person (as is more common in the De mulieribus). Boccaccio uses the episode of the Minyan women to demonstrate the depth of love felt by these wives towards their husbands who had been imprisoned and were awaiting execution. Just under half of its length is devoted to the courage and devotion of the wives, presented as an ideal in their relationship with the opposite sex.

The episode of the wives of the Cimbrians relates a much darker story. After the Romans had defeated their husbands, the women asked to be admitted as vestal virgins. Their request was refused so they first murdered their children and then committed mass suicide. The focus in this account is not so much on the status of the women as wives, as on their attitude towards their conquerors and the courageous defence of their pudicitia (chastity). Hence the two new chapters complement each other, both offering images of courageous wives/mothers who defy their more powerful enemies. The two chapters combine to elucidate the idealized behaviour of wives. The first case insists on their loyalty, and the second on the necessity of sexual purity. The loss of a husband does not mean the abandonment of female sexual mores—on the contrary! These episodes form a signifying pair, although in the final version of the De mulieribus they are separated by about fifty chapters. Both have quite extensive commentaries appended to them to leave no room for misinterpretation. They consolidate strands in the text which, although quite strong, were in need of further strengthening. This suggests that the writer wished to focus attention more forcefully on women who adhered unambiguously to those tenets of pagan doctrine that could be applied to Christian society, especially marriage and chastity.

The additional commentaries inserted at this time offer insights into the adjustments made by Boccaccio after the composition of the greater part of the text.[8] Significantly, the discussion of the importance of Latin culture in chapter XXVII reinforces the more indirect statements found in Cornificia's biography. Although separated in the text, ideally they should be read together because of their similarity of theme and proximity of composition. The exhortation to industry in chapter XXVI is also connected to the Cornificia chapter—she becomes a poet only through conquering a natural 'female' tendency to non-activity. The commentary on good government appended to the chapter on Athaliah (LI) seems out of place in a treatise which programmatically appears to eschew overt political issues involving the institutions of power. It would have been more at home in the *De casibus*. The text seems to be renouncing the political values of a Florence from which Boccaccio was 'exiled', both physically and spiritually, in his last years.

Boccaccio introduced another major revision into his text when he was carrying out alterations stimulated by his imminent journey to Naples. The final chapter of the work, originally entitled "De feminis nostri temporis" ["Concerning the women of our time"], became the "Conclusio" (stage 6). The "Conclusio" is a shortened version of the superseded chapter which, in a final display of humanistic knowledge, contained the names of over forty women. By the time of the revision, Boccaccio must have considered these examples superfluous and so they were eliminated. They were mainly figures from classical mythology, owing more to the ethos of the *Amorosa visione* than to the *De mulieribus claris*. Some emphasize illicit sexual liaisons with the gods, such as Zeus' violation of Danae in a shower of gold, or Callisto who was loved by Zeus and then transmuted into a she-bear. In others, brief descriptions of unhappy and criminal loves follow one another inexorably—Omphale is mentioned, as is the gory tale of Progne and Philomela.

It is understandable that Boccaccio deleted these names from the final version of the text, as they do not sit well with the more conventional messages which were the intended centre of the work. Love is no longer considered the matrix of female action (at least not deadly passion which overrides all social conventions and relationships), and so 'romantic' love is greatly reduced in the *De mulieribus claris*. The fascinating tales of love which were listed almost impersonally in the superseded conclusion do not find a place in the revised text. However, there was a change of emphasis in the "De feminis nostri temporis" itself, with a gradual recognition of married love as being more consonant with the concerns of the writer's later humanist period.

Boccaccio included a reference to Laodomia who arguably would have been a close candidate for inclusion in the text proper. Inconsolable after the death of her husband Protesilaus at Troy, she was unable to find peace and committed suicide, even after Hermes had brought him back from Hades for a few hours. Her exclusion may have been due to the emphasis on the pagan supernatural in the story or to the writer's unease with the pedagogical lessons to be drawn from the heroine's suicide. The last section of the original listing places the focus on conjugal love as an antidote to the even longer list of tragic and fantastical or mythological loves. It is only in the final sentence that Boccaccio shifts his focus to historical women. The last group is Roman, repeating the grouping which is superseded with respect to the B-version of the *Amorosa visione*.[9] The decision to omit it altogether represents a move away from the Dantesque vision of feminized Roman history. This aspect will be discussed in a later chapter (V).

Boccaccio continued to tinker with his text after this period of febrile activity, but did not make any major additions between 1363 and 1366 (Zaccaria's stage 7). The final version of the *De mulieribus claris* brought to us in the autograph manuscript was written in 1370 with additional minor corrections in 1375.[10] In compositional terms, the years 1361–62 represent the period of maximum intensity and concentration on the work. It is interesting that Boccaccio did not seem to let go of it, in spite of the repeated failures to obtain patronage from Niccolò Acciaiuoli. Once the work had acquired its definitive shape, Boccaccio did not abandon it, but kept on making corrections until he wrote the final autograph. Certainly, the *De mulieribus claris* was a critical sign of his commitment to humanistic studies.

Visions of Women

𝕿he *De mulieribus* brings together the biographies of over a hundred women in a single anthology to produce the first contemporary repertory of this kind. The general principles of selection are clear enough, since the majority of the women are from the Graeco-Roman world. Yet Boccaccio's rationale for the selection of individual women is not always immediately clear from the structure of the text. Apart from some generalities expressed in the prefatory material, reasons for inclusion and exclusion are not made explicit. The Introduction stresses the open-ended nature of the text by explaining that the title, especially the adjective "clarus," is not necessarily a positive evaluation of the women.[11] Thus the term creates *ab initio* a sense of ambiguity about these women. The historical process of 'recovering' women, of granting them historical validation competes with the standard moral categories that for centuries had denied women narratives in which they figured as protagonists.

Boccaccio had originally conceived of the *De mulieribus claris* as a humanist encyclopedia which emphasized female achievement in the classical world. Boccaccio does include medieval women, but they are few in comparison to their classical counterparts. Of 106 women only six belong to the Middle Ages and of them two are later additions brought about by Boccaccio's impending trip to Naples (Zaccaria's stage 6). There is not the slightest hint of universal coverage of postclassical women. It would appear that Boccaccio was chiefly concerned with demonstrating his humanist credentials, avoiding as far as possible any contamination between pagan and Christian women. He exhibited an increasing preoccupation with demonstrating the moralizing possibilities of classical *exempla*, shown by the need to add further commentaries to already existing chapters.

The chronological sequence of classical women closes with Zenobia [C], who is depicted as extraordinarily chaste as well as courageous in battle. This signals a positive end to the varied depictions of ancient women, even though Zenobia is eventually defeated by the Romans. The jump to the next biography is both chronologically and morally dramatic in the re-ordered arrangement of the biographies (Zaccaria's stage 6). For its subject is no other than the 'mythical' Pope Joan [CI] who negates all the qualities displayed by the previous subject, Zenobia. The following chapter [CII] contains the biography of the Empress Irene, whose behaviour and ambition hark back to the earlier women of imperial Rome, previously recorded in the *De mulieribus claris*. The Empress Constance [CIV] represents a moment in which power politics were of greater importance than Christian fidelity to one's vows. Gualdrada's [CIII] modesty is played out before the Emperor Otto IV. Indeed, all the postclassical *exempla* before stage 6 have Rome or the Roman Empire as their focal point. It is an empire that has been christianized, but now in serious decline. Boccaccio chose not to look at other female rulers of the Middle Ages, some closer in time than the examples selected for the *De mulieribus claris*. He introduced only two such figures [Camiola and Constance] for a precise tactical purpose in 1361–62. Unlike the *De casibus* which vaunts its medieval heritage through its structure and content, the *De mulieribus* restricts itself to the classical world and to the influence of the Roman Empire in the later period.

The construction of the *De mulieribus* takes the form of a series of representations of women, set side by side. Unlike the *Genealogie*, there is a minimum of cross-referencing to the other women mentioned in each individual chapter. The narrator rarely refers to previous or later biographies in the course of the work. In this sense, Boccaccio's Latin works reflect his growing awareness of the need for scholarly apparatus: from *De casibus*, where dramatic representation of the characters submerges the critical activity of the author, through *De mulieribus* in which one finds a much more analytical/historical approach. This approach then culminates in the *Genealogie*, which cites sources much more rigorously than the work on women; furthermore, the *Genealogie* has an internal referencing system, and more completely subdues narrative in favour of analytical discursive practices.

The women, therefore, are very much 'alone'. They are not supported by the use of a *cornice* or framing device—they are loose women. In fact, the reader, moves from one woman to the other without really knowing what kind of woman to expect next. It is true that some of the women fall into thematically coherent units, but the design of the text is along chronological lines. Boccaccio underplays the moral cohesiveness of the lives as an organizing principle. The text does overtly engage with moral, social and political issues, but in a sporadic fashion, from within the discrete narratives. Therefore, the writer has privileged the humanistic study of history over other concerns so that the women's exemplary power is rather diluted. The *De mulieribus claris* makes an art of fragmentation and discontinuity. The text deals in fractured, incomplete discourses that declare the impossibility of producing a coherent picture of woman.

Structures and Sub-Structures of the *De mulieribus claris*

𝕋he discontinuity of the text is sometimes belied by the appearance of chronologically contiguous groupings of women who share similar characteristics. These groups of women are unheralded in the text and can easily be broken or interrupted by the insertion of an 'alien' woman whose chronology happens to coincide with that of the group. Boccaccio is happy to sacrifice thematic development to the cause of an accurate time-scale in the later versions of the *De mulieribus claris*. The opening biography of the series, Eve, may be considered a necessary starting point, but she stands alone except for the negative biblical *exemplum* of Athaliah. There is no sustained attempt to weave in biblical figures to provide a sacred chronology from which a comparative perspective could be gleaned.[12] Boccaccio is much more interested in providing a critical reading of pagan religion, deconstructing its beliefs and rituals.

Goddesses and Demons

The discussion of the pagan goddesses (III–X) presents to the reader a cohesive group of women at the beginning of the *De mulieribus*. Boccaccio has the luxury of developing a number of themes connected with pagan religious cults and, at the same time, emphasizes the humanity of these exceptional women by liberating them from their mythological foundations. It is likely that Boccaccio was testing out his theories of classical mythology, presenting in embryonic form brief excerpts from his researches into the pagan gods.

There are obvious differences between the respective approaches of the *De mulieribus* and the *Genealogie* that are instructive about Boccaccio's intellectual position in his collection of female biographies. The case of Opis (IV) underlines the contrasting perspectives in the two works. It is immediately noticeable that the *Genealogie* entry on the goddess is more scholarly. The variants of her name do not figure prominently in the *De mulieribus* ("Opis seu Ops, vel Rhea") whereas in the *Genealogie* they form a topic of some consistency and interest.[13] In the later work, Boccaccio's discussion is informed by a stronger need than in the *De mulieribus* to identify his sources and to account etymologically for the names. Although Boccaccio is considerably more thorough in the *Genealogie*, he still resorts to the less precise method of vaguely stating that some writers take an alternative view without identifying the dissonant voices.[14] This was the basic procedure used in the *De mulieribus claris* where no source is precisely identified by the author. The difference in methodology points to a fundamental shift in the implied readership. For the *Genealogie*, Boccaccio was certainly addressing himself to a republic of humanist scholars, most definitely male, who were interested in the minutest details which could then be checked for their veracity and precision.

The *De mulieribus* is more a popularising work which suppresses those scholarly niceties that may have impeded an appreciation of his historical approach to the goddesses. An excessive accumulation of names and etymologies would have made the text unreadable for its target audience of women and men of the elite classes. Boccaccio does not mention the particular objects associated with the Opis cult or their intricate symbolism. In the *De mulieribus*, his interest lies elsewhere. Furthermore, the central part of the narrative is not constituted by the mythical story of Opis' deception of her brother, Titan, recounted in the *Genealogie*,[15] but by the account of the political importance of the goddess to the Romans in a moment of military crisis, taken from Livy. The latter episode is framed by a self-satisfied understanding that pagan religion was based on erroneous foundations. It is this strongly expressed belief, also common to the *Genealogie*, which appears to be the main point of the chapter (biography is subsumed into the historical survival of a cult). Boccaccio has well-defined moralistic intentions: twice he refers to Opis in Christian terms, stressing the partisanship of the narrator who insists that Roman history and antiquity need to be read with Christian eyes.[16] Opis' 'biography' sets the pattern for the other goddesses. There is hardly any interest in retelling the myths associated with them.[17] The biography of Ceres is submerged by a meta-commentary that ponders the effects of civilization on contemporary society.

The divide between the two works is not always as great as may appear from my analysis of Opis. Genealogy is not at all absent from the *De mulieribus* as Boccaccio is always concerned to locate his famous women in an abbreviated family tree. Certain biographies of goddesses are, in fact, extremely close to the form they will take in the *Genealogie*. Isis' genealogy is the subject of prolonged discussion in the *De mulieribus* and covers similar territory to the *Genealogie* chapter, though in a less detailed manner. He notes the disagreements between historians on Isis' origins, but without the mathematical precision of the *Genealogie* which deploys the Eusebius-Jerome *Chronicon* to favour one interpretation over another (II, xix; pp.220–222). In both cases, Boccaccio chooses to follow the more generally accepted attribution of Inacus as Isis' father.[18] In comparison to the *Genealogie*, Boccaccio considerably reduces the amount of space given over to the paraphrase of Ovid (three paragraphs in the *Genealogie* and less than one in the *De mulieribus*) and to the historical interpretation of the episode.

A similar process is at work in the biography of Europa (IX) where Boccaccio is not reticent in exhibiting his knowledge of the classical sources, including issues of dating which form an integral part of his discussion. The medieval writer appears keenly aware of the variant versions of the Europa myth in the *De mulieribus claris*. Moreover, he does not remove such questions from the text to produce a racier narrative, as might have been expected. The desire to demonstrate his credentials as a scholar ensures that he registers problems he has encountered in constructing the biography. In the chapter on Europa, Boccaccio is on the point of becoming entangled in an intricate genealogical question involving the paternity of Europa's sons. "Other sources could be cited," but Boccaccio chose not to do so because a discussion of that nature did not constitute the essential material of his book.[19] It *will* be discussed in the *Genealogie* using the *Chronicon* to throw light on conflicting dates (XI, xxvi; pp.1124–1126). Boccaccio does not ignore problems of dating in the chapter: he lists the various alternatives, but without detailed referencing or discussion, tentatively favouring one hypothesis as more convincing than the others.[20] In a similar vein, a bronze statue dedicated to Europa serves two different rhetorical purposes: in the *Genealogie*, it helps clarify the date of her abduction whereas in the *De mulieribus* it is a sign of her worldly glory.

The usefulness of the *De mulieribus claris* was perhaps limited for a humanistic audience by the fact that Boccaccio all too often provides scant information on his sources, an omission that some of the later writers on famous women will rectify. He is partially sacrificing scholarly thoroughness to readability. The *Genealogie* will be much more painstaking in its pinpointing of sources.[21] Indeed, his last work, the *Esposizioni*, bears witness to a refinement of his humanistic methodology whereby he attempts to pin down Dante's sources as accurately as possible. This can be seen as a recognition of one of the shortcomings of his earlier humanist encyclopedia, perhaps, closer than intended to medieval compilations in which the acknowledgement of sources did not play a fundamental role. The *De mulieribus* can be seen as a transitional work in which his target audience might not have appreciated a completely scholarly apparatus.

In one major respect, the goddesses of the *De mulieribus* are treated differently from their counterparts in the *Genealogie*. They have been grouped together at the beginning of the compilation as notable women who substantially contributed to the foundation of civilized society. The *Genealogie* includes this theme but does not allow it any prominence. The *De mulieribus* establishes that certain exceptional women played a fundamental role in creating the *polis* and inventing letters, the sign of civilization itself. Ceres [V], Minerva [VI], Isis [VIII], and Nicostrata [XXVII] were all involved in the creation of civilized values.[22] Their achievement is recorded in a variety of tones and contexts which do not permit an easy evaluation of these figures. These biographies are crisscrossed by a series of competing discourses—critiques of ancient pagan cults, scholarly discussion of genealogy, and in some cases, a commentary that focuses attention on other issues. The result is that it is difficult to determine how the diverse discourses interact with each other.

The fact that pagan goddesses are ridiculed as objects of cultic veneration may effect our reading of the embedded discourse on their contributions to civilization. The line separating these two areas, of necessity becomes blurred. In addition, the commentary on Ceres casts her achievements in a negative light. In the midst of such worthy inventions and discoveries, Venus' biography 'celebrates' her invention of brothels and prostitution. Although the order of presentation is basically chronological, it does have an impact on the generation of ambiguous messages by mixing together contrasting biographies. If the goddesses are meant to provide the earliest indications of exceptional women, they also signal the unstable connotations of female ingenuity in a context where pagan achievement is devalued because it is 'unchristian' and praised because it demonstrates that female potential was actualized in ancient times. Boccaccio peels off the religious paraphernalia surrounding the goddesses so that what remains is the value of humanistic scholarship and, more ambiguously, the worth of exceptional mortal women. His emphasis on their mortality indirectly makes them more human, if not more imitable; the goddesses have been brought to earth. His insistence that there may have been more than one Minerva also ironically renders the goddess more accessible by reducing her status as a superhuman entity and placing her achievements within range of mortal women.

Historical and Poetic Women

Although Boccaccio consciously set out to privilege chronology over thematic development, this did not mean that he abandoned other kinds of internal organization. From a close reading of the *De mulieribus* it becomes clear that Boccaccio was more interested in certain classes of women than others in spite of the fact that there was an attempt at encyclopedic coverage. Therefore, the women mainly chosen for their exceptional deeds, are not as isolated as one might think, because their situations and/or skills are regularly repeated through the text. Boccaccio does not draw attention to the repetitions that bind women together, preferring to create the impression of their isolation from one another. However, Boccaccio indirectly demonstrates the recurrence of particular types of women indicating that their primary function (queen, military leader etc.) was not unique, but repeatable and imitable across time. Such repetitions form a substratum of the text offering an alternative way of viewing its procession of exceptional ladies. Boccaccio's propensity to favour Livy and Valerius Maximus as his basic sources is highly suggestive of a methodology which unevenly, and not always successfully, tries to accommodate both the chronological and thematic approaches. Indeed, his aim of making known sources that were unfamiliar to the later Middle Ages can be seen in those groups of women whose actions are further enhanced by reference to more esoteric texts, such as Tacitus and Homer. In this way, the writer is stressing his humanist authority and originality.

Boccaccio's approach in the *De mulieribus claris* can be broadly described as historical. On the macroscopic level, he is closer to the concept of the chronicle, exemplified by Eusebius-Jerome. The individual biographies themselves are subject to historical criteria of investigation, some more developed than others. The classical goddesses who form a coherent group near the beginning of the *De mulieribus* (III–X) are discussed not solely or even principally according to the poetic myths associated with their names. The emphasis falls on a discussion of variants to find the most acceptable, regarding the lineages of the goddesses, dating, and the demolition of their cults from a historical point of view. After dismissing the mythical elements, in a systematic way consistent with an evehemeristic approach, Boccaccio investigates the historical achievements of these goddesses, treating them as exceptional women who often laid the foundations of society.

This methodology is clarified in the later biography of the 'goddess', Flora (LXIV) in which the poeticized myth of Zephyr and Flora is discounted as a fabrication on the part of the Roman senate. Boccaccio deconstructs the poetic myth preferring an historical explanation of the games celebrated in her memory. He treats the Ovidian *fabula* of Zephyr with disdain, consistent with the evehemeristic approach taken in the principal block of goddesses. Boccaccio's historical method enables him to introduce a critical element into the interpretation of the Flora myth. It debunks pagan religion even further and reveals the mechanisms by which cities create false myths about themselves for political ends.

Even if he momentarily loses patience with evaluating variants, Boccaccio the historian is nonetheless still concerned enough to note them.[23] His interest in them is sometimes spurred by his sense of a good story whether veracious or not to reinforce the moral point of his analysis. Boccaccio appears extremely sensitive to the different textures of the discourses he was examining in the *De mulieribus*. The biography of Flora demonstrates his overriding concern to arrive at as clear a picture as possible of the historical record. His method hierarchizes the genres so that some are more valued than others in the reconstruction of the biographies. Here, poetry is seen as defective from the perspective of biographical reconstruction and stands in contrast to the methodology employed in the *Genealogie*. The goddesses of the *De mulieribus claris* are the clearest sign of Boccaccio's Christian humanist agenda: they are treated historically, within the limits of his methodology, as women who lived and who were capable of founding civilzations as well as vitiating them through their innate sexual urges (Venus, Flora).

Boccaccio is particularly attracted to the idea of the powerful woman who represents a recurring figure in the text (Semiramis [II], the Amazon queens [XI–XII, XIX–XX, XXXII], Camilla [XXXIX], Dido [XLII], Nicaula [XLIII], Tamyris [XLIX], Athaliah [LI], Artemisia [LVII], Sophonisba [LXX], Berenice [LXXII], Cleopatra [LXXXIX], the two Agrippinas [XC, XCII], Symiamira [XCIX], Zenobia [C], Pope Joan [CI], Irene [CII], Queen Giovanna I [CVI]). Many of them have strong negative connotations, confirming the disorder that is unleashed by allowing women political influence or even direct leadership. The rare positive female ruler could be seen as the exception that proves the rule. Of the powerful women listed, eleven (out of twenty-two) may be considered positive. Yet even that figure can be further reduced, because of the sheer otherness of some of these women (Marpesia and Lampedo, Camilla, Tamyris, Berenice, Irene) in terms of the value system used by the contemporary reader.

To categorize these powerful women into positive or negative is often an extremely delicate matter. A case in point is the Empress Irene [CII]. The fact that she reigned for ten years with her son receives no special comment in the text. However, when mother and son enter into an overt power struggle which ends with Irene imprisoning him and taking control, the narrative presents some ambiguous signs for the reading of the episode. Boccaccio is always clear up to this point about Irene's fundamental virtue, even if it involves fighting her son for the right to rule. She is described as a "woman of great spirit," but this is tempered by the annotation that she "thirsted for power."[24] However the "imperandi avida" does not entirely vitiate Irene, as one might have expected: after she imprisoned her son, she reigned "cum gloria."[25] Therefore, her governance was not unduly influenced by the means she used to achieve it. Unlike her son, she did not commit atrocities once in power. Her sole aim was to acquire it through whatever method was necessary, including blinding her son.

There is no commentary appended to the narrative or any further details of Irene's reign that may have assisted in the elucidation of the chapter. It is tempting to read as ironic any of the indications which praise the Empress. Her "noble spirit," her glorious rule, her courage seem out of place in a drama in which the thirst for power is so great. But she did not behave as an Athaliah or a Cleopatra. The biography emphasizes that when she ruled she ruled brilliantly.[26]

Admiration for Irene expressed in the text is always in danger of being pushed in the opposite direction. It does not happen probably because Irene's desire for power was not excessive in the way Athaliah's was. The narrative chronicles the peripeteias of her life in a sympathetic light: the last of the men to deceive her is called a "wicked man."[27] Boccaccio is walking a tightrope, restraining his denunciation of morally dubious actions performed by Irene, a Christian empress. He seems more at ease with her power since the "enormitates" are kept within bounds. The obsession with power is seen as a sign of the decline of the Empire. If not exactly positive, the Empress is caught between the twin poles of her characterization: "ingentis animi mulier et imperandi avida." The two cannot be separated in her biography so that the power of attraction comes from her forcefulness of character, her capacity to rule, and her desire for power. Irene's biography illustrates the neces-

sity neither to rush to judgement nor to render the biographies too black
and white. The *De mulieribus claris* is virtually framed by the biographies
of Semiramis (II) and of Queen Giovanna (CVI), two conflicting versions
of queenhood that the text does not resolve.

Other themes recur across the chronological extension of the *De
mulieribus* that are equal in significance to the *exempla* of women in
power. Boccaccio shows special interest in the sexual status of women as
wives, widows, and virgins. Often their sexual *persona* is in competition
with other aspects of their activities. Women's sexuality is a given which
either impedes or advances activities in other areas. It is not normally
neglected—if it is then that is quite noticeable.

The role of the wife, the faithful wife is prominent in the *De
mulieribus*. Hypermnestra, Argia, wives of the Minyans, Penelope, Gaia
Cyrilla, Virginia, Tertia Emilia, Hypsicratea, wives of the Cimbrians,
Curia, Sulpicia, Pompeia Paulina, Triaria. The unfaithful wife has a certain currency in the *De mulieribus* (Pocris, Clytemnestra, Helen,
Olympias, Sabina Poppaea), but compared to faithful wives they constitute a definite minority. Widows also feature prominently. In most
cases, widowhood is not the main point of the biography, but forms an
important substratum: the commentary on Dido accentuates this aspect
of the narrative and carries it over into the present. The biography of
Antonia [LXXXIX] is entirely dedicated to an *exemplum* of perfect widowhood. There are a number of women whose virginity forms the centre-piece of the biographical narrative: Cloelia, Hippo, Virginia,
Gualdrada.

At times, it is difficult to allot a predominant theme to a particular
biography since it can be intersected by several thematic lines. Dido,
Artemisia, and Zenobia are good examples of this type of intersection. It
means that sexual status cuts across other areas of action contending
with them for the significance of the biography. Sexual purity can
enhance a life or can constitute its entire meaning. Boccaccio introduces both kinds of biography into the *De mulieribus*, paradoxically
opening up the potential for women not to be completely signified by
their sexual status. The situation is complex because women who break
the rules of virginity and chastity are not *a priori* excluded from heroic
actions (Laeana, Epicharis). The text has no interest in the enclosed life.
In fact, the commentary on Rhea Ilia [XLV] condemns enforced religious
enclosure. That sort of Christian heroism does not find an equivalent in
the *De mulieribus* where family life and public action are its fulcra.

The role of woman as mother does not receive emphasis: Niobe [XV]
is the principal (negative) example. The chapter on the "iuvencula
romana" [LXV] presents a reversal of the normal situation of mother
suckling baby. Faithful wives and loyal widows project an image of

women which idealizes a concept of the family that does not sit well with other active models (queenship, intellectual achievement, public action) set out in the *De mulieribus*. It does not necessarily conflict with them in the text but, functions as a kind of sub-structure guaranteeing the integrity of the extraordinary actions. If a woman has chosen the opposite path of breaking sexual taboos and patriarchal structures, the text condemns her, though not necessarily totally. Clearly, to reject the roles of wife, widow, or virgin constitutes a challenge to the foundations of society. In most cases, the text treats these exceptional women as ignoble failures for whom one can feel some admiration tempered by loathing for their sexual conduct.

The other major grouping in the *De mulieribus*, women intellectuals and artists, can be sub-divided into several strands:

i) founders/inventors of disciplines, sciences, and processes. This category overlaps to a degree with the chronological grouping of the goddesses, some of whom are accorded praise as founders and discoverers of vitally important arts. To this list, one can add Eve (I) who is credited with the invention of spinning with the distaff, according to some traditions. This reported fact implicitly links Eve to the pagan goddesses who were responsible for similar foundational inventions. Other female inventors are included after the main group of goddesses: Arachne (XVIII), Nicostrata (XXVII), Pamphile (XLIV). Arachne's biography is considered in the same historical terms as the goddesses already treated in the *De mulieribus*.[28] She is credited with the invention of nets and the discovery of the uses of woven cloth. Her contest with Pallas Athene is just another fact along with others and so does not receive extensive coverage. About half of the chapter is concerned with a diatribe against those who aim for primacy in their given areas of expertise. Similarly, Pamphile is credited with the invention of processing cotton. Inventions connected to spinning perform an ambiguous function in the text since they confirm a subordinate, domestic role for women. The inventors may have been extraordinary, but their legacy to future women was quite different. It fell to some of the women described in the *De mulieribus* to break the bonds symbolized by the invention of spinning.

ii) Prophetesses (Erythraea [XXI], Almathea [XXVI], Manto [XXX], and Cassandra [XXXV]). Boccaccio includes two of the Sibyls, Erythraea and Almathea, in his collection. To foretell the future required study and/or divine intervention.[29] Erythraea who foretold the advent of Christ represents the model of a female savant. Almost as an afterthought, her sexual purity is mentioned in the last paragraph of the biography to underline the extent to which she is a model of intellectual perfection. Although not all writers share the view that she was a virgin, the historical narrator makes a personal intervention, not for the first time in the chapter, stamping his authority on the issue ("I can easily believe this" [*FW* 87]). Boccaccio is at pains to indicate that Erythraea was not an empty receptacle into which God poured knowledge of his future intentions. She was deserving because of her learning ("ingenium" and not "astutia") and her religious devotion. The text specifically employs the word "meritum" in relation to her qualities.[30] Thus, Erythraea provides a model for female intellectual endeavour that aims at the closest rapport between writing and Christian inspiration.

iii) Artists (Tamaris [LVI], Marcia [LXVI], Irene [LIX]); (iv) Writers (Sappho [XLVII], Cornificia [LXXXVI], Proba [XCVII]); (v) Intellectuals (Nicaula [XLIII], Hortensia [LXXXIV]). Pliny the Elder provides most of the information on the female painters who form a coherent group in spite of their being scattered throughout the text.[31] Although the artists, writers and intellectuals are a small group, their significance for the text as a whole goes far beyond their numerical presence. If considered alongside the prophetesses they are suggestive of the crucial role women could play in society that is neither power politics nor domesticity. Nicaula, the Queen of Sheba, is an example of the way in which learning acts as a safeguard for the state: "Despite the pleasures which riches can bring, we read that Nicaula did not abandon herself up to idleness or feminine luxury" [*FW* 183]. Boccaccio had diagnosed excessive wealth as a reason for the decline of states. Therefore, it is implied, a way to avoid this is to place considerable value on learning and hence, wise government. The sentiment echoes the commentary on the Sibyl Almathea which takes the form of an exhortation to flee idleness and to exploit one's natural gifts ("ingenium"), aimed principally at men. In this case, women's achievements act as a stimulus to men. The emphasis on learning in society represents a general call for humanistic intervention in government. However, the *exempla* in this group should not just be read in this limited way—they are representations of the potential for female learning and creation.

Poetry against History: The Presence of Thisbe and Pocris

T̲he *De mulieribus claris* is an intensely historicist text. Boccaccio places historical/archeological sources above all others in the search for information about his subjects. There is an effort to be systematic even when poetic sources are the only ones available to him for some women. Evidence for Circe [XXXVIII] only exists in poetic texts, therefore, Boccaccio follows the praxis that will be developed in the *Genealogie*: a brief résumé of the mythical narrative followed by a moralizing interpretation. Boccaccio's interest in Circe was probably aroused because her story was also told in Homer.[32] He also depends on poetic sources, predominantly Ovid, to recount episodes from the love life of Hercules (Iole [XXIII], Deianira [XXIV]). The two chapters together constitute the nadir of Hercules' existence leading to his death. The emphasis is on love that causes his eventual downfall.[33] Iole's biography contains a passionate diatribe against love's power over men.

The presence of the tale of Pyramus and Thisbe [XIII], modelled on Ovid's *Metamorphoses* complicates matters since it portrays a pathetic, and ultimately sympathetic, view of love—an antidote to the message of Hercules' unhappy experiences. The fact that Dante includes mention of the episode in *Purgatorio* (XXVII, 37–9) may have influenced Boccaccio's decision to insert this somewhat atypical story in the *De mulieribus*.[34] It is a story of true love, thwarted by parents, culminating in the tragic death of the two young lovers. The story-line itself is not a common one in the *De mulieribus* although it would not have been out of place in the *Decameron* (and indeed there are echoes of the tale in the vernacular work). The *De mulieribus* rarely dwells on innocent love, preferring to concentrate on married love and faithfulness (and their opposites), and on exploits to defend one's chastity (and its opposite). Unmarried women in the *De mulieribus claris* are not often involved in illicit sexual activity: they are generally depicted as virgins (Hippo [LIII] is emblematic of the situation, committing suicide when she discovers that her virginity is under threat).

The story of Pyramus and Thisbe possesses only the slimmest degree of historical veracity. In spite of the poetical source, Boccaccio attempts to create an illusion of historicity by abandoning all reference to the metamorphic aspects of the Ovidian version, that is, the mulberry berries changing their colour from white to red as a result of being bathed in Pyramus' blood. Boccaccio creates the illusion of Thisbe as a historical figure by having the narrator state at the beginning of the chapter that he had been unable to find the names of Thisbe's parents (a procedure similar to that employed in the more historical biographies). In order to present the veneer of an objective narrative, Boccaccio employs only indirect speech in the passage preceding the lovers' flight. On the other hand, Ovid had ensured that the pathos and poetic intensity of the episode were fully exploited: "'O envious wall,' they would say, 'why do you stand between lovers?'"[35] In contrast, the Boccaccian text maintains a conservative distance from the two lovers by not entering into the minutiae of their love, but by dispassionately analysing it. Boccaccio's version indirectly portrays the lovers as more mature than their some- what pathetic Ovidian counterparts who kiss the wall before parting from each other!

Boccaccio's treatment of Thisbe's death also differs from Ovid's ver- sion. The medieval writer christianizes the episode so that he is able to show sympathy for Thisbe and not ridicule her faith in the gods upon whom she calls before committing suicide. His paraphrase of Thisbe's final speech emphasizes the soul, and the joining of the two souls in death: "[she] begged him to look upon his Thisbe at least in death and to wait for her soul as it departed her body, so that they could go together to whatever might be their resting-place" [FW 59]. Boccaccio increases the pathos of this final scene by allowing Pyramus to open his eyes (some- thing that he did not do in the Metamorphoses). Pyramus' action con- tributes to the creation of a bond in death between the two lovers ("amor"/"dolor"). Their unfulfilled desires are placed at the centre of Boccaccio's narration rather than the consequences of their death: "Straightway Thisbe fell upon the young man's breast and then upon his sword, poured out her blood, and followed the soul of her now dead lover" [FW 59]. Boccaccio makes no mention of the burial arrangements referred to by Ovid.[36] It is likely that he filtered the Ovidian account through readings of medieval romance and his own vernacular experi- ments in the short story.[37]

Thisbe's story is not permitted to stand without commentary. The text attempts to limit the number of interpretations that could be attrib- uted to the tale by enclosing it in a moralizing reading. The story of the two unfortunate lovers does not sit easily alongside Boccaccio's diatribes against female sexuality since it is a story which seems to bear the hall- mark of the Decameron, emphasizing "the outcome of her tragic love"[38] and the misreading or innocent deception which leads to the deaths of both lovers. The story could have easily been inserted into the Decameron in the rubric of loves with unhappy endings; the chance arrival of the lion fits well into that kind of scenario. A similar sentiment is found in the Decameron as the concluding statement to the eighth story of the fourth day dedicated to unhappy loves: "and they whom love could not join together while alive, were joined inseparably in death."[39]

The commentator of the De mulieribus takes a partisan approach to the lovers' fate, asking the reader to be sympathetic towards them: "Who does not shed at least a single tear for their tragic end?" [*FW* 59] The theme of recalcitrant parents and ingenious means of breaking their prohibitions occurs in the vernacular text with a certain frequency. Unlike the polyphony of the *Decameron* where women are able to express themselves and make assertive statements about the meaning of the stories, the male commentator of the *De mulieribus* seeks to be reductive, cutting out those layers of meaning which conflict with the moral intensity of the message he is trying to convey. The commentator attempts a rather contorted justification of the narrative: "To love while in the flower of youth is a fault, but it is not a frightful crime for unmarried persons since they can proceed to matrimony" [*FW* 61]. The commentary makes every effort to tame the narrative, to justify its pleasurable aspects in the name of Christian morality and social order. As a consequence, sexual passion, which is not mentioned in the account proper, becomes linked in the commentary to lawful procreation. Although the commentator pleads for understanding in treating the excesses of youth, it is in the context of marriage. The moral argument which suggests that Christian instruction can be drawn from the tale shifts attention away from its literariness and potential amorality. It brings closure to the possible proliferation of its meanings.

Almost as an afterthought, Boccaccio introduces the theme of parental control in the concluding paragraph whereas in Ovid it is an essential part of his narrative and explains the actions of the lovers.[40] The commentator gives advice on how to manage young people, particularly in matters of love. His attitude in general could be described as somewhat patronising, creating the impression of someone who has earned the fruits of experience. The episode seems to have triggered a peculiar reaction here that belongs more to the ethos of the *Decameron* than to the hardened morality of the *De mulieribus*. Boccaccio's compromise is to walk a tightrope between condemnation and acceptance of youthful physical desire: "Passionate desire is ungovernable; it is the plague and the disgrace of youth, yet we should tolerate it with patience."[41]

I have examined the 'moral' of the Thisbe chapter at some length in order to illustrate the way in which Boccaccio attempted to channel the anarchic tendencies of the story itself into the more rigid reality of the older commentator. In this chapter, one can notice the gulf between the story, vibrant with youthful passion, and the commentary of an older man. In a sense, the chapter can be regarded as the attempt by the writer to justify the contenutistic choices of the *Decameron* through the addition of moralizing material and the subtraction of too explicit references to the details of love. Hence, Boccaccio distances himself from the *Decameron* without quite rejecting it. Thisbe's biography is characteristic of a style of writing that was the idiolect of the younger Boccaccio whereas the commentary represents his more 'mature' moral approach to literature and life—the *Decameron moralisé*. The commentary attempts to limit the pleasure/seduction of the narrative, to circumscribe love with enough prohibitions to render it acceptable to the general moralizing tone of the book. The inclusion of Thisbe indicates that there were still residues of the *Decameron* present in the text, but they had to be the object of historical and/or moral analysis.

Thisbe is not the only problematic and unexpected Ovidian character to find her way into the *De mulieribus*. Pocris [XXVIII] is the subject of a chapter related to the theme of the corrupting influence of monetary values.[42] In Ovid's version Cephalus, the husband of Pocris, professes his love: "...it was Pocris I loved: Pocris was in my heart, Pocris was ever on my lips."[43] This perfect love was not destined to endure. The husband's jealousy (augmented by the intervention of the goddess Aurora) leads him to test his wife's fidelity by arranging to have her seduced with promises of gain. To his grief, he discovers that she is corruptible. The story uses disguise and subterfuge to illustrate its themes in ways that are again reminiscent of the *Decameron*. However, Boccaccio pares the original Ovidian account to its bare bones, omitting long digressions concerning the gifts Pocris gave to her husband (*Metamorphoses*, VII, 759–93).

The Ovidian account is narrated in the first person, which has the effect of making Pocris a hapless victim of the jealousy of both the goddess and Cephalus. Boccaccio transforms the story into a third-person account, which prevents an intimate understanding of either of the spouse's feelings. In the medieval text, there is not one instance of the husband using direct speech. Aurora uses it once, indicative of Boccaccio's continuing interest in narrative, since it is rarely employed in the *De mulieribus claris*. Boccaccio frames the story with a strong moralizing structure. He provides a single sentence of introduction to present the two protagonists and then launches into a diatribe against women, leaving no doubt as to the position of the narrator. The story is not allowed to speak for itself: the reader is asked to interpret the tale in accordance with the clear instructions of the text.

Any sympathy for Pocris that may have been generated by the story is dissipated before the narrative even begins: "Her greed gained her in equal measure the hate of honest women and the approval of men, because through her example the faults of her sex were revealed."[44] Thus the opening commentary reinforces the stereotyped view of woman as avaricious. It stresses Pocris' function as a generalized symbol of woman's grasping nature. However, the concluding commentary, although it does not exactly negate the impression created by the opening statement, goes a long way towards mitigating its effect. The (male) commentator does not go so far as to find excuses for the woman's behaviour—he does, however, shift the focus on to men and society as a whole. In spite of the fact that Pocris is called "foolish" ("insipiens," *DMC* 122) because of her desire to enrich herself, it is remarked that she is not alone in this foolishness; that, in fact, most people possess the same defect (and they are referred to as "stupid" ["stolidi," *DMC* 122]). Secondly, the husband's activities are called into question and seen as a sign of weakness—the antithesis of virility: "In my opinion, jealousy is a ridiculous sickness of the mind caused by the pusillanimity of the people who suffer from it" [*FW* 115]. Therefore, the husband's dishonest behaviour is blamed for leading to his wife's downfall, indicating a crisis in the interpretation of the story. From the strong opening statement where blame is seen as residing with women, the commentator inserts the wife in the broader question of social values and male behaviour (in this case jealousy which is seen as a crisis of masculinity—a kind of impotence). In the end, Pocris' conduct is explicable through an analysis of the social conditions under which she lived.

The attraction of this story for Boccaccio resides partly in the fact that it illustrates the corrupting force of money on human values. So even in this Pocris is only partially to blame for her misfortunes. Through the promptings of Aurora, the husband sets in train a series of events that totally undermines his relationship with his wife, eventually leading to her death. It is perhaps one of the valuable lessons of this chapter, sporadically applied elsewhere in the text, that women are part of a society which is dominated by questionable male values and therefore should not have to carry the sole blame for the particular forms their behaviour takes. From a clear, unambiguous opening paragraph, the conclusions of the commentator cast doubt on how the reader should interpret the culpability of Pocris. The early straightforward condemnations of the female sex are caught up in a complex web of contradictions and, more tellingly, in a purposeful undoing of conventional wisdom.

The use of poetic sources is limited in the *De mulieribus claris.* Boccaccio was more inclined to deconstruct them or find alternative discourses, as was the case with Flora. He does not eliminate them altogether but applies the criteria of historical analysis as far as possible. The biographies of Thisbe and Pocris are exceptional. In both tales, the narrative dynamic is maintained and the analytical, historical approach is subordinated to the moralizing commentary. This would seem to indicate that Boccaccio, although more interested in the analysis of texts, was still open to producing a seductive narrative. However, it had to be under the control of the other discourses (historical, moral, analytical).

· · · · · ·

II

𝕭occaccio the 𝕳umanist

The *De mulieribus claris* can be read as a conscious effort by Boccaccio to confirm his credentials as a humanist writer who was part of that avant-garde movement presided over by Petrarch. He certainly copied works by Petrarch whenever he was able and regarded him as a model writer and scholar. However, to think of Boccaccio as the disciple, simply following his master's example is rather misleading. One should perhaps think more in terms of reciprocity: the relationship between the two humanists benefited both of them and stimulated the two writers to launch out in directions that were only possible because of this sense of mutuality.

Boccaccio made clear his debt to Petrarch with respect to the *De mulieribus claris* by indicating a precise model for his series of female autobiographies in *De viris illustribus*. The debts to Petrarch do not end here. There are other, less well-known, Petrarchan texts which form part of the structure and content of the *De mulieribus*. The *De mulieribus* can be called Petrarchan because of its self-proclaimed modelling on the *De viris*, and also because of its focus on the classical Roman world, with a similar adhesion to values that Petrarch himself championed. At the same time, the *De mulieribus* appears to me to be marked by an effort to distinguish itself from the model and assert its own identity. This is not to say there is an open break between master and disciple, but Boccaccio brings his own interpretation to the practice of humanism, a *contaminatio* of Petrarch's methods and aims with his own vast cultural baggage, including his experience as a writer of prose in the vernacular.

Boccaccio's work on women is suggestive of the formation of his humanist personality. He places considerable emphasis on his own rediscoveries of the classical past. In particular, Boccaccio displays his

Greek scholarship, perhaps with the aim of indicating his difference from Petrarch. References to Homer, and to Greek culture in general, are a noticeable feature of the work.[1] It may be true that Boccaccio is solely adding a patina of Greek culture to figures which were well known to the later Middle Ages through Latin texts. Yet, the fact of alluding to and making use of his knowledge of Greek was a sign of his commitment to extending humanism to include the study of Greek. Further, Boccaccio's deployment of Tacitus in the *De mulieribus claris* may be seen as a conscious enlargement of the parameters of early humanism. The recovery of such an author was a distinguishing feature of the text that enabled Boccaccio to add details to some of his biographies that were not available elsewhere. Boccaccio was seeking his own voice while aware that he was closely bound to the master. He was rechannelling his creative energies into the ordered world of humanist endeavour.

Man-Made Women: Boccaccio and Petrarch's *De viris illustribus* (Concerning Illustrious Men)

In his introduction to the *De mulieribus claris*, Boccaccio explicitly refers to Petrarch as the author of the *De viris illustribus,* a series of humanistically inspired biographies of (mainly) Roman heroes.[2] The reference to this particular Petrarchan text was not a casual one: Boccaccio expressly adopted this model because it had been endorsed by the most prestigious scholar and writer of the day. The imitation of the open structure of the *De viris* allowed him to manipulate and remould Petrarch's male heroes—substituting women for men—to appeal to a prospective audience appreciative of the new humanistic studies.

Although in some ways the *De casibus* is closer to the *De viris*, it does not have the same 'open' structure.[3] Boccaccio implicitly asked that his text on women be judged and evaluated against the *De viris*, not only in terms of the structure of the individual texts, but also in the sense that, if taken together, the two writers present a humanistic overview of the role of both sexes in history and society. Indeed, the comparison serves to highlight the originality of the Boccaccian text by its very choice of subject—women. The choice of subject-matter was not a simple substitution of women for men, but implied a view of society in which women should not be absent from humanistically inspired texts.

The final version of the *De viris* had been limited quite stringently to the heroes of ancient Rome, whereas Boccaccio felt no such constraint. It may well be that he had been instrumental in encouraging Petrarch's aborted attempt in the period 1351–53 to extend the scope of the *De viris* by introducing figures from outside Roman history (Petrarch wrote twelve new biographies from Adam to Hercules, including an 'honorary' man, Semiramis—the second figure in chronological order in the *De mulieribus*). Both biographies exhibit enough similarities to strongly suggest that Boccaccio was at least familiar with this redaction of the *De viris illustribus*, if not the mover behind it.[4]

Boccaccio sets his women within the framework of an extended chronological structure. He feminizes the male origins of the human race (Eve instead of Adam) before proceeding to other historical eras, although nearly always avoiding specific treatment of biblical or Christian women. The similarities between the *De viris* and the *De mulieribus* seem to end here. Petrarch's work has more in common with Boccaccio's *De casibus virorum illustrium* than with his text on women. Nevertheless, there appears to be a common historical method discernible in both works in so far as Petrarch talks about gathering together scattered information into one text; a strategy employed quite literally by his disciple who includes dissonant versions of historical/biographical events.[5] However, Boccaccio applies the historical method much more haphazardly—although he does appear to be more aware of the problems involved in producing an historical account when there is more than one version of the 'facts'.

A good example of the strengths and limitations of Boccaccio's 'historical' method, can be found in the chapter on Semiramis [II] in the *De mulieribus*. From his sources Boccaccio notes the conflicting views on the queen's sexual partners—whether she was the lover of her son, or whether she had many lovers whom she ordered to be killed immediately after intercourse (Orosius). The fact that he notes conflict amongst his sources indicates the beginnings of a more rigorous historiographical process which, however, he does not follow through. He does not state which might be the more likely version in view of his scholarly investigations. Petrarch, in his search for a tight narrative, avoided the structure employed by Boccaccio since it opens the text to doubts and uncertainties, not only about what actually happened, but also about the author's message.[6]

Petrarch had privileged the message and clarity of organization so that the ideality and moral purpose of his collection of biographies made the fullest impact. He had no doubts about the function of history, which for him was a series of *exempla* designed to fulfil a specific moral role. In the *De mulieribus claris*, Boccaccio seems to be following his master's interpretation of history as an appropriate means of encapsulating the ideological structure of his work: [7]

Indeed, this is, unless I am mistaken, the fruitful goal of the historian: to impart those things that the readers must either imitate or avoid so that in either case there is an abundance of illustrious examples.[8]

In the *De viris* there is an obvious model of military and moral virtue in the person of Scipio Africanus through whom the key values of "gloria" and "virtus" are expressed (*Prose*, p.218).[9] Scipio incarnates the ideal of a warrior who is not vitiated by base ambition and is motivated only by "true and lofty glory."[10] Indeed, Scipio banished any sign of the feminine from his physical appearance.[11] The inference is clearly that truly heroic behaviour can only be attributed to men, mainly military men. This may help to explain the presence of so many military women in the *De mulieribus*, by implication ranked alongside outstanding male generals.[12]

The *De viris* and the *De mulieribus* are indirectly comparable only in so far as they present structural similarities: individual portraits of the famous (and in some cases the infamous) require the reader to make sense of the single lives and then draw general conclusions from a reading of the entire text. In Petrarch's case, the biographical subjects are much more homogeneous than the disparate women of the *De mulieribus claris*. Boccaccio's attraction to the *De viris* owed much to his humanist aspirations and the desire for his work to be considered favourably alongside Petrarch's. By using this model, Boccaccio raised expectations about the women contained in the text, something that contributes in part to the difficulties in gaining a clear sense of the work's signification.

Petrarch's Men and Women

Boccaccio was not the first to list or catalogue famous women, although he himself was not aware of a classical precedent for such a literary/historical text. Plutarch's *Mulierum virtutes* was completely unknown to him. It became common currency only after the publication of the Latin translation in 1485, offering some variation and correction to the Boccaccian *exempla*.[13]

It is probable that Boccaccio was familiar with Petrarch's epistle to the Empress Anna (wife of the Holy Roman Emperor Charles IV), datable to 23 May 1358.[14] Petrarch wrote in response to a letter from the Empress informing him of the recent birth of her daughter, Elizabeth. Petrarch associates the moment of writing with the failure on the part of the woman to produce a male heir.[15] Thus, in spite of the title of the epistle in the *Familiares*: "To the Empress Anna, congratulating her on the birth of her child, unfortunately a girl, and using the opportunity to recount many things in the praise of women,"[16] its thrust is more in line with a *responsio consolatoria*. The discourse links female failure to the male politics of dynastic continuity and to the structure of the social universe in which women must act in conformity with male-imposed statutes of behaviour. The text's relationship with the woman's biological body is a complex one: it recognizes her role as (re)producer, but defines her only partially by that function. The humanist word, by presenting diverse models of behaviour, hints vaguely at the possibility of liberating woman from the traditional version of the female body. Petrarch does not offer a program for change—indeed, he insulates himself from such a need by grounding his presentation of literary and historical women in the reality of dynastic politics (the primary function of women to produce male heirs).

Petrarch argues the case for a changed perspective on women using exemplary figures organized along thematic lines. He does so principally with reference to the classical world, occasionally alluding to Christian sources (Saint Augustine is mentioned but once). One can discern the influence of Valerius Maximus' *Factorum ac dictorum memorabilium liber* in which the Roman writer arranged the digest of historical incidents and curiosities under various headings to emphasize the moral aspects of history. Indeed, a number of Petrarch's examples are culled from that source.[17]

A strong case can be made for Boccaccio's awareness of the Petrarchan epistle. There is not only the biographical possibility namely, a visit during which Boccaccio may have copied, or seen the letter in question, but also the highly suggestive fact that nearly all the classical women described therein reappear in Boccaccio's work, representing about a quarter of the *De mulieribus*.[18] Given that Petrarch was breaking new ground in gathering his *exempla* from disparate sources and welding them into a coherent, evaluative discourse, it seems most likely that Boccaccio consulted the epistle for knowledge of these women. The clarity of Petrarch's moral purpose is achieved by grouping the women around certain themes—unlike Boccaccio who preferred a chronological structure.

The first group of women in the Petrarchan epistle constitutes an acknowledgement that, in some circumstances, women may be able to achieve recognition as humanists. The correspondent has opted for female intellectuals and writers as a sign of his own interests, and of the possibility that women might be appreciated for their intellectual gifts. The fact that Petrarch begins with Minerva and Isis is also significant for the way in which Boccaccio concentrates ancient goddesses at the beginning of the *De mulieribus claris* to demonstrate the weaknesses of classical explanations for the origins of material culture. Petrarch, anxious to ensure that the Christian side of his discourse on women is not lost, on two occasions chooses figures which explicitly urge the connection between writing and Christian duty.[19] Petrarch renounces the idea of the woman as lover who might throw the moral program of the new Latin humanism into disorder, as Boccaccio will do in a less systematic manner in the *De mulieribus*.

Military women occupy a comparatively large space in the letter although, their stories are compressed as much as possible with the exception of Hypsicratea, Tamyris, Zenobia, and especially Semiramis whose stories are told in relatively more detail. The warlike determination of Semiramis is illustrated by an episode which was well-known from classical sources: the queen, who was combing her hair when she heard the news of the rebellion of Babylon, immediately took up arms and did not complete her coiffure until the insurrection was quashed. To celebrate her victory, a statue was erected showing her with half her hair combed and the other half loose.[20]

It is significant that Petrarch chose to illustrate the life of Semiramis by selecting a single event and granting it privileged status. Most other writers who venture into this genre adopt a similar methodology; that is, a meaningful fragment is exhibited for the purpose of proving a particular point about the woman in question. There is no sense in which the illustrious women have autonomous or complete lives of their own. Boccaccio himself was aware of the gaps in his knowledge of classical women. Although his biographies are fragmentary, he frequently alludes to missing pieces of information so that the reader is conscious of the effort to complete the lives. His inability to discover more information about his subjects after the accomplishment of the deed(s) for which they were best known—often in the form of a statement acknowledging that he could not find out when they died—is suggestive of a desire and an intent to go beyond Petrarch's methodology. The expanded biographical form favoured by Boccaccio represents an attempt to break away from Petrarch's restricted vision of female lives. The problem for Boccaccio was that in the process the moral kernel might be lost, hence, his addition of moral commentaries.

Petrarch enshrines Semiramis in art. Her statue, to which the writer alludes, represents this process of 'freezing' the female figure in a pose which defines her absolutely. In his epistle, Petrarch says nothing about Semiramis' sexual indiscretions, frequently discussed by classical and medieval writers (including Boccaccio). Such a discussion would have led Petrarch into the area of female sexuality, a topic he normally avoids throughout the text. This registers the extent to which he wished to be 'positive' about women in a humanist reconstruction of women's history, and indicates his possible discomfiture with the subject of sexuality in this context. Petrarch's message for women is circumscribed by the general emphasis on their sexual probity.[21] The brief text seems to offer a bewildering variety of female activities, but relies on linking them to social institutions—the family in particular—as a means of suggesting ideal feminine behaviour beneath the fictions of diversity.[22]

Strangely enough, in the same section, Cleopatra and the extraordinarily chaste Zenobia are placed side by side.[23] The account focuses on their eventual defeat by the Romans rather than on their contrasting sexual *mores*. Such a pairing highlights the problem of interpreting the illustrious women genre. The common destiny of these two women—defeat—brings them together, yet they are inevitably separated by their opposing sexual practices, seen through the eyes of a Christian male valorizing the concept of chastity. What is the relationship here between the female body and male politics in the case of the infamously unchaste Cleopatra and the extraordinarily chaste Zenobia? It would seem that in the epistle to the Empress Anna sexual practice had no effect on the end result. Petrarch does not raise the possibility that Cleopatra may have been victorious had she been more chaste nor that she might have been more favourably judged by male history. In the epistle, Cleopatra's sexuality is a side issue which would be utilized by Boccaccio as a metonymy for female debility.

The remaining sections of classical *exempla* offer a series of women who show an extraordinary devotion to family values. Except for a brief excursus into the female names of continents and some Italian cities, approximately half of Petrarch's letter concerns the sacrifices made by women, either as daughters or wives. Petrarch presents an ambiguous picture of the woman as nurturer. Related to this theme is that of family values which, in the case of Cornelia (mother of the Gracchi), sees her watching her twelve sons being put to death with the greatest stoicism, a calamity "that would have crushed even virile souls."[24] The fact that her courage might be considered greater than that of a man is the literal limit of the mini-treatise—the metamorphosis of the imperfect woman into the perfect man. The case of the daughter who suckles her father indirectly associates the woman with incest taboos.[25] The *exemplum* raises general issues of representation in collections of biographies of famous women. The use of an extreme example to make a point about 'normal' behaviour runs the risk of rendering all female conduct aberrant. The epistle and Boccaccio's collection of biographies are always addressed to men as well as to women. They implicitly exhort men not to be 'outdone' by exceptional women promoting the role required of males as 'natural' leaders. They also appeal inevitably to men as both voyeurs and judges of female behaviour.

Pushed to the margins of Petrarch's discussion are references to biblical (Old Testament only) and Christian figures. Although not excluded totally, they do not hold centre stage in terms of moral authority. This is an effect of Petrarch's humanism in that the classical exemplary tradition is considered a valid pedagogical tool with which to inculcate moral values in Christian women, replacing the well-worn Christian *exempla* that formed part of the everyday culture of many women. In fact, Petrarch dismisses the saints and martyrs in one sentence![26] The Old Testament women fare slightly better—they are not mentioned by name, but described in such a way as to make their identity clear. In this way Abraham's wives and concubines, and Judith find a place.[27]

The authoritative language of Latin emphasizes the controlling function of male discourse in the *De mulieribus claris,* excluding the many men and women who could not read Latin and hence could not participate in the humanist movement. Latin is the language of domination, authorizing a body of Christian texts which is alien and generally unsympathetic to women. The text speaks to men in so far as it provides a humanistically acceptable arsenal to contain women, and marks out acceptable and unacceptable female behaviour by telling stories about women. Boccaccio has not chosen to enter into discursive argument about the social and religious status of women, but rather to illustrate and comment on them, categorizing them for men.

It is only with difficulty that one can distinguish between the pride taken in humanist research (the unearthing of rare and little known *exempla*) and a preoccupation with producing role models relevant to contemporary women. The latter function is severely truncated in Petrarch's epistle because of the framing of the *exempla* in the context of an acceptance of male dynastic politics and its priorities. The brief mention of Matilde of Canossa[28] provides a relatively recent example of a warrior-queen, comparable to the Amazons who are mentioned earlier in the letter. Matilde combines warlike courage (she is described as undertaking military action "with manly courage")[29] with other moral virtues, particularly her "munificent, and more than feminine, generosity."[30] She overcomes female weakness, defeating the innate grasping nature of her sex, to become a ruler. It is implicitly understood that to attain a position of power a woman must publicly emulate male behaviour, yet in private she must follow rigid rules of propriety which would have usually excluded her from public life. It is difficult to escape the conclusion that paradox lies at the heart of the illustrious women treatise: its pedagogical intention seeks to produce rules for normative behaviour out of extraordinary *exempla*. The famous women themselves have a space, defined by male writers who seek to contain the impact of examples that might upset the controlling ideologies of the text and society.

As indicated above, Petrarch's letter to the Empress Anna seems to have inspired Boccaccio's collection of biographies of famous women. The *De mulieribus claris* is much larger and more complex than Petrarch's text in so far as female virtue is scrutinized in an elaborate historical context losing some of its clarity of definition. The biographies themselves are less 'symbolic' and, in general, less assimilable to the representation of a single, straightforward virtue. The neat sections of Petrarch's letter are lost in Boccaccio's 'translation', but this does not mean that he disregarded the categories that the humanist had devised. In fact, women as warriors, leaders, and writers form the basis of the *De mulieribus claris* as well as the female virtues associated with them.

Petrarch's letter refers to only one woman who could be seen in a negative light—Cleopatra—whereas Boccaccio introduced a systematic principle of mixing together 'good' and 'bad' women in his own work. Such a procedure places the entire encomiastic project under stress because of the subsequent uncertainties and ambiguities created by the presence of women who threaten to undermine the positive fabric of the text.

In other respects, the *De mulieribus claris* presents basic similarities to Petrarch's epistle. The addressee remained a woman connected to a powerful male political figure (Andrea Acciaiuoli for Boccaccio). There were hardly any medieval women in both texts (the use of recent 'local' illustrious women was expanded to a degree by Boccaccio, but only at a later stage in the composition of the *De mulieribus*). Essentially the biographies had been explorations into the topic of classical women using an experimental humanist methodology. Boccaccio's marginalization of biblical and Christian women was more rigorous than Petrarch's who still retained a residue of such women. Therefore, Petrarch's letter to the Empress Anna gave a stimulus to Boccaccio's treatise on women, bringing about the (re)birth of this form, associated with a birth of a different kind!

The Search for Classical Women

Petrarch's choice of women provided Boccaccio with an invaluable starting-point for his research. Once Boccaccio had adumbrated a plan for the *De mulieribus claris* he needed to flesh out the bare bones of the information found in Petrarch's letter and to seek out new women for his compilation. Most likely, this work was undertaken after Boccaccio had viewed the letter: it was begun probably in 1359 during his visit to the master and continued until 1361, the date of the first draft of the *De mulieribus*.

Boccaccio's search for 'suitable' classical women led him inevitably to two major classical writers who were known to him from his youth: Livy and Valerius Maximus. The *Factorum et dictorum memorabilium libri* could be likened to a treasure-trove of historical figures used for moralistic purposes. It had already been employed by Boccaccio in the *De casibus*.[31] It is therefore likely that he used Valerius Maximus as a first guide to the 'availability' of suitable women. One of the characteristic features of Valerius Maximus is the thematic division of subjects under various headings associated with moral categories, either positive or negative.[32] Petrarch probably had such a schema in mind for the composition of his letter to the Empress Anna. Boccaccio chose to ignore the Roman author's methodology. This decision indicates a certain freedom towards his sources, dictated by a desire for completeness and by a complex political, social, and moral agenda. It was a means of reasserting the importance of biography as a genre which would lend prestige to the nascent humanist movement. Boccaccio added a twist to the genre by 'inventing' the female biography, making it a serious object of scholarly inquiry.

Although Boccaccio found the same story in different authors, and sometimes much more extensively treated (particularly in Livy), Valerius Maximus stressed a certain number of themes which were to be explored by the Florentine author who was extremely careful about his choice of exemplars. In fact, from Valerius Maximus' sixth book on chastity Boccaccio selected only two out of thirteen Roman *exempla*—the reason being that seven of them are concerned with men alone and the others contain no sense of female heroism or sufficient detail to make a 'good' story.[33] However, he selects all three of the foreign examples.[34] It is probable that the choice of these narratives was due to the fact that Boccaccio found more extensive accounts in Livy which confirmed their authority and 'fame'. In addition, he makes use of all three *exempla* in the section on the fidelity of wives towards their husbands (Tertia Aemilia, Turia/Curia, Sulpicia [VI, 7, 1–3]).[35]

Boccaccio subjected the moral schema of Valerius Maximus to his chronological arrangement of the same *exempla*. Obviously the organization privileged by the *De mulieribus* resulted in a dilution of Valerius Maximus' carefully crafted moral analysis of the best and worst in Roman and other societies. Boccaccio confused 'good' and 'bad' women so that the reader does not know what to expect in moral terms from each successive biography. In this way, Boccaccio can play with readerly expectations. This re-ordering of the biographies did not of necessity entail the abandonment of a moral plan beneath the relentless historical procession of female personages. Indeed, on the key issue of widows not remarrying the moral attitude of Valerius Maximus did not conflict with Jerome's *Against Jovinianus*.[36] His emphasis on sexual restraint, and its opposite, was a means of showing right and wrong forms of behaviour. This method was also used by Boccaccio in his collection of women.

Although Boccaccio was not a slavish disciple of Valerius Maximus' interpretations of individual women, he did tend to express similar doubts about them. Valerius Maximus' section dedicated to Sempronia begins with a question that seeks to undermine the point of what follows: "What have women to do with public speaking? Nothing, if ancient tradition is to be maintained."[37] This is part of the pattern of misogyny which is apparent in the text. For example, Hortensia (the daughter of a famous orator) is praised in such a way that the encomium itself undercuts her achievement:

> if the men of later generations wanted to imitate her forcefulness, the great heritage of Hortensius' oratory would not have finished with the oration of a woman.[38]

Such double-edged compliments whereby female achievement is viewed as a lack of virility on the part of men are frequently to be found or hinted at in the *De mulieribus*. Both texts are really an encouragement to men to conform to certain types/standards of 'male' behaviour. In Sempronia's biography [LXXVI], Boccaccio did not employ the direct form of doubt about women's public role in society, but uses instead other, perhaps more subtle, means. The first is a reminder about female nature, Aristotelian in origin:

> Perhaps some who will object that, although Sempronia deserved it by right of ancestry, nonetheless she should not have been included among famous women on the grounds of constancy since women are instinctively obstinate and unbending in their opinions about everything. I do not deny this, but I believe that women ought to be praised if they rely, as Sempronia certainly did, upon the truth. [FW 319]

This argument concerns the so-called natural characteristics of woman. It contrasts the "some" who represent a hard-line view on women with the commentator who is presented as more conciliatory. The latter does not deny the accepted view of female nature but suggests that some of these seemingly negative qualities in certain circumstances may be used positively. This is a typically ironical ploy in the *De mulieribus* whereby there is a slight amelioration to a biological observation that nevertheless still maintains the status of a fundamental truth. The term "constantia" ["constancy"], often applied to the steadfastness of Christian martyrs confronted with the perverted punishments of tyrants, is implicitly undermined.

The introduction of the first-person into the discourse at this point (the penultimate paragraph of the chapter) is indicative of the way in which the commentary intends to subtract the positives from the historical account reported by the text. In the biographical narrative, Sempronia had been praised for her courage and her "constantia" ("constantia animi"; "constantissimo pectore"). Her intelligence allowed her to deduce that the man who presented himself as her nephew was an imposter. Therefore, the narrative concerning Sempronia rejects the conservative notions attached to the episode, implanted in its very action by Valerius Maximus. Boccaccio separates out the historical narrative and the commentary in a way which is contrary to the Roman writer's methodology, but which uses the commentary to direct the reader back to Valerius Maximus' position.

The final paragraph of Sempronia's biography owes its tone to Valerius Maximus and contrasts strongly with the preceding heroic narrative which is thereby deconstructed.[39] Indeed, the commentary on Sempronia is carried even further in the *De mulieribus*: in the very last sentence Boccaccio introduces another group of interpreters ("She is also reported by some sources...").[40] These newly introduced documents suggest that Sempronia carried inflexibility to the point where she became an accomplice in her husband's death. The commentator makes no explicit intervention here, allowing the assertions to remain uncontested and creating a final, negative impression on the reader. Boccaccio has fashioned two Sempronias the second of whom is created by a reportage of voices dissenting from the narrative of the 'first' Sempronia. The last paragraph weaves together dubious assertions held by a minority of historians and a negative view of female nature to create a pastiche which compromises the positive version of Sempronia. It does not appear to have the same status as the biographical section, but the insertion of the commentator's opinion on female obstinacy is certainly intended to bolster a view of women that would make the reader rethink the heroic action of Sempronia.

Indirectly, the commentary demonstrates the facility with which male discourse belittles women's achievements by insinuation, even if the statements are not solidly factual or rationally deduced. It is perhaps one of the ironies of the text that the commentary is an example of a non-humanistic approach which perpetuates anti-female sentiments. It indicates the power of such discourses, and in some ways, is asking the reader to distinguish between two types of 'evidence' about women, historical (humanist-based) and traditional (unquestioned assumptions drawn from a variety of sources) .

In trying to uncover a pattern of choice in Boccaccio's selection of women, one inevitably finds a case which does not seem to fit into any pattern; for example, Dripetrua [LXXV], who receives only the barest of descriptions in Valerius Maximus. Her one remarkable feature is a double set of teeth ("duplici ordine dentium" [I, 8, ext. 13]. The other detail of her life on which the Roman author passes comment is that she went with her father (King Mithridates) into exile. In the *De mulieribus*, Boccaccio draws an implicit parallel between Dripetrua and Hypsicratea who followed her husband into exile, courageously supporting all the hardships that such a venture entailed. Hypsicratea assumes heroic proportions, whereas Dripetrua is handicapped by a chance of nature: "If we can trust the accounts of ancient authors, Dripetrua, who was born with a double row of teeth, presented a monstrous spectacle in her day to all the people of Asia" [*FW* 315].

Boccaccio's choice of Dripetrua symbolizes in perhaps its most extreme form the struggle between nature and culture which is central to his quest of defining and analysing woman. Her handicap graphically crystallizes the idea of woman as a defect/freak of nature, but who can partially redeem herself (notwithstanding her deformity) in her social and cultural performance. In the *De mulieribus*, the concept of female weakness is generally expressed through uncontrollable sexual urges but in this instance difference is made visible in a body which externalizes innate female monstrosity. However, as with female sexuality, the text urges that it is possible to overcome natural 'disadvantages': "they [the teeth] did constitute a notable deformity. This, as I have already indicated, she mitigated by a loyalty deserving of praise" [*FW* 315]. Her moral virtue does not totally compensate for physical disability which is a sign of her reification into an object of horror. Her faithfulness, mentioned three times in the space of a brief paragraph that constitutes the chapter, is part of the text's valorization of the family unit offering the vision of a submissive daughter against the odds. Nature still defines what a woman is in this biography. The cultural elements do not eliminate nor neutralize her natural deformity nor do they permit her to rebel against the values imposed on her—submission (both to nature and to the family) is the key message of this biography.

It is probable that Valerius Maximus provided confirmation and a degree of systematization to some of the key themes of the *De mulieribus*; most notably, female sexual restraint. The knowledge Boccaccio acquired from this text had to be supplemented by information obtained from other sources such as Livy, known to Boccaccio from his early studies.[41] From both these writers, Boccaccio extracted a core of women. They conformed to the thematic interests of the classical writers but were judged by Christian notions of sexual *mores* and female behaviour in general. Indeed, Livy viewed his history as a series of negative and positive *exempla* which would make Romans think about and question their own behaviour.[42]

In some ways Livy is closer than Valerius Maximus to the structure adopted by Boccaccio in that the episodes selected for the *De mulieribus* centre on an action, or a series of connected actions, performed by a woman in a chronological framework. Livy's episodes have a strong narrative base and offer a relatively subdued moral commentary on the deeds presented in the episode. Without undue difficulty, they could be removed from their context of a chronological account of the Roman republic and still retain their sense of being 'monumental'. In a number of cases, Boccaccio follows the Livian version of events almost to the letter; for example, in the biographies of "Orgiagontis reguli uxor" and Theoxena.[43]

In the Theoxena episode, there is a slight change of tone in the description of the premeditated suicide Theoxena organizes for herself and her family. Livy calls her "ferox" (XL, 4, 13) whereas Boccaccio who wishes to bestow greater gravity on her uses the adjective "austera" (*DMC* 290). Since, for Livy, the episode constitutes part of a continuous narrative, he is able to insert it into a more complete political frame than Boccaccio, who is more interested in the singularity of the action. For Livy, the suicide of an entire family had precise political consequences: "The horror of this act added, as it were, a new spark to the resentment against the king, so that people generally were cursing him and his sons."[44]

Boccaccio's treatment of Veturia [LV]—the mother of Coriolanus— illustrates the ways in which the *De mulieribus* distances itself quite significantly from its Latin sources. The episode is treated extensively by both Livy and Valerius Maximus. Therefore, it provides an opportunity to gauge the way in which these sources were used. In his treatment of this episode, Boccaccio scarcely deviates from Livy's account, perhaps attracted by the dramatic nature of the confrontation between mother and son. On the other hand, Valerius Maximus plays down Veturia's *active* contribution to Coriolanus' decision to refrain from attacking Rome—the mere sight of his mother is sufficient to make him change his mind: "As soon as the son saw her he said, "You have conquered and defeated my anger."[45] In Livy's account, Veturia persuades her son to abandon his plan of attack using rhetorical argument.

At this point the similarities between Boccaccio and Livy cease. Livy ends his narration by describing the positive effects of Veturia's action on the future status of women in Rome:

> There was no envy of the fame the women had earned, on the part of the men of Rome—so free was life in those days from disparagement of another's glory—and to preserve its memory the temple of *Fortuna muliebris* was built and dedicated.[46]

Boccaccio however makes a distinction between the action and its consequences (historical narrative and commentary). The *action* by a brave individual may be praiseworthy but does not necessarily pave the way for positive change in women's condition in society. The commentor focuses attention on the fact that as a consequence of Veturia's action women were permitted to inherit, which, in his view, threatens the very structure of society. Women are seen as non-productive dissipators of male wealth. The mere possibility of control shifting from male to female hands results in the emasculation of the male sex: "This is a woman's world, and men have become womanish" [FW 231]. The confusion of gender roles is anathema to Boccaccio since it entails a reversal in power relations; holding wealth gives the real possibility of power to women and it is this that Boccaccio decries.

Money is seen as a major, deleterious influence on social interaction, which may help to explain why the *De mulieribus* is in favour of a return to a Golden Age where a primitive economy prevails. The world could be turned upside down by a change in the balance of economic and political power. Thus Boccaccio makes a precise link between economics and gender, whereby economic control is essential to man's virile image and a sense of himself. His strategy is to discredit the results of Veturia's action. The concluding paragraph 'demonstrates' the consequences of removing power from the hands of the men and allowing women too much control. Boccaccio does appear to have a social program, one that intends to enforce women as economically powerless and unproductive:

> Let women applaud Veturia, then, and honour her name and worthy deed whenever they adorn themselves with precious jewels, with purple cloth, and with gold brooches; whenever men stand up as they go by; and whenever they calmly calculate the wealth of dying testators.[47]

·   ·   ·   ·

Obviously, the above discussion does no more than indicate some of the most fundamental materials used in the construction of the *De mulieribus*. Of the Roman historians and moralists, Livy and Valerius Maximus were the most favoured but by no means the only ones. Boccaccio was also keen to show off his latest and more recondite finds; perhaps no more so than in the chapter on Penelope [XL] where he utilized his faltering knowledge of the original of the *Odyssey*.[48] The urge to provide a full historical coverage for women meant that Boccaccio could use another of his important 'discoveries'—the *Annals* of Tacitus (and, to a much lesser degree, the *Histories*)—to supplement the information he found in Sallust.[49] The deployment of Tacitus established his work as part of the new humanism in which the re-discovery and re-use of ancient texts constituted an essential element. The use of 'new' texts aimed at putting the *De mulieribus* at the forefront of new patterns of knowledge. It was also a means by which Boccaccio stamped on the text his own 'original' contributions to the movement. The use of materials such as Homer and Tacitus marked Boccaccio out from the other humanists, conferring on him a sense of his own re-elaborated identity as a writer. If the *De casibus* exhibited its debt to medieval systems of thought through its literary structure, and only belatedly makes limited use of Tacitus, the work on women breaks with those structural chains and explores a different way of classifying and presenting knowledge.

Imperious Women

The imperial women of the *De mulieribus* (Agrippina, wife of Germanicus [XC]; Agrippina, mother of Nero [XCII]; Antonia [LXXXIX]; Epicharis [XCIII]; Pompeia Paulina [XCIV]; Sabina Poppaea [XCV]; Triaria [XCVI]; Cleopatra [LXXXVIII] could also be included in the group) form a select band, not thematically homogeneous but chronologically attiguous. They constitute one of those rare occasions in the *De mulieribus* where women from the same sources are close both in time and textual space. Of the eight biographies under consideration here, four can be described as 'negative' and four as 'positive'. No less than four have a commentary attached to them. The exposition of these imperial women poses a number of awkward questions about whether the work can be said to have a dominant ideology, given that half of them took part in morally reprehensible actions. Boccaccio's increasing concern with making Tacitus more readily accessible may have been at the expense of a coherent diagram of women. However, he seems to have had a firm idea of which imperial women he wished to exclude; specifically he omitted Octavia who is treated sympathetically by Tacitus in the *Annals*. Octavia may be described as one of the many victims of the various power struggles taking place in early imperial Rome. Although she was the first wife of Nero, Tacitus baldly states:

> Octavia had virtually died on her wedding day. Her new home had brought her nothing but misery. Poison had removed her father [Claudius], and very soon her brother [Britannicus]. Maid had been preferred to mistress. Then she, Nero's wife, had been ruined by her successor [Sabina Poppaea]. (*Annals*, p.343)

Certainly drama was not lacking from Octavia's biography. After her murder, she was decapitated and her head sent to Sabina Poppaea (the subject of one of the chapters of the *De mulieribus*). Her exclusion from Boccaccio's work is intriguing because she represents the tragic human consequences of the imperial power struggle. It may have been due to the fact that she was not the author of any notable actions, but rather a victim of the intense power struggles at the imperial court.

The chapter on Agrippina (mother of Nero) is surprising for its lack of openly condemnatory statements, especially when compared to Tacitus' depiction of her in the *Annals*. To Boccaccio she is outstanding because of her "famous actions" (*FW* 385) which include numerous assassinations, political intrigues, and an incestuous marriage. This underlines the ambiguity of the adjective "clara," suggesting that the connotation 'notorious' was as attractive to Boccaccio as 'famous'. The chapter is marked by understatement and irony. Boccaccio refers to Agrippina as "a very shrewd woman indeed" (*FW* 387; "astutissima... mulier"), a term he uses to describe women whose intelligence can be defined only as underhand cleverness. The account is restrained when compared to others in the collection. The conclusion makes no moral statement whatsoever, but notes a variant view of Agrippina's burial. Tacitus was much clearer in his condemnation of Agrippina whose thirst for power was called a "masculine despotism" (p.255). In Tacitus' account "this always terrible" woman (p.289) does receive retribution in so far as her own son, for whom she sought supreme power, orders her murder. Boccaccio seems more interested in recounting the deeds of this extraordinary woman, reconstructing her story through his reading of the *Annals*. It may be that the fascination of her biography was greater than the moral message the writer could draw from it.

Sandwiched between Agrippina and Sabina Poppaea, both obsessed by power, are two other women who demonstrated a fierce adherence to values which no longer appear to have held much sway in imperial Rome. Epicharis [XCIII] receives unambiguous treatment in the *De mulieribus*. Her refusal to betray the names of her co-conspirators against Nero leads her to commit suicide. As in the chapter on Penthesilea, this allows Boccaccio the opportunity to rail against male degeneration and the failure to follow traditional masculine values. Boccaccio elaborates on this concept which he found in a less developed form in Tacitus' criticism of the decadence of Roman men:

> So, shielding in direst agony men unconnected with her and almost strangers, this former slavewoman set an example which particularly shone when free men, Roman knights and senators, were betraying, before anybody had laid a hand on them, their nearest and dearest. (*Annals*, p.373)

The Boccaccian commentator does not miss the opportunity to make the same point, but extends it to ensure that it has clear contemporary relevance for men. His discourse is quite complex, making concessions to women on the one hand, and withdrawing them on the other. He concedes that woman, like man, receives a perfect soul. One may be tempted to think that the natural consequence of such a premise is that women are the equals of men. Boccaccio recoils from such a statement, stressing sexual difference. He views men and women as engaged in a struggle for superiority, the outcome of which should be obvious from the outset. Harmony and social stability can come only from a return to stereotyped gender values:

> In my view, men should be ashamed to be defeated, not so much by a wanton female, but by a woman [Epicharis] who had steeled herself to endure any difficulty. If, in fact, we are the stronger sex, is it not fitting for us to have the stronger resolve? If this is not the case, we are as effeminate as the conspirators and appear with as good reason to have deviated from sound morals.[50]

Paradoxically, the exceptional woman represents a call to arms for men. In political terms, Boccaccio is concerned with male cowardice and the failure to oppose tyranny. The commentary underlines an obsession with men's behaviour so that there is no interest in this *exemplum* as a model for other women taking political stands. Men constitute the 'superior' gender and the expectations by which they are bound are illustrated negatively both by Tacitus and Boccaccio (the latter making explicit the Roman historian's indications). Boccaccio constructs a discourse of male domination into his commentator's point of view, skewing the narrative perspective of the historical account which had emphasized the exceptional heroism of Epicharis.

Boccaccio's commentaries become the site of conservative discourse, ensuring that any conclusions to be drawn from the historical narratives are kept within the bounds of contemporary discourse on women. We can see a similar situation in the biography of Pompeia Paulina who wished to commit suicide alongside her husband Seneca. The entire episode is framed between the conventional stereotypes of the woman as wife and widow (the latter of special significance in the *De mulieribus*). Boccaccio imposed interesting changes on his source to maximize Pompeia Paulina's heroic devotion. Tacitus reports that because Seneca "was afraid of weakening his wife's endurance by betraying his agony, or of losing his own self-possession at the sight of her sufferings" (*Annals*, XV, 63; p.376), he sent her away to another bedroom. If one wanted to construct an exemplary episode from Pompeia Paulina's behaviour, this detail might be judged anticlimactic. Boccaccio expunged any mention of it, so that the image he creates is one of intense heroism: "Fearlessly, at the same moment as her husband, Paulina stepped into the warm water and opened her veins to pour out her spirit" [FW 401]. He makes a further change to the Roman text, omitting a version that Tacitus suggests had some circulation at the time—that Pompeia Paulina's decision not to die was coloured by Nero's lack of animus against her. Indeed, Boccaccio seized the occasion to stress that after Seneca's death his widow led a life of "exemplary widowhood" (FW 401). His reading of the episode was such that he wished to energetically propose a perfect image of Pompeia Paulina as wife and widow, without the need to detract from it in any way.

It is no accident that the biography of Sabina Poppaea follows immediately on from that of Pompeia Paulina. Chronology allows the medieval writer on this rare occasion to utilize consecutive biographies to contrast female behaviours. Boccaccio follows Tacitus' account of Sabina Poppaea in the *Annals* very closely, sometimes adding a negative comment in order to ensure that the signals for understanding her behaviour are read properly. Beauty is singled out as her principal negative quality:

> If she had been of good moral character, she would not have lacked other womanly attributes. In fact, Poppaea was unusually attractive and resembled her mother, who in her own day was the most beautiful of all the Roman women. [FW 403]

Beauty is connected with unbridled sexuality; it is a powerful negative force that upsets the balance between the sexes. It is noted Sabina Poppaea "practised lasciviousness, that common feminine vice" [FW 405]. At the very end of the chapter, there is a short, concluding comment by the commentator which is, to a degree, tongue in cheek: "But I have decided to leave out these matters lest I seem to be writing satire rather than history" [FW 409].[51] Indeed its very brevity seems to underline Poppaea's excesses, emphasized by the omission of a diatribe in the *De casibus* style. In Tacitus, the narrative itself carries enough clues for a 'correct' reading of Poppaea's rise to power and consequent fall.[52] It is also an assertion of his humanist methodology, a partial rejection of the *De casibus*.

Poppaea is followed by another 'fierce' woman (Triaria) who appears to be the parody of the wifely devotion seen in Pompeia Paulina. Her biography tellingly precedes that of the Christian Proba. Triaria's representation in the narrative is somewhat negative, the noun used to describe her behaviour being "ferocity" (FW 409).[53] This epithet is due to the active role she played in a surprise night attack on an enemy city during which she killed many sleeping soldiers. The commentator's attitude can be described only as parodic of the perfect wife. It links conjugal love with excessive violence as symbolic of the decadence of imperial Rome. Her conduct breaks the rules of feminine propriety in such a way to undermine the precise rules of wifely devotion. Furthermore, her actions fall between the 'manly' and the 'barbaric', thus, implying the sense of imbalance that accrues to 'male-coded' deeds carried out by women caught in the double-bind of feminine and masculine behaviour. The example of Triaria allows Boccaccio to implicitly contrast her with Pompeia Paulina, emphasizing limits that should be placed on a wife's behaviour. It is a condemnation of power politics as particularly unseemly for women. Without a moral purpose, becoming like a man (or even superior to a man) is dangerous and destructive of all values. Imperial Rome, through the perspective of Tacitus, allowed Boccaccio to choose extreme examples of female behaviour—both positive and negative. Women become the touchstone of a society's health or decline— heroism in a disordered society can come from unexpected quarters, as in the case of Epicharis. The women of imperial Rome provide a convenient guide to the limitations to be placed on women. Female involvement in power politics is generally considered a negative, although in some cases it is not condemned as harshly as one might have expected. Conventional feminine behaviour receives the approbation of the text. However, against these stereotyped judgements of women's actions, the figure of Epicharis demonstrates the possibility of overcoming the rigidities of the expected norms of female conduct.

· · · · ·

III

Constructing Discourses

MEDIEVAL PATTERNS AND CHRISTIAN MODELS

*A*n analysis of the *De mulieribus claris* may suggest that while humanist scholarship appears to order the text, other discourses are introduced to buttress its authority. The seeming neutrality of historical discourse is undercut by commentaries that draw on contemporary experience with the purpose of restraining the implications of humanist research. Boccaccio introduced a developmental thesis into the *De mulieribus claris* whereby pagan women give way to Christian women towards the end of the book. The Christian women are so few and exclude those exemplars which define Christianity—saints and martyrs— that it is hard to say whether they bring about any noticeable change to the pattern of the text. Boccaccio does not exclude Christian ideals from his book—far from it! The *De mulieribus claris* is permeated by the fundamental rules of Christian conduct which aim to demonstrate the compatibility between classical *exempla* and Christian behaviour.

St Jerome's *Against Jovinianus*

*B*occaccio would have been aware of the tactical uses of exemplary women in earlier treatises—in particular, St. Jerome's *Against Jovinianus* which provided a ready-made basis for an anthology of famous women. Jerome's text would not have provided the exact ideological frame for Boccaccio because it had a precise aim: to demonstrate the superiority of virginity over marriage.[1] Marriage is viewed as a rather positive experience in the *De mulieribus claris*; faithful wives are valued highly in the text. Gaia Cyrilla (XLVI) is included in the text principally because of her connection with ancient Roman marriage rites. She represents a view of marriage that is pure and free from the corruption of later social developments, particularly from increasing wealth that contaminates *simplicitas*, recalling the commentary to Ceres' biography (V).[2] Such an outlook is reinforced by the biography of Megullia Dotata (LIV) which again praises the *simplicitas* of her age as against the contemporary obsession with wealth and its display. Chastity is a norm to which wives are expected to adhere otherwise they are the object of the severest remonstrances. Virginity has a less prominent role in the text, but is especially valued for those women who display artistic or intellectual genius. This discrete group eschews social commitment in the form of marriage in order to offer total dedication to its 'higher' vocation.

St. Jerome's views on female sexuality are problematized in the *De mulieribus claris*. Boccaccio shares them to the degree that sexual purity is a fundamental value for all his women. Though he regularly includes women who break these rules of sexual behaviour, he just as regularly admonishes them. The institutionalized virgin is almost completely absent from the anthology (the Empress Constance is forced to leave the monastery and it is only after her departure that her fame is secured). Therefore, Boccaccio is attracted by the actions of his chosen women who may transgress the rigid rules of Jeromian sexuality. Consequently, he sets up his own emphases, which are not those of the saint.

For the most part Jerome relies on biblical writings in *Against Jovinianus* to support his assertions, but he does have recourse to the "tribunal of worldly wisdom."[3] Of approximately twenty examples of pagan virgins, six are to be found in the *De mulieribus* (Camilla, the Sibyls,[4] Cassandra, Claudia Quinta,[5] Minerva[6]). A second listing in Jerome concentrates on chaste widows who refused to marry a second time—a key theme of both *Against Jovinianus*[7] and Boccaccio's collection. From a total of around twenty chaste widows, only five will find their way into the *De mulieribus* (Dido, Artemisia, Penelope, Portia and Lucretia).[8] It could be argued that these famous women had such wide currency in the Middle Ages that Boccaccio had no necessity to consult Jerome. However, the presence of these famous women in Jerome confirmed their relevance to Christian writing and justified their use by later writers. It is suggestive of the Christian status that had accrued to classical women and which Boccaccio was keen to exploit.

There is a definite parallel between the earlier writer's obsession with widows not marrying a second time and Boccaccio's own insistence on the prohibition of second marriages in the *De mulieribus*. Indeed, Boccaccio takes up this theme with alacrity. In the chapter on Dido alone (XLII), he devotes ten paragraphs (out of twenty-six) to widows remarrying; an act that is considered inexcusable. When applied to the contemporary context, the prohibition forms an integral part of Boccaccio's concern for a return to basic Christian morality.

Boccaccio does not accept all of Jerome's positions on female sexuality. The saint was implacable in his attacks on marriage, as illustrated by the impressive array of troublesome and unfaithful wives in *Against Jovinianus*. In this, Jerome was himself drawing on the classical tradition, particularly Juvenal's sixth satire, probably known to Boccaccio as well, and Theophrastus. However, the *De mulieribus claris* used only two of the *exempla*, Clytemnestra and Helen, and to very different effect.[9]

Indeed, one of the notable features of the *De mulieribus* is the number of *exempla* given over to faithful wives. In contrast to *Against Jovinianus*, Boccaccio changes the emphases in his own work to accommodate a positive version of the wife. There is little of Jerome's anti-wife sentiment present in the *De mulieribus*, and subsequently slightly less emphasis placed on virginity. However, Boccaccio places equal, if not more, stress on chastity (fidelity and sexual restraint in marriage). He has no problem in implicitly assenting to Jerome's evaluation of chastity: "In every grade, and in both sexes, chastity has the chief place" (I, 35; p.373). Also in general: "All the virtues of the Spirit are supported and protected by continence, which is as it were their solid foundation and crowning point" (I, 38; p.376). To these statements, the author of the *De mulieribus* gave his wholehearted assent.

The Jerome model of sexual purity is applied to most of Boccaccio's female subjects, but does not constitute the only test of their worth: rather it enters into an uneasy relationship with the other elements of a woman's public performance. In some cases, female heroism can even appear to excuse sexual 'impurity'; for example, Leaena [L], in spite of the fact she was a prostitute, acted heroically in refusing to reveal the names of the tyrannicides whom she knew personally.[10] The account of her heroism is sandwiched between two narratorial interventions, the first justifying the concept that heroism and sexual purity are not necessarily related. However, the second and concluding discussion attempts to deradicalize the earlier proposition by introducing the idea that Leaena was a prostitute through no fault of her own.[11] The only way in which the constant threat to female integrity can be overcome (and only in the most exceptional circumstances) is through "her manly strength" [*FW* 207]. By biting off her own tongue to avoid betraying the conspirators, Leaena becomes a "virilis femina" whereby her sexuality is made subordinate to socially inspired actions. It is this moment that appears to interest Boccaccio: the point at which women deny their sexually tainted bodies to behave like asexual and strong men. By biting off her tongue, Leaena breaks with the stereotype of the garrulous woman to become the strong, silent (wo-)man.

Leaena is a crucial *exemplum* of the *De mulieribus claris* since it overtly challenges Jerome's version of woman's sexuality as the only marker of female heroism. Further, she is able to participate in the classically inspired basis of male intercourse, *amicitia*, which binds men together outside the traditional family alliances because of shared humanist beliefs.[12] Her 'manliness' is realized because of her espousal of *virtus* through a remarkable action.[13] The act of transgendering occurs because of the narrowly defined limits of womanhood in the Christian tradition.

Thus, while subscribing to Jerome's notion of sexual purity, Boccaccio appears unwilling to make women totally submit to that Law or to have their actions answerable only to protecting or furthering their chastity. This is surely one of the reasons why he sought a much more varied list of women's deeds than that found in *Against Jovinianus*. Ensuring such variety involved consulting other sources for more heroic women. Boccaccio would also have found in Jerome's text confirmation of the pedagogic utility of searching for *exempla* from pre-Christian history: "Seeing they [contemporary women] despise the fidelity which Christian purity dictates, let them at least learn chastity from the heathen" (I, 47; p.383). This sentiment is echoed in the dedication to the *De mulieribus,* wherein Boccaccio states that Andrea should feel shame if she is beaten in virtue by a pagan (*FW* 5, 7). Boccaccio intuited that men and women could learn a great deal more than "chastity from the heathen," and so extended the range of women on show in the *De mulieribus.*

The question of Boccaccio's eventual choice of women, and their provenance, is not merely scholarly activity for its own sake. In the early modern period, the *De mulieribus* was one of the first texts to which a writer on women turned for examples to support his or her position. Although there was a certain flexibility in interpretation, Boccaccio's selection of famous women exerted enormous influence on future writers who reacted in different ways to the archetypes of the *De mulieribus claris*. His choice is also extremely informative about the peculiar characteristics of his humanism. To study Boccaccio's selection procedures is to note the polemical thrust of his own humanism in its relation to his master, Petrarch.

Finding a Decent Woman: Dante's *Divine Comedy*

ne of the most notable features of the *De mulieribus* is the heterogeneous nature of the materials used and the variations in the 'factual' status of the women included in the collection. It cannot be an accident that approximately just under one-third of the women who make up Boccaccio's *exempla* are mentioned in the *Divina Commedia*, a work which may well have provided a convenient starting-point from which to build.[14] A significant proportion of the *De mulieribus* women pertain to the structured universe of the *Commedia*. This adds another layer of source materials that interacts with and impacts on the classical impetus that is the hallmark of Boccaccio's Latin text.

Boccaccio's interest in and admiration for the *Commedia* can be readily documented. His last work, *Esposizioni sopra la 'Comedia' di Dante*, closes the circle in so far as Boccaccio re-uses some of the biographies from the *De mulieribus* in the commentaries on individual cantos. He is more precise in his acknowledgement of sources and corrects or enlarges upon points made in the earlier work.[15] However, the clarity of Dante's condemnations and encomia is lost in the *De mulieribus claris* because of the later writer's lack of a guiding frame, and the fact that he occasionally follows a different textual tradition (as, for example, in the case of Dido).[16] This is just one of many radical adjustments that Boccaccio makes to the range of his women with respect to Dante. For example, the figures of the Virgin Mary and female saints are absent from the *De mulieribus*. Unlike Dante and Jerome, Boccaccio depends almost entirely on pre-Christian women to convey his Christian and social messages.

It is true that Dante's indications often provided only the skimpiest descriptions of the women in whom Boccaccio takes an interest. Consequently he sought further corroboration and additional information elsewhere. At times, Boccaccio may have used the slightest of indications found in the *Commedia* as a point of departure: "Cleopatràs lussuriosa" (*Inferno*, V, 63) is expanded and amplified in the *De mulieribus* to form the substance of an entire chapter. In the case of Semiramis, Boccaccio does not deny her sexual appetite, as alluded to in Dante ("A vizio di lussuria fu sì rotta" [V, 55]), but 'completes' the picture by emphasizing her military talents. Boccaccio does not appear to be bound by the more 'judgmental' Dante where one sin is singled out by the poem. For example, the closure imposed on Semiramis' life, caught up in the overthrow of human and divine laws, is opened out by Boccaccio on to other vistas of her story.

Although Boccaccio was keen to show off his classical learning, he did not reject medieval sources of information on women. The *Commedia* assumed the status of a classic for Boccaccio. If he knew of medieval sources which provided details useful to his exposition he did not hesitate to use them.[17] He effected a kind of *contaminatio* whereby classical sources were amplified or bent more consciously towards a Christian ethic.

The *De mulieribus* and the Christian Historians

nother strategy employed by Boccaccio was to re-read pagan history through the eyes of Christian writers, in particular Eusebius-Jerome, Justinus, and Orosius. Eusebius-Jerome's *Chronicon* can be considered central to the *De mulieribus* as it provides a chronological ordering of world events that assisted Boccaccio in arranging his own work. Furthermore, it offered a comparative chronology of the world's civilizations, placing their histories in a Christian framework.[18] Boccaccio certainly does not foreground this preoccupation for parallel histories but the implied methodology offers a justification for his interest in classical women. Implicitly, Boccaccio is making it clear that women are an essential part of history and their chronology fits into the universal history of civilizations. By developing his own variation on the *Chronicon*, the medieval writer is proposing that women's contribution to society must be seriously considered: the sequence of women in history renders them visible/mainstream, inserting them into the grand plan of historical development. Eusebius-Jerome names a number of the female personages who will appear in the *De mulieribus*.[19] They help create a sense of women's history the details of which Boccaccio was able to expand from other sources. The use of the *Chronicon* is a way of implicitly claiming a Christian perspective on a body of pagan texts and figures.

Boccaccio may have availed himself of other universal chronicles in order to create a solid chronological base for the *De mulieribus*. He shows an interest in the evolution and development of certain key institutions, such as the Roman Empire, as evinced by his notes in the *Zibaldone magliabechiano*.[20] Therefore, one cannot exclude the use by Boccaccio of medieval encyclopedias and chronicles, especially those that embedded a variety of classical sources in a chronological frame. One of the most influential and widely diffused was Vincent de Beauvais' *Speculum maius*, and in particular, the *Speculum historiale*.[21] It often identifies the sources used as well as providing an *excerptum* of the cited texts. It contains references to a number of the women found in the *De mulieribus claris*, a few of whom can be considered amongst the more recondite selections made by Boccaccio—Athaliah, Harmonia, Olympias.[22]

On a number of occasions Vincent de Beauvais conveys information that will find its way into Boccaccio's compilation. Vincent's discussion of the Amazons offers the reader a sense of the warrior women's otherness by using the rejection of spinning as an indicator of their refusal of traditional feminine roles. Boccaccio will develop this theme not only in the chapter on the first Amazon queens, but throughout the *De mulieribus claris*.[23] Vincent de Beauvais also provides the variants of Semiramis' death that are used in the *De mulieribus claris*, particularly Justinus' and

Orosius' accounts. In both cases Boccaccio will likewise refuse to supply a clarifying overview or historical judgement.[24] On another occasion, Vincent refers to the confusion between Artemisia and Archemidora, but again without forming a judgement, therefore allowing Boccaccio to consider the two figures as one in the manner of the medieval encyclopedist.[25]

A reconstruction of Boccaccio's sources for the De mulieribus claris must take into account the availability of texts such as the Speculum historiale, sources which Boccaccio's work mediates and freely appropriates. The presence of Vincent amongst others in the De mulieribus claris seems to suggest that Boccaccio was not a 'purist' in his humanist historiography, but appreciated the medieval contribution to historical knowledge. Unlike Petrarch, both Vincent and Boccaccio were keen to record variants to a story without feeling the necessity to impose a hierarchy of verisimilitude amongst their sources. Petrarch himself came out strongly against this procedure and recommended a more rigorous humanistic approach to source materials.

Boccaccio availed himself of Christian historiographers of the pagan world who added their voices to the chorus of classical writers. Not least among them is Paulus Orosius' Historiarum adversus paganos [Histories Against the Pagans]. The principal thrust of this work is to demonstrate the difference between pagan and Christian times. The former are characterized by "death eager for blood,"[26] and further distinguished in the following terms: "[those times] were all the more terribly unhappy in relation to their distance from the remedy of the true religion."[27] Although not a major theme for Boccaccio, political violence is a recurring motif in the De mulieribus, perhaps as a reminder of the devastating consequences of the pursuit of power for its own sake outside a Christian vision of society.

Female subjects in Orosius are always tainted with blood: his depiction of Semiramis is far less restrained than Boccaccio's. Although Boccaccio imitates the double perspective (political/military achievement and female sexuality) used by Orosius, there is a notable difference in tone between the two writers. Orosius sees nothing positive in Semiramis' political actions—for him they are merely examples of bloodthirsty violence, typical of pagans. Thus, unlike the version we find in the De mulieribus, it is not a matter of Semiramis' sexuality betraying her brilliance as a general and a leader. Orosius portrays her sexuality as uncontrolled and uncontrollable, "burning with passion" ("libidine ardens," I, iv, 7; p.48). It is a position accepted by Boccaccio but mentioned only in the second part of his account. Orosius 'reports' the most extreme details about Semiramis' sexual activities which even Boccaccio does not accept as 'fact'. Indeed, the later writer included only selected details in his account of her life. Orosius portrays Semiramis as a completely negative example of the anarchic pagan tendency to destroy both self and others, whereas Boccaccio extols the queen's political and military skills. Orosius included in his survey other women whose sexual licence led to destruction and death; for example, Medea whom he describes as "wounded by cruel love."[28]

It is not surprising, given the themes of his history, that Orosius saw fit to include the Amazons who brought devastation to Europe and Asia. In a similar manner to Semiramis, Tamyris is presented as a bloodthirsty queen. Boccaccio is faithful to most of the indications offered by Orosius except that he is less negative than the early Christian historian. When Tamyris decapitates Cyrus and places his head in a leather container filled with blood as revenge for his blood lust and the death of her son, Orosius observes that her accompanying statement was "not a lady-like thing to say."[29] In contrast, Boccaccio comments that the fame of Tamyris was all the greater for having defeated a person as great as Cyrus. Preceding this, Orosius had noted that instead of crying over the death of her son, Tamyris decided to seek revenge. This is seen as unnatural and pagan, whereas Boccaccio makes a small but significant change: "But she did not burst out weeping as women usually do" [FW 203]. Her determined attitude is viewed by the Italian writer as positive—a suppression of 'weak', feminine tendencies.

In the case of Olympias [LXI] (the mother of Alexander), Boccaccio follows Orosius very closely, although here too he makes minor changes. For example, he omits the names of the Macedonian elders listed by Orosius, perhaps to avoid overloading the text with too many inconsequential names. Boccaccio is determined to portray female heroism wherever he can find it. In spite of the fact that Olympias was pitiless in killing off rivals, his final image of this queen is testament to the nobility of a woman who courageously accepted the harsh treatment she so freely dealt out: "[she] voluntarily offered her body to their blows, as if she scorned what even the bravest of men are wont to fear."[30]

For Boccaccio Orosius also confirmed the validity and 'Christianity' of certain classical *exempla* of women whose chastity was under threat: the Livian Virginia finds a place in the *De mulieribus*, as do the Cimbrian women who killed themselves and their children rather than be taken into captivity by the Romans.[31] Orosius provided Boccaccio with particulars about the lives of some of his subjects and even, in the case of Olympias, with most of the biographical information.

Overall, Orosius provided an example of the use of a biographical method embedded in an historical discourse (similar to Livy in structure) in which the classical *exemplum* was revised to provide a new, Christian perspective. Instead of merely recounting tales of wars, Orosius concentrates on their horrendous effects, undermining the militaristic values underpinning the ancient Roman world. In the *De mulieribus*, Boccaccio does not completely share Orosius' world-view. On the contrary, he wished to highlight the military exploits of some of his women to demonstrate the potential equality of women in an area where history is decided. At the same time, Orosius vindicated the study of pagan civilization, creating a precedent which undoubtedly encouraged Boccaccio to continue his study of ancient *exempla*.

Sourcing the Women

It is clear that Boccaccio did not necessarily tie himself down to a single source for each biography. For example, he might ground a biography in his reading of Livy, but introduce other available sources to provide alternative readings, or to insert details not present in the principal source. In a sense, he is imitating the method of Macrobius who stated in the *Saturnalia*: "Let us gather then from all sources and from them form one whole as single numbers combine to form one number."[32] Although this may indeed have been Boccaccio's working method and his intended aim, he does not always achieve a successful outcome. Often the seams are too visible, mainly because the writer makes little effort to hierarchize conflicting readings, being content simply to list sometimes quite considerable variations. It appears that Boccaccio did not generally wish to exclude one reading in favour of another.[33] He will list a series of alternatives, which has the effect of creating an open-endedness about the historical narratives. What is remarkable is the fact that this methodology is grounded in an attitude that can be described as non-Petrarchan. In the first preface to the *De viris illustribus*, Petrarch argues forcefully against historians who do exactly what Boccaccio does in the *De mulieribus*:

> In doing this I have thought that I have been able to avoid the imprudence and sterile diligence of those authors who, having collected the words of all the historians—so that they seem to have not neglected anything at all— have really contradicted one authority with another so the entire text of their history is lost in cloudy ambiguities and inexplicable conflicts.[34]

History was not so straightforward for Boccaccio as it seems to have been for Petrarch. Boccaccio was captivated by the possibilities that contrasting accounts offered, adding to the richness of the narrative. While one could denounce Boccaccio's lack of evaluative skills, it is perhaps more interesting to speculate that he was concerned with the polysemic nature of discourse, a concern which translated into a reluctance to reduce the pleasures of the historical narratives. This is a recurrent feature of many of the chapters and forms a strong contrast with the decisive position adopted in the commentaries.

However, on rare occasions, the narrator does assume a partisan position; for example, in chapter VI where he agrees that there was probably more than one Minerva: "I shall gladly agree with them in order to increase the number of famous women" [FW 39]. This is not a well thought-out historical position, but part of an unveiled attack on pagan religions, extended so that the very concept of the classical goddess is itself undermined.[35] As a consequence, the achievements of the Minervas are at least the achievements of 'real' women. In the biography of Venus, queen of Cyprus (VII), Boccaccio states that "there is disagreement as to her parents" [FW 39]. However, he makes no attempt to resolve the issue, dismissing it as of little or no importance: "No matter who her father was."[36] His irony can be read as a sign that the woman in question is to be read negatively because of her lack of known illustrious parentage. At times, it is clear that Boccaccio has little interest in uncovering the historical truth of a particular set of circumstances. He may faithfully report all the versions known to him, but they do not affect the moralistic intent of the biography, indeed they may even enhance it.

A similar pattern is seen in the biography of Harmonia [LXVIII] wherein Boccaccio notes some doubts concerning her marital status and/or her virginity. The problem is 'resolved' in the following fashion: "Of these alternatives one may choose whichever one prefers since the divergence of opinion does not detract in the least from Harmonia's courage and loyalty."[37] Here we have a clear exposition of the way in which history is subordinated to exemplary concerns. History is not ignored in the pursuit of moral lessons, but it sometimes takes second place.

Boccaccio tends to accept the majority view, simply because it is the majority view and not for any intrinsic historical merit it may have. He also supports the majority view in the dispute over Hecuba's parentage [XXXIV]).[38] Isis [VIII] clearly demonstrates the limitations of Boccaccio's historical methodology. He lists four conflicting statements about the period in which she lived and the identity of her parents. However, he makes no attempt to distinguish the authoritative from the non-authoritative nor to introduce other historical evidence. Indeed, his procedure is to accept the majority view as he did in the biography of Minerva [FW, 43, 45].

In his biography of Penelope [XL], Boccaccio cites the one dissenting voice which alleged that she was not as chaste as Homer claimed her to be. The narrator does not simply dismiss the claim as that of a crank but gives it some credence by the terms of his rebuttal:

> Far be it from me to believe that Penelope, whom many authors have cele-
> brated for the purity of her morals, was anything but completely chaste just
> because one writer states the opposite. [*FW* 163]

As an exposition of his historical 'method', this could be read as ironically undermining the popular image of Penelope. Had there been more
writers of the same opinion, would the narrator have changed his mind?
It is an illustration in reverse of the majority verdict in history that
Boccaccio tended to follow.

In the latter part of the text, particularly following the chapter on
Cleopatra, references to conflicting interpretations virtually disappear. In
some cases, this is probably because the number of sources available to
Boccaccio for the later women, particularly post-classical women, was
considerably reduced compared to those treated earlier. In others it is
due to a greater consensus about the meaning to be attributed to particular women, such as Cleopatra.

The above analysis demonstrates Boccaccio's recognition of the
obstacles involved in trying to reconstruct an ancient biography.
However, the limitations of his methodology should not disqualify him
from being regarded as a humanist historian in embryo. He is aware of
the limits of his sources and resists the temptation, as a writer of fiction,
to fill in the sometimes too obvious gaps. For example, at the end of the
chapter on Tamyris he states that nothing else is known of her apart
from what he has recounted.[39] It is an acknowledgement of the insurmountable obstacles involved in the recovery of a life. It reinforces the
centripetal structure of the historical narratives by concentrating on a
single event or connected events that define the historical subject. The
historical account structured as a narrative is acknowledged by the historian to be an incomplete fragment. Boccaccio's confessions of a fruit-
less search for other information that might have completed the
biography suggests that his humanist studies seek to provide an ideal
completeness to the women's lives in the *De mulieribus*, but history prevents this through gaps in the historical record.

Exemplary Women

In this context I believe it is worthwhile considering the *De
mulieribus* as a series of exemplary biographies which lose moral
effectiveness because of the lack of a consistent point of view.
Without a frame, 'rival' discourses do not constitute an easy hierarchy;
the readability of Boccaccio's moral discourse is compromised by the
changing focus from chapter to chapter. The exemplarity of some of the

figures is multiple and contradictory. The commentator makes desperate attempts to impose a reductive reading on the text's polyvalences—not always with great success. As characterized by Boccaccio's usage, the *exemplum* has at base a narrative event which is offered up erratically to moral interpretation.

I am positing here that at least some of the readers of *De mulieribus claris* will have been women. Studies of *exempla*, particularly of human-istic ones, do not often address the question of gender in their research. It is true that *exempla* of humanist derivation mostly deal with public, male issues of concern. Ancient writers normally excluded women from them because of prohibitions on their public activities.[40] The fact that Boccaccio reinstates women as the subject of exemplary discourse is a moment of considerable importance in the evolution of the *exemplum*.

It is not simply a question of substituting a female *exemplum* for a male one. The mere fact of having a woman who is neither saint nor martyr at the centre of a narrative discourse urges a different set of ques-tions on the reader. In some instances, the woman replaces a man in the performance of a particular function, such as bearing arms. In these sit-uations, the reader may be challenged in his or her thinking about the role of men and women in contemporary society. In other circum-stances, the male reader may have their views confirmed or even inten-sified, coming away from the text more convinced about the limitations to be imposed on women in society. The *exemplum* can therefore contain important messages for both male and female selfhood: confirmation of the life led by the female reader, or suggestions that it is too restrictive and could be released but without precise instructions on how to achieve change.

It is essential to note that the Boccaccian *exemplum* does not form part of a concerted, continuous discourse such as a sermon on which the majority of *exempla* studies have concentrated their attention.[41] The *De mulieribus claris* presents narratives of women's lives without their being nested in a structuring, didactic discourse; the *exempla* have little overt support from an authoritative discourse. Thus, the primary function of the *exemplum*, as theorized by the ancient rhetoricians, of clarifying the points of another discourse, is not properly fulfilled in the Boccaccian collection of women.[42]

The use of *exempla* collections was certainly prevalent in the Middle Ages, particularly as a moral-didactic tool for the education of the laity and for use in sermons and larger narrative texts.[43] The *exempla* were often of Christian inspiration: biblical women, female saints and martyrs. In the *De mulieribus claris* Boccaccio renews this genre from a humanist perspective. By selecting women from principally classical sources, he expands the possibilities of the new humanism, whilst presenting a conventional Christian view of his subjects in the commentaries which form part of certain biographies. A model for the *De mulieribus* could certainly have been those collections of moral *exempla* which were inserted at will in sermons, although in Boccaccio's case the women are arranged neither alphabetically nor according to subject-matter. His subjects are arranged in historical order which may owe more to classical historians than to any Christian writer except Eusebius through St. Jerome.

Furthermore, at least on the surface, Boccaccio's collection challenges the rationale behind Christian exemplary women, replacing the saints, martyrs and 'religious' women with a different set of subjects. The biographies of classical women challenge the accepted subject positions available to women. However, they are not easily translated into action. Indeed, Boccaccio attempts to frame them in such a way that they do not overly disconcert male readers and reinforce fundamental notions of female behaviour. In some cases, by their depiction of excess and prohibition, the Boccaccian biographies titillate the reader, for example in the descriptions of Cleopatra's 'depravities'. On other occasions, certain biographies seem constructed to produce a frisson of fear or stupefaction at the events narrated (the Amazons, Tamyris), perhaps for the particular benefit of male readers.

One can regard Boccaccio's biographies as exemplary narratives which highlight exotic or extraordinary behaviour as a means of problematizing female conduct. They are not as straightforward as sermon *exempla*: the *De mulieribus claris* only partially ties women down to stereotypes (whether by design or not is unclear) although they share the similarity of concentrating attention on one particular aspect of a woman's life through which she acquires meaning. This meaning is one that has been imposed on the material by a desire for order in accordance with a male agenda. The biographies are characterized by their fragmentary nature because the narrative discards material which is not central to its ideological or narrative purpose, as seen by the male writer. Any sense of a woman's integrity is lost in the chase for meaning and in the attempt to fit woman into a scheme of things which does not displace man from the centre.

Boccaccio's Audience and the Use of *Exempla*

The intended audience for the biographies of illustrious women is a problematic issue. It can be argued that, in some cases, women were not the intended primary audience. In the *De mulieribus claris*, Boccaccio seems equally interested in addressing men about their own gender problems as he is concerned about the role of women in society.[44] Female *exempla* also implied a relationship with men. Men could interpret the extraordinary acts of women in a number of ways: as sheer titillation (women breaking the accepted boundaries of female behaviour and exciting the male imagination); as pure fantasy (having no anchor in the real world); as a confirmation that female endeavour always fell short of male achievement; as a guide to men on how to improve women's conduct; as a confirmation of the reader's own views and sense of 'maleness'; and occasionally as a challenge to male dominance and modes of behaviour, and to current thinking on women. If the exemplars set up imitable forms of behaviour, then both men and women needed to navigate the contradictory messages of the text. In many of the accounts, the actions of a woman spark a crisis in men. The women's deeds are sometimes so extraordinary that they can challenge male superiority and accepted modes of behaviour. The text sends out ambiguous messages about female behaviour: Boccaccio sees it in function of sexual and social codes, but there exists the possibility of breaking them.

To compare Boccaccio's treatment of the story of Hercules and the Amazons with Christine de Pizan's is to appreciate the disparate ideologies that are inscribed in each narrative; the social programs conflict in their conceptualization of patriarchal society. It is striking that de Pizan uses the same basic material as the Latin writer (with the addition of a possibly invented episode), but reverses the significance attributed to it. In Boccaccio's version, the defeat of the women signifies a serious setback to the kingdom of the Amazons—a return to 'proper' gender relations in which men restore their primacy in combat. Boccaccio's account emphasizes the inadequacy of the women when faced with Theseus and Hercules (the two great heroes of antiquity); the Amazonian challenge to male authority and virility is put down with a resounding victory by the men.

Christine de Pizan reverses this male victory, presenting it in terms which discredit the Greek heroes and redound to the credit of the Amazons; the implication is that brute strength should not be the sole indicator of power. She describes Hercules at the beginning of the chapter as a man at the pinnacle of male physical achievement who was "victorious over all" (p.44). However, such fulsome praise reveals the hypocrisy and vanity of male glory by its juxtaposition with the revelation of Hercules' cowardly action in launching his assault on the Amazons by night: "[Hercules] did not dare to come into port nor to land during the day, so much did he fear the great power and daring of these women...Orithya heard the news that the Greeks, without provocation, had fallen upon their land at night and were slaying all whom they met" (pp.44–45). Not only are the men (Hercules, Theseus and their fleet comprising the flower of Greek youth) seen as having taken an unfair advantage but, significantly, as having had no motive for their attack apart from a desire to express their 'maleness', to dominate women who had escaped the yoke of male control.

This tale could be construed as a metaphor for women's unequal position in society. De Pizan adds an episode not mentioned in Boccaccio in which the two Greek heroes are unseated in battle by two of the Amazons—an addition which serves to illustrate the point that if the challenge had been fair, the warrior women might have achieved victory. Christine de Pizan uses comedy to discredit male historians who make excuses for the heroes' discomfiture at the hands of the two women by blaming the horse! Even the eventual 'defeat' of the Amazon nation is portrayed as a moral victory for the women who preferred to save their comrades rather than achieve glory in battle. The fact that the heroes eventually took the two Amazon maidens prisoner does not diminish their stature as fighters—especially as Theseus falls in love with Hippolyta and marries her. The result is peace between equals.

These polar versions of the same episode stem from two contrasting views of men: de Pizan sees their fallibility, vanity and weakness; whereas Boccaccio is trying to re-establish a code of virility by which men will rule and women know their 'rightful' place. However, the latter's problem is that the dominant position of men is always under threat from exceptional women. The fear that strong women means weak men is never far from the surface in episodes such as the Amazonian one discussed above. The complexities of Boccaccio's *De mulieribus claris* stem partly from the contradiction between representing strong women who shame men (possibly into action to assert their virility), and the fear of the consequences of such behaviour for the social order. Later writers will try to address this problem in various ways—by advocating a return to traditional norms; by paying lip-service to change without suggesting radical movement; or by putting forward the idea of a compromise between women and power and, most rarely, the possibility of decisive change.

· · · · · ·

IV

Fallen Women, Fallen Texts

FROM THE *DE CASIBUS* TO THE *DE MULIERIBUS*

Boccaccio's monumental Latin work, *De casibus virorum illustrium* dates to the mid-1350s but underwent revisions for many years after. It does not only deal with the fall of famous men; women play an important, if somewhat veiled, role in the text. Their inclusion allows the writer to meditate on female sexuality and to sermonize stock ideas about women—possibly as a reaction to perceptions about the *Decameron* and as a defence of his own conventionality in such matters. The *De casibus* is Boccaccio's first major Latin prose work and is much closer to his vernacular production than the *De mulieribus claris*. In some ways, the *De casibus* presents itself as a continuation of his interest in the drama of narrative in which the concept of character is a crucial feature. The emphasis now falls upon historical characters caught up in a literary text which fictionalizes their dramatic moment of confrontation with the narrator or with other characters in the manner of Dante. *De casibus* is strongly marked by this difference from the *De mulieribus*, yet in other ways the two texts bear some resemblance.

The *De casibus* makes fiction out of history while the *De mulieribus* makes history out of fiction whenever the possibility arises. The *De mulieribus* rejects the structure of the *De casibus*; it prefers the new humanism to the 'old' forms of vernacular literature. The *cornice* is also rejected as part of the push towards the new forms of humanist writing. Analysis replaces the narrative urges of the *De casibus*, though not completely. The differences between the two works are notable: the display of erudition *per se* in the *De mulieribus* can be understood as a sign that the humanist has taken priority over the writer of literary texts. The extended Dantean frame of the *De casibus* has no place in the *De mulieribus*.

It is perhaps no accident that the formal structure of the *De casibus* resembles an expanded medieval sermon in which general axioms are supported by *exempla* taken from ancient history, the bible, and contemporary or near-contemporary history. Although the number of references to the New Testament are much reduced, there are a few remaining from the Old Testament. The statements of a general nature that pepper the text serve as the vehicle for a vehemently conventional Christian viewpoint, ensuring that the exemplary figures are beyond misinterpretation. In this way, the *De casibus* is a conscious rejection of the system of the *Amorosa visione*. There are no longer female voices to explain and protect the famous women—they are replaced with a repressive male voice, speaking for all men. The positions adopted by the male voice are often more extreme than those which will be found in the *De mulieribus*. The women who clearly belong to the 'legend of bad women' are either omitted in the later text, or treated in a more ambiguous fashion. The male commentator of the *De mulieribus* is more sporadic and less strident, almost an afterthought in the humanist text, delineating its Christian parameters more sharply.

The 'sermon' *In mulieres* appears in the first book of the *De casibus* [I, xviii] as a reflection on the biblical episode of Samson and Delilah—the latter a notorious medieval *exemplum* of female treachery and cunning.[1] In Samson's biography, Boccaccio does not refrain from moralizing his subject's predicament in order to emphasize its misogynist message: "This is what happens to a credulous person, to an amorous person, to a person who puts too much faith in a woman" (*The Fates*, p.40). By not understanding woman's nature, Samson is deceived and defeated by Delilah, and becomes "as weak as a woman" (p.40). In the Boccaccian account, Samson does not redeem himself by his death—it is still considered "an unworthy death" (p.41) despite its heroic proportions. Thus, the account emphasizes the theme of female sexuality as a weapon of destruction against men, who thereby lose all the authority they possess. This is not the only time that Boccaccio will utilize a story of a great, or potentially great, man destroyed by his sexual desire. In the *De mulieribus*, Hercules will fulfill much the same function in a classicizing vein—in fact, a well-established connection between the two heroes is duly noted:

> There have been those who called the lion that he killed a Nemean lion, and they thought Samson was Hercules. I do not support this view: yet I do not know anything that contradicts the testimony.[2]

Thus Boccaccio is able to make the same point in both Latin texts because of a common identification of the two heroes in the medieval mind. However, the absence of Delilah from the *De mulieribus* renders the point less obvious. The *De mulieribus* is more subdued since it does not place its women under rubrics like "In mulieres" nor does it always go for the most obviously negative *exempla* that were an integral part of medieval culture.

The presence of both Samson and Hercules in the chapter *In mulieres* is a sure sign that it will take a misogynist line. Boccaccio's diatribe is, in fact, triggered by the Samson episode. The anti-women attack is unremitting for the greater part of the 'sermon'. The concept of beauty as a trap for men animates most of the discourse (also alluded to in the *De mulieribus*). Implicit is the notion that men are superior to their own bodies and capable of imposing sexual restraint upon themselves. Susceptibility to the female sexual body and the illusion of beauty created by women is the one weakness that brings about men's downfall, a theme with which the *Corbaccio* is preoccupied.[3]

In the *De casibus*, distrust of female beauty leads to a series of negative *exempla*: the first of these, Eve's 'seduction' of Adam, reappears in the *De mulieribus claris* in similar terms. Indeed, the introductory chapter of both texts concentrates on the sins of the first parents although from differing perspectives, each suited to the theme of its respective book. In the *De casibus*, Adam and Eve were responsible for the introduction of *fortuna* (change and degeneration) into human affairs; their perfect situation being transformed into utter misery![4] The earlier work takes the perspective of Adam who informs the narrator that the flight from Eden is the archetypal story of the Fall which will be repeated throughout the text: "no one except us can provide a more appropriate beginning for that which you are seeking."[5]

The title of the chapter in the *De casibus* differs from that in the *De mulieribus*. Whereas in the former "Adam et Eva" are given equal prominence, in the latter text only Eve is mentioned. Such a difference is a good indicator of the point of view of the discourse, affected by the diverse contexts. Adam speaks in the *De casibus* and is the central mediator in the description and interpretation of the Fall. The *viri* of *De casibus* are generally granted primary access to speech, emphasized by the male discourse of the 'sermons'. The narratives are dominated by accounts of men acquiring and losing power; women sporadically take centre stage, but are more often on the fringes, their voices subdued by the louder tones of the men.

Thus, the first mention of Eve by name is as Adam's wife, but it is not a neutral comment: "and she was joined to him not to be a bane to him, *as are today's wives*, but a comfort" (my emphasis).[6] This remark is not to be found in the *De mulieribus* version of the episode. While a general, critical attitude pervaded by cynicism and disgust at current female *mores* does surface regularly in the later work, with respect to Eve,

Boccaccio preferred to remain silent and write in a more restrained manner. Rather than turning every opportunity into a moralistic tirade, he seems interested in presenting a more subtle account, drawing on his biblical source in a less impassioned fashion.

The restraint of the *De mulieribus* derives from the suppression of tendencies that were allowed to surface in the *De casibus* account. The overtly moralizing tone of the *De casibus* is further enhanced by its basic structural pattern of having biographies followed by 'sermons'. Although the moral commentaries are still present in the *De mulieribus* (even if more sporadic and fragmented), they are integrated into the biographies and not granted the prominence of separate chapters. The structures of the two chapters on Adam and Eve are therefore quite different. In the *De casibus*, about a third of the chapter is devoted to a description of the garden of Eden (paras.4–9), thus emphasizing the extent of the loss, the entry of reality into a utopian existence, and the subsequent contrast with life outside the Garden, a topic which receives extended attention of a negative kind (paras.12–15).

The *De mulieribus* account concentrates, obviously enough, on the biblical story with Eve as the central character. She is described as an extraordinary being, and, in particular, as a beautiful woman, replacing the description of the garden in the earlier text. This is not only a changed perspective in line with the new subject-matter, but also a different kind of history. In the *De casibus*, it is public history, or the history of rulers underpinning its narrative assumptions, whereas the *De mulieribus* offers a view of these episodes from the point of view of the woman's body and its effect on the man. Thus, what at first sight seems an *excursus* on Eve's beauty, is in reality pivotal to the thesis of the text:

> We can imagine, besides, how marvellously beautiful her body was, for whatever God creates with his own hand will certainly surpass everything else in beauty [*FW* 15].

The fact that beauty is subject to change mirrors the fall: time is an agent of decline causing beauty to fade. The archetypal woman is described neither in terms of power nor of her relations to authority and its institutions. Her body determines her ambiguous place in the social order. The writer's comment on the role of beauty in society as a purely female issue is particularly telling:

> Yet, since women count beauty among their foremost endowments and have achieved, owing to the superficial judgment of mortals, much glory on that account, it will not seem excessive to place beauty here and in the following pages as the most dazzling aspect of their fame [*FW* 15].

The ironic tone is unmistakable here. The use of adjectives suggesting the superlative value of beauty creates the impression that women are to be judged by this single criterion, rather than by others which might be more in keeping with Christian visions of women or with praiseworthy public actions. The writer insinuates that beauty is to be tagged as a negative because of its social/psychological consequences on men. Boccaccio recognizes that female beauty is an essential part of male culture: an element that indicates the prime weakness of men is their sexuality. The imposition of chastity on women seems to be a one-sided male counter-measure to protect their fragile sexuality. Boccaccio seems to be *playing* a double game here: mocking beauty as an absolute value, and contemporaneously declaring it a value to which many men and women adhere (perhaps including the author himself in the not so distant past). Beauty is therefore a double-edged weapon: its very fragility induced Boccaccio to ridicule those women who artificially sought to maintain or improve their natural beauty, against nature. The *De casibus* and the *Corbaccio* are particularly brutal concerning this aspect of female behaviour; putting forward an uncompromising and reductive view of woman as the sum total of her artifices.

A new emphasis, with respect to *De casibus*, can be found in the second part of the *De mulieribus* version of the story of Eve: once the couple have been expelled from the Garden they both have to become (re-)productive, to become workers. From being an object of contemplation, Eve is reconstituted as an active subject who performs work that actively transforms nature:

> There, [in the fields of Hebron] while her husband tilled the soil with the hoe, this distinguished woman [egregia mulier], famous [clara] for her above-mentioned deeds, discovered (so some believe) the art of spinning with the distaff.[7]

The irony with which the passage begins, referring to the act of disobedience to God, underlines the irony or duality which characterizes the *De mulieribus* as a whole. The reference to the title of the book could not be clearer—'clara' takes on the double significance of both infamous (Eve's role in the Fall and its consequences) *and* notable for her supposed invention. It may seem that the mood of the *De mulieribus claris* is captured perfectly by the first biography—an ironic record of the 'great' deeds of women.

Boccaccio did not stop his account of Eve at her expulsion from the Garden. In a similar fashion to the *De casibus*, he continues the story but adds a significant detail, absent from the earlier work. He attributes the invention of spinning with the distaff to Eve. This is not just an idle detail, but one crucial to the text's ideology: it recognizes and explains the origins and development of woman's place in the Judeo-Christian

tradition. Her archetypal role of homemaker and mother, the first function characterized by spinning, sets the pattern for Christian women.
The loss of Eve's beauty ("Finally she reached old age, tired out by her
labours, waiting for death" [FW 17]) contrasts with her former good looks
and idyllic existence. The profound fracture between these two images
of a woman's life emphasizes what is to become the stereotype of a
Christian woman: on the one hand a domestic being, and on the other a
dangerous sexual creature whose beauty can overpower men. This
dichotomy is shared by the De mulieribus and becomes one of the staples
of Boccaccio's biographical method instituting the double bind of female
sexuality and public/private life.

The De casibus fulfils an intermediary position between the Epistola
consolatoria a Pino de' Rossi and the De mulieribus.[8] This hypothesis
receives qualified support from an analysis of those women whose
names appear in the titles of individual chapters in De casibus.[9] Such a
sounding is significant from a number of perspectives. First, the text is
primarily concerned with the fates of famous men since it is they who
generally have political control. Hence, the mention of women in this
context is of necessity less frequent. However, powerful women are not
ignored. This explains why so many women are 'hidden' in the titles of
individual chapters (for example, in the chapter on Samson, Delilah
receives no mention in the title). Secondly, the choice of women named
in chapter titles indicates a switch in interests and priorities when it
comes to the composition of the De mulieribus—under fifty per cent of
them make it to the later work.[10]

The motives behind these omissions seem to me critical to an understanding of the shift in emphasis from the one work to the other. The De
casibus appears to be a clear continuation and expansion of the Amorosa
visione, particularly from a structural perspective.[11] The use of the
Dantean visionary structure in both works allowed Boccaccio to confirm
Dante as an authoritative literary figure who lent credence to his
attempts at inventing and renewing literary genres, whether in the vernacular or Latin. Thus Dante's continuing influence can be seen at work,
providing not only a literary antecedent for 'direct contact' with men and
women of the past but, in the De casibus, an obvious moral slant. This
particular morality permeates the entire text with hardly a variation,
condemning the excesses of desire for sex and power, which lead to ruin.
In the De mulieribus, Boccaccio abandoned such an approach to signal its
difference from his previous works. It could be considered a sign of
greater commitment to the historical subject-matter rather than to the
narrations as such, also indicating a change of genre.

The De casibus structures history in accordance with a meta-histori-
cal principle, placing it in the straitjacket of a single interpretation, as

ineluctable to the reader as it was to the historical figures paraded in the book. The chapter heading which presents a single character predominates in the *De casibus* (as it will do even more obviously in the *De mulieribus*). However, the effect of a series of single characters passed in review is interrupted, the single characters juxtaposed to a crowd from which one or two speakers are detached. This literary technique, borrowed from Dante, renders the moral message more visible as well as importing into the text the prestige associated with its model.

The desire to include in the text as many historical personages as possible is one of the hallmarks of *De casibus*. The sheer bulk of *De casibus* points to its encyclopedic scope, emphasizing the significance of the proper noun, while aiming to demonstrate that historiography has moral goals. An uneasy equilibrium is established between these disparate elements of the textual strategy. The historical processes are subjected to an uneven analysis, sometimes forced to fit the transcendental framework. The same, repeated emphases reduce the characters to a one-dimensionality from which it is difficult to escape.

History is not fictionalized in the *De mulieribus*, indeed, the problems of reconstructing the past form part of its texture, emphasizing gaps in knowledge, variant readings of particular events, and obscurities that refuse clarification. Notable is the much reduced use of direct speech with respect to the *De casibus*. It is hardly used at all. In the *De casibus* one can talk about characters, even if they have a solid foundation in history, principally because of the use of direct speech and dialogue in the Dantesque manner. This practice lends a sense of fictionality to the text in combination with its clear, moral purpose defined by the structure of the work. The opposite impulse is at work in the *De mulieribus*. Ventriloquism is not a vehicle for the humanistic approach promoted in the *De mulieribus*.

Many of those historical women from the *De casibus* who arguably produced some of the most 'thrilling' episodes for the reader do not reappear in the *De mulieribus*. In particular, women from the early medieval period do not readily find a place in the collection of female biographies. The few who do appear do not form a consistent block (some were the result of later revisions made for contingent reasons). This is in part due to the narrower focus of the text which features classical culture as *the* cultural choice for Boccaccio, thus reducing the space available for more recent examples.[12] Undoubtedly, as a group, the early medieval women of power suffered most in the transference from the *De casibus* to the *De mulieribus*. In most cases, sexuality is the defining trait of the *De casibus* women, and often there are no 'mitigating' circumstances. Rosmunda (VIII, xxii), for example, is characterized solely by her sexuality which is viewed as entirely destructive of all those bonds that hold society together. However, the narrative does provide some indications which might convince the reader that socio-political motivations go a long way towards explaining her behaviour.[13] The episode is followed by a second chapter entitled *In mulieres* which emphasizes the virtue of restraint as a general warning to all women who challenge male-defined social and cultural paradigms. This kind of female anti-exemplar is common in the *De casibus* and forms a definite type.

There are also other women who do not reappear in the *De mulieribus*. Of the medieval exemplars, perhaps the most notable who falls into this category is Romulda, duchess of Friuli (IX, iii). Not by accident is she related to king Alboinus of Rosmunda fame and, in a sense, outdoes her predecessor in terms of sexual outrage. Romulda only has to view the invading king Catanus, and all moral codes are flung to the four winds:

> She put aside her tears for Gisulphus [her husband] and all care for the common good. She concentrated her mind on the virile vision of the enemy, desiring nothing more than to taste his embraces.[14]

Romulda offers to betray her country in return for marriage to Catanus. The conqueror accepts the proposition, but reveals a distorted morality by atrociously punishing her for her promiscuity. He finally transfixes her to a pole by her genitalia (a phallic symbol of male domination?), causing her death. The episode has a Dantesque flavour. It shows the crime and then concentrates on the punishment as *contrappasso*, appropriate to a woman who subordinates everything to her sexual urges. The punishment, however, is also part of the fantasy, the 'attraction' of the historical episode. It puts on show a woman who is available to everyone and who has an inexhaustible fund of sexual energy. That danger is symbolically and literally excised. The display of her sexuality is countenanced because it has a didactic purpose. The particular violence of this medieval episode may not have been so congenial to the classicizing *De mulieribus*. The punishment, graphically described by the text, is at least on a par with the offence. Its barbarity finds no place in the work on women.

Boccaccio does not include many of the classical women from the *De casibus* in the *De mulieribus*. Errant sexuality alone is generally not enough for inclusion in the latter work. This point is vital to understanding the change towards women in the *De mulieribus*. Female sexuality is still a central aspect of the collection, yet the focus shifts to women's achievements in a variety of fields, at times challenging the stereotype of the sexually charged woman.

In the *De mulieribus* Boccaccio did not include Valeria Messalina—one of the best known anti-female emblems from antiquity onwards.

Messalina's infamy derived from the circulation of Juvenal's sixth satire in which she is depicted as a woman wholly subject to her uncontrollable sexual passion, which she tries to satisfy by becoming a prostitute.[15] Thus, to later ages and particularly the Middle Ages, she was *the* sign of unbridled female sexuality. Boccaccio was undoubtedly aware of the currency of such a reductive interpretation and it certainly touches some of his later writings, especially the *Corbaccio*.

However, I would argue that Boccaccio works some quite remarkable variations into the standard theme and, in many ways, reforms Messalina's character. First of all, this example of sexually debased womanhood is not condemned on its own terms. She is compared to two men, two notorious Roman emperors (Tiberius and Caligula), so that vicious, uncurbed sexuality is shown to exist in men as well. Messalina enters into a heated discussion with the emperors on their relative culpability for the lives they led. Boccaccio-narrator (the severe moralist of the mature years) plays a secondary role in the framing of the debate. The narrator is drawn towards the trio; to their "almost pleasurable, though obscene, quarrel" ("iurgium fere delectabile, licet obscenum" [p.584]). It is a central and compelling question to ask what constitutes the pleasure of the dispute for the narrator. The grotesque nature of the sexual perversions performed by Messalina and the two emperors seems to exercise an obscure fascination on him. It cannot be rationalized as simply moral satisfaction at the debauched behaviour of pre-Christian society, although that is undoubtedly an element.[16]

A moral ambiguity, thoroughly unexpected in the classical tradition, permeates the character of Messalina. Such ambiguity has profound implications for the interpretation of her story. Surprisingly absent is a straightforward condemnation of Messalina as a transgressor of sexual rules, especially those of marriage. The narrator does not deny the 'sins' of Messalina, but he subtly shifts the emphasis by asserting the value of her intelligence as expressed through restrained discourse: "But that woman with a severer expression and more controlled speech than you might think such a licentious woman capable of, said to those trying men..."[17] We can note that Boccaccio is here breaking with the stereotypical representation of Messalina as a sexual body who expressed herself solely through corporeal desires and needs. The fact that she speaks in the first person, in a manner that might be considered part Ovidian and part Dantesque, is suggestive of an ambiguous sense of personal power, even when faced with two emperors who were once the most powerful men in the universe. It is this speaking voice which generates a disturbance in the accepted medieval model of the feminine. It is not only the fact that Messalina speaks (a condition bestowed on numerous women in the *De casibus*) but, more interestingly, that she speaks on subjects other than those confined to her individual life story, always equated with her sexuality. Her intervention examines the behaviour of Tiberius and Caligula as case studies of how absolute power destroys ethical and collective values. She rigorously examines the emperors' conduct in order to make clear the breakdown in Roman values.

By rationalizing her female body, Messalina breaks with the image men have constructed of her—an image that posits female sexuality at the centre of most discourses on women. In this way, she can be compared to Dante's Francesca who apportions blame to the dominant male ideologies which frame male-female relations. However, Messalina blames fortune for her actions, not love or literature. Such an attitude is questionable since *Fortuna* fulfils a moral function in the *De casibus* by punishing those who have transgressed against the laws of human decency and collective morality. Messalina's destiny, like Francesca's, is as inescapable as her own body.[18] Like Francesca, Messalina wishes to be excused for her sin, about which she talks directly: "although I redden I will not deny it. I was lascivious and wanton, guilty of adultery and always desirous of sexual pleasure."[19] These excuses read like a compendium of the faults of which women were often accused in the Middle Ages and later. Messalina's main point is that sexual desire is to be regarded as a defining feature of women—the constituent element of the female self. Hence it is regarded as 'natural' but, because of dominant ethical systems, is always closer to being amoral. Such an analysis could go unremarked if it were not that it is a woman 'confessing' to the perceived fault; a device used to render Messalina's confession more 'natural' so that it becomes the confession of all womankind. This strategy appears to be one of allowing women to be their own accusers; of having them identify themselves in terms of their sexuality and its potentially monstrous aspects. As such it appears to present a perfectly formed misogynist view of women.

The alluring simplicity of this view (a woman condemning herself out of her own mouth) does not account for the fascination of Boccaccio's creation. Messalina is not just a mechanical device used to condemn women: her direct assault on the emperors' (mis)conducted government reveals the extent of her political and historical knowledge, in that implicitly she lays down the criteria for good rule.[20] Her ironic address to Caligula as "princeps optime" ("great prince!") emphasizes that she is speaking from a 'moral' position on the issue of state governance.[21] This *disputatio* brings the issue of the double standards used to oppress women to a head. Although Messalina is acting from a position of weakness, she exposes the two emperors' sexual perversions in order to expose the means by which men succeed in denigrating women; that is by concentrating on female sexuality to perpetuate the idea of double standards.[22] A woman breaks the silence, or taboo, about male sexual-political behaviour. Messalina makes the following point about the relationship between private and public morality: without the former, the state becomes an image of disorder, corruption, oppression and universal inequality.

Boccaccio's portrait of Messalina seems to suggest blurred contours and complex perceptions of women, which hindered him from subscribing fully to the totally stereotyped picture of medieval woman. His imaginative formulation of a character like Messalina allowed him to play with the possibility of a woman, completely defined by her body in life, demonstrating the importance of the intellect over the physical body, but only after her death.[23] Messalina's attack on the emperors uses the traditional hierarchy of male superiority and female inferiority in order to reverse it:

> I know that you (Tiberius) are iniquitous in your soul, I in my body; you in your thoughts, I in my actions. Your acts were harmful to the entire human race, mine to no one (except for the shame I put on womanly chastity).[24]

Although Messalina subscribes to the traditional definition of female sexuality, by placing her life in parallel with the emperors', she raises important political issues about the relative gravity of social transgressions. By giving a female voice to the criticism of imperial Rome, Boccaccio is giving voice to the unheard. This strategy renders his critique all the more potent and expressive. Any direct suggestion that woman's rule would be more humane and rational is undermined by the fact of Messalina's sexual 'depravity'. She represents a model of female behaviour which does not allow for facile moral judgement, but sees woman as the site of contradictory and conflicting impulses. Messalina implicitly recognizes her future silence by paying tribute to chastity as the one female virtue *par excellence*, whilst simultaneously acknowledging that women are generally characterized by a rampant sexuality. Ironically, it is this which permits her to speak, breaking the law of female silence intended to protect female chastity. Her forthright and open speech has an immediate effect on the narrator and, by extension, on the male reader:

> She narrated these things with a sort of a broken vivacity and I had listened all ears, not only without boredom but with the greatest enjoyment. The wild men, confused, showed by their silence that she had won.[25]

Although her lack of morals is roundly condemned, Messalina not only emerges from the debate 'cleaner' than the men, but she manages to hold the moral high ground despite her shameful past. Here Boccaccio seems to have been willing to admit the complexities and contradictions of placing women in the straitjacket of official male sexuality.

.　.　.　.

A complex process of reassessment seems to have gone on in the period between the composition of the *De casibus* and the *De mulieribus*, perhaps influenced by Petrarch's epistle to the Empress Anna. The Boccaccio of the *De mulieribus* is less interested in the tragic circumstances of his chosen heroines and so less influenced by the Senecan model of tragedy than he was in the *De casibus*. Some of the most memorable women of the *De mulieribus* resist the swings of fortune and emerge victorious (Artemisia). Boccaccio was testing a different, wider range of emotions in his collection of female biographies: they may include gory finales, but also wifely faithfulness, familial devotion and other similar virtues. The *De mulieribus* is also more clearly a work of humanist inspiration: there is no division here into the numerically significant nine books of the *De casibus*. Instead, there is a more determined 'scientific' approach to the material, with less overt emphasis on the role of fortune and destiny.

It is noteworthy that some of those women who were most prominent in the misogynist tradition are not mentioned at all in the *De mulieribus*. The chapter *In mulieres* [I, xviii] in the *De casibus* displays a knowledge of archetypal 'bad' women. They are Delilah, Eriphyle, Danae, Arachne, Phyllis, Sylla, Clytemnestra, Semiramis, Iole, the daughter of Pharoah, Cleopatra, Sabina Poppaea, Sempronia, Medea, Progne. Just under half of these women will reappear in the *De mulieribus* but they will not be concentrated, as here, in a single consistent grouping. They will be dispersed throughout the text and placed side-by-side with 'good' women. In this way, there is a dilution of the anti-woman stance, so noticeable in *De casibus*.

Thus, the *De mulieribus* creates the impression of a more balanced and 'objective' picture of women through the interweaving of 'good' and 'bad' subjects. This impression is heightened by the absence of a clear, stated ideological frame urging the reader to assume a particular attitude towards women. The commentaries do act in this capacity to a degree, but are themselves dispersed throughout the text. At the same time, some of the stock examples of anti-female literature are still present, and represent one of the poles around which the discourse of the text circulates. It should be added that Boccaccio provided a stimulus to the anti-woman tradition by adding new *exempla* of female iniquity, culled from his eclectic readings of classical and other texts.

The moralizing strain of Boccaccio's writing generally covered the fissures revealed by the figure of Messalina. The *De casibus* and to a lesser extent the *De mulieribus*, oscillate between the dominant definition of womanhood, and an altered definition, one that highlights the positive results of sexual repression or entertains the possibility of escaping definition altogether through exceptional endeavour.

Considering Boccaccio's labour of research for the *De casibus*, and its apparent relevance to the later project, the absence of women such as Messalina from the *De mulieribus claris* is significant. As we have already seen, a number of women fulfil the conditions of re-use in the later text and hence appear in both. Yet it is interesting to note that a number of them take on a new lease of life in the *De mulieribus*. For example, the mother of Coriolanus, Veturia, does receive a mention in the *De casibus*, but she is not referred to by name and only in passing (III, v). The actions of this mother, pious towards both Rome and her own son, will receive extended treatment in the *De mulieribus* (LV). Other 'positive' women who are identified by criteria other than their sexuality do not find a place in the later text; for example, Arsinoe, Queen of Macedonia [IV, xv], whose interest resides wholly in the way fortune treats her—not a central theme of *De mulieribus*. Indeed, overall, the figure of Arsinoe in the *De casibus* is rather colourless. The same can be said for Sophonisba who, although not entirely neglected in the *De casibus*, plays a minor role in the narrative which has as its focus her husband, Syphax (VI, vi). The narrative is taken up from the perspective of Sophonisba in the *De mulieribus*, perhaps as a reflection of Petrarch's interest in the subject-matter.

Common Woman: A Shared *Exemplum*
from the *De casibus* and *De mulieribus*

*E*ven when Boccaccio used the same figure in both texts, the emphases are often diverse. The specialized focus of *De casibus* gives way to a more generalized meditation on female behaviour in the *De mulieribus*. The brief mention of Tamyris (II, xxi) in the earlier text (again to be extended in the *De mulieribus*) is inserted in the context of male conquest and aspiration to vast empire. Tamyris' vengeful act of throwing Cyrus' head into a cask of blood is not considered a matter of great praise for her victory over such a powerful ruler, but a humiliating end for the tyrant, perhaps not quite deserved. Two thirds of the episode in the *De casibus* is taken up with a *declamatio*, lamenting Cyrus' downfall. It is important to note that Tamyris herself is not seen as the architect of Cyrus' defeat; her stratagems which contributed to his death are not mentioned here. Instead, the book's general theme on the power of fortune is repeated. Cyrus is an "exemplum" (p.184) of human fragility and the intervention of God into human affairs. His head left in the blood "imperio mulieris" (by the order of a woman [p.184]), and the image of a woman cursing the mutilated corpse, are the substance of Boccaccio's narrative at this point. The ignominy of Cyrus' death catches the attention of the writer in this version. The greatness of Tamyris' achievement does not merit a mention.

The perspective changes dramatically in the De mulieribus once Boccaccio decided to provide the figure of Tamyris with motivation and depth. Human agency, including female agency, returns as the pivotal force in human affairs, thereby granting biography almost an autonomous status in which the subject struggles to achieve recognition and power. Greatness is no longer seen as its own punishment. Both Cyrus and Tamyris acquire motivations, no longer puppets of a higher destiny. For Cyrus it is the desire to conquer for the sake of conquest. Boccaccio's annotation is crucial here: the potentate desired to conquer Tamyris' land "more as an enhancement of his own glory than an expansion of his empire" [FW 201].[26] Such a detail is significant in the new context. It places the queen on a level of equality with the great emperor, granting her a status not even contemplated in the De casibus where she is implicitly regarded as a woman of little worth. In that work, the distance between the man and woman is depicted as being insurmountable: a great man humiliated by a woman whose qualities are not even minimally suggested.

The contrasting perspective of the De mulieribus allows Tamyris to claim a certain degree of gloria in the sense that the new situation permits her, no less than Cyrus, to demonstrate her prowess, and to have it consigned to history and the memory of future generations. The terms in which this is defined—especially the use of the word "clarius" (FW 202)— suggest a determination on the writer's part to redress the interpretation of De casibus by a more thoughtful revaluation of the Scythian queen, placing her amongst famous female warriors such as Camilla.

The contest between such exceptional generals is described with full military particulars to show that Tamyris was in no way inferior to Cyrus. In the De mulieribus, Boccaccio accepted that the queen was fighting for reasons which were more serious than those of her rival since they involved her own survival, the survival of her people and, later, revenge for her son's death at the treacherous hands of Cyrus.

The queen is generally presented in the most positive light possible. In the first place, she is described as a widow—a detail that places her alongside other widows of the De mulieribus, most notably the chaste Dido. This is a clear indication that she is independent and does not owe allegiance to any man, particularly not to a husband. Secondly, her exceptional status is confirmed by separating her from the stereotyped perception of womanhood as fearful, even when faced with the awesome power of Cyrus. This procedure is a common one in the *De mulieribus*. Tamyris demonstrates the possibilities of women in historically determined circumstances—an opportunity for the author to suggest that certain exceptional females can be equal or superior to men in the conduct of public affairs. However, this entails abandoning the accepted notions of femininity, unquestioningly marked as negative:

> she did not, like some timid female [femina territa], look for a place to hide, nor did she seek terms of peace through the mediation of an ambassador. Instead she gathered her forces and became their commander [dux] during the war [FW 201].

The contrast between "femina territa" and "dux," the latter obviously masculine in gender, helps to differentiate the everyday definition of a woman from a more radical re-definition, based on a woman's potential to emulate male behaviour. Tamyris has had to take on male-defined qualities and cast off 'feminine' ones in order to be granted the status of exceptional woman. Such a procedure negates the specificity of the feminine and sets up maleness as the most desirable goal for both sexes. Although it is easy to criticize Boccaccio's position, as it has been, it nevertheless permits him to document women in different spaces other than the enclosed ones of domesticity. The exercise of power by a woman disturbs conventional notions of the feminine—Tamyris' barbarity seems to present a male recoil at the operations of female power.

Tamyris' exceptional gifts are indicated by the adjective "sagax" ("wise" [FW 201]), employed to describe the brilliant tactics she used to defeat Cyrus. This adjective is rarely found to describe female behaviour in Boccaccio's tract. He prefers to use descriptive words deriving from nouns (for example "astutia"), which underline the concept of cleverness in the sense of female trickery, often for immoral or unworthy purposes. In this case, Tamyris' level-headedness is contrasted to "Cyrus' fury" [FW 201]) to stress the reversal of behaviours possible—even with Cyrus, the most powerful ruler of his day. Significantly, Cyrus himself is described as "astutissimus" [FW 202]. He brought about the death of Tamyris' only son by deception in a 'female' way, adopting the criteria used to judge women in the *De mulieribus*. The narrative at this point emphasizes the fact that Tamyris abandoned typical female behaviour and rejected the standard norms of female psychology as viewed by men. It is precisely because of this that finally she was able to defeat Cyrus:

> Tamyris, already a widow, grieved deeply for the death of her only son. But she did not burst out weeping as women usually do. Anger and a lust for vengeance restrained her tears [FW 203].

It would be hard to find a more explicit description of a woman redefining the hierarchy of sentiments in order to favour action/agency against female inactivity and, in textual terms, excessive emotionalism. However, towards the end of the account, it seems that one kind of emotionalism is replaced by another—anger becomes Tamyris' guiding principle and places her in the realm of the irrational: "and his bloody death satisfied the widow's wrath" [FW 203]. The dramatic finale of the account contains elements that were present in the shorter version of the *De casibus*. The ferocity of Tamyris is especially highlighted so that she becomes the negation of all sentiments representing human warmth. Her behaviour is partially explained by the fact that she belongs to that small group of heroines who can be defined as 'wild' or 'barbarian'; sometimes they are tamed, as happens with Zenobia, other times they are victorious as is the case here. The death of Tamyris' son is caused by the contamination of his natural state with the refined civilization of Cyrus in the form of exquisite food and wines, previously unknown to the Scythians. Thus, on another level, Tamyris rejects civilization as an agent which weakens and destroys the fighting spirit. The downside of such an attitude is that her final actions tend to invalidate those aspects which have received the highest praise in the rest of the story. We are left with the image of a woman whose exemplary value lies in denying the feminine within her, but to such an extent that it might be considered reprehensible.

The account of Tamyris in the *De mulieribus* is evidence of Boccaccio's deepening awareness of female potential beyond the sexual. At the same time, this awareness is hedged around with a variety of compromises and double-edged concepts that both add to and detract from the idea of women acting outside narrowly conceived domains.

·   ·   ·   ·   ·

V

𝔙ulgar 𝔚omen

BOCCACCIO'S VERNACULAR WRITING
AND THE *DE MULIERIBUS*

𝔗he *De mulieribus* can be regarded as a revaluation of Boccaccio's own previous work, which, in differing degrees, had touched on the classical traditions of the representation of women. It can also be regarded as a crisis-point, seeking 'new' ways of inscribing women in male discourse. The following analysis will concentrate on three texts: the *Decameron*, the *Amorosa visione*, and *Il Corbaccio*. Although one can trace continuities between them and the *De mulieribus*, the discontinuities appear equally important. An analysis of these works reveals that the names of antique women appear in Boccaccio's vernacular works from an early date (including the more recent *Lettera consolatoria a Pino de' Rossi*), indicating an interest in collecting a body of female characters whose significance was underpinned by their classical origins.

Decameron

𝔍n many ways, the *De mulieribus claris* appears to be a systematic re-writing of the *Decameron*. The role of female sexual desire and romantic love has been curtailed. There are no calls to the "amorose donne" who have been displaced from their position as arbiters of the text.[1]

De mulieribus was certainly designed to attract a different readership, if only because it was a Latin work. Its difference from the vernacular text is signalled by a systematic researching of relevant classical sources that are integrated into the discursive structure; the abandonment of Boccaccio's most obvious sign of literariness—the framing device—and the introduction of a single narratorial voice with the sporadic, additional use of the metahistorical commentator. In contrast, the *Decameron* grants a large space to women who become voices for the narratives, the fiction also allowing them to comment on and discuss the protagonists of the *novelle*. They mediate the readers' responses with frequent apostrophes to women. The multiple female voices of the *Decameron* are reduced in the Latin work to the male voices of the narrator and the commentator who attempts to impose a single interpretation on the discourses. The women of the *Decameron*'s *cornice* are able to sit in judgement on the morals of the stories, but there is dissension and, often, no clear-cut definition. The story of Solomon's judgement (IX, 9) illustrates this point nicely. The reaction to the narrative is divided along gender lines: "This story of the queen's produced one or two murmurs from the ladies, and one or two laughs from the young men."[2] In the Latin text, the male voices, especially the commentator, speak with monologic authority, signalling a break with Boccaccio's earlier literary texts and the creation of a new and quite different genre.

An obvious difference between the two texts lies in their respective attitudes to sexuality. While the sexual elements are not completely written out of the *De mulieribus*, in respect to the *Decameron*, they are drastically reduced. In large part, female sexuality is redefined negatively. Openness to female sexuality has disappeared and a more coherent moralistic framework imposed. The positive sexual consequences of female beauty for the male beholder have been censored; 'piacere' has been mostly eliminated from the *De mulieribus*. Love has been replaced by chastity. Women's sexual desires are described solely in negative terms and as a trap for men, bringing about their possible loss of power.

In the *De mulieribus claris* beauty is not a purely aesthetic category, but is closely associated with female sexuality, and hence constitutes the greatest danger to 'masculinism'. As we have seen, in the first biography, Eve's, Boccaccio constructs beauty ironically, imploding what is generally considered to be a woman's greatest asset. The archetypal *exemplum* in this sense is that of Iole (XXIII) and Hercules. From the beginning of the narrative, she is characterized, as "the most beautiful girl in her country" [FW 91]. Her emasculation of Hercules is made possible by the hero's perception of her sexualized beauty. There is no sense that sex is neutral or life-giving; it is generally viewed as a threat.

If adultery was one of the most frequent scenarios in the *Decameron*, in the *De mulieribus* this has been partially replaced by a more insistent effort to portray faithfulness in marriage as *the* desirable social and theological goal of women. Inconceivable in the Latin work is the mistress of Azzo da Ferrara, a widow (II, 2), who sleeps with a passing stranger. Boccaccio attempts to eradicate all traces of the positive attitude towards female sexuality, evident in his previous writing. However, the act of repression is not complete: the story of Thisbe, in particular, bears witness to a sporadic resurfacing or incomplete suppression of the *Decameron* vein. The commentator is sympathetic to the youthful demands of passion but claims that it is acceptable only as a stimulus to procreation and should lead to marriage [*FW* 61]. The commentator assigns love to youth; in old age, it is to be repressed and other values take on greater relevance. In this sense, *De mulieribus claris* is to be read as a work of 'old age' which seeks to lend decorum to a literary career that was marked by the 'excesses' of the *Decameron*. The introduction to Day IV is suggestive in this respect. One of the criticisms levelled against Boccaccio was that "it is not good for a man of my age to engage in such pursuits as discussing the ways of women and providing for their pleasure."[3] Although the author provides a response to such accusations in the same introduction, it is not hard to hypothesize the *De mulieribus* as a book of Boccaccio's maturity in which he attempts to arrive at a more conventional and more easily assimilable reading of women. Indeed, the lawlessness and disorder, brought about by the plague, as described in the *Decameron*, explains in part the composition of the *De mulieribus*. The *Decameron* narrator claims that those women who survived the plague were less chaste afterwards.[4] Hence, the need to put women back on the path of proper moral behaviour underlies the Latin work.

Parallel to this transformation of the *Decameron* is Petrarch's reworking and transposition into Latin of the last *novella*, the tale of Griselda. It will be useful here to rehearse its main features because it helps us to understand the re-formation of Boccaccio's reputation as a Latin writer of moral tales. Petrarch's short story is not merely a work of translation carried out because of his stylistic and rhetorical interests: the motives run deeper. He wrote to Boccaccio that he had leafed through the *Decameron* but the text did not entirely please him, mainly because of the presence of salacious subject-matter. The text was too lightweight for someone who had aspirations as a humanist writer. From the entire corpus of the *Decameron*, Petrarch was impressed only by the story of Griselda: "which seemed to me very different from the others."[5] His decision to translate it into Latin had the effect of separating it from the rest of the *Decameron* and bringing it into line with the *De mulieribus*. Petrarch made a serious attempt to redeem Boccaccio's reputation by deliberately misreading the Griselda story, emphasizing, almost as a final image for the writer, the exceptionally obedient wife. The changes he introduces normalize the text, removing any ambiguities which might have prevented a straightforward moral interpretation of the story. Petrarch's translation converts the multi-faceted vernacular narrative into an example of humanistic endeavour, both stylistically and morally.

This is not to suggest that it is necessary to ascribe to Boccaccio a total rejection of the *Decameron*. What can one make of the possibility that Boccaccio was revising the *Decameron* during the same period that he was composing the *De mulieribus*?[6] Both reflect woman as a contradictory creature, capable of good and evil, thus rendering the act of interpretation problematic. There are 'links', though not substantial ones, which suggest a residue of classical reference in the *Decameron* with respect to women: the name of one of the *racconteuses*, Elissa, is the Phoenician version of Dido; the first part of the story of Bernabò and Zinevra (II, 9) is a rewriting of the opening of Livy's account of Lucretia.[7]

Zinevra is presented as the archetype of the exceptional woman in the merchant environment. She combines noble pastimes with skills that would allow her to participate in the business world of the Genoese merchants: "her skill at horse-riding, falconry, reading, writing and book-keeping, at all of which she was superior to the average merchant."[8] The admixture of aristocratic and merchant skills is not present in the *De mulieribus* where the emphasis falls squarely on noble women. Hence, the possibility of a woman proving herself in the merchant world is excluded. Classical models are the only acceptable ones in the *De mulieribus*. In the *Decameron* Zinevra's domestic skills are also accorded respect, unlike the hard line taken by *De mulieribus claris* against such 'womanly' activities.[9] Finally, she is both beautiful and chaste,[10] continuing to love her husband, in spite of his 'betrayal'. Zinevra herself represents an intermediate position between the bourgeois wife and her noble counterparts of the *De mulieribus*: "for not only was she endowed with all the qualities of the ideal woman, but she also possessed many of the accomplishments to be found in a knight or esquire."[11] If the biographical narratives completely reject the merchant ethos of the *De mulieribus*, the commentaries often attempt to re-read the narratives from that perspective. The moralizing sections reinstate bourgeois notions of decency and propriety that seem appropriate for a readership of young women and their parents from the Florentine merchant class.

Critics have noted connections between the *Decameron* and the *De mulieribus* in terms of narrative technique and, to a much lesser degree, content.[12] Only a couple of chapters in the *De mulieribus* have received critical attention as exemplars of narrative writing, namely the biographies of Paulina [XCI] and Thisbe [XIII].[13] Such selective attention understates the narrative pulse of the *De mulieribus*, since overall the text presents biographical fragments that lend themselves to narrative treatment. The writer stated in the *proemio* to the vernacular collection of *novelle*:

> In reading them, the aforesaid ladies will be able to derive, not only pleasure from the entertaining matters therein set forth, but also some useful advice. For they will learn to recognize what should be avoided and likewise what should be pursued.[14]

A similar statement appears in the preface to *De mulieribus claris*:

> Hence I have decided to insert at various places in these stories some pleasant exhortations to virtue and to add incentives for avoiding and detesting wickedness. Thus holy profit [sacra utilitas] will mix with entertainment and so steal insensibly into my readers' minds. [*FW* 11]

Although the statements complement each other, they have different consequences. The Latin work specifies that the moral lessons are Christian in inspiration whereas the parallel passage in the *Decameron* refers to vaguer "useful advice." The *Decameron* does not make univocal declarations that stand unchallenged for the duration of the text. It is often difficult to decipher the 'correct' moral message.[15] The moralizing commentaries of the *De mulieribus* present a restricted view of female conduct. They assume an increasingly important function in the economy of the text since Boccaccio progressively adds to and strengthens their presence in the work. The moral impulse focuses the more diffuse researches of humanistic inspiration on to the everyday behaviour of Florentine (and other) women.

On one level, the relationship between the two works, can be described as relatively straightforward: the *De mulieribus* is intended to clarify a strong moral position on women where the *Decameron* slid into potentially radical proposals about female sexuality and behaviour. If the *De mulieribus* was more traditional in this aspect, by unearthing classical women whose actions, behaviour, and morality were not governed by Christian principles, Boccaccio allowed for the possibility of instability and ambiguity at the centre of this later work. Classical women may be judged retrospectively by Christian standards, but parts of their biographies can be recalcitrant to contemporary *mores*. While representing a simplification and clarification of the purported moral intention of the *Decameron*, the *De mulieribus* is itself not a paragon of clarity or simplicity. The mindset of the *Decameron* has been revised, but still the urge to narrate lives persists in the *De mulieribus claris*.

Amorosa visione

The literary relations between Boccaccio and Petrarch are not always easy to unravel, particularly in texts which have a more direct bearing on the genesis of the *De mulieribus*. Especially thorny is the question of the relationship between Petrarch's *Triumphi* and Boccaccio's *Amorosa visione*. The matter is of considerable interest because it throws light on Boccaccio's development as a humanist, particularly his preoccupation with exemplary female conduct. Their similarities are interesting for a study of the *De mulieribus* because of the use of female *exempla*, many of which appear in both works. There are conflicting views about which text takes precedence over the other. One theory proposes that the *Triumphi* owe their existence to the Boccaccian archetype, while the opposing view suggests that Petrarch had invented his schema before meeting Boccaccio. It is suggested here, however, that regardless of which text came first, there was considerable osmosis between the two works during their composition.[16] The evidence suggests that there was a significant degree of intellectual intercourse between Boccaccio and Petrarch from their first meeting, especially throughout the 1350s and during the composition of the *De mulieribus claris*.

There are strong indications that Boccaccio imbibed the concerns of the master. A convincing consequence of their relationship can be seen in Boccaccio's revision of the *Amorosa visione*, originally composed in the early 40s, probably between 1342 and early 1343, when he returned to Florence from Naples. If Branca's persuasive hypothesis is correct, Boccaccio was involved in revising his text in the period 1355–60, but the process of revision may have begun much sooner, even as early as the first meeting between the two writers; a view rigorously pursued by Billanovich.[17]

Boccaccio's return to a poem he had written in the vernacular at a time when he was increasingly concentrating on prose (and Latin prose in particular, in the later 50s), renders more convincing the hypothesis that he had seen fragments of the *Triumphi*. He may have wished to match Petrarch's standard of citation and reference within the strict limitation of his chosen form, with its acrostics and other stylistic difficulties.[18]

Boccaccio's revisions did not aim at a complete rewriting of the poem: they do however indicate an increasing concern with its moral tone, probably under the influence of Petrarch. He adjusted what he now perceived as some of the most glaring faults of the *Amorosa visione*, adding and subtracting a minimal number of male and female figures from the earlier version, but refraining from doing more because of poetical restraints and, perhaps, because he did not wish to expend too much energy rewriting what was clearly a juvenile work.

Some twenty-nine female figures from the *Amorosa visione* find a place in the *De mulieribus*; that is, just under a third of the women in the Latin work.[19] In many ways, Boccaccio's poem provides a basic nomenclature and structure for his Latin treatise. It would be incorrect to speak about a break between the vernacular and Latin texts. Rather, Boccaccio's revisions of the poem should be seen as an attempt to achieve a certain continuity, rendering it more consonant with the concerns of his later period. The change from verse to prose allows the writer to enter into more complex patterns of discourse than those permitted by the catalogic form of the *Amorosa visione*. At the same time, it suggests that there remains a 'poetic' strand to the Latin text. One may have expected more severe censorship than is actually to be found in the *De mulieribus claris*. The Ovidian love stories of the *Amorosa visione* have not been eliminated altogether—indeed both Thisbe and Pocris are not only present, but their tales are recounted in a form of extended prose poem.

The revision of the *Amorosa visione* permitted Boccaccio to take stock of the classical knowledge he had acquired by the 1350s, to assess the difference in the quantity and quality of his knowledge at the time of writing the early version of the poem and to measure it against Petrarch's learning and writings. This operation may have acted as a further stimulus for him to take up Latin prose in a committed manner, and to search for new methodologies and genres based on his humanist research.

In the *De mulieribus claris*, Boccaccio rejects the thematic unities of the *Amorosa visione* by placing the illustrious women in approximate chronological order, an approach which emphasizes the humanistic and 'scientific' at the cost of a defining, moral stand towards his subjects. In spite of the wide gulf between the two texts in a number of key areas, there are overlaps between them, especially in the areas of moral commentary and cultural acquisition.

The number of women Boccaccio 're-uses' later on is not the only relevant factor in assessing the extent to which he reworked the poetic text, although it is certainly important in reconstructing the parameters of his cultural vision of women. Importantly, his attitude towards a single woman might undergo substantial change in the process. Dido is the best example of this phenomenon: from the Virgilian temptress she is converted to the chaste founder of Carthage who dies on the pyre rather than remarry.

Some of the groupings of the *Amorosa visione* are respected in the *De mulieribus* in so far as they represent chronological as well as thematic homogeneity. After the fundamental accounts of Eve and Semiramis, the Latin work has a survey of classical goddesses as its first major 'series' of women, covering chapters III through to IX.[20] Five of these goddesses had already appeared in the *Amorosa visione*—significantly grouped together—in the company of other female deities subsequently excluded from the *De mulieribus*. However suggestive the repetition of certain female goddesses may be of a continuity in Boccaccio's thought, more striking is the change in tone and attitude towards his ancient material. Firstly, one can note the writer's increasing desire to systematize fragments of knowledge into encyclopedic form. Secondly, it is essential to take into account the 'scientific' re-reading of the goddesses in contrast to the poetic narrative of the *Amorosa visione*. I will take the contrasting representation of Juno in the two texts as my example. The poem focuses on Juno as the betrayed wife of Jove, long-suffering and vengeful, a portrait drawn from the Ovidian accounts of her activities. Her revenge on Semele and her own husband is exemplary. At the beginning of the episode she is described in the following terms:

> Dressed as an old woman and full
> of grief, there was Juno, envious[21]

Juno combines pain and grief over her errant husband with the latent (soon to be realized) possibility of revenge. In the space of a few lines, her desire becomes actualized as she tricks Semele "behind false appearances";[22] in much the same way as her husband seduced and conquered hapless virgins on countless occasions. In the poem, Juno does not constitute the central figure of these episodes; rather she appears in the interstices of Jove's numerous loves and lusts. The sources of her characterization lie in a potent combination of powerlessness to prevent Jove from betraying her, and the desire and capacity to end his illicit relationship of the moment. Thus, there are two sides to the way in which she is depicted: one aspect shows her as the grieving wife who employs all her available resources to keep her husband within the bounds of matrimony (the 'good' wife who shows loyalty to her god). On the other hand, she is a schemer who uses deceit to achieve her goal of revenge. These contrasting images render Juno a problematic character, with the 'positive' being undermined by the negative trait of untrustworthiness and vengefulness.

In the *De mulieribus*, Boccaccio cannot help but pour ridicule on Juno's role and functions as a goddess: "[they] entrusted to her conjugal rights, the protection of women in childbirth, and many other things that arouse our amusement rather than our belief" [*FW* 29]. The image of Juno as goddess of conjugal rights and duties above all attracts Boccaccio's scorn. Her behaviour does not fit the stereotype that seeks to predominate in the Latin text, that of the wife in accord with the Christian version of marriage.

The narrative verve and the lyrical intensity of the mythical episodes of the *Amorosa visione* were no longer considered appropriate to the *De mulieribus claris* since they rendered obscure any moral lessons which may have been derived from such tales. Jove does not repent of his immoral behaviour. He does not become a model husband and Juno's behaviour, whilst understandable, is less than exemplary. Thus, when it came to writing Juno's chapter in the *De mulieribus*, Boccaccio consciously refused to compose an entertaining narrative, or even to acknowledge that such dramatic narrations existed. To do so would have lent credence to erroneous beliefs, seducing the unprepared reader into a fantasy world beyond morality. Boccaccio takes an extreme line in this chapter by omitting any mention of Jove's adulterous behaviour and Juno's reactions.[23] Such poetic fantasies, although not completely alien to the *De mulieribus* (one can recall the episode of Pyramus and Thisbe, also present in the *Amorosa visione*) are kept in check. They are hedged around with the defences of moral stricture and sometimes extraordinary re-editing—as in the case of Dido, who is transformed into a chaste widow. Thus Boccaccio was distancing himself from his earlier positions on classical culture. Now, in chapter IV of the *De mulieribus claris* he reneges on (or at least regrets) *part* of his poetic past as a producer of amoral love fantasy:

> Nonetheless, it is easier to speak of Juno's singular good fortune than to relate any great deed of hers that is worthy of comment. [FW 27]

Juno is one of the most obvious examples of Boccaccio's effort to break with his past, cementing his metamorphosis from *poeta* to *humanista*. His defence of poetry in the *Genealogie* attempts to resolve the problem of the morality of reading (and writing) poetry by positing a hidden, moral truth in all poetry, especially classical. In the *De mulieribus*, Boccaccio shifts the focus on to a historical and logical reconstruction of Juno's cult, following clearly in the euhemeristic tradition of deconstructing pagan religion and opening it up to historical evaluation from a Christian vantage-point.[24]

Aside from the classical women who form a significant stratum of the *Amorosa visione*, Boccaccio introduces women who act as spiritual guides to the poet-narrator. The latter's reactions to their moral lessons and guidance are of some assistance in measuring the moral and thematic distance between the *Amorosa visione* and the *De mulieribus*. Dante's archetype is never far away from Boccaccio in this poem, although it is much modified to permit the narrator to make choices of his own. The role of the female guide ensures that the poem has a certain coherence. The threat of fragmentation is warded off through this unifying function.

From the opening lines, Fiammetta (the poet's beloved and one of

the female guides) lends an ambiguity to the kind of love evoked in the
poem:

> A new desire moves my bold mind,
> lovely lady, with the wish to sing,
> telling what love made known to me.[25]

This purpose is characterized by the poet's love for Fiammetta. The
central theme of the poem concerns the conflicting definitions of love
which cause alternations in the behaviour of the male protagonist.[26] The
protagonist is misguided in spite of the best efforts of the celestial guide
and Fiammetta. He has not got quite right the message of the lessons he
is meant to absorb, and is seduced by the representations of love in history and mythology depicted on the walls of the palace.[27]

The *De mulieribus* takes a strong stand against the notions of love that
are ambiguously explored in a text like the *Amorosa visione*. Love in its
various guises no longer acts as a galvanizing factor in the *De
mulieribus*.[28] Consequently, there are no presiding female deities to provide a sharp, central focus to the *De mulieribus* as there were in the
Amorosa visione. The dedicatee, Andrea Acciaiuoli, cannot, and does not,
play that role. Women are no longer made coherent by the spiritual (and
not so spiritual) bonds that tie the writer to an individual woman.

While using the *Amorosa visione* as a base for his investigations of
classical and later women, Boccaccio continued to find 'new' women
from sources previously known to him as well as ones that he had
recently discovered. The limitations of his knowledge in the 1340s would
have become clear to him on his re-reading of the poem in the 1350s. It
was not simply a matter of adding new names and a greater depth of
detail. It was a re-reading in all senses of the term: a rethinking of the criteria of exclusion and inclusion—a meditation on those qualities that
constituted an exceptional woman.

One example will suffice in order to explore Boccaccio's critical reading of his early text. In the last ten lines or so of canto X of the A-version
of the *Amorosa visione*, the poet mentions four Roman women: Cornelia,
Martia, Julia and Calpurnia. By the time of the revisions of the B-version,
these women have been reduced to three.[29] Marcia has been sacrificed
according to criteria that will become clearer after analysis of the *De
mulieribus claris*: in this text the original four women are further dimin-
ished to one—Julia. Boccaccio's probable source for his original listing is
Dante who mentions: "Lucrezia, Julia, Marzia, Corniglia" (*Inferno*, IV,
128). As has already been noted by critics, there is no mention of
Lucretia in the *Amorosa visione*: she was substituted by Caesar's loving
wife, Calpurnia. The omission of this famous classical *exemplum* is a
telling indication of the writer's lack of interest in chastity in the

Amorosa visione.[30]

The *De mulieribus* reinstates Lucretia, keeps Julia, and eliminates Calpurnia, Cornelia, and Marcia. It is interesting to note, however, that in the closing section entitled "De feminis nostri temporis" ["Concerning women of our time"], omitted from the final redaction of the text, Boccaccio mentioned all three of the eliminated women as examples of model wives: 'Martia Catonis, Cornelia Pompei, Calpurnia Cesaris dictatoris" (*DMC*, p.557). Clearly their appearance in previous texts had not been forgotten and their complete eradication was only a late initiative; an indication that Boccaccio believed their names, although not their complete biographies, were still useful if used in a subordinate position in the text.

The reasons for this 'game of musical chairs' are complex and go to the heart of the writer's changed ideology. Marcia's disappearance can be attributed to Boccaccio's obsession in the Latin text with widows and the absolute necessity that they *not* remarry at any price. Marcia's life history necessitated her exclusion. She divorced her first husband Cato in order to marry Hortensius and, on the death of the latter, asked to be taken back by Cato in order to be remembered only as his wife.[31] The same argument holds for Cornelia, who is to be identified as the second wife of Pompey. She herself had been married previously—a compelling reason as to why she is not recalled in the *De mulieribus*. Thus, in spite of Cornelia's tragedy—of seeing her husband murdered—the moral imperative of the Latin treatise places particular ethical considerations above dramatic, human situations.

The case of Calpurnia does not appear to be so clear-cut. Calpurnia is the model wife of Caesar, even warning him not to go to the Senate on the day he is murdered. Yet in the *De mulieribus* Boccaccio prefers to select Lucretia as one of his models of Roman behaviour—perhaps because her reputation was much more firmly established in the medieval mind than the little discussed Calpurnia. In contrast to both Lucretia and Julia, Calpurnia was a survivor and lived on in relative obscurity after the death of her husband. By the nature of their deaths, both Lucretia and Julia affirmed their attachment to the values of chastity and married life in the most dramatic and narratively interesting manner possible. They are both emblematic of the absolute value of marriage, which leads to their death: they are framed by that moment which declares their total dependence on male institutions for their identity. Calpurnia, by continuing to live, does not offer the same dramatic possibilities of sacrificial womanhood.

Other exclusions that the *De mulieribus* makes, can be more simply explained. Even though the *Amorosa visione* draws on characters from medieval romances, Boccaccio lays the groundwork for their deletion from future works. This revision takes place in the period of the B-version of the text, and shows the evolution of a historical consciousness in the writer. He refers to the fanciful historical reconstruction of medieval romance as "fola scritta" and "ombra di istoria," an indication of his greater interest in classical history moulded by more 'trustworthy' historians.[32]

The most popular female figures of romance enumerated in the *Amorosa visione* offer another type of difficulty for the older writer—their stories are often far from moral. The story of Guinevere is a prime example: her adulterous affair with Lancelot could not remain unproblematic, even in the revised version of the *Amorosa visione*. Thus in the *De mulieribus* queen Guinevere could have no place.[33]

In the *Amorosa visione* Dido died on the bed where she had made love to Aeneas; a setting that could not have remained even if Boccaccio had fully maintained the Trojan's part in her story.[34] Wherever possible the prose text represses and suppresses all expressions of the power of a woman's love, especially of its spiritual qualities. A woman's love is subordinated to social considerations of place and authority, generally represented as a negative effect, acceptable only within the bounds of matrimony. Reason seems to have won out in the competition with desire which characterized so much of the vernacular poem. Love no longer provides a single, unifying goal for female behaviour, as it did in the *Amorosa visione*. It appears in the *De mulieribus* only sporadically, and certainly not in the guise of a guiding spirit. It is just one possibility amongst many for women and so loses that exclusivity it had previously held for Boccaccio. In one sense, the relative absence of love in the *De mulieribus* reduces the opportunities for female control over men, whilst opening up the text to a wide range of other possibilities for women. These include state power, military action, and involvement in spaces far from the domestic hearth.

Il Corbaccio

It should be increasingly evident that Boccaccio's later works present a disconcerting range of messages to the reader. In spite of certain similarities, the two Latin works, *De casibus* and *De mulieribus*, provide contrasting emphases. The *Corbaccio* can be read in relation to one's interpretation of the *De mulieribus claris*. If the view is held that the Latin work is generally misogynous, then it is only a short step from the *Corbaccio*. In that case, it is unnecessary to formulate hypotheses about changes or volte-faces. If, on the other hand, one attributes to the *De mulieribus* even the slightest hint of 'progessive' thought on women, then interpretation becomes more complicated.

The *De mulieribus* can be envisioned as standing at the crossroads of a number of genres: humanistic biography, sacred hagiography, sermon, narrative. On the other hand, the *Corbaccio* belongs to the genre of anti-female satire and, as such, emphasizes elements which are more muted in the Latin text. In other words, the *De mulieribus* dealt with the exceptional, whereas the *Corbaccio* no longer exhibits faith in the exceptional woman. Therefore widows who appear in the biographical collection tend to be virtuous, while the subject of the *Corbaccio*'s acidic prose is a widow who projects a most negative image of womanhood.

In this context, the much-disputed question of chronology comes into its own. Rather than being simply an academic exercise, it underlies the different interpretations given by critics to the text. There are two distinct lines of thought concerning the dating of the *Corbaccio*. One places it in the mid-1350s or even earlier; and the other much later, some time after the composition of the *De mulieribus*.[35] Recently, it has been noted that there are textual bridges between the two works in the form of what appears to be unmistakeable references to the *De mulieribus* in the *Corbaccio*.[36] The presence of such passages suggests that the *Corbaccio* was written after the *De mulieribus* as a partial reflection on it. Extending this hypothesis even further, by the time he wrote the vernacular work, Boccaccio seems to have entertained doubts about the efficacy of the *De mulieribus claris*. If indeed the *Corbaccio* is a later work, some of the commentary can be read as clarification of the *De mulieribus*. By far the greater part of the Latin text recounts the stories of ancient women and these the *Corbaccio* treats in glowing terms:

> ...we came to speak of worthy women; and having said many things of the ancients, praising some for their chastity, some for their magnanimity, and others for their bodily strength, we came down to the moderns, among whom we found a very small number to commend, although he who took up the discussion at this point did name some from our city.[37]

The passage idealizes the content of Boccacccio's treatise on women, perhaps to the point of falsification, suggesting that the "valorose donne" from ancient times offer a perfect model to modern women who, in general, represent a decline in morals, needing such *exempla* to help them improve. For a reader familiar with the Latin work, it is no surprise to find that chastity is the first-mentioned virtue. The other two virtues chosen by Boccaccio to characterize ancient women reveal his fantasy of the strong and valiant martial women who are amply represented in the *De mulieribus*. Modern women, by contrast, do not match up to ancient *exempla*. This is reflected in the *De mulieribus* itself where the number of modern women is miniscule.

Summing up the widow's 'achievements', the *Corbaccio* again refers to "ancient worthy ladies"[38] to illustrate graphically the distance between ancient and contemporary women. However, the widow herself is ironically compared to Alexander:

> and he endeavoured to show her (beyond the nature of womankind) an Alexander, recounting some of her acts of liberality, which so as not to waste time in anecdotes, I do not care to relate.[39]

The comparison recalls the technique of the *De mulieribus* where a few exceptional women are able to overcome their Aristotelian shortcomings. Here, it is used to ironical effect, especially since the text exhibits a refusal to recount the actions that would have been central to a humanist compilation of biographies. The refusal to allow the narration of "anecdotes" ("novelle") confirms a change of perspective from the *De mulieribus*: the moral force of the *exemplum* is put in question.

The Corbaccio represents the reverse side of the *De mulieribus* in so far as the exceptional women have been replaced by an equally exaggerated single woman who personifies all female faults. Indeed, the Spirit resembles the conservative commentator of the *De mulieribus*, but taken to extremes, almost a parody.

In the *De mulieribus*, Boccaccio presented a more ambiguous view of the women of antiquity than is suggested by the black and white terms used in the *Corbaccio* to denigrate the widow. Moreover, in this vernacular text Boccaccio ironizes the use of *exempla* for moral edification, exploiting the ways in which examples can be manipulated to justify misogynistic attacks. As a result, rather than being utilized as a constructive tool in the moral education of women, the *exempla* are used to consolidate the construction of an anti-model. Adapting a Dantesque image, Boccaccio despairs of the possibility of moral improvement through instruction: "and our women have willingly lost the path; nor, of course, would they want it to be shown them again."[40] For example, in the *Corbaccio* the Sibyls seen as the incarnation of knowledge in pre-Christian times because of their prophecy of the advent of Christ, are used to ridicule the intellectual arrogance of contemporary women: "just as if every one of them should be the eleventh!"[41]

In the *Corbaccio*, the writer seems to have lost faith in the humanist endeavour to recover the past and integrate it into the framework of Christian morality. The text serves as an alternative mode of exemplary writing, drawing on a disparate tradition from that encountered in the *De mulieribus*. The commentaries of the *De mulieribus* make it clear that Boccaccio's view of contemporary women was *not* irreconcilable with the *Corbaccio* since there are numerous criticisms made of them in the Latin work. The belief in the moral, educational value of *exempla* has fallen away—a loss of 'faith' in their relevance to contemporary society.

The figures of the Virgin Mary and the female saints, presented in the *Corbaccio* as antitheses of the widow, are surprisingly absent from the *De mulieribus*. Their absence suggests to me that, at the time of writing the latter, Boccaccio was confident of the power of classical *exempla per se* to induce changes in moral behaviour. The *Corbaccio* dramatizes the crisis point of this theoretical structure wherein the only models which may be salvaged are the Christian ones of the Virgin and female saints:

> The other few who strove to resemble this most reverend and true Lady with all their might...Instead of wrath and pride, they possessed mildness and humility, and overcame and vanquished the rabid fury of carnal desire with admirable abstinence by showing wondrous patience in torment and temporal adversity.[42]

Here an extra-historical model replaces the lengthy list of historical *exempla*, embodying within a single, unified subject a choice of Christian virtues, emphasizing passivity and chastity, in contrast with the more dynamic representation of female virtue found in the *De mulieribus claris*.

The situation, as I have briefly outlined it, helps us to understand how, after composing the *De mulieribus*, Boccaccio may have conceived the *Corbaccio*. The focus of the Latin text is on a range of historical women who demonstrate that, in spite of fundamental flaws in the female sex, a few women are worthy of praise (within the bounds of clearly drawn male parameters). The relationship between past and present is a didactic one in that history is utilized as a tool to teach men and women to improve their behaviour in the present—although the present in the *De mulieribus* is partially repressed in favour of a humanistic approach to learning through history. On the other hand, in the *Corbaccio*, Boccaccio wrote in the vernacular and switched genre so that the text appears to be clearly in the anti-woman camp. Also, he returned to using a *cornice* of a type employed in the *Amorosa visione*.[43] Boccaccio's final comment on saintly women, although consonant with the tone of the *Corbaccio*, has its parallel in the *De mulieribus*:

> I would say that she [Nature] had cruelly sinned against such women [saints], subjecting and hiding such great spirits, so virile, so constant and strong within such base limbs and within such a vile sex as the female; because, if you well consider who these ladies were and who those are who wish to mingle in their number and be honoured and revered among them, you will see quite well that the first group ill-matches the second, or rather, that they are completely opposite to one another.[44]

A similar comment can be found in the Latin work apropos of one of Boccaccio's most fascinating heroines, Artemisia:

> As we admire the deeds of Artemisia, what can we think except that the workings of nature erred in bestowing female sex on a body which God had endowed with a virile and lofty spirit? [FW 241, 243]

Masculinity and Parody in *Il Corbaccio*

Both the *Corbaccio* and *De mulieribus claris* take it for granted that masculinity is superior to femininity and that the most successful women are closest to a supposed male ideal. In both works, it is implied that all is not well with contemporary masculinity, and indeed, in the Latin work, there are numerous references to its failings. The superior male virtues do not appear to be present in the two 'heroes' (the narrator and the guide) of the *Corbaccio*. Robert Hollander describes them as two "male hysterics."[45] I take the term to indicate a loss of masculinity, understood as control and authority over women—in fact both male principals have been emasculated by the widow. The narrator clearly exhibits this loss in the episode in which he is humiliated by his would-be lover. Though a scholar, he fails to read the widow correctly. The *Corbaccio* seeks to reinstate male identity, lost through the power of sexual desire, parodying a humanist encyclopedia such as the *De mulieribus*. Revenge is central to the *Corbaccio* because it allows the two men to reassume their male identities. The revenge is a scholarly one since, through literature, women are revealed for what they are.

On the other hand, the guide has been condemned to Purgatory for two sins. The first is avarice (presumably to keep his wife in the luxury she desired) and the second, revelatory of the loss of his masculinity, is "the improper patience with which I bore the wicked and shameless ways of her upon whom you would wish you had never set eyes."[46] The term "pazienzia" is often regarded as a feminine virtue, used to praise the sacred passivity of female martyrs. Thus, the adjective "improper," refers to the guide's lack of dynamism and activity which befits a man. There has been a confusion of gendered behaviours by the guide; such 'feminine' behaviour is viewed negatively in both the *Corbaccio* and *De mulieribus*. It reinforces the idea that when faced with his wife's behaviour he played the part of a martyr instead of the more correct role of an authoritative husband. His condemnation to Purgatory is a clear illustration that as a husband he broke the rules of male domination and, on several counts, failed the test of manhood. The *Corbaccio* presents to the reader two negative *exempla* of male figures who failed to read a particular woman correctly. Their failure is generalized so that all women are blamed for the 'faults' of the widow.

However, these two men do not exhaust the possibilities of the masculine in the *Corbaccio*. There is another male character who acts as a counterpoint to the narrator and the guide, disparagingly called by them the "second Absolom."[47] Compared to them he has been successful: sexually virile enough to seduce the widow; he was subsequently instrumental in the narrator's humiliation. For both these reasons a terrible revenge awaits him, prophesied by the Spirit. The widow's lover is identified as the author of the fatal letter which ensures the narrator's downfall and, as a kind of *contrappasso*, a significant part of their revenge will be the production of a more authoritative text for public consumption: the *Corbaccio* itself. The spitefulness of the two men is in no small part due to their impotency, sexual in the first place, but also intellectual in the context of the embedded narrative. The profound irony of the text lies in the fact that the so-called scholar is not a scholar at all. He may be able to write, but his use of knowledge is biased and uncritical. Such a stance contrasts strongly with the methodology employed in the *De mulieribus claris*, where, despite tendencies towards an overt misogyny, the text does not reduce women to one-dimensional objects of derision.

The *Corbaccio* is much more extreme than the *De mulieribus* in a number of key areas. Female beauty, while viewed with considerable ambiguity and disdain in the Latin text, is treated with ferocity in the *Corbaccio* where it is deconstructed and revealed as completely false. The same point can be made about the treatment of love in the two works. It is not totally condemned in the *De mulieribus*, although female sensuality is marked clearly as negative. However, Boccaccio's commentary narrows down the conditions in which love can operate, that is, it must lead to matrimony. Nothing of this is left in the *Corbaccio*.[48] The *De mulieribus* points towards the *Corbaccio*, especially in its commentaries which sometimes catch the tone of the later text, but is generally more restrained.

The *Corbaccio* ruthlessly parodies the *De mulieribus*, with a number of classical references underlining women's misuse of positive female *exempla*. Indeed the classical references may be read as a humorous side-swipe at the seriousness of the Latin treatise.

Certainly, the humour is still there without taking the *De mulieribus* into consideration. However, it gains depth when placed alongside the Latin solemnity of the biographies of the Sibyls, for example. The *Corbaccio* demonstrates the merciless manipulation of the *exempla* for purposes for which they were not originally intended: the scholar has lost control of them. The basic premise of the existence of exceptional women is further parodied in the continuation of the same passage cited above:

> It is a wondrous thing that in so many thousands of years that have passed since the world was made, amid so great a multitude as has been that of the feminine sex, only ten wise and celebrated women have been found among them; and each one thinks she is either one of them or worthy to be numbered among them.[49]

This is a parodistic reversal of the argument that exceptional women provide concrete evidence of the possibility, *albeit* slight, for contemporary women to overcome stifling stereotypes—the argument that subtends the *De mulieribus*. Indeed, the social relevance of *exempla* is questioned in the *Corbaccio* to such a degree that the *De mulieribus* implicitly becomes a problematic archaeological inter-text for the vernacular work.

.   .   .   .   .   .

VI

The Dangers of Dedication

DE MULIERIBUS CLARIS
AND CONTEMPORARY POLITICS

During the composition of the *De mulieribus claris* Boccaccio's life underwent major revision: from being a man of some authority and prestige in Florence he went into self-imposed 'exile' in Certaldo. He had to look outwards for solutions to his economic woes, making another attempt to establish himself in Naples under the tutelage of Niccolò Acciaiuoli. At the same time, it appears fairly sure that Boccaccio did, in fact, become a priest, perhaps with parish responsibilities, in the period 1360–61. This biographical 'fact' helps us to understand the hardening of his position towards sexual purity in women, such that in practical terms he silenced the language and subject-matter of the *Decameron*. The sermon-like qualities of the commentaries in *De mulieribus*, with their hard line on the issue of parental control over children and the need for a return to proper Christian values are also becoming to his new ecclesiastical dignity. Boccaccio's desire to develop Petrarch's Christian humanism, boosted by his stay with the humanist in 1359, was certainly another factor contributing to the complex cultural circumstances of these years.

It would be no exaggeration to refer to a personal crisis precipitated by the conspiracy in which Niccolò di Bartolo Del Buono and Pino de' Rossi were deeply implicated at the end of 1361. The first, the dedicatee of the *Ninfale fiesolano*, was executed; the other, addressee of the *Lettera consolatoria*, was exiled. Boccaccio's scornful attitude towards the Florentine regime of new men constituting the *Signoria* is made explicit in the *Consolatoria*. An insistent feature of the *Lettera* is the damage done to Florentine society by the accession to power by the *homines novi*. Boccaccio is outspoken in his denunciation of the "disonesti uomini assai," accused of a variety of actions against the commune, including

the Dantesque sin of barratry.[1] The ruling elite is accused of placing personal gain before the "comune bene"; corruption is seen as endemic to
the political system in Florence.[2]

Such views are not alien to the *De mulieribus claris*, although not
expressed with the same openness and directness, the Latin work manages to find ample space for political representation. Boccaccio tends to
generalize from his personal experience of the breakdown, as he saw it,
in the traditional values that guided the commune. He translated the crisis in Florentine politics into classical terminology and imagery, but it is
no less intense than the heartfelt language of the *Consolatoria*. The addition of further commentaries to the *De mulieribus* would seem to indicate
that there was a double movement between the *De mulieribus* and the
Consolatoria. On the most obvious level, the re-use of classical *exempla* of
the wife, already researched for the Latin work, create an aura of learning and erudition in the vernacular text. They also implicitly ennoble the
concept of wife, taking it out of ordinary usage and giving her a dignity
which may have otherwise been lacking.

In the other direction, one can note the circulation of political ideas
and commentary in the *De mulieribus*. Its composition coincides precisely with Boccaccio's voluntary exile to Certaldo, mirroring Pino de'
Rossi's own enforced exile. It seems possible that the writer could have
been working on both texts simultaneously. The *De mulieribus* was
started in the summer of 1361 and the *Consolatoria* shortly afterwards,
probably in the latter part of the same year.[3] In the *De mulieribus* direct
reference to contemporary political events is excluded, but this does not
mean that the generalized, humanistic observations have no relevance
to the actual situation in Florence.

What may appear to be a commonplace assumes heightened significance because of Boccaccio's political analysis in the *Consolatoria*. For
example, his statement in the biography of the goddess Ceres that the
Golden Age is preferable to the present one is repeated, with slightly different emphasis, in the *Consolatoria*. The epistle emphasizes a point that
is not made explicit in the Latin text, namely that civilization enervated
masculine values. Such an explanation makes sense of Boccaccio's
doubts about the efficacy of the city and the consequences of civilized
living expressed in the *De mulieribus*. It is difficult, if not impossible, for
the refined male to live up to traditional expectations of his gender. In
these circumstances, exemplary biographies of famous women are a subtle reminder to men of their gender, a novel means to renew the
depressed moral climate of their city.

Florence itself does not get much explicit mention in the *De
mulieribus*, as one would expect from a work that is intended mainly as
an exposition of classical women. The most obvious exception is that of

Gualdrada [CIII] who teaches her father a lesson in correct morals. The last paragraph of the chapter emphasizes the contrasting moral standards between Gualdrada's generation and the writer's own. Moral standards are indicative of the well-being of a society or otherwise. The fact that Gualdrada's ordeal ended in marriage on the direct instruction of the Emperor fits into the pattern of the De mulieribus where marriage is for the good of the community.

The tale is also concerned with dynastic foundations since the family into which Gualdrada married, the Guidi, was one of the major feudatories of the Tuscan contado. There is an evident anti-imperial slant to the biography (the Emperor is described as suppressing his 'German barbarity'[4] in this instance and Gualdrada's father is willing to prostitute his daughter to curry favour with Otto IV). However, fealty to the Emperor is rendered complicated in the narrative because the Emperor himself chose a suitable husband for Gualdrada, from one of his feudal vassals. Therefore, in spite of the doubts about the Emperor, the story alludes to the continuation of a feudal house in Florentine territory through marriage to a woman who shows courage and daring in being able to stand up to both her own father and the Emperor.[5] Thus, the Guidi accept into their family a woman who is able to bring with her values that have not been tainted by political manoeuvrings and clientelism. Boccaccio shows his Guelf colours more clearly in the following chapter (CIV), and without any hint of compromise, when he declares the Emperor Frederick II a monster and a pestilence since, in his time, he had threatened Florentine independence.[6]

Gualdrada is the only Florentine woman in the De mulieribus claris. Camiola (CV) is Sienese and her narrative concerns Sicily rather than Tuscany. Camiola does offer certain similarities to Gualdrada's biography. The Sienese widow refuses to accept the deceit of Orlando d'Aragona whose ransom she had paid on condition that she married him. She had required this surety as the only way of safeguarding her reputation. Orlando's refusal to accept the condition leads Camiola to denounce him publicly. Her speech emphasizes those values that have led her to pay his ransom: truth, sincerity, compassion, and loyalty to the royal house [FW 461–67]. Her speech shames Orlando into repentance, but Camiola will not be moved and refuses to wed him. It is a woman from a northern Italian commune who incarnates the values of true nobility, like Gualdrada. Camiola has everything except royal blood to call herself royalty. Her wealth is described as "almost royal" [FW 455]. Further, she states that her proximity to the ladies of the court inculcated royal values in her:

> I admit that I am not a woman of royal blood. But from my childhood I have
> been in the company of the daughters, daughters-in-law, and wives of kings,
> so it is not surprising that I have acquired their manners and spirit. And this
> is sufficient for me to assume the noble state of royalty. [FW 465]

Although the De mulieribus insists on noble bloodlines for most of its
women, it occasionally makes exceptions. Camiola is hardly an exception because of her remarkably noble deportment. The discourse against
blood nobility without the concomitant understanding of the required
behaviour might be read as a message from a Tuscan woman to the
Florentine magnates and to all the aristocracy concerning the ethics of
nobility and the essential importance of keeping faith.

The only other woman in the De mulieribus claris to have close relations with Florence is the goddess Flora (LXIV). No specific reference is
made to Florence or even to a tradition that associates her with the city.
However, for a Florentine reader the association would have been clear.[7]
The Anonimo Fiorentino claims that Florence was first called Flora,
although he does not recall the goddess. The further association with
spring, fertility, prosperity was undoubtedly propitious for a newly found
city:

> And in that place and the surrounding countryside where the city was built
> flowers and lilies were always in bloom. Therefore most of the inhabitants
> agreed to call it Flora because it was built in flowers, that is, amongst many
> delights.[8]

The most celebrated example of the Flora myth can be found in
Botticelli's Primavera. And the goddess appears in Vasari's The Story of
Gualdrada (1561), identified by her holding a bunch of flowers.[9]
Medicean art seems to have systematically expoited the goddess as a
guardian of the city and associated her closely with the dynasty. But this
does not preclude an earlier pre-Medicean tradition which emphasized
the Flora/Florence connection. In this respect, Boccaccio's alternative
readings of Flora are not innocent.

The creation of the Ovidian myth of Zephyr and Flora was in
response to the unsavoury historical reality of her origins as a prostitute
according to the De mulieribus. The state rewrote the story of Flora for
political ends to bring respectability and a sense of mythical origins to
the games celebrated in Flora's memory. Boccaccio urges the view on the
reader that Flora was a prostitute [FW 269]. He unmasks the mechanism
by which political myths are created by establishing a historical critique
of their operation in a social context. If, as I have argued, the chapter is
an indirect barb at Florence and its claim to divine origins through the
'goddess' Flora, the biography stands in contradiction to the Gualdrada
story by presenting its founding divinity as a prostitute. This is not so far

off from some of the criticisms Boccaccio made of the new men in the *Consolatoria* a few of whom ply questionable trades, such as pimps.[10] They have prostituted Florence for personal gain.

In political terms, the *Consolatoria* does not spare Florence's political arrangements. The government comes under fire for its lack of morals, and more importantly, for the insinuation of the *novi cives* into powerful positions in the commune.[11] In an exaggerated sketch of their rise to power, the writer claims that their trickery (almost akin to that of Ser Cepparello) played a large part in their being accepted into government.[12] The *Consolatoria* provides as clear a statement as one can find on Boccaccio's alignment with a magnate position at the time of composition of the *De mulieribus claris*. Boccaccio has some harsh words for his fellow citizens whom he castigates as overly ambitious and underhand in their dealings. In particular, he does not hold back his negativity towards the "moltitudine indiscreta" which is also the object of abuse and mistrust in the *De mulieribus*.[13]

Boccaccio's moral disgust is also the political conviction that Florence is in bondage to factional, self-seeking individuals. His closeness to Pino de' Rossi and the point-of-view expressed in the *Consolatoria* made inevitable his distance from the regime. His self-imposed exile may have stimulated a rethinking of his political position that led to the different, more democratic views indicated in the *Corbaccio*, but certainly at this political juncture, Boccaccio saw Florence as a city in decline subject to the moral depravities of the new men. The emphasis of the *De mulieribus*' discourse is on traditional values, a return to moral integrity, both sexual and political, accounting for the novel emphasis on the wife as upholder of such values. The wife in the *Consolatoria* becomes the sole safeguard of traditional values in society. Her opposite, the unfaithful wife, cited also in the *De mulieribus*, serves to underline the dangers of uncontrolled female passions, including those of wishing to increase their 'grande stato'.[14]

By linking his name to the magnate Rossi family, Boccaccio was obviously cutting down his options for career advancement in his native city and leaving himself open to accusations of colluding with the conspirators of 1360. On the other hand, it could be hypothesized that he was taking a calculated gamble in a different game. Niccolò Acciaiuoli, the Florentine who had become so powerful in the Kingdom of Naples, had strong magnate sympathies and possibly some involvement in the conspiracy against the *Signoria*, if only indirectly. It does not seem incidental that in December 1360 Niccolò Acciaiuoli was declared ineligible for the Signoria.[15] Such details affect our picture of Boccaccio in this period. Firstly, it is well known that our writer had or wished to have close relations with Acciaiuoli; friendship may be too strong a word, but Boccaccio definitely had ambitions which he felt he could satisfy through him. Secondly, the *De mulieribus claris* undergoes significant changes, including the dedication to Andrea Acciaiuoli, because of Boccaccio's invitation to Naples by her brother. One might interpret this in part as a reward for his support of Pino de' Rossi and compensation for his voluntary exile.

Andrea Acciaiuoli: Escape and Desire

The decision to go to Naples in search of more favourable fortune marks a turning-point in the history of the *De mulieribus claris*. It required the addition of new elements, especially the dedication. It is not dedicated to the Grand Seneschal of the Kingdom as that act might have been too provocative given the circumstances of the conspiracy. Moreover, the choice of a woman and someone no less than the sister of Niccolò Acciaiuoli, was more effective in the context of a collection of female biographies.

Clearly the dedication of the *De mulieribus* to Andrea Acciaiuoli was part of Boccaccio's strategy to ingratiate himself with her brother. The dedication itself contains much to interest the critic studying the significance of the collection of female biographies. It is important, however, to bear in mind that the dedication represents a later stage with respect to the majority of the biographies, which had been written before it was composed. The dedication presents a 'public' interpretation of the collection. Providing guidelines for a 'correct' reading of the text, it imposes a single, unified interpretation. In the absence of a larger frame, it is obvious that the dedication assumes greater importance because of the reader's need for points of reference in an apparently seamless text. Yet the dedication is not without its problematic aspects: Andrea Acciaiuoli herself presents an image of womanhood which perhaps does not suit a text designed as the pendant of Petrarch's *De viris illustribus*.

Re-Reading Boccaccio's Dedication

Boccaccio's dedication in the *De mulieribus* does not represent a clear-cut, positive attitude towards a female patron. But his declaration that due to its subject-matter, the *De mulieribus* should be dedicated to a woman is double-edged. An early remark is most perplexing and requires comment: Boccaccio states that he had originally planned to dedicate the treatise to Giovanna, Queen of Naples: "...that unique glory not only of women but of rulers" [*FW* 3], but that he con-

sidered his work too minor to merit the attentions of so great a queen—
hence the present dedication![16] Such an apparent faux-pas can be
explained as an extremely subtle compliment to Andrea Acciaiuoli, considered second only to the queen herself![17] The mention of the queen
allays any fears that she had been slighted. The denigration of his own
book is a courtly compliment that serves to raise the prestige of
Giovanna I.[18] However, this positive evaluation does not completely put
the contemporary reader at ease. It seems to show a Boccaccio uncomfortable in the world of courtly compliment, especially since he utilizes
most of the dedication to sermonize his subject in the manner of a
prickly preacher. From this point-of-view Andrea Acciaiuoli was a safer
target for this form of discourse than the queen would have been! In fact,
the dedication bears close resemblance to the moralizing sections of the
main text. Andrea is an imperfect subject on whom the exemplarities
illustrated in the text can exercise a beneficial influence.

The dedication does not honour Andrea wholly in her own right:
implicit is the political knowledge that her brother holds power in
Naples. Thus, she can be seen as an instrument used to further
Boccaccio's ambition. She was a means of insinuating himself into
Niccolò's favour by flattering his literary sensibilities.

The irony of the writer exploiting a woman within the parameters of
a text which purports to praise women should not be lost on the reader.
It also helps to explain why Boccaccio did not dedicate the work to queen
Giovanna. His choice is based on the realization that real power in the
Kingdom is in the hands of Niccolò Acciaiuoli to whom Boccaccio
believed he had special rights of access. Thus, the dynamic, contemporary part of the text is given over to his sister. Queen Giovanna does not
exert the same hermeneutical influence over the work as a whole. In her
place of honour, as the last biography of the *De mulieribus*, she fills a cer-
emonial position. Her presence ensures that no possible source of
patronage is alienated.

This situation was further complicated by the vacillating sentiments
nurtured by Boccaccio towards the Acciaiuoli, particularly Niccolò.
Contrary sentiments had been expressed once before, using the sister as
the medium, in a game of male jealousies and petty politics. In the
Amorosa visione, ostensibly referring to Andrea, Boccaccio pronounced a
negative judgement on the family:

> ...with humble demeanour, came she who was born of stock which, first
> sharpening their wits on base material, then passed themselves off as noble
> at others expense, so increasing in numbers as in wealth.[19]

In this interpretation, Andrea is tainted by the family's *arrivisme* and
thirst for power. The focus is not on her personality or actions, but solely

on her as a representation of the family's obsession with making money and climbing the social ladder. It is quite obvious that Boccaccio was using Andrea in the *Amorosa visione* to revenge himself on Niccolò whereas, in the *De mulieribus*, he used her to repay a favour (the invitation to Naples) in the hope of receiving further reward.

It is with this background in mind that Andrea becomes an ambiguous figure, seemingly ill-equipped to carry the hopes of all womanhood. Another disturbing feature of the dedication is that she had remarried by the time of the later revisions. Such an event may not in itself appear exceptional—after all, even Queen Giovanna was not immune from the 'stigma' of remarriage, although Boccaccio suppressed this fact in her biography. Nevertheless, remarriage is an important object of enquiry and moral outrage in the *De mulieribus*, the text never missing a chance to reprehend those women who seek more than one husband. For example, the episode concerning Pompeia Paulina (XCIV) is manipulated to provide yet another occasion for the commentator to castigate contemporary women for their lax morals:

> Alas, what wretches we are! To what depths have our morals plunged! The ancients, who were naturally inclined to purity, used to regard a second marriage as disgraceful, much less a seventh; they also held that after remarriage it was wrong to permit such women to mingle with respectable wives. The women of our day are quite different. [*FW* 403]

The contrast between Paulina's exemplary moral conduct and contemporary *mores* is particularly pertinent in the context of the dedication to Andrea Acciaiuoli. In the final analysis perhaps political considerations were too weighty at such a late stage to allow Boccaccio to begin thinking about replacing Andrea as the dedicatee, or to reflect on the double standard implicit in praising an individual who negates one of the moral foundations of the text.[20] The accommodation sought by the writer between political realism and his Pauline idealism concerning the remarriage of widows, means that the second attitude remains in uneasy juxtaposition with the first. The irony in the dedication is produced by the imposition of pressures which fall outside the ideologies expressed in the body of the text. It is true that in the rush to complete the manuscript Boccaccio did not foresee the unexpected consequences of a few loose words.

The ambiguity surrounding Andrea Acciaiuoli renders interpretation of the dedication slippery in relation to the avowed intentions of the text. The problem does not lie solely in the generalized description of the dedicatee, which could be adapted to the praise of any well-born woman, so that she becomes a mirror in which her female contemporaries might see themselves reflected. Andrea's individuality is obscured behind those general characteristics which serve either as a guide to other women, or to confirm the type for the male reader.

Andrea's description is idealized only to a point, although Boccaccio does not fail to impress upon the reader her moral rectitude: "outstanding probity, women's greatest ornament" [FW 3]. However, in the same breath, he mentions other social gifts which suggest that she had a role to play in court circles, particularly her "elegance of speech" ("verborum elegantiam"). This highlights the importance of conversation and social intercourse in court society, in contrast to the Pauline ideal of the silent woman; a theme that Castiglione will take up and amplify in the *Libro del cortegiano*.

Women are seen quite explicitly in Boccaccio's text as defective beings, and males as the standard against which they are measured. The only way Andrea can 'shape up' is by increasing her distance from the majority of other women, thus creating two distinct regimens.[21] Yet Andrea does not clearly belong to the group of exceptional women. Her nobility is not all that it seems since she owed her position to the wealth of the family. She has not been selected for any notable action and shares in the defects of her sex. Her ambiguity, whether intended or not, destabilizes the text, leaving it open to conflicting interpretations.

In the dedication Boccaccio portrays his book as a practical guide for female conduct and improvement: "Nor will the perusal [of the book] have been vain, I believe, if it spurs your noble spirit to emulation of the deeds of women in the past" [FW 5]. The surface meaning suggests that Andrea could become like the heroines of classical antiquity, but there is no hint that she is capable of acting as audaciously as many of the ancient women described in the biographies. It could also be interpreted ironically; as an insinuation that the pagan women could be models even for powerful Christian women who did not enjoy the former's dignity and power. In a crucial passage, Boccaccio describes this difference between pagan and Christian women, to the detriment of the latter. The presumed inferiority of gentile women (at least in certain areas) is not wholly borne out by the representation of Andrea Acciaiuoli. Indeed, one can note an imbalance in the book between the narrative space of the biographies and the restrictions of the social world of contemporary Christian women, highlighted by the discursive parts of the text:

> Whenever you, who profess the Christian religion, read that a pagan woman has some worthy quality which you feel you lack, blush and reproach yourself that, although marked with the baptism of Christ, you have let yourself be surpassed by a pagan in probity or chastity or resolution.[22]

Boccaccio proposes here that the biographies of pagan women be read reductively to diminish their ideological distance from the model of a Christian woman. Boccaccio urges his reader to view the text as moral *exempla,* not as historical examples that can be imitated. Implicit is a directive to Andrea on how to read these narratives in a way that does not altogether conflict with traditional stereotypes. The encomiastic nature of the dedication inflates the worth of Andrea, but in a way which is revelatory of the text's ideological limitations. Andrea's name becomes the subject of word-play (it is the Greek for man), allowing Boccaccio to show off his knowledge and underline his idea of female perfection; in other words, renunciation of the defective feminine. On a more realistic note, Andrea appears close to those contemporary females who are berated by the commentator in the course of the *De mulieribus,* and who are in dire need of education in the ways of proper Christian female behaviour.

Implicit in this discussion is the sense that contemporary men and women have to live up to the ideals of Christianity. Boccaccio does not compare classical and contemporary society from an historical perspective since this may have led him to make general comments on institutions and arrangements of power, thus removing his analysis from the level of individual ethical choice. Andrea is exhorted to direct her intellect towards outshining not only her contemporaries, but also her classical counterparts, in virtue and spiritual excellence. Boccaccio limits this personal growth to moral categories which constrain female sexuality.

The difficulty with interpreting the dedication is further augmented by the fact that many of its statements are not as straightforward as they may first appear. The opening sentence contains two statements which are particularly troublesome. The first is that the "libellus" ["little book"] was written "in the highest praise of the female sex." Now, such an affirmation may appear conventional and not in need of special attention—except for the fact that it does *not* faithfully reflect the contents of the *De mulieribus.* Clearly the text is not merely a listing of positive women. It contains a number of subjects such as Clytemnestra and Medea who, in medieval culture, were archetypal bad women. The dedication sanitizes the contents of the volume in order to create the appearance of a suitable gift for a noblewoman. Boccaccio only refers to this mixing of good and bad women in the preface to the text. It was not something to which he wished to draw attention in the dedication.

The second statement goes to the heart of the problem. Boccaccio states that he wrote the text for "amicorum solatium" ("my friends' pleasure" [FW 3]). This implies that it was written primarily for a male audience of humanists, probably including Petrarch.[23] The book was to be the object of male admiration for Boccaccio's construction of women – the result of his humanist erudition. Further it suggests that the *De mulieribus* was not conceived as a political work, in the sense that women were not seen as potential actors on the public stage. This is a way of reading the text as 'safe' or non-threatening, or, at least of presenting it as such to its implied audience. In contrast to the *De casibus* where the reader is meant to draw political conclusions from the array of fallen princes, the women rulers of the *De mulieribus* offer messages of a moral nature.

Generalizing Women: The Preface of *De mulieribus claris*

The general preface to the work is the matrix from which we can draw some of the principles of the *De mulieribus*. Boccaccio discusses the genre of the *De mulieribus*; that is, in the first instance, the form of the biographies themselves. In the dedication he stressed the pleasurable nature of the lives ("you will find delight in the virtues of your sex and in the charm of the stories" [*FW* 5]), together with their potential for inspiring personal development in the reader, particularly the implied female reader. In the preface he goes into more detail about the shape of the biographical accounts, emphasizing that length is an important structural feature—especially for women, who know little about history.[24] Clearly, one of the purposes of the text is to serve the educational needs of women, but only those of the higher social orders with some access to Latin, thus mirroring the nobility of many of the subjects of the work. Here Boccaccio makes no secret of the fact that he plans to use narrative as a device to render his text of interest to the female reader. He has not completely abandoned the *Decameron* in his mature, Latin works. According to the preface, his anticipated audience is still female and he is trying to combine textual pleasure ("hystoriarum delectationi") with moral instruction although in a more direct and emphatic fashion than in the earlier work.[25]

However women are not the exclusive audience for the book. Boccaccio suggests that men will find it equally interesting: "It is my belief that the accomplishments of these ladies will please women no less than men."[26] The importance of such a declaration should not be underestimated since the intended readership is critical to understanding the book's implied purposes.

At this point Boccaccio strongly emphasizes the equality of male and female readership, even though the next sentence states that the text is directed particularly towards women. This contradiction is more apparent than real. If the text encourages the exceptional female reader to open her horizons to the women of the past (freeing her momentarily from the servitude of the present), the emphasis on pleasure encourages a belief that the text is a game and that any alternatives are not serious. Whilst women are thus locked into a rigorous moral position, the appeal of the text to men is on a slightly different level.

The text conveys a message to male readers about certain women and their potential: it shows women acting heroically, far beyond ordinary expectations. The crucial problem is the relationship between past and present. Can contemporary women behave like their elder sisters? Certainly bad behaviour is to be avoided, but what about that designated as 'good'? As has already been noted, the commentator truncates any possibility of the stories being taken as literal transcriptions of possible female behaviour in the present, preferring to have them read as allegorical messages of moral conduct. This is a way of dealing with the danger female power poses to male readers, channelling it into manageable forms. This might have been considered necessary by the writer, given that the implied male reader could be characterized in general terms as having an Aristotelian attitude towards women—a staunch defender of the *status quo*. Boccaccio's text offers few clues as to how classical values and models might be enacted in the late Middle Ages. Indeed, for the male reader the moral commentary reinforces the patriarchal values which underpin the subordinate position of women in his society.

The message of the text seems more specific for the male reader. He is addressed in terms that purport to inform him of his decline from a virile model of masculinity. The *exempla* of fierce, warlike women can be read as part of a strategy to shame him into rediscovering his masculinity according to the traditional stereotype of man as warrior, leader and guarantor of social order. Thus, the text can also be read as an admonition to men who have become too like the traditional notion of women urging them to assume their leadership role. Strong women are a sign of masculine weakness and loss of integral male values. It is one of the unresolved contradictions of the text that if men acted with traditional vigour (according to accepted patterns of behaviour) then it would have been unnecessary to write the *De mulieribus*. The spotlight on women, therefore, hides another agenda, no less critical for Boccaccio: the crisis of masculinity. The 'digressions' of the commentary assume greater centrality once they are integrated into a discourse on the failings or impotence of contemporary manhood.

An example of this reading can be found in the chapter on Penthesilea (XXXII). The last paragraph has its conclusions separated along gender lines, the main point being that "usus" ("social practice") is dependent on the norms of individual societies. Theoretically this should leave the way open to a reform of women's condition, yet Boccaccio closes off this interpretation in order to open up another which is more socially acceptable.[27] He transforms the notion of *usus* into a trope which insists on a carnavalesque vision of the world turned upside down: women being more warlike than men, and men betraying their nature by conforming to a wrongful notion of *usus* which sees them metamorphosed into "helmeted hares."[28] The virility of the women serves only to highlight more explicitly the emasculation and effeminate behaviour of men.

Boccaccio on *Gloria* in the *De mulieribus*

𝕋he great deeds of the classical women are turned to socially useful ends that often concern men more than women. The "facinora" ["great deeds"] of women provide evidence, albeit some of it negative, that they are more than just biological reproducers, or passive creatures at the disposal of men. Boccaccio notes from his reading of ancient history that: "some women have performed acts requiring vigour and courage" [*FW* 9]. He does claim in the preface that, as for famous men, female achievements are measured in relation to *gloria*. Yet this term is peculiarly ambiguous with regard to the famous women of the *De mulieribus*. To the disadvantage of the pagan women, the writer distinguishes between two kinds of *gloria*. The lesser kind of *gloria*, represented by the powerful women of the text, is based for the most part on worldly actions. True *gloria* is for Christian women alone, and is achieved by a completely different kind of behaviour.

One could make a further distinction by contrasting male and female *gloria* in general. It should suffice to look at the paean to glory which Boccaccio makes in connection with Alcibiades in the *De casibus*—in some ways similar to that employed by Petrarch in the *De viris*. In this latter text, Petrarch's most favoured hero, Scipio Africanus, has a single aim in life: to acquire *gloria*. He acts always in accordance with principles that ensure that he becomes "illustris" rather than simply "clarus." Boccaccio's equivalent figure in the *De casibus*, Alcibiades, is the object of intense veneration because of his appreciation and pursuit of *gloria*. In this biography, Boccaccio enters into a poetic appreciation of *gloria*, viewed as liberation from bodily needs and desires: "Our soul is implanted with a divine gift comprising a fiery strength, a divine beginning, and an insatiable desire for glory."[29] Such a statement does not find its equivalent in the *De mulieribus* where the term *gloria* is mentioned very rarely in relation to women, and never with the same enthusiasm as in the passage cited above. It would seem that there are two different measures applied to *gloria* dependent upon gender, which tends to limit female aspirations through the importance given over to other factors, such as sexuality.

In the *De mulieribus* Boccaccio mentions two specific types of *gloria*. The first kind is explicitly excluded from the text—this is the *gloria* which is associated with biblical women and saints who would have been at the top of the female hierarchy. The second, and inferior, kind of *gloria* is that pursued by the gentile women which has worldly fame as its goal. In contrast, Christian saints seek "eternal and true glory" ("eternam et veram gloriam"). The emphasis on "true" introduces an element of uncertainty into the text: by neglecting women who have been illuminated by divine truth and concentrating on those who have not, the writer is dividing women into categories; implying that some are less equal than others. Whilst maintaining that pagan women are a proper area of study for the new humanism, Boccaccio is careful not to lose sight of a Christian perspective. He achieves this throughout the text by the insertion of moral statements which generally recall readers to their Christian duties. The ancient women are not permitted to seduce the reader into an amoral, pre-Christian world.

By concentrating on pre-Christian women Boccaccio cannot help but emphasize the differences and contradictions between classical and Christian cultures. Not only are the goals of the women different (earthly vs. heavenly), but their modes of behaviour are in total conflict. Christian women are characterized through the saints whose virtue is defined as a capacity to suffer in the face of the most extreme adversity.[30] Thus female saints are defined as essentially passive in their heroism (and, as a consequence, so are the majority of Christian women who follow them). Pagan women, on the other hand, are the exact opposite: they limit *gloria* to this world and the emphasis is on the deeds they have performed.[31] Classical women are all action and activity in the present world. The contrast could not be sharper. Christian women deny the flesh and look towards eternal salvation, whereas their pagan counterparts find the strength and energy to perform great deeds within themselves, in their 'instinctual nature'.

What the preface does not say is that in the texts of the individual biographies female nature might produce powerful women capable of defeating men, yet simultaneously the nature of these same women can be their undoing as it is also the equivalent of their female sexuality. If directed towards 'valid' ends, the energy unleashed by these pagan women is approved by the text, but should it be diverted into sexual power then it is obviously condemned. The sexual ideology inherent in the female saints cannot be ignored in the biographies proper: the notions of virginity and chastity are in fact central to the writer's evaluation of pagan women. He has attempted to christianize them. The women most favoured by the text are those who manage to combine sexual purity with the pagan bent for action (for example, Dido, Artemisia and Zenobia). From this perspective, Boccaccio is attempting a synthesis of the passive and active aspects which he sees as characterizing the two contrasting civilizations. Thus the complexity and ambiguity of the *De mulieribus* is partially the result of an attempt to bring together irreconcilable opposites in the biographies of individual women.

·　·　·　·　·

VII

Creating Lives

THE FORMS OF FEMALE BIOGRAPHY

Parameters of the Text

occaccio's decision to compose the *De mulieribus claris* marks a profound change in his approach to writing. Of primary importance is the way he structures his collection of female biographies, discarding the all-embracing *cornice* which was common to his vernacular texts and to his preceding Latin work, the *De casibus.* It is a sign that this text is not to be considered literary in the way his previous works were, but a work of 'objective', historical analysis.[1] Certainly the influence of Petrarch's *De viribus illustribus* is clearest here. Petrarch's single biographies of famous men, in rough chronological order, are to be read as exemplary figures whose presence emphasizes the distance between Roman *gloria* and contemporary decline.[2]

The literary structure of the *De casibus* had drawn heavily on the *Divine Comedy*, where the boundaries between fiction and history are consciously blurred. Both these texts emphasize the drama of history, narrating it in the first person, whereas the *De mulieribus* assumes the third person to distance itself from the events narrated and to create a sense of historical truth.

In the *De casibus* it is possible to discern the biographical structure which will characterize the *De mulieribus*. However, the biographies are doubly embedded: in a literary structure imitative of the *Divine Comedy,* and in a discursive, moralizing frame which intersperses narrative with sermon.

In the *De mulieribus claris* an obvious effort is made to reduce the impinging structural elements of the *De casibus*. It is not simply a case of eradicating the moralizing sections—Boccaccio still wishes to make moral points about women.[3] Yet, it will be argued that he does so in different ways, thus freeing the literary structure from its medieval apparatus, so apparent in the *De casibus*. The visible collapsing of the moral structure that had served Boccaccio in his earlier work does render interpretation more ambiguous. There are moments when the text assumes a more overtly moralizing tone of the type one would expect from the author of the *De casibus* and the *Corbaccio*. The major difference is that the *De mulieribus* has not programmed its moral responses into an overarching structure. The moralizing interpolations are more sporadic and do not offer absolute guidance to the overall meanings of the work. Although a number of common themes occur in the text, it lacks a sufficiently clear framework to make interpretation automatic or simple. In this sense, the *De mulieribus* might be defined as more 'open' (in other words, more open to conflicting interpretation) than the *De casibus* where the monotone message was pushed relentlessly, both in the biographical chapters and in the *cornice*. Unlike the *De casibus*, the *De mulieribus* is rigid in the structure of its individual entries, creating the impression of an impersonal encyclopedia based on historical research.[4] This emphasizes its reliability and objectivity, thus making it a future object of interest to a wide range of compilers.

Most chapters of the *De mulieribus* begin with a discussion of the protagonist's lineage; a strategy which was dictated by more than the author's historical enthusiasm and desire for accuracy. The biographies are framed by the introduction of 'scientific' research based on original sources, so that the stories he relates are considered to be historically truthful and not vehicles for moralizing. Thus a chronological ordering was considered more appropriate than a grouping of historical *exempla* according to moral precepts. The example of Petrarch's *De viribus* comes of age in the *De mulieribus* where selection criteria seem more rigorous and so less inclusive (unlike the monumental *De casibus*). There has been some attempt to introduce structural regularity into each chapter.

Boccaccio's opening statement of origins can fall into a number of categories. The most straightforward of these is the simple statement of fact concerning the subject's closest family. The female subject is usually described as a daughter and/or wife. She is therefore enclosed in traditional forms of relationship which are either confirmed or negated in the course of the chapter. This is an important device to limit implicitly the field of female action, but can also be employed to measure how far women can go in achieving a different set of goals. Hypermnestra [XIV], for example, is defined in the opening sentence of her biography simply as wife and daughter.[5] Both functions play a determining role since Hypermnestra refuses to obey her father's order to murder her husband and, eventually, her husband kills her father.[6] Occasionally, Boccaccio introduces other family relations, such as a brother or sister: Deianira [XXIV] is defined as the daughter of Oeneus and the sister of Meleager. Her marital relations cannot be described so succinctly because they are at the heart of the story.

A second and much less common category emerges when Boccaccio is unable to identify the family origins of his women. He makes meaningful the lack of information itself, frequently through an ironical reading. One such example is the case of Venus, queen of Cyprus [VII], whose parentage is unknown. The writer tells us "there is disagreement as to her parents,"[7] followed shortly afterwards by the offhand comment: "no matter who her father was." Boccaccio's abrupt dismissal of the importance of family origins serves to emphasize Venus's lack of moral values and her commitment to promiscuity (described in some detail in the chapter).[8] On rarer occasions, the absence of information about parents is related in a neutral manner: for example, Penthesilea [XXXII], queen of the Amazons, does not have documented forebears, but Boccaccio simply writes without further comment "I have read nothing about her parents."[9]

Women are often involved in a complex series of actions which only obliquely concern their familial status. It is sometimes problematic to ascertain whether one aspect of their ties is more important than another. Although the text is careful to the point of pedantry in ascertaining the family relations of the illustrious women, in many cases, these relations slide into the background once the biography proper gets underway. For example, the chapter on Nicostrata [XXVII] identifies her as the daughter of Ionius, but this has no bearing on the account. In addition, she is the mother of Evander, but only a small portion of the chapter [paras.3-5] is devoted to that relationship. The greater part of Nicostrata's biography concerns her intellectual achievements and the legacies she bequeathed to the Romans. From this perspective, the *De mulieribus* is far from consistent, but there is a tendency to underplay family ties in favour of identifying women in ways other than those prescribed by the chapter headings. Nonetheless, this aspect cannot be ignored, and in some cases it provides an essential reference point for the exemplary behaviour of certain women.

Nobility in the *De mulieribus*

With a few exceptions, a distinctive feature of the *De mulieribus* is that a great majority of the women belong to the nobility — indeed, as a norm high rank is regarded as a prerequisite for their inclusion in the text. This is a position diametrically opposed to the theoretical statements in the *De casibus*, where rank is not deemed necessary for a person to be called 'noble'.[10] In the *De mulieribus*, gender has become pertinent to Boccaccio's definition of nobility. That is, he brings into play a more restrictive notion of nobility; allowing only a limited number of 'common' or non-noble women access to virtue. This ensures that the social structure is not shattered by an influx of women who demand the privileges and rights associated with nobility. It suggests also that women generally lack those spiritual values used to designate a noble person. Boccaccio's emphasis on nobility signifies that women generally are to be excluded from public affairs unless they meet certain criteria, one of which is obviously noble origins—and even then it is not clear whether the text provides any kind of *imprimatur*. Unlike the *Decameron*, where the various classes are involved in a dynamic interplay of social forces, the *De mulieribus* documents a closing-in and reduction of possible participants.

The final chapter of the *De casibus* on Filippa of Catania who advanced her career by becoming very close to the future Queen Giovanna confirms Boccaccio's unease with women climbing the social ladder and, at the same time, looks forward to the change in emphasis apparent in the *De mulieribus*. In this chapter the *excusatio* stresses Filippa's humble origins, calling attention to them at every juncture. The text employs a particular terminology that creates the impression of the wrongfulness of her social ascent as a woman ("a plebian and degenerate woman").[11] In this connection, the use of the term "clara" is particularly revealing. In the Filippa episode, a distinction is drawn between "clarus" and "nobilis" (p.854), with only the former possessing a negative implication. Such a contrast is not operative in the *De mulieribus* because generally the two terms are inseparable: the subject's noble birth is a precondition of her fame. Yet "clara" does maintain a sense of inferiority in the *De mulieribus*, perhaps with respect to other conditions of fame ("illustris").

Few indeed are the women from non-noble backgrounds in the *De mulieribus*. One rare example is the semi-mythical Arachne (XVIII), "an Asian woman of the common people" [*FW* 79]. Arachne is not condemned for her lack of ancestry in the opening to her biography: "Although her lineage was undistinguished, she deserves nonetheless to be praised for several meritorious deeds" [*FW* 79]. The fact that she is famous for manual work, does not in itself bring condemnation from the narrator. The text compares her skill as a textile worker to that of a painter, a comparison which looks forward to the biographies of female artists elsewhere in the text.[12] The narrator draws back from the radical nature of the comparison by stating immediately that "a woman skilled in such tasks [weaving] is by no means to be despised" [*FW* 81], a view which is flatly contradicted in the biography of the Greek artist Tamaris [LVI] who is praised for *not* participating in traditional female roles. The activity of spinning *per se* is generally regarded throughout the text as a sign of feminine inertia, an anti-model with respect to the exceptional women. Arachne almost manages to make the narrator accept the importance of this *ars*. He resists the temptation because it would mean re-evaluating women as a group and empowering them by assigning greater value to their quotidian activities.

Arachne is condemned for her desire to be superior to Minerva, the institutionalized authority. The source of Arachne's downfall is shown to be her overweening pride in her work and the contest she enters antisocial and destructive of the social fabric. Certainly it is not seen as a legitimate means of challenging the distribution of power. Boccaccio's commentary is taken up by a discussion that threatens the entire *raison d'être* of the *De mulieribus*. This commentary propounds the idea that achievement is possible for all, suggesting that everyone can "become brilliant and masterly through effort and practice" [*FW* 83]. Given that Boccaccio used 'nobility' as a filtering device for the women to be included in the *De mulieribus*, and given the attitudes generally espoused throughout the text, the message here amounts to a surprising and disconcerting conclusion.

The arguments Boccaccio put forward in the commentary on Arachne might have signalled a theoretical refashioning of gender relations. Suggesting the equality of the sexes, they potentially overturn Aristotelian thought on female incapacity:

> Stimulated by that same Nature, we are all carried forward by a desire for the knowledge of things, although not all with the same degree of skill or success. If this is so, what is there to prevent many of us from becoming equally skillful in the same occupation? [*FW* 83]

The answer to that question is provided in the negative by the *De mulieribus* itself. The question may seem to render the entire project paradoxical, if it not does not deconstruct its major premise of exceptionality. Gender is not specifically at issue so that the reader is left wondering just how inclusive are the plural verbs? The question is suffocated by the mass of the text which overall actively withholds an answer. In the chapter on Arachne, the meditation is used to denigrate her achievement: exceptional deeds are within reach of everyone, so an individual (especially a woman?) should not regard herself as different from the masses. Again, such an argument undermines the thrust of the *De mulieribus*. It would appear that any point is good as long as it keeps women in their place. An unintended consequence of the discussion is that great deeds are within reach of all women.

To similar effect, Boccaccio adopts a different strategy in the chapter on Leontium [LX], with one of the clearest statements on noble birth in the book:

> Since she was so brilliant in such a distinguished field of study, I will not easily believe that Leontium was of humble plebeian origin. It is rare indeed for sublime genius to spring from those dregs, for even if genius is sometimes implanted there by heaven, its radiance is darkened by the shadows of lowly estate. [FW 253]

Leontium's social origins and her lack of sexual restraint are seen as undermining her intellectual gifts. The body nullifies her social origins as well as her spiritual and intellectual achievements. And lastly, similarly to Arachne, Leontium challenges authority and, perhaps even more threateningly, male intellectual superiority: "prompted either by envy or feminine temerity, she dared to write an invective against Theophrastus, a most famous philosopher of that period."[13] Boccaccio's women are often caught in a double-bind: berated for not breaking stereotypes and criticized when they do if the rupture threatens male hegemony. For women to be truly exceptional, they must be absorbed into the fictions which society creates about itself.

Boccaccio whose mind-set insists on the conjunction of social and intellectual 'quality' forcefully insists on Sappho's [XLVII] nobility. The writer acknowledges that absolutely no external evidence exists to prove that Sappho was of noble birth. However, this does not deter him from arguing that her poetry is sufficient in itself to impute noble ancestry to her:

> But if we consider her *métier*, we will see restored to her part of what time has destroyed: namely, that Sappho must have been born of honourable and distinguished [claris] parents, for no ignoble soul could have wanted to write poetry, nor could a vulgar one have actually done it.[14]

The clarity of this statement suggests that Boccaccio is urging an acceptance of the binomial of social and intellectual nobility: restricting access to writing to the dominant class. However, the supposition of nobility does not only apply to intellectuals. Cloelia [LII], for example, whose claim to fame is as protector of virginity (both her own and that of others) left no trace of family origins and status. Since the conservation of virginity looms large in the ideological structure of the *De mulieribus*, Cloelia is viewed in a particularly positive light. Thus Boccaccio has no qualms in equating her "noble spirit"[15] with a presumed nobility of her origins: "but we can assume with some confidence that she was born of an illustrious family."[16] Again, it is vital to note that Boccaccio chose the adjective "clarus" to define the family of Cloelia. This emphasizes the relationship established in the text between the 'correct' behaviour of a chosen few, and the great variety of female misbehaviour documented, presupposed or alluded to therein. Yet extraordinary behaviour on its own is not sufficient. It needs the support of social rank to render it acceptable to male eyes, to ensure that these acts performed by women can be absorbed by the social order.

Exemplary Behaviour

The opening paragraphs of individual chapters also prepare the ground in other ways by setting up paradigms which filter and direct reader responses. Some of these are quite blunt and their prominent position ensures that they colour the reader's interpretation of the biography.

Boccaccio's standard procedure is to connect a general opening statement to a description of the family origins of the woman in question. In this way the subject is well and truly 'fixed' by male discourse before the narrative speaks of the woman's actions. Boccaccio thus carefully guides the reader's response to the narrative. There are variations to this standard format: sometimes (but extremely rarely) he introduces a story without using such a device for example, Camilla [XXXIX].

There are different levels of explicitness, the most clear-cut type being when the writer states categorically that the subject is to be considered the embodiment of a particular vice or virtue. In other words, Boccaccio is 'telling' the reader that the narrative is serving the purpose of presenting a moral fiction that proposes models of female behaviour. The term *exemplum* is seldom employed, only three women are sufficiently privileged to have this status explicitly attributed to them: Penelope [XL], Artemisia [LVII] and Antonia [LXXXIX]. All are positive representations of women from a textual viewpoint. Boccaccio's praise of Penelope enshrines her as the most potent illustration of marital fidelity: "wife of Ulysses, a man of great activity: for married women she is the most sacred and lasting example of untarnished honour and undefiled purity" [FW 159]. This declaration forms part of the introductory sentence which opens by stating that Penelope is the daughter of King Icarius. Thus, the connection between highest birth, honourable marriage, and exemplary value is made explicit at the very start of the biography. The deployment of a 'christianized' series of adjectives ("exemplum sanctissimum et eternum") raises Penelope above most women and grants her the status of a lay saint. This suggests that her activities are to be imitated by other women as if she were, indeed, a Christian saint. In this way, the text clarifies the position of the new humanism vis-à-vis classical *exempla*. Boccaccio takes the same line with Antonia whom he presents as "a lasting example of outstanding widowhood" [*FW* 233]. The chapter on Artemisia fuses together the language of the previous two *exempla* to create an image of pious widowhood: "Artemisia, queen of Caria, was a woman of great character; to posterity she is a lasting example of chaste widowhood and of the purest and rarest kind of love" [*FW* 233]. One can note the similarity to the opening statements previously mentioned, perhaps rendered more forceful by the fact that the reader is provided with a precise indication that the *exemplum* has the practical goal of encouraging like behaviour.

Boccaccio employs other terms when discussing divergent forms of significant behaviour. For example, "documentum" is used to describe Medea's [XVII] notorious deeds, a term which tends to underline the historical foundations of his investigations more than the overtly moral narrative of the *exemplum*: "Medea, the cruellest example of ancient treachery" [*FW* 75]. The same term is used to express the exemplary form of Hecuba's plight [XXXIV].[17] Other words such as "specimen" or "testimonium" are occasionally used to describe the function of the forthcoming narrative.[18]

As this analysis makes clear, Boccaccio only rarely refers to his subjects as exemplary. However, the absence of such explicit terminology from other chapters does not signify any shift of emphasis. Rather, only a few of the biographies fall into the category of *exempla* so perfectly and so powerfully that the writer insists on their particular structure in order to impress upon the reader the superiority of a few, restricted types of behaviour for women.

In most cases, Boccaccio guides the reader's interpretation towards a moralistic reading of the biography. Thus the text often pronounces on the moral content of the story before the unravelling of the narrative elements. For instance Niobe [XV] is described as having seven sons and seven daughters. However, before her story is allowed to run its course, Boccaccio the narrator interjects a declaration that has a negative impact on any assessment of her character: "It is certain that this achievement, which to a wise woman ought to have been a source of good, was to her, in her pride, a source of destruction."[19] The commentator has the last word in the chapter so that the message of the episode is clear to the reader, particularly the female reader. Niobe broke the Aristotelian code of female behaviour, and by so doing, reinforced its value for all women.[20]

History for Boccaccio cannot be separated from moral categories: an encyclopedic approach to the material certainly does not mean the jettisoning of a moral re-reading of the historical narratives. The act of recovering a particular figure is partially governed by the exemplary reading that can be furnished for her, as well as other factors including chronological position and fame.

Boccaccio is particularly keen to alert the reader to the nefarious conduct of women, especially those whose behaviour is considered reprehensible according to the parameters constructed by the text. There is no sense in which readers will be allowed to judge for themselves. Thus the name of Cleopatra [LXXXVIII], which was well known to the medieval reader, is glossed by the text in order to ensure that there would be no mistaking the tone of reprehension adopted by the writer. After stating that Cleopatra was "the subject of talk the world over,"[21] Boccaccio adds:

> but she succeeded to the rule of the kingdom only through wickedness. Cleopatra had no true marks of glory except her ancestry and her attractive appearance; on the other hand, she acquired a universal reputation for her greed, cruelty, and lust.[22]

This is not the only occasion on which Boccaccio closes the discourse on his subject even before beginning to tell her life story. In the chronological stretch of the *De mulieribus* covering the later Roman empire, one finds a number of similar examples: Paulina Romana [XCI], Sabina Poppaea [XCV], Triaria [XCVI][23], and Symiamira [XCIX]. The very first sentence of Paulina's biography, without revealing the exact nature of the subject's actions, attempts to constrain the attitude of the reader towards her: "Paulina, a Roman woman, gained practically indelible fame for a certain ridiculous naïveté" [FW 381]. The notion of the "indelebile nomen" is essential to Boccaccio's project in so far as it is a question of naming or, more specifically, of creating or confirming a series of stereotypes for women. In this way, Boccaccio is able to equate a particular female quality (positive or negative) with a story and make it memorable for the readers. It is also a means of reining in the possibilities of a narrative before the reader has the chance to develop his or her response to it. These 'stage-directions' enforce limits on the reader's imagination, to try and ensure that the writer is able to direct and control whatever self-discovery may be afforded by the *exempla*.

Split Personality: Narrator and Commentator

$\mathfrak{I}$n all of the biographies, the genealogical/moral introductory material is followed by the focal point of each chapter, the story of one
woman's life (or, in exceptional circumstances, more than one
woman). The biographical material concerns only the principal episodes
that the writer wished to commemorate and, in this sense, the account is
really only a fragment, its unity a fiction created by the male writer for
purposes beyond the single life. The biographical subject is defined by
one (sometimes a limited series) of outstanding actions. Boccaccio does
not attempt a biography in the mode of Suetonius where the stages and
achievements of the emperors' lives are carefully charted. Boccaccio is
drawn by the dramatic moment: always scornful of the everyday, mun-
dane activities of women, the *De mulieribus* is founded on the narrative
possibilities of the extraordinary.[24] A model may have been the miracu-
lous acts performed by female saints.

Frequently, the narrative is embedded in another set of discourses
which comment on the material presented in the chapter. These discourses are rendered in the first person singular. There are sometimes
brief authorial comments inserted into the historical account. While
these rarely substantially interrupt the flow of the narrative, the historical narrator does not completely efface himself, at times drawing attention to historical problems associated with a particular episode, or
commenting on its historical veracity. Furthermore, and quite distinct
from the historical narrator, there is also a moral commentator for some
chapters. This commentary is distinct from the body of the historical
episode. In some senses it is digressive in that it is used to address a variety of topics not strictly related to the narrative.

The narrator of the historical biography makes it clear that he has
taken the greatest care in evaluating his sources (although on occasion
he makes hypotheses which are not supported by any evidence). If he
cannot reach a decision about which source is the most trustworthy, he
provides various and sometimes conflicting versions. Expressions such
as "others however write" [*FW* 22]; "yet another version claims" [*FW* 22]);
"some people think" [*FW* 39]; "some sources claim" [*FW* 42]; "some
authorities, however, say" [*FW* 100]; "a different version recounts" [*FW*
120]; "other accounts relate" [*FW* 130]; "in some versions" [*FW* 152] are
not uncommon. Gaps and doubts about particular moments or events in
the subject's life are sometimes admitted: "we are unsure" ("nobis incer-
tum est," *DMC* 266) and the search for evidence is sometimes mentioned
in the first person to indicate the commitment of the historian to try and
uncover all the relevant documentation. In relation to Leontium [LX], the
writer notes that an invective against Theophrastus was attributed to her

in the ancient sources but explains that: "I have not seen this work" [*FW* 251].

This general adherence to sources does not exclude hypotheses (especially on the family origins of the women) even if not based on genuine historical deduction.[25] However, within the confines of Boccaccio's hesitant historiography (following on from Petrarch's with its emphasis on the moral lessons of history), such assertions are considered by the narrator to be acceptable interpretations of the historical situation.

This care in expressing an opinion about the past is in direct contrast to the assertiveness of the text's moral commentator. The contrast could hardly be more striking. The 'I' of the later 'moral' sections is strident in his opinions and statements, providing an intensity which is absent from the mainly third-person narrative account. The moral commentator is not necessarily concerned with history, or even directly with the female biography in question. He aims to provide a moral conclusion to the chapter, but frequently introduces issues which were not central to the narrative. Not all of the closing remarks are directly concerned with women and are based on the writer's own reading of the biography in the light of his interests in social order and disorder.

The regular division of chapters into two parts (narrative followed by moralizing meta-commentary) is suggestive of the conflicting ambitions of the writer. On the one hand, as we have seen, there is the active reconstruction of history, a task made difficult by contradictory accounts which require either a choice based on an historical assessment of their validity or a simple listing of variants. The historical narrative is often characterized by uncertainty and gaps in knowledge. However, when the sources do not conflict, history moves closer to the modes of fictional narrative in that Boccaccio relates stories in which psychological motivations often play an important role. He is not content merely to register events: for him the reactions of people to the historical situations in which they find themselves are equally critical.

The second 'I', reminiscent of the preacher of a sermon, overwhelms the first narrator by his incandescent discourse. The moral of the story becomes easy and recognizable with the introduction of the contrasting style of discourse. This additional voice is clearly recognizable as Christian; in fact he positively parades his Christianity.[26] Certainty is restored to the text and women are generally put back in their place.

The contrast between the narrative and commentary can be described in other terms. The narratives often represent women in the world of power, far from the domestic hearth, involved in combat, culture, and acts of exceptional heroism. The moralizing commentaries express concern about women's place in these spheres. The narratives might be described as romances of non-merchant societies, regulated by queens, empresses and the like. They are far from the merchant society of Florence and its rationalist, economic-based values in which women are theoretically held in subaltern positions, particularly in the role of the unassuming, obedient wife (Petrarch's rewriting of Griselda). This is where the voice of the commentator comes in. His discourses on women are the voice of the conservative thinker, found in numerous Florentine texts, particularly sermons and other religious documents. They seek to bring women under the control of male discourse so that they behave in a manner befitting Florentine society. Thus, the commentator directs his instructions to women who are neither expected nor encouraged to behave in any extraordinary way. The male 'voice-over' institutes a relationship of superiority-inferiority between the commentator and the contemporary women to whom he is most often addressing his remarks.

A number of the commentaries fall under this rubric and form an underlying pattern in the text. The *De mulieribus* constructs precise parameters for the comportment of women, notwithstanding the scattering effect produced by commentaries that parade as part of the narrative.[27] The freedom to look, and therefore, to make choices of one's own, is denied women on the example of Medea [XVIII]. Boccaccio's commentator makes the connection between the gaze and female lust, creating disorder and disaster. Self-restraint and control are the key messages of the commentary in contrast to the 'good' or 'bad' exceptional behaviour of the women in the biographies. The direction of the gaze is taken up as part of the moral instructions to women in the conclusion to Sulpicia's biography [LXVII].[28] The codification of female behaviour permits no escape from the reduction of possibilities in contemporary everyday life. The exceptional women of history serve to confirm a style of woman consecrated by church doctrine and relegated to mediocrity, directing all her energies towards her husband and the maintenance of chastity.[29] Through the agency of chastity, ancient women are transformed into the model of the house-bound wife whose foremost thought should be the control of her sexuality.[30]

However, homilies on chastity do not overly dominate the text: a paragraph in praise of Hippo [LIII], a brief comment on Virginia [LXIII]. A remark at the end of the chapter on Gualdrada [CIII] renders her biography openly didactic, confirming the use of commentary as a strategy for social reform by looking back, in this case, to earlier Florentine history.[31] In this narrative, historical detail is subsumed by the desire to inculcate ancient values into a society that has lost all sense of direction. That is why many commentaries arising from the biographies, through their changed perspective, criticize the development of institutions and the decline in standards of behaviour.

The commentator is particularly irked by sexual passions, as can be seen from the biography of Iole [XXIII] where love is forcefully denied as a life choice. The moralizing commentary represents more than half the length of the chapter. Its principal focus is the effect of love on men and as such, the extensive segment can be regarded as a critical element in the text's strategy to insist on a traditional definition of virility and masculinity. The commentator takes up the threat of the powerful woman who has the potential to create sexual disarray in society. He offers the reader a procession of women and situations which reflect the overturning of male power/domination. He strives to facilitate a return to stereotyped gender relations by pointing out to men their duties and failings. Hercules represents the shortcomings of all men who submit to love with its ensuing loss of masculinity. Passionate love is no longer an acceptable part of the male psyche. It is a weakness that contributes to the undermining of societal values. The conclusion to the chapter on Penthesilea [XXXII] is instructive here as it concerns a matter which was not raised in the body of the text and has little to do with Penthesilea or the other warrior women. In effect, rather than concentrating on the exceptional skills and capacities of the women themselves, the conclusion insists on the failure of men to live up to their gender-expectations as warriors.

Passionate, sexual love is rejected as a valid form of relationship and another kind, a considered love within the institution of marriage, replaces it. This forms the substance of the commentary on Hypermnestra [XIV], Argia [XXIX],[32] Virginia [LXIII], and Tertia Emilia [LXXIV]. Along with brief remarks in the chapter on Portia [LXXXII], the loyalty of Curia [LXXXIII] and Sulpicia [LXXXV][33] receive positive comment. Pompeia Paulina's absolute loyalty towards her husband [XCIV] and the love of the Minyan women for their husbands [XXXI] are also persuasive *exempla* of the theme. Overall, Boccaccio's commentator demonstrates a decisive commitment to social order through the regulation of sexuality, indicating a firm attachment to the values of marriage and the family, social stability and tranquillity necessary for studious pursuits. Indeed, Boccaccio is asserting the positive value of marriage in the face of serious opposition from medieval clerical thought.[34] He is subtly aligning humanist thought with marriage as a combination that might ensure social stability and the success of the new intellectual practice.

In this context, the book's prohibition on second marriages and the insistence on chaste widowhood is suggestive of this obsessive desire for social stability based in part upon the suppression of female desire and the negation of the marriage market with its related pressures. One of the most remarkable diatribes is to be found in the chapter on Dido [XLII] in which ten paragraphs (from a total of twenty-six) relate to wid-

ows remarrying.[35] The same theme occurs in the biography of Pompeia
Paulina [XCIV] where the commentator exclaims:

> Alas, what wretches we are! To what depths have our morals plunged! The
> ancients, who were naturally inclined to purity, used to regard a second
> marriage as disgraceful, much less a seventh.... The women of our day are
> quite different. [FW 403]

The decline in morals and the possibility of learning from the heathen become leitmotifs in the commentaries. For this reason, the commentator lavishes praise on the wife of Orgiago for her attitude towards
chastity [LXIII].[36] Irony is frequently employed by the commentator to
reinforce the idea of a topsy-turvy world where a pagan society is seen to
be more moral than the Christian one.[37] Boccaccio utilizes many of the
devices constantly used by writers of sermons: the insistent use of
rhetorical questions, use of the iussive subjunctive to emphasize the
moral imperative of women to change and the dramatic insertion of
direct speech by anonymous women to underline ironically important
points.

The Moral Commentaries as Contemporary Critique

𝕴t becomes clear from the commentaries that contemporary society needs a mirror in which to view its faults. In this mirror, a contemporary reader may view solutions based on historical *exempla*,
but *exempla* that the commentary often subverts or distorts. Numerous
commentaries are political in nature, if by that we mean they seek to
find remedies to social ills that beleaguer the writer's society. The commentary is not only interested in berating women about their lack of
sexual morals or praising chastity in the abstract. The reflections on
gender also entail a deeper critique of the values or lack of them that
hold sway in people's lives.

The commentaries are particularly interested in the behaviour of
parents who through the raising of children have an inordinate influence on the future direction of society. The text is perhaps surprisingly
moderate on the strictness of controls that should be used to ensure that
children, especially females, conform to male-created laws.[38] 'Correct'
behaviour is taught in the parental home [FW 157]. The narrative on
Rhea Ilia [XLV], the mother of Romulus and Remus, allows the narrator
to plead with parents not to use convents as dumping grounds for
dowryless daughters. Enforced claustration is seen as a violation of the
daughter's limited 'rights'. This unnatural form of servitude is used to
explain her consequent failure to remain a virgin in the convent. As a

consecrated vestal virgin, Rhea Ilia's punishment for becoming pregnant was to be buried alive.[39] It is this aspect of the episode which provides the link with the commentary: vestal virgins and nuns are brought together by a degenerate and illicit sexuality. Forbidden sexuality instrumentalizes the historical account of Rhea Ilia to make a point about the dowry system and its effects on the young women who are its victims. Boccaccio does not spare the parents who have taken away their daughters' freedom of choice [FW 189]. The De mulieribus, therefore, proposed quite a radical break with this aspect of patriarchal society by valorizing the importance of limited 'rights' and the need for proper parental guidance free of dehumanizing motives that treat female children as property.

This shifting movement between historical narrative and commentary dislocates the text. In the chapter on Rhea Ilia, the commentary is longer than the historical account. By using two genres, each competing for control over the other, Boccaccio creates f[r]ictions of freedom and rigidity. It might be described as a conflict between 'telling' and 'showing', whereby the narrative 'shows' various possibilities for women. The commentator 'tells' women what to do. However, Boccaccio sometimes shifts the emphasis away from what may be construed as the principal point of the narrative. [40] This is the case with the conclusion to the chapter on Penthesilea [XXXII], but it is not an isolated example.

Indeed, some commentaries are less concerned with gender than with more overtly political issues, often treated in generalizing humanistic terms. The political dimension of Boccaccio's work owes something to the De casibus, but perhaps more to his meditations on Florentine politics in the aftermath of the conspiracy involving Pino de' Rossi. Boccaccio does not specifically mention Florence, but the commentaries can be viewed as an attempt to theorize, in humanistic terms, a more equitable and less oppressive society.

Boccaccio does not seem to mind the consequences of dismantling the premises by which Ceres [V] had achieved fame and renown. He is preoccupied with the state of contemporary society, but is not content just to describe present ills. He makes humanistically-inspired comments to resolve some of its contradictions. In a chapter consisting of 13 paragraphs, only five deal directly in any way with the biographical subject, the rest examining the consequences of Ceres' efforts to civilize humankind. The conclusion to the long discussion is that the Golden Age is preferable to modern civilization. In the commentary on Ceres (consisting of more than two-thirds of the chapter), Boccaccio paints a bleak picture of the effects of proto-capitalism and conspicuous consumption on lifestyles and class differences, accentuating the latter. The commentator expresses his concern at the way in which economic divisions engender social and political conflict. "Invidia" [envy], brought about by the politics of the city-state, results in political enmity and exile. The distance separating the more positive view of merchant society glimpsed in the *Decameron* and the entirely negative view it receives here could not be greater. Such comments are more than humanist nostalgia for a passed Golden Age. In the context of the *De mulieribus* they represent, a judgement against contemporary politics.

Boccaccio's commentary to the chapter on Ceres is a digression, but one that does have relevance for the gender issues raised in the book. The writer provides an alternative version of the Fall, one which does not place the blame on Eve for the corruption of society. Ceres only indirectly brings about this fundamental change in societal values. Indeed, one might argue that the *De mulieribus* is a search for those lost values— an investigation into whether classical women might provide modes of behaviour to counterbalance contemporary proto-capitalist attitudes and ideologies.[41] Looking back on pre-Christian times, Boccaccio analyses female comportment and social position, imbuing it where necessary with the requisite Christian reading. He seems to be seeking the difference between male and female behaviours across chronological time to provide exemplars of women who contradict the preoccupations of both sexes in his own period.

Critique of Money

Che commentator is deeply concerned with the role of money in society. He views it as the major cause of social conflict. Associated with the desire to possess and dispossess, money distorts social relations to such a degree that a cohesive society is impossible.[42] The discussion on the corrupt judiciary, stimulated by the plight of Virginia, daughter of Virginius [LVIII], also links this corruption with the failure of values brought about by a society based on money.

One of the most dramatic denunciations of wealth found in the text, in the chapter on Veturia [LV], the mother of Coriolanus, is gender-specific, creating a deep semantic divide between narrative and commentary. Veturia dissuades her son from attacking Rome, and her intervention in public affairs is decisive in saving the city. The commentary does not see fit to be positive about her intercession (the subject of the historical narrative), but examines the consequences of her act for future generations of women. The Senate's decrees (enacted as a sign of Roman gratitude) are condemned by Boccaccio for overturning the established order. The writer's criticism focuses principally on the ruling that women were allowed to inherit, a right previously denied them.[43] The possession of power by women, and the considerable social control they could achieve through money, is condemned.[44] Boccaccio does not end his criticisms at this point. He draws out the implications and claims that the upgraded status of women introduced by the Roman Senate has turned the world upside down in terms of gender: "But what can be done? The world is effeminate and men have turned into women" [*FW* 231]. The satirical touches of the chapter (such as the image of men languishing in poverty while their wives parade like peacocks in expensive clothes) demonstrate the fear and disgust with which Boccaccio viewed real control by women. The commentary places Veturia's actions in an entirely unexpected light and underlines one of the obsessions of the text—the chaos which results when the relationship between the sexes is no longer bound by the Aristotelian fixity of gender. The praise of frugality in women, for instance, can be interpreted as a means of preventing women from entering into those economic exchanges that constitute society, hence also cutting them off from other forms of exchange [*FW* 333].

The commentaries on sexuality effectively frame exceptional women in a conventional structure, creating an irresolvable dialectical tension. There is an effort to subordinate narrative to commentary and, in general, to mute such pleasures of the narrative texts as the rediscovery of neglected sources, the narration itself, and the depiction of powerful women by imposing a moral closure on a significant number of biographies. This ensures that any possible subversive elements of the narrative text are eliminated from any final interpretation. The commentaries constitute an effort to 'control' woman by male discourse and, at the same time, to present a more general critique of society which has falsified basic moral principles. Thus it can be seen that the commentaries are far more than a tirade against women: they are a reflection of the writer's unease with contemporary society.

. . . . . .

VIII

In the Family/ Out the House

WOMEN IN PUBLIC

Motherhood in the *De mulieribus*

On the surface, the family status of Boccaccio's subjects is crucial for the text, enabling the women to be placed within existing institutional structures. However, some aspects of family life play a rather subdued role in the *De mulieribus:* even the traditionally sacrosanct role of the mother is not heralded above other possible female functions. Of the few women singled out as mothers, almost all have negative connotations. The one exception is Veturia [LV].

The biography of Berenice [LXXII] goes some way towards explaining the writer's lack of interest in mothers. The narrator puts forward three possibilities to justify her inclusion in the collection; firstly, that she was of a noble family. The other two reasons are interconnected and concern motherhood:

> Berenice of Pontus, known also as Laodice, may seem to have gained a place among famous women by reason of her noble birth. Yet she is thought to deserve it much more, not for the fervent love she had for her son (for this is something most mothers experience), but for her remarkable audacity in avenging him. [*FW* 303]

The narrator indirectly indicates one of the criteria of choice—it is the extent to which women are able to overcome their 'female' natures which makes them candidates for inclusion. Thus mothers and maternal love (viewed as the norm for female behaviour by other writers) are not favoured by the *De mulieribus*: these aspects of female identity are seen as natural and not culturally exceptional.[1] The text is uncomfortable with this stereotype because, in most instances, it is too static, unheroic and therefore unsuitable as a focal image for women. The sole reason for the inclusion of Berenice lies in the way she exacted revenge for the death of her son. In fact, her actions transform her into a man: "in her grief Berenice forgot her sex."[2] Yet, Berenice's feat is caught ambiguously between a denial of the feminine and a confirmation of 'natural' female behaviour. The commentator provides a more traditional explanation:

> Good Lord, how invincible are the forces of Nature, how indomitable is the strength of Love! What greater, what more marvellous deed could they have done? [FW 305]

The commentator proposes that Berenice's audacious act of revenge is the result of instinctive maternal love, and hence not meritorious in the sense that her actions neither enhance nor deny her femininity. It is implied that her actions are extraordinary not only because they exhibited virile courage, but principally because they represented a unique moment in her life, brought about by grief and rage. However, Boccaccio cannot escape the fact that to carry out her vengeance required courage and skill, both implicitly denied to the majority of women. Berenice represents a difficulty for the text in that her motivation originated in nature (maternal love), but the resolution to act required a cultural transformation.

Berenice forms a pair with Theoxena [LXXI] who killed herself and her children rather than allow them to be enslaved. Her action remains more ambiguous than Berenice's because it involved the killing of her own children. The achievements of the archetypal mother Niobe [XV] are not highly valued and so receive short shrift in the *De mulieribus*. It is implied that the production of children is hierarchically inferior to other exploits. The discourse on motherhood seems to cut two ways: a liberation from a role that domesticates and stereotypes women and simultaneously a devaluation of one of the very few roles allowed them in the *real* world. It ambiguously suggests that women need to create a social identity which is not solely based on their reproductive role.

Faithful Wives in the *De mulieribus*

The *De mulieribus* is peopled by what appears to be a relatively low number of faithful wives—just under twenty from one hundred and six biographies.[3] Although the number of faithful wives is just sufficient for them to constitute a thematic strand throughout the text, there seems to be some effort to make their presence felt more strongly than the actual numbers would suggest. In this respect, one can note that there is a certain amount of concentration, particularly between chapters LXXIII and LXXXV, which contain eight biographies of faithful wives. There appears to be a concerted effort towards the end of the work to put forward a clear model of behaviour for women, one that gains in clarity because of its juxtaposition with anti-models. For example, Cleopatra [LXXXVIII], the personification of uncontrolled sexuality, is placed immediately before Antonia [LXXXIX], an *exemplum* of chaste widowhood. This type of alternation is particularly evident in the latter part of the book and serves to clarify the pedagogical implications of reading Roman history in the feminine—a rhythm which seems to override the casual patterns thrown up by chronology, imposing upon them an ideological structure which privileges a certain type of female behaviour.

However, there are some biographies that seem obvious candidates for moralizing *exempla,* but instead serve to render the discourse on sexuality yet more tortuous. Boccaccio introduces the biographies of two prostitutes who, in spite of their uncontrolled sexuality, turn out to be more courageous than the men of their period: Leaena [L] who bites off her tongue to prevent herself from revealing the names of her fellow-conspirators, thus earning the title of "manly woman";[4] and Epicharis [XCIII] who commits suicide rather than betray the would-be assassins of Nero. These two women contribute to a sense of disorientation regarding the importance of sexuality in assessing the actions of women. The commentator feels obliged to make excuses for them because they contravene the seemingly cast-iron rules concerning female sexual behaviour. Their position in the text suggests that they are strategically placed to encourage the reader to think about female sexuality and how it does not prevent women from acting heroically.

In a number of the biographies, Boccaccio is explicit about the role of marriage. Argia (XXIX), the wife of Polynices, is a good example of the writer's discourse on married love. She is presented to the reader as having "left to posterity a flawless, splendid, and eternal record of conjugal love" [FW 117]. The narrative illustrating the love she bears her husband is concentrated on her determination to give him a proper burial in spite of an edict forbidding it on pain of death. Argia's heroic action comes about through the suppression of those wifely characteristics that constitute the ideal model of a meek, submissive spouse:

> Casting aside royal splendour, the comfort of her chamber, and womanly weakness, she immediately set out with a few companions for the battlefield. [FW 117, 119]

The commentator states the obvious by reiterating the motivations behind Argia's seemingly foolhardy actions, so that the exemplarity of her behaviour will not be lost on even the most obtuse of readers:

> Such were the deeds taught her by true love, total devotion, the sanctity of marriage, and an unshaken chastity. For these merits Argia became a woman whose praise, honour, and glory should be announced with shining trumpets. [FW 121]

Married love allied with chastity is the model of behaviour for women in society; heroism no longer comes from devising ingenious means to deceive one's husband and satisfy one's natural instincts. This love acknowledges no other authority than the husband's: the heroism of an exceptional wife is centred on him. This is a way of 'taming' the heroic impulses of women into a channel which most benefits men, reducing or eliminating the challenge to society that other forms of action might initiate.

A similar principle is enunciated in the chapter on Tertia Aemilia [LXXIV], who discovers that her husband (Scipio Africanus no less) is having an affair with a slave girl. The biography concentrates on the wife's reaction which is seen to be out of the ordinary from three points of view. The first juxtaposes a description of Tertia Aemilia's behaviour with one of 'normal' female conduct: "The female is a very suspicious creature, either because of the weakness of her sex or because she does not have a good opinion of herself" [FW 313]. The general rule is broken in this particular case: Tertia Aemilia's exceptional behaviour is construed as a distant goal towards which women are encouraged to aspire. Secondly, the narrator intervenes in the first person to reinforce the general patterns of behaviour in such circumstances, expressing sympathy with the outrage wives feel at being betrayed. Thirdly, the commentary emphasizes that Tertia Aemilia's actions towards her late husband's lover are exceptional by listing the possible responses of an 'ordinary' woman. The main point of contrast between Tertia Aemilia and the hypothetical 'ordinary' wife is made clear: the former is characterized by her "patient silence" whereas the latter noisily focuses all attention on her betrayal, destroying the harmony of the relationship as well as her husband's reputation.

Such a position conflicts with the stand taken by numerous other women in the text. One has only to think of Sempronia ([LXXVI], the wife of Scipio Aemilianus, who defended the purity of her line from an imposter, a defence that took place in public and required her to make a convincing speech. The biographies of Tertia Aemilia and Sempronia are separated only by the chapter on Dripetrua. At this point, the problem of interpretation becomes particularly complicated because chronological order confuses logical or thematic order. The placement of the two biographies in such close proximity creates confusion about the 'right' role for women: whether they should have a public face, or whether they should act 'behind the scenes' solely for the well-being of their men. It is unlikely that Boccaccio was oblivious to such contradictions. He was, after all, the author of the *Decameron* in which contradiction forms an essential part of the textual strategy.

In Sempronia's biography the situation is further complicated by the fact that the heroic battle of wits described in the narrative section is undermined by the commentary, which supports the Aristotelian view of women. The commentator agrees that all women are stubborn, "I do not deny this" [*FW* 319] (a commonplace of medieval misogyny) but allows Sempronia her place in the female pantheon because she relied on the truth to make her stand. Aristotelian biology still holds true even for the exceptional woman. The text suggests here only that 'defects' such as obstinacy can be turned to good account. Yet this 'concession' is undermined in the case of Sempronia by her supposed consent to the death of her husband, stripping her of any remaining moral authority. Boccaccio's ambiguous use of sources, the status of which remain unverified in the text, isolates the subject's praiseworthy action by suggesting that she was capable of other, socially more dangerous acts that confirm the basis of Aristotle's observations on women. On the basis of certain unnamed authorities, the last paragraph of Sempronia's biography suggests that she consented to her husband's death thus, undermining her earlier heroism. Within a single chapter, a woman is subject to diverse interpretations which corrode a unified, positive view of her 'character'.

Not all wives stay at home. Boccaccio is able to construct an image of the heroic wife ("endowed with a manly spirit" [*FW* 325]) through such figures as Hypsicratea [LXXVIII] who followed her husband, Mithridates, into war and exile. The description of the abandonment of the "ease and softness in the royal bedchamber" [*FW* 325] and the subsequent hardships she suffers leads to another paean of married love, perhaps even more intense than that dedicated to the wife of Polynices.

The biographies of Argia and Hypsicratea are complemented by a group of biographies in which all the women commit suicide following the death of their husbands (or presumed death in the case of Julia)—the wives of the Cimbrians [LXXX], Julia [LXXXI] and Portia [LXXXII]. Portia's devotion to her husband Brutus elicits the remark: "How inexhaustible is the force of love! How lucky the man with such a wife!" [*FW* 343]. Such interjections are common in the chapters on faithful wives, and serve to illustrate the level of devotion to which a wife should aspire. The proximity of these chapters helps to construct a series of powerful images of wives who are heroically bound to their husbands and their chastity.

The chapter on Curia [LXXXIII] immediately follows that of Portia, providing in ideological terms an alternative to suicide. It can be viewed as a counterpart to the adventures of Hypsicratea. Instead of fleeing, Curia's husband, who has been proscribed, is hidden in his own home by his wife. The episode demonstrates a particular brand of heroic behaviour on the part of the wife: domestic heroism. Boccaccio breaks into a lyrical fantasy that transposes the roles of the husband and wife: the husband dares not move out of the house whereas the wife is forced to employ her histrionic skills in order to save him. In other circumstances, Curia's deceptive behaviour would have been condemned as duplicitous except that here it is being used to protect her husband. The writer indulges in a fictional reconstruction of Curia's behaviour to give the reader a sense of wifely devotion and to legitimate her conduct which is described in almost mystical terms as a "holy deed" [FW 347]. The word used to define the measure of Curia's actions is "claritas" without the slightest hint of ambiguity or derision. Her fame is justifiable because it highlights the complete abnegation of all desire except that which is centred on the husband. As such, the example of Curia represents the culmination of the figure of the wife whose active qualities serve paradoxically to fix her even further in a passive, submissive role.

Wayward Women

The *De mulieribus* counterbalances the picture of the faithful wife with stories of women who betray their husbands and families. In these cases, the text concentrates on the sexuality of the wives; Boccaccio does not fail to include, as one of the yardsticks against which to evaluate unfaithful wives, the archetype of the violated wife, Lucretia [XLVIII].[5] Clytemnestra [XXXVI] is roundly condemned for killing her husband Agamemnon. Her biography is followed by the archetypal unfaithful wife, Helen of Troy [XXXVII], whose life story allows Boccaccio to concentrate on errant sexuality as cause and signifier of social disorder. Helen's story relates the negative effects of sexuality upon men who have made a cult of female beauty.[6]

The narrative proper portrays Helen more as a victim than a prime mover. Her first contact with men occurred when, still a virgin, she was seized by Theseus: "Although he had in fact been able to take from her nothing except a few kisses, he nevertheless left some doubt regarding the matter of her virginity" [FW 145]. With some deliberate ambiguity, Helen is held not altogether responsible for the subsequent events leading to her flight to Troy.[7] To describe her abduction by Paris, Boccaccio uses the same verb "rapire" as he uses for her unlawful seizure by Theseus. This leads to more uncertainty about the full extent of Helen's guilt, a reading helped by the text not taking a *parti pris* until the siege of Troy actually begins. At this point, Helen looks out over the battlements and sees the land being laid to waste with many people dead, and the narrator/commentator devastatingly notes: "Helen could recognize the worth of her beauty" [FW 149]. From this moment on, there is no longer any hint of ambiguity. Helen commits more acts of moral outrage. On the death of Paris, she marries "the younger Deiphobus," eliciting the narrator's comment: "as if she thought she had not sinned enough the first time" [FW 149]. Helen's greatest betrayal is when, in order to regain the love of her first husband, she helps the Greeks enter Troy.

Boccaccio borrowed a number of personages from the *Iliad* to suggest the wave of human misery caused by this one woman as well as to suggest his familiarity with one of the architexts of classical civilization. Undoubtedly, this series of biographies owes something to the conceptual position of the *De casibus*, yet these other figures (Polyxena [XXXIII][8], Hecuba [XXXIV][9], Cassandra [XXXV], and Clytemnestra [XXXVI]) trace the consequences of Helen's betrayal of marital fidelity. Clytemnestra is connected with both the preceding biography of Cassandra, whom she murdered, and the following one of Helen, with whom she functions as a pair of 'deadly' women. By having their biographies placed side by side there is less reason for commentary on Helen— it is condemnation by proximity. Polyxena joins the select group of those women in the *De mulieribus* who managed to overcome both their female nature and their social conditioning in order to face death courageously.[10] As on other occasions her bravery also becomes an object lesson to men on how to conduct themselves in such desperate circumstances [FW 133].

Virgin Women

𝕵emale sexual power is a defining characteristic of the majority of women in the *De mulieribus*. Nevertheless, one of the messages which can be teased from the recesses of the text is that female sexuality can be repressed (at least in some cases) by women themselves. Sexuality is considered a given of female nature—yet it is ambiguous: it sometimes has the effect of propelling women into the public arena, a driving force which can be diverted to higher purposes. At other times it can destroy or compromise the exceptional qualities displayed by the protagonist. In certain cases, it reifies women. One has only to look at the treatment accorded Virginia (LVIII), whose opening definition holds true for her entire biography: "Virginia, a Roman, was a virgin in name and in fact."[11] The narrative regards her as a sexual object over whose destiny the fathers (of both state and family) have complete control, her own father killing her to save her from being deflowered by a Roman official. Virginia's story is similar to Lucretia's (XLVIII) in so far as both their deaths brought about a political revolution in Rome, a result which followed from the violation of their chastity, and one which had not been foreseen.[12] Virginia is certainly the object of male discourse and violence. Her death provides another occasion to sacrifice the text to male interests of political change.

Virginity is highly regarded in the text although it is not given the coverage one might have expected. Boccaccio does not slavishly follow St. Jerome's insistence on the superiority of virginity over marriage. Indeed, it could be said that he reverses the hierarchy set up in *Against Jovinianus*. Of about sixteen virgins specifically mentioned in the *De mulieribus*, the virginity of approximately one-third of them has no real impact on their actions, and is mentioned only in passing.[13] The chapters in which virginity takes centre stage are rare indeed. We have already noted Virginia—to this can be added the episodes of Hippo [LIII], Cloelia [LII], and Gualdrada [CIII]. These narratives are not, however, from the same mould as Virginia's. Most importantly, they privilege active, enterprising young women who take control. Admittedly, for Hippo this means committing suicide to escape violation, but for Cloelia and Gualdrada it means safety and honour while still alive. Cloelia carried out a daring escape from captivity; Gualdrada, refuting her role as a chattel in the hands of her father, refused to kiss the Emperor. Gualdrada's rebellion gets its reward—she is married to a man of the Emperor's choosing! We are not told whether her reaction is favourable or unfavourable. In fact, we learn only about the reaction of her family. The protagonist literally disappears from view once she is betrothed in accordance with the wishes of her elders [FW 449]. Ironically, her heroic act leads to a confirmation of woman's inevitable destiny. After her courageous defiance in the face of paternal and political authority, all she leaves as a sign of her fame is her offspring: "In due course she had many children and at her death she left her husband's illustrious house adorned by her own noble progeny" [FW 449]. This biography reinforces the general message of the *De mulieribus* which seeks to find a new heroism in married life, with virginity inevitably leading to marriage or death.

It is no accident that Gualdrada's biography is followed by that of the Empress Constance [CIV], which more or less repeats, in general terms, the previous narrative. This time the female protagonist is an institutionalized virgin, a nun in a cloister. For political reasons, it is decided that she should marry, notwithstanding that by now she is a "wrinkled crone" [FW 453]. In spite of her objections, Constance is married. The text does not lose sight of its biographical subject and her reaction (so different from Gualdrada's) to the situation which has been imposed upon her: "She went into the imperial chamber, entered the marriage bed, and *against her will* lost the eternal virginity she had dedicated to God" [FW 453; my emphasis].

Social forces present themselves as being more potent than pure virginity. Gualdrada and Constance demonstrate that the 'true' destiny of women is to ensure the survival of the family. This is almost the final image of women in the book: fated to bear children whatever the circumstances.

In a limited number of cases, virginity enters into a productive relationship with other forms of being, in particular woman as an intellectual. Although virginity is not an exclusive quality for this type of calling, it suggests that a different path is open to virgins other than institutional enclosure or eventual marriage.

The intellectuals discussed according to this alternative model are Erythraea [XXI], Almathea [XXVI], Manto [XXX][14] and Martia [LXVI]). Virginity plays an ambiguous part in the presentation of these four women as exceptional although, for the Sibyl, Erythraea, the question is not discussed until the last paragraph of the chapter and seems, almost an afterthought. Erythraea's virginity is intended to underpin her achievements, particularly her prediction of the coming of Christ:

> Some accounts further claim that she preserved her virginity. I can easily believe this, for I do not think that so clear a vision of the future could have shone forth in an unclean breast. [FW 87]

Clearly, this statement has been included to reinforce the authority of the Sibyl—a necessity as the commentator declares her to be the most worthy of fame amongst the women of classical antiquity [FW 87]. This is an important directive to a 'correct' reading of the *De mulieribus*. Boccaccio's establishment of an apparent hierarchy amongst his subjects seeks to ensure that the 'right' message is heard, in spite of the more problematic biographies. The biography of Erythraea is that of an intellectual who can be assimilated into the Christian world. Her position in the text does not appear to be fortuitous: she is placed between two Amazon queens [XIX–XX] and Medusa [XXII] who herself is followed by Iole [XXIII] and Deianira [XXIV]. Position is meaning at this point in the *De mulieribus*. In ideological terms, the Sibyl predicts history, but does not take any real, meaningful part in it. The emphasis given to Erythraea's superiority over other pagan women does not pertain to her

inherent qualities as a woman. The gift of prophecy, for which she is
famous, is a gift from God. However, the narrator does propose that there
is an active element in her gift, "attentive study" [FW 87]. This places her
on the same level as other classical female intellectuals. If Erythraea is to
be understood as superior to the other women in the book, I would argue
that it should be for the combination of active study and the gift
bestowed upon her by God (study alone could not account for her
prophecies). Erythraea represents a negation of the values of those subjects that surround her in the text, the Amazon queens and Medusa.
Against military aggression, wealth, beauty, and sensual satisfaction, the
Sibyl asserts the twin virtues of study and Christian piety, using her
intellect to guide men towards true religion.

Though a central tenet of Boccaccio's view of women, virginity is not
at the critical heart of the text's discourse on female sexuality. Chastity
claims centre stage—sexual restraint within marriage and after the death
of one's husband. Widows (as we shall see later in the chapter) play a
noticeable part in the text. Taking them together with dutiful wives, a
picture emerges of a society in which women will have to take on roles of
heroic proportions in order to return society to older, more conservative
values. But these roles will always be the traditional ones, revivified by
an adhesion to Christian values and uncorrupted by the false values of
sexuality and money.

Woman as Artist

$\mathcal{A}$ small but coherent group of women in the *De mulieribus* seek self-
definition through aesthetic and intellectual means, and constitute a thematic thread throughout the work. This group
comprises three painters, eleven intellectuals and writers. Together these
figures can be described as the founding mothers of written culture and
the flag-bearers of female intellectual activity.

From the first category we may take as our example the Greek artist
Tamaris (LVI): although this woman's actual paintings had not survived,
Boccaccio attempted to commemorate her achievement through writing.
It is one of the few occasions in the text where he applies the term *gloria*
to a pagan woman without ironic intent: "she gained such acclaim [glo-
riam] for her painting" [FW 233].

The female artists in the *De mulieribus* appear to offer women the
possibility of overcoming domestic stereotypes by achieving *gloria*
through art.[15] In this account, Boccaccio repeats certain phrases which
emphasize Tamaris' rejection of her expected role, crossing over tradi-

tional gender lines: "Tamaris scorned womanly tasks and practised her father's craft with remarkable talent" [*FW* 231, 233]. This comment indicates an opening out of the social space made available to women, artistic talent enabling Tamaris to become involved in activities that break with the stereotyped mould. It emphasizes that activities designated 'feminine' receive scant acknowledgement in the text. In this sense, women artists represent a challenge to accepted norms of female behaviour. At the end of the chapter, the writer remarks that Tamaris' achievement was all the more remarkable "if we compare it with the usual spinning and weaving of other women" [*FW* 233].

The same principle is applied to Marcia [LXVI], who is described as "scorning womanly occupations" [*FW* 275], to highlight the difference between her and most other women. In the chapter on Irene [LIX] Boccaccio states categorically that "the art of painting is mostly alien to the feminine mind" [*FW* 251]. These artists underline the basic tenet of the *De mulieribus* that only a few women are able to overcome both their own natures and social restrictions. Their exceptional gifts are the only means to remove the double bind of 'inferior nature' and social oppression. The female artist exemplifies Boccaccio's view of women who through a quirk of nature are endowed with exceptional talent which they manage to exploit. His silence on the personal/sexual lives of the Greek painters may be due either to a lack of historical information in the *Natural History* or to a conscious desire to withhold any information which might detract from his exegesis on the ennobling powers of art.[16]

Marcia, the sole Roman artist included in the text, is treated in far greater detail than her Greek counterparts and is the only one of the painters to have her sexuality discussed. Her biography follows a pattern which is almost standard in the *De mulieribus*: a bipartite division in which nature and culture are juxtaposed. From the very start of her biography, Boccaccio places the emphasis on Marcia's sexual purity, "a virgin all her life" [*FW* 275]. Indeed, it is not until the third paragraph that the reader realizes she is being celebrated for anything other than her virginity. The text stresses the point that her virginity was the result of a conscious choice, neither imposed upon her nor taken up unthinkingly. This is important in Boccaccio's conceptualization of women because female sexuality not only threatens men, but also prevents women from achieving their full potential. Marcia's self-control is viewed as instrumental in granting her the space to become a painter.[17]

Boccaccio brings sexuality and art together in the last section of the biography where he hypothesizes about the reasons for Marcia not painting male figures. For the narrator the reason is her *pudor*. However, the phenomenon is open to other readings, which he attempts to close off by his authoritative interpretation. Marcia's rejection of male artistic val-

ues and of men themselves in her art is suggestive of a conscious difference explored in her representations of women. They are depicted as
subjects rather than the naked objects of male desire.

In Marcia's biography, sexual abstinence is not an end in itself, nor is
it viewed as superior to worldly actions and glory. It allows the female
artist to break with the conventional female role, to avoid *otium* [idle-
ness], a trap which induces sexual promiscuity, and to be regarded as
superior to male artists. In this chapter, Boccaccio is not clear whether
Marcia's artistic ability has its source in teaching or in a natural gift. He
is, perhaps, unwilling to decide one way or the other, because such a
decision goes to the heart of his thinking about the intuitive (or otherwise) nature of art and about women's ability to change through learning. In this particular case, to pronounce decisively one way or the other
would signify either that women possess innate gifts not requiring male
tutelage, or that with instruction women might go beyond male achievement. This conundrum of the text, therefore, remains unresolved.

Women as Writers and Intellectuals

When Boccaccio discusses female writers (Cornificia [LXXXVI],
Leontium [LX], Proba [XCVII], Sappho [XLVII], and Sempronia
[LXXIX]), he almost invariably mentions their sexuality. The
figures of Leontium and Sempronia are of considerable interest since
they present a sharp contrast with Marcia.

Unlike Marcia, Leontium is characterized by her promiscuity, which
has a determining effect on the way she is represented (in comparison
to the emphasis on Marcia's uncompromising virginity). The text pro-
claims that Leontium's sexuality had a detrimental effect on her literary achievement:

> If she had preserved her matronly honour, the glory attached to her name
> would have been much more radiant, for she had extraordinary intellectual
> powers. [*FW* 251]

Thus, because of Leontium's uncontrolled sexuality, or as an ana-
logue to it, her literary achievements are not viewed positively. One of
her lost works was an invective against the philosopher Theophrastus,
and it is this work which causes Boccaccio to view his subject even more
negatively. He does admit that the longevity of its reputation down the
centuries means that it must have been a worthwhile piece, but he cannot accept the premise on which such a polemic rests: that of a woman
challenging a man's authority—an eminent philosopher. Indeed,

Leontium's critical work is considered an act of temerity or envy. Sempronia [LXXIX] is also a writer, but does not challenge male authority by this means.[18] She was part of Catiline's conspiracy against the Roman republic. Her errant sexuality is connected to her errant politics. In both cases, Sempronia transgressed the boundaries and is punished both in history and by retrospective judgement on her conduct.

In contrast to the female painters such as Marcia, Leontium directly challenges the male monopoly of knowledge. Leontium's sexuality is a convenient label used by the writer to discredit all her intellectual activity. She is not a helpmate; she has transgressed on to male territory. This is the precise limit of Boccaccio's ideological position: once women challenge male authority they are ruthlessly damned by the text. Perhaps the most striking example is that of another female intellectual, Pope Joan [CI].

Pope Joan bears more than a passing resemblance to Leontium in that both women are guilty of transgressing male territorial rights: Leontium engages in an intellectual dispute with a man, and Joan usurps the highest post Christendom has to offer men. Both women are sexually active and both are highly intelligent. Joan is reminiscent also of Semiramis in that disguise as a man is an essential element for her gaining power in a world controlled by men—the Church is the symbol of this *par excellence*. Joan's disguise enables her to exercise power like a man but, once she is discovered, that moment marks the end of her authority and her 'manhood', unlike Semiramis. The text emphasizes that her learning glows most particularly during periods of sexual abstinence.[19]

Some authors could construe her ascension to the papacy as a positive event in that a woman had attained to the highest honour à la Christine de Pizan (though, ironically she omits Joan in the *Cité des dames*).[20] Boccaccio views Joan's accession to the papacy with the utmost negativity. Indeed, the very foundations of Christendom are threatened: God is invoked so that Joan's punishment is not only exemplary but also divinely inspired. This has the effect of demonstrating the enormity of her deception. The intervention of God restores order and puts the woman back in her place, a biologically ordered place as Pope Joan becomes pregnant.[21] This is the most targeted of punishments since it reveals woman as fundamentally bound to 'nature' in spite of attempts at acculturation in a male-dominated society.

Particularly towards the end of the *De mulieribus*, Boccaccio does manage to create effects of dramatic contrast by juxtaposing figures that present opposing images of womanhood; for example, the extraordinarily chaste Zenobia precedes Joan. The shift between the sexually pure pagan and the sexually corrupt Christian woman is abrupt, presenting 'correct' and 'incorrect' conduct side-by-side, thus making clear the rules that should govern female morality.

In the same way, Proba [XCVII] appears amidst a group of unchaste women and presents an equally clear message to the reader. The opening statement leaves no room for doubt about the way in which her biography will be approached: "Proba, an excellent woman in reality as well as name, is worthy of remembrance for her knowledge of literature" [FW 411]. This is one of the few occasions on which Boccaccio explains the reason for his subject's fame right at the beginning of the chapter. It is not fortuitous that she is the only Christian writer included in the entire collection. Proba can be read as providing a possible model for writing in the later Middle Ages. As the author of two *Centos* that used the poetry of Virgil and Homer respectively for the Christian purpose of retelling the Bible in classical verse, she personifies the attempt to marry humanistic studies (both Latin *and* Greek) to religious belief.

Proba is a model intellectual whose example should stimulate both men and women. As far as men are concerned, the chapter contains a number of sharp barbs against the contemporary state of learning, especially the study of the Bible.[22] She represents a kind of ideal to which Boccaccio himself would have liked to aspire. Indeed, she also represents the negation of those narratives which Boccaccio had been engaged in writing: the *novelle* of the *Decameron*:

> Would that her example was favourably regarded by those women who yield to pleasure and idleness, who think it wonderful to stay in their rooms and waste irrevocable time in frivolous stories. [FW 415]

Proba's biography represents the ideological centre-piece of the *De mulieribus*, the work in which an alliance between Christianity and the new humanism is proposed, together with a denial of the literary strategy of the *Decameron*. The *De mulieribus* represents a new kind of storytelling where the 'trivial' has been replaced by historical narratives based on research grounded in a moral determination to serve conventional standards. The *De mulieribus* does not deny narrative, but brings it under the partial control of historical enquiry. Proba stands as a monument to the idea of literary fame based on the alliance between biblical and classical pasts.

Women Warriors, Widows and Queens

𝕮 hapter headings in the *De mulieribus* often contain the titles of their female subjects; that of queen being one of the most common. Equally often, these titles have little bearing on the aspects of a woman's life, which are highlighted in the text.[23] Nevertheless, Boccaccio specifically treats the reigns of some fifteen queens, including the still living Giovanna I, queen of Naples. Yet the queens do not form a coherent group. This is due to the encyclopedic principle shaping the *De mulieribus*, that of chronological extension having precedence over thematic cohesion.

A feature common to most of the female rulers treated by Boccaccio is their competence in war. The Amazon queens are dealt with in some detail in the *De mulieribus*, precisely because they represent a sharp image of 'otherness'. They formed a society in which their distance from patriarchy measured female achievement, symbolized by a rejection of the domestic. The chapter suggests and warns that women, cut loose from the weight of the family, are able to achieve goals generally only available to men.[24] Cutting off the left breast in order to facilitate shooting with a bow, indicates a rejection of nurturing as primary activity in favour of a more active, masculine-centred role. Boccaccio himself remarks at the beginning of the first set of Amazon biographies [XI–XII] that their "hystoria" is "peregrina" [extraordinary].[25]

The first Amazons are marked by their ferocity. In this sense they are the ideological 'mothers' of a number of women in the text, such as Camilla [XXXIX],[26] Tamyris [XLIX] and the wife of Orgiago [LXXIII]. These women exhibit an overriding sense of justice combined with a highly developed notion of vengeance, often carried out in a bloodthirsty manner. Similarly, an attack on the liberty and livelihood of the Amazons leads them to take justice into their own hands without waiting for men to act [*FW* 51, 53].

One can note here that the Amazons take personal responsibility for their safety only when their husbands are dead. I do not believe this to be a coincidence, for the simple reason that, statistically, nearly half of Boccaccio's queens are widows: Semiramis [II], Dido [XLII], Tamyris [XLIX], Athaliah [LI],[27] Artemisia [LVII], and Zenobia [C] are the most noteworthy. It is almost as if widowhood is a prerequisite for assuming the reins of power—indeed, the demise of the husband is seen as a unique chance for women to exert authority. The majority of the widows of the *De mulieribus* do not withdraw from the world and, although outcomes may not be positive for all of them, most do decide to act on the political stage.

Widows who withdraw from the world are very much in the minority

in the *De mulieribus*. The most outstanding example of this type is
Antonia (LXXXIX). Following the death of her husband, Antonia lives out
her life chastely in the matrimonial chamber, her behaviour gaining the
full approval of the authorial voice: "[she] thought that an honourable
woman should wed only once" [*FW* 375]. Antonia places in vivid focus
the widowhood of the text's female rulers, resulting in an implicit comparison between extreme renunciation and extreme liberation.

The complexity of reading the two positions cannot be underestimated. Does one line of conduct nullify the other? Is one closer to the
ideological concerns of the implied author? The problem lies in the fact
that the *De mulieribus* has no overarching framework that ranks one position definitively over the other. To tackle such questions requires interpreting textual markers that are hard to read, difficult to find, and often
contradictory. Antonia's biography bears the message that widowed
chastity is to be valued in its own right—and certain of the queens
emphasize this value in all of their actions (Dido, Artemisia, Zenobia).
Thus, it might be argued that total sexual renunciation allows women to
access real power in the *De mulieribus*. In the lives of the queens, chaste
widowhood becomes a justification for women's claim to power.
Government and female sexuality come together, sometimes positively,
sometimes negatively, supporting or attacking the notion of supremely
powerful women.

It is clear that the ideal of women marrying once, and only once,
forms an integral part of Boccaccio's vision of widowhood in the *De
mulieribus*. Boccaccio presents women who do not remarry as heroic on
a number of levels, usually for their military prowess and leadership
skills. But even Antonia, whose widowhood may be thought passive, falls
into this category. Antonia denies her beauty, represses her natural
instincts and imposes a rigid discipline upon herself, enabling Boccaccio
to set up a stark contrast to the behaviour of contemporary women,
which he criticizes throughout the text in the strongest possible terms.

The other widows mentioned in the *De mulieribus* go out of their way
to leave their mark on society, both politically and militarily. The
Amazons, in particular, manage to invert the image of the male conqueror. The wars of the Amazons are against 'softness'—that trait which
renders men effeminate and women lascivious through over-indulgence.

However, the account of the Amazons is not as straightforward as
might appear at first sight. The second and third generations of the
Amazon queens all fail in different ways. For example, Hercules defeats
the Amazon warriors in one of his labours (XIX–XX). The women are
proven fallible and subject to the power of that embodiment of virility
itself—Hercules. Such an impression is reinforced by a description of
Orithya's expedition against Greece, which resulted in her defeat.

It is ironic that the defeat of the Amazons by the Greek hero is the only time in the *De mulieribus* that we see Hercules as truly virile; controlling and subjecting women. Indeed two further chapters—XXIII (Iole)[28] and XXIV (Deianira)—present the enslavement of Hercules to one woman, and his death through the unwitting compliance of another. Thus, although Hercules appears on one occasion as a victorious warrior (*albeit* against the Amazons without their queen), he remains more memorable as the puppet of his beloved Iole who is a pre-figuration of the biblical Delilah.[29]

It is important to note the reversal that takes place in the gendered roles of the two lovers, undermining the authority of the male. The illustrious hero illustrates graphically what happens when a man loses the signs of his maleness and hence of his power. The loss of Hercules' bow and arrow reduces him to a level lower than that of the Amazons whom he had defeated in an earlier chapter. Iole progressively strips him of his virility and dresses him in dainty robes, to the extent that he might be considered a transvestite, wearing rings and perfumes and adorned with "girlish garlands" [*FW* 93]—no longer the hardened man of former times. A story such as this confirms the traditional gender boundaries, exerting pressure on the male reader to condemn the foolishness of Hercules as well as the perfidy of Iole. Hercules is now no more than an ordinary woman characterized in the same way as the anonymous mass of women engaged in spinning wool. His defeat could not be spelt out more clearly. The hero has been reduced to a perfect model of female passivity, obeying the orders of a woman, with the verbs "imperavit," "precepit" reinforcing the picture of his disempowerment:

> Finally she forced Hercules—by this time totally effeminate—to sit in the midst of her servant girls and tell the story of his labours.[30]

The emasculation of Hercules serves as a warning to men about the destructive power of love, a message conveyed especially through the long commentary condemning passionate love in chapter XXIII. Hercules failed to tame the desires of his body through the use of his reason and, hence made himself vulnerable. Fear of the sensual body leads the mature Boccaccio to reject the physical love of woman as an unacceptable facet of nature. Love is to be feared because it creates disorder; signifying for Boccaccio female domination leading to the destruction of the stability of the male-controlled social order and male dignity.[31] Hercules is defeated because he is made to relinquish his stereotyped role, and in the process loses his "gravitas." There is no longer any reason for him to be considered superior to Iole. Love opposes the 'rational' order, and with it man's ability to control woman and to preserve the status quo.

Love and sexual desire form an uneasy background to a number of the biographies of queens in the *De mulieribus*. Different biographies, however, place different emphases on sexual desire. Although one cannot deny that control of sexual instinct looms large in the text, the writer aims to show that exceptional women are capable of traditional male activities. This interpretation is confirmed in the chapter on Semiramis [II]. Her biography, derived from an amalgam of classical and Christian sources, is divided into two distinct parts. The first, like so many of the *Decameron* stories, centres on a deception: following her husband's untimely death, the Assyrian queen disguises herself as her son, whom she considers too young to wield power, and rules the kingdom in his stead. It is noted in the text that Semiramis' beauty is comparable to that of her young son. This detail is significant for the development of the narrative as it insinuates a certain naivety on her part, as well as sexual slippage between the two roles of woman and boy. The interest of the text in its first part lies in the achievements of the queen resulting from the denial of her female sexuality and her adoption of the role of transvestite. The consequences of this act of trespass are twofold: firstly, her son is emasculated: "As though he had changed sex with his mother, Ninyas languished idly in bed while she exerted herself in battle against her enemies" [*FW* 23]. Secondly, the dynasty is tainted by this reversal of roles.

The second stage of Boccaccio's account can be calculated from the moment Semiramis reveals that she is a woman, and is concerned entirely with her sexuality. The description of her boundless sexual desire can be read in counterpoint to her desire to build an ever vaster empire and, indeed, represents a parody of her ambition. The two senses of conquest underscore the potential dangers to the contemporary political and social system, as represented by a woman who manages to gain power through trickery and deception. By repeating the diverse accounts of various historians (including Orosius's claim that Semiramis killed her lovers immediately after copulation) and refraining from selecting one definitive version of the story, Boccaccio intentionally adds to the myth surrounding the queen's sexuality. Her failure to control the feminine aspect of her nature leads to her disgrace and downfall, whereas when disguised as a man she was able to achieve great glory. Female sexual instinct is regarded as an irresistible force which, when unleashed, is capable of wreaking untold havoc and destruction.

The two parts of the biography are emblematic of the struggle between two views of what it is that constitutes a woman. The first part displays a woman with considerable political acumen who understands the necessity of overcoming the limitations of her sex ("mentita sexum" as understood by the male author).[32] The episode in which Semiramis leaves her hair only half-combed until she recaptures Babylon is inserted by Boccaccio to demonstrate the queen's will-power and military energy in times of crisis—in short, to emphasize that she was a good ruler.

The second part of the biography concentrates on her incestuous relationship with her son, Ninyas. The language is now morally charged and introduces the concept of contamination, that is, the pollution of the queen's political, public qualities by her uncontrollable sexual urges. The private thus becomes a public issue in the text and replaces the political as the measure by which Semiramis is to be judged. The terminology is similar to that employed by Boccaccio in the chapter on Iole [XXIII]: both these women are guilty of rendering men effeminate, perhaps their greatest crime.

The reading of Semiramis' biography is a complex process involving the definition of the relationship between its constituent parts. Does the second part necessarily invalidate the first? I think not because the early narrative presents the forceful image of a queen who surpasses even her husband as a conqueror. The second part indisputably sets out to 'stain' the regent's reputation, ensuring that her biography ends on an entirely negative note.[33] However, the positive image of Semiramis as an active and skilful politician/general lingers in spite of Boccaccio's best efforts to reduce the effectiveness of his portrayal of the warrior queen.

As we have seen in the chapter on Semiramis, Boccaccio does not necessarily oppose or openly vilify the involvement of women in public action—he is at least prepared to depict them performing deeds of public value. What he does object to is women's use of their sexual power to effeminize men. This is exactly what Cleopatra [LXXXVIII] does.[34] The Egyptian queen is introduced in the first paragraph in terms designed to induce the reader to view her in a totally negative light. Her "claritas" is due to nothing more positive than her physical beauty—the most ambiguous compliment in Boccaccio's store of feminine praise. For the rest she is described in traditional, stereotyped terms, with emphasis placed on her "avaritia" [avarice], "luxuria" [lust], and cruelty. She is presented almost exclusively as a slave to her bodily desires, "burning with the desire to rule" [FW 363]. Her acquisitiveness is seen as instinctual rather than as the result of a conscious, political process or policy. There is no separation here between imperial conquest and sexual depravity, as was the case with Semiramis. All Cleopatra's activities are permeated by her sexuality. Her politics are the politics of the body. Her history is the sexual conquest of Roman heroes, beginning with Julius Caesar who becomes, in Boccaccio's interpretation of the episode, "the lusty prince" [FW 363].

Technically, Cleopatra becomes a widow after the murder of her brother/husband, and so her behaviour is in breach of the restrictive principles which Boccaccio enunciates throughout the text. Her politics are ruled by the pleasure principle which subordinates all humanitarian values to those of the self and its aggrandisement. The powers of the female body are to be feared, as the loss of Hercules' masculinity to Iole makes more than clear. Similarly, in the story of Cleopatra, Antony is described as "effeminatus" because he subordinates the values of Rome to love and lust.[35]

Semiramis and Cleopatra are not permitted to exhaust the possibilities of the feminine ruler. In contrast Boccaccio offers a different kind of queen whose government is based on a regimen of sexual abstention. Cleopatra and Semiramis are situated at one end of the spectrum, whilst at the other end are the examples of Artemisia [LVII] and Zenobia [C].

Standing apart from the women rulers heretofore discussed is the widow-*cum*-warrior Artemisia. It is significant that Boccaccio begins this narrative by emphasizing Artemisia's attachment to her late husband, describing in detail how she drinks his ashes and begins the construction of the famous mausoleum in his honour: "Thus the conjugal love of Artemisia gained renown, and even more so her perseverance in widowhood and mourning" [FW 237].

The second part of this same chapter bears little resemblance to the first which had insisted on the perfect marital love between husband and wife, followed by the perfect devotion of the wife now widow. Not only does the latter part show a different side to Artemisia, but (as the writer admits) the woman described was probably a completely different historical character. However, this slight complication does not seem to bother Boccaccio at all in the *De mulieribus*. The second Artemisia leads her people into battle twice (once to defend her city against attackers, and once as an ally of Xerxes), employing stratagems worthy of the most cunning general. Indeed, describing a combined naval battle which Xerxes observes from the safety of the sidelines, Boccaccio writes: "Artemisia, in the midst of her admirals, was seen urging on her men and fighting bitterly; it was almost as if she had changed sex with Xerxes" [FW 241]. The writer seems determined to preserve the fragile 'unity' of his character in spite of historical and logical evidence to the contrary but does not argue his case at all convincingly, part of his conclusion reading: "Whoever my readers are, let them believe what they prefer. Whether one or two women were involved, each undertaking was still that of a woman."[36]

The fact that Boccaccio's narrative is fractured by the extreme difficulty of reconciling Artemisia-widow and Artemisia-general, suggests that he nurtured an ambivalent desire for women to fulfill simultaneously two mutually exclusive roles: they should be faithful to their husbands (either as wives or widows) and they should be free to break out of constricting social bonds and enter into the world of men.

A parallel case can be found in the figure of Zenobia [C], an extraordinarily chaste woman and powerful military leader (depicted in many ways as being similar to Camilla [XXXIX]). However, neither Zenobia's chastity nor her military prowess are sufficient to deter Boccaccio from describing in detail her public humiliation at the triumph of the victorious Roman general.

On Zenobia: Distinguishing the Methodologies of Boccaccio and de Pizan

occaccio portrays Zenobia as a fearless maiden whose youth is spent contesting the harshness of nature. She is a hardened hunter whose strength has its source in the rejection of men and love: "It was her practice to scorn the love and companionship of men and to place great store by her virginity."[37] Her denial of the female self is so complete that she avoids the fatal disease of "mollicia" and becomes more virile than her male contemporaries. Zenobia appears to be the most perfect model of the warrior queen, combining superhuman strength and endurance with sexual purity and chastity. She is described as being so virtuous that "according to our ancient sources, ..she ought to receive precedence over other pagan ladies for her illustrious reputation" [FW 427]. The chronology allows Boccaccio to place Zenobia as the last of the pagan women before he enters Christian territory.

Zenobia's chastity does not, however, exhaust the possibilities of her perfection. She had strong intellectual interests, spoke a number of foreign languages, and is reputed to have put together a compilation of historical writings. Yet, in spite of this positive representation, Zenobia suffered defeat at the hands of the Romans. It is perhaps surprising that Zenobia's defeat evokes from the commentator no long tirade against injustice, nor other laments of a similar nature. A passing comment suffices to illustrate the humiliation she endured at the Roman triumph, conveying the pathos of her fall from ultimate power:

> burdened by her crown and royal robes and pearls and precious stones, she was exhausted by their weight and often had to stop, despite her inexhaustible vigour. [FW 437]

The once powerful figure is crushed by Roman might in spite of the fact that, as a woman who conforms to the dictates of Boccaccio's most stringent standards, victory should have been hers.

The response of de Pizan is instructive: using the *exemplum* of

Zenobia she follows Boccaccio's account closely, but, she makes no mention whatsoever of Zenobia's defeat and humiliation at the hands of the Romans. The omission of this salient fact transforms Zenobia from a spectacular failure into a positive model whose manifold virtues are properly rewarded. From this example, de Pizan can be seen rewriting history, offering an ideal 'feminist' reappraisal of events. Exceptional women are not oppressed by male domination—more often than not they reverse the 'unnatural' order. Coherence in establishing a pro-woman program of positive role models overrides the need to write complete historical accounts. Clearly Boccaccio and de Pizan adhere to contrasting views of history. For Boccaccio, it is a case of reconstructing the past, of giving priority to historical detail and inclusiveness (and inconclusiveness?) over any programmatic assertions or overviews. Constant reference to 'ancient sources' emphasizes that his text is a work of historical reconstruction. He also draws attention to his unsuccessful attempt to discover the identity of Zenobia's parents, and to the fact that his text is based on the work of others.[38]

In the closing lines of Zenobia's biography, Boccaccio introduces an element (one de Pizan certainly does not take up) which provides a good example of the archeologizing mentality he evinces in the *De mulieribus*. Rather than closing with a morality message or a *declamatio* bewailing Zenobia's fate, he informs the reader that the queen lived for the rest of her life on an estate near Tivoli which became known as Zenobia: "not far from the palace of the emperor Hadrian, in the place which the inhabitants called Conca" [*FW* 437]. This final piece of information would be totally superfluous if the focus of the biography were solely on an ideologically inspired picture of Zenobia. Instead, it fills in a detail for the reader interested in the reconstruction of ancient Rome. Piecing together the classical past can be seen as an important consideration for Boccaccio in the *De mulieribus*, and is one of the reasons for his inclusion of incongruous details about Zenobia's life (again omitted by de Pizan). He notes, for instance, that as a young woman the virtuous Zenobia was able to defeat men of her own age in wrestling contests! Details such as this, combined with the assertion that she joined her captains and various princes in drinking sessions, create the impression that she wanted to be 'one of the boys'—insinuating perhaps that she was involved in superficial, unheroic and possibly questionable activities which might throw some doubt on her acceptability as a model of perfect political and sexual governance. It comes as no surprise that Boccaccio includes a report from an unverified source suggesting that Zenobia might have been responsible for the deaths of her husband and stepson. The inclusion of such an accusation (which may well have been completely unfounded) was unacceptable to de Pizan on the grounds that it contradicted the general tendencies displayed by Zenobia, detracting from the efficacy of her portrayal as a woman of action and, moreover, as an utterly chaste woman.

Although both authors discuss Zenobia's intellectual gifts and her attitude to learning, de Pizan gives them extra emphasis by placing them at the end of the chapter. Also, the female writer's hierarchy of achievement is different from that implied in Boccaccio's account: "the high point of her virtues which I have to tell you was, in summary, her profound learnedness in letters" (*City of Women*, I.20.2; pp.54–55). Learning is one of the hallmarks of the women in the *City of Women*. It is used as a sign of their capability to re-read what men have written, as a sign of female independence, and as a bid to break away from male interpretation. By giving such importance to learning and structuring Zenobia's biography so that it gives a rounded picture of her, de Pizan presents the female ruler on her own terms. The queen's actions can be judged by the reader as exceptional, yet within the capabilities of an 'ordinary' woman.[39] There is no indication that the rest of womankind is inferior to her, or incapable of reaching such heights. Boccaccio, however, cannot resist interpolating comments about female sexuality into the flow of his narrative: "Very rarely indeed will you find women of this stamp" [*FW* 433]. The deletion of such comments from de Pizan's narrative is indicative of a profound distinction between the attitudes of the two writers towards women. While Boccaccio is prepared to accept that occasionally a woman is able to overcome her own sexuality, he emphasizes the rarity of the occurrence. Christine de Pizan, on the other hand, renders her model more positive by showing her virtuous character as a possibility for all women.

In the *City of Women*, it is striking that the biography of Zenobia is immediately followed by that of Artemisia, whereas in Boccaccio these two women are separated by forty-three chapters. The distance the Italian writer places between them is not merely chronological: Boccaccio dwells on the defeat of Zenobia, describing her humiliation in Rome. For de Pizan, there is little or no difference between Artemisia and Zenobia—they are both celebrated as victorious generals. In order to try and make sense of Boccaccio's paradoxical treatment of these two female figures, it might be argued that he has reintroduced, although in a much less systematic way, the kind of divisions which are to be found in the *Decameron*:—stories with happpy and unhappy endings. Similar situations produce opposite results, emphasizing the weakness of human endeavour in the face of *fortuna*, a structure which permeates the *De casibus*.

The text of the *De mulieribus* betrays a 'Romanocentric' view of the past whereby any woman challenging the authority of Rome must be punished.[40] The story of Zenobia might be read in an alternative way, as the reassertion of Roman power, to be understood as the archetypal masculine. Zenobia's husband, Odenatus, was able to achieve his aim of extending his territories only when the Roman empire itself was weak. Thus, the figure of Zenobia is intended to contrast with those male rulers who had betrayed their virility and succumbed to soft 'feminine' luxury. Boccaccio contrasts the queen as a supreme military commander with the effeminate Romans.[41] The eventual defeat of Zenobia is brought about by a return to those Roman values which had been held in contempt by previous emperors—Aurelian moved against the queen "for the purpose of redeeming the dishonoured Roman name and acquiring immense glory" [FW 435]. Of course, the shame lies in the fact that it is a woman who defeats the 'might' of Rome. By the end of the biography order is restored in the sense that Zenobia is humiliated and lives out her days with her children, deprived of access to power and the occasion to display any of those skills previously mentioned.

Zenobia and the Internal Contradictions of the *De mulieribus*

𝕿he following chapter which deals with the life of Pope Joan seems to consolidate the structure of Zenobia's biography: another gifted and intelligent woman attains a remarkable place in society before being humiliated and ejected from the (male) sphere of action. Yet, in contrast to Joan, Zenobia retains a positive dimension, mainly through the long descriptive passages relating her achievements. It is tempting to read her biography as a moralistic sermon on the eventual surrender of the woman ruler to superior forces. The figure of Artemisia represented an attempt to weld together these two conflicting concepts—Christian theology vs. classical history—although to my mind the seams are obvious. The text as a whole seems to revolve around these two polarities, including even those women who infringe the rules of female propriety, since they act as anti-models of behaviour to be shunned at all costs. Such a duality accounts for the large number of women in the *De mulieribus* representing an impossible attempt to reconcile the extraordinary deeds performed by the pagan women of antiquity with the *mores* of Christian morality. This is yet another example of the way in which the text represents the difficult fusion of two types of exemplary writing. The first is the narrative account in which the reader is left to draw conclusions with only the implicit guidance of authorial intervention (or, at most, brief comments), and the second is the direct moral imperative to draw a constructive lesson from the given *exempla*.

The *De mulieribus* closes with a chapter on Giovanna I, queen of Naples. Following the extensive array of biographies on ancient female rulers, this modern queen represents the possibilities of female power in contemporary Italy. It is interesting to observe the singular way in which Giovanna is depicted, as opposed to Boccaccio's presentation of the more ancient queens of the *De mulieribus*. The text emphasizes her royal origins (more than is usual in the other historical biographies), particularly on the French side. Whilst not denying that this might be considered normal encomiastic practice, it appears to be a necessary confirmation and validation of the rule of a contemporary female regent. In other words, instead of Giovanna's lineage acting as a springboard for some extraordinary deed, it textually replaces such actions and, in a sense, sets limits to the space of her efforts to seek personal glory. Similarly, Boccaccio's praise of the territory over which she rules might be considered a normal procedure, but this too, by associating the queen with a land obtained through the efforts of others, denies her any glory in her own right. Indeed, Giovanna stands in striking contrast to most of the queens discussed hitherto: rather than an Amazon striding off to war, she sends generals in her stead.[42] On the whole, Boccaccio adopts the modes of Christian sainthood to describe the political experiences of Giovanna: no longer the doer—the active figure—but a female ruler who 'sits out' the storms around her ("perpessa est," *DMC* 446). Moreover, in spite of Boccaccio's efforts to represent her as politically astute by comparing her favourably with a male ruler, the impression remains that it is the men who carry through the active politics of the kingdom.

Holding the crucial position of last biography in the text, Giovanna confirms the ambiguous status of the woman who holds power. She must be praised for exceeding the limits of normal female behaviour, but she must also be restrained. Such ambiguity explains why interpretation of the *De mulieribus* is fraught with difficulty; its 'doubleness' rendering interpretation perilous—'just like a woman'. At once threatening and vulnerable, the female body is nonetheless for Boccaccio a crucial restraint, or limit, continually drawing women back into the natural order. And yet the text does not always use the male authoritative voice to speak openly about what a woman is. A woman can be reconstituted in various ways by different readers, thus allowing readings of differing degrees of negativity and positivity. The fifteenth century will use the lack of a central explanation to convert the text into strangely contrasting and conflicting artifacts.

·   ·   ·   ·   ·

Conclusion

Boccaccio's *De mulieribus claris* is a text that is apt to raise the hackles of many contemporary readers. It does not provide satisfaction for a feminist-inclined readership because of the numerous references to female inferiority and stereotyped behaviours. Even sympathetic readers can be caught out by the text's intransigence on matters of female sexuality and the dearth of radical proposals for change. In a sense, the mixture of positive and negative *exempla* is not so far from the procedures of the *Decameron* except for the major difference that there is no framing device to group the biographies by theme. It is this difference, perhaps more than any other, that makes the *De mulieribus* such frustrating reading.

There are few interconnections between chapters facilitating the reader's search for an overall meaning in the text. The chronological arrangement of the biographies only adds to a sense of semantic disorientation. From one chapter to the next the reader has little idea of the type of woman to expect. The text is encyclopedic and could be consulted as such since the range of women it provides represents a considerable part of its pleasure and usefulness. Structural inconsistencies do not make for a cohesive reading of the text; in particular, the fact that not all chapters have commentaries creates an unevenness of presentation. The commentary draws attention to a particular biography, as especially significant in some way, while underlining points of more general interest. This strategy further complicates a reading of the text because a number of the commentaries deal with wider political and social issues, sometimes not even particularly concerned with women.

The mixing of genres—narrative and homiletic—can be explained in part by the question of readership, divided, I suggest, like the text itself.

Women readers are cajoled into conventional behavioural patterns by the voice of the commentator. At the same time the text provides the possibility for some female exemplars to partially escape categorization. Here, the potential for new self-mirroring or awareness of one's capacity for change is much stronger in spite of the rigid guidelines on how to read the women laid down in the commentaries. The *De mulieribus* is hesitant about this latter possibility since it frequently presents ambiguous *exempla* that show exceptional women flawed by sexual vice. The reason for this ambiguity may be the other audience, that is the men. The Latin work indicates that Boccaccio was signalling to a male audience that he should be taken seriously on the subject of women. Boccaccio's 'ideal' male reader was most notably Petrarch, who was not generally impressed by the vernacular *Decameron*. The revised image of women in the *De mulieribus* was intended to meet a number of fundamental criticisms of the *Decameron*, especially the criticism concerning the open treatment of female sexuality. By restricting his treatment and tolerance of female sexuality in the *De mulieribus*, Boccaccio announced his readiness to enter fully the humanist club that viewed chastity as the basis of female behaviour.

However, female behaviour is not the only object of correction: in the *De mulieribus* there are frequent references to errant male conduct. Yet clearly any critique of men has implications for the representation of women. That is, if women have the slightest possibility of matching men in any area of endeavour, the writer faces the challenge of accommodating this equality, by reconceptualizing social organization, or, alternatively, by reinforcing gender stereotypes. Boccaccio does not seem to make a clear choice. On the one hand, there are elements in the *De mulieribus* that suggest a readiness to conceptualize gender roles differently, at least with respect to pagan societies. This radical approach is often submerged in traditional thinking about women and their possibilities. The commentaries frequently represent an act of closure, and more rarely, an opening into new spaces.

Boccaccio views men as part of 'the problem' requiring resolution. Contemporary men do not live up to the conventional expectations of their gender. Boccaccio is particularly concerned about role-reversal, evincing a contradictory attitude towards women assuming male authority. In the chapter on the wives of the Minyans (XXXI), the voice of the commentator concludes: "To sum up: I do not hesitate to affirm that these wives were tried and true men, while the Minyan youths they impersonated were women" [*FW*129]. The force of this expression depends on the reader acknowledging the accepted and acceptable roles of each sex and the potential for dramatic reversals. In the following chapter on Penthesilea, the conclusion highlights the 'effeminacy' of contemporary men, a theme that surfaces regularly in the *De mulieribus*. However, such a simple explanation does not suffice since Boccaccio is at pains to point out that the Minyans were also wives. Moreover, the greater part of the commentary focuses on the ideals of marriage which are to be heroically defended if necessary: "When their husbands were in danger, they gathered their wits and found stratagems which *normally* they could not have discovered" [*FW* 127; my emphasis]. The Minyan women's courage is empowering, but is limited to the protection of the fundamental social institution of marriage.

Marriage as a sign of social stability and continuity is established as pre-eminent in the *De mulieribus claris*. The text makes a number of assumptions about female sexuality in general which tend to emphasize the centrality of this institution. Widowhood is connected to the discourse on marriage in so far as it arises from the refusal to contemplate more than one marriage. It requires adherence to a rigid code of behaviour centred on a single husband for a lifetime, based on the concept of chastity. The family is re-engineered in the *De mulieribus* to provide a formative, morally instructive environment for its children. Parents transmit morally acceptable doctrine so that social peace can be achieved by imposing certain restrictions and goals on their children. It is this didactic aspect of the biographies that receives extensive attention in the commentaries, even at the cost of trivializing or distorting the narrative.

The commentaries that are stitched on to the historical narratives serve the function of seemingly *ad hoc* annotations suggested by the subject-matter of each biography. Yet if examined together, the commentaries constitute a pattern of political and social analysis. The two elements that form many of the chapters, narrative and commentary, are not often fused in a seamless whole. The stitching becomes visible. If there is not a rupture between the two components of a chapter, there is at least a hairline fracture, sometimes degenerating into a tear. On its most obvious level, there is a disjuncture between past and present—the historical past of the biographical subject and the contemporary present. The present does not name individual women nor does it single out great acts. It does not germinate exceptional behaviour, indeed, the aim of the non-narrative discourse is quite the opposite, to encode female comportment in a rigid practice. That practice excerpts only a small number of codes from the narrative to be utilized in the discursive segments of the text. The commentary functions to reduce the significance and magnitude of the exemplary women; it asserts a particular meaning for 'exemplary' that flattens the biography into conventional shape emphasizing those reproducible elements at the expense of the exceptional or unique which thus remain embedded in the biographical narrative without being granted contemporary relevance.

Where they appear in the *De mulieribus*, the commentaries have the function of limiting the horizons of contemporary life for women. The narratives tantalize the reader with the prospect, however remote, of recovering the pagan past. The commentaries cumulatively generate a picture of a society that advocates only certain values from the classical past. The negative *exempla* are also used to confirm 'right' behaviour for women, as is the case with Cleopatra.

Boccaccio's mixture of 'good' and 'bad' women wreaks havoc with the interpretation of the text. Even without considering the text's basic conservative tendencies, Boccaccio presents no decisive genealogical 'line' for the women, confusing the question of whether the *De mulieribus* is radically challenging medieval female stereotypes or reinforcing them. The question may seem irrelevant if one regards the text as a compilation or a display of Boccaccio's knowledge of classical women. However, his increasing concern to add commentaries to the narrative suggests a preoccupation with pointing readers towards very specific moral responses. The encyclopedic expanse of the *De mulieribus* is hence reined in to provide a more coherent and reductive reading of the women's life stories. But such a procedure is not enough to ensure the general cohesion of the text.

Later Editions and Translations of the *De mulieribus*

The chronological ordering of women is counter-balanced by their discursive disordering. The *De mulieribus claris* was the subject of numerous re-writings and translations, and of many attempts to 'close' it, all of which were in no small part due to the openness of the text. About thirty years after publication, the potential of the text to appeal to a wider readership was fulfilled; the courts of northern Italy provided an excellent environment for a work on women. The first translation, emanating from the humanist circle associated with Petrarch and Boccaccio, was the work of Donato degli Albanzani.[1] His translation rather tentatively extends the original work by including additional material concerning Naples and the queen of that state, Giovanna I. This particular translation was the direct result of a commission from Niccolò d'Este, marquis of Ferrara, as is made clear in the text itself. Albanzani's project represents an attempt by a humanistically trained intellectual to introduce the Latin works of the masters to the courts of northern Italy; a milieu in which Latin was not the *lingua franca*.[2]

It is no accident that his translation was dedicated to Niccolò d'Este,[3] initiating a relationship that was to make Ferrara perhaps the most important centre of pro-woman writing in the Italian peninsula about a century later.[4] In a sense, the first vernacular translation confirmed that court women were a presence to be taken into serious consideration. A theoretical revision of their role was about to commence with greater access to the ambiguously charged *De mulieribus*.

It is interesting to note that even in the first translation of this collection Albanzani did not fail to make an addition to the original text—that is, he makes an attempt at closure by updating the biography of queen Giovanna of Naples. This addition, which brings the biography up to the death of the queen, demonstrates, albeit minimally at this stage, the malleability of Boccaccio's text. Moreover, Albanzani deconstructs the last chapter of the *De mulieribus claris* in order to expose its ideological underpinnings and encomiastic aspirations, openly criticizing Boccaccio's position, although fully aware of the forces that helped create it. His intervention perforce leads the reader to reflect on other 'hidden agendas' that may lie beneath the seemingly lucid structure of the *De mulieribus*. Albanzani is acute in his recognition of the pressures of patronage discernible in Boccaccio's chapter on queen Giovanna: "...with the greatest care he adorned the queen with marvellous praise so that this work should come into her hands."[5] The result was a falsification of the truth—a distortion which the translator aimed to correct, from an apparently disinterested perspective, by proceeding with an 'objective', historical narrative.[6] The translator's continuation of the chapter resembles Boccaccio's *De casibus* rather than the *De mulieribus* because it insists on linking political history to the notion of the reversals of fortune.[7]

Abanzani's text was not the only translation of Boccaccio's *De mulieribus claris*. Indeed, another fourteenth-century translation acquired greater authority when it became the basis of the first printed translation of the *De mulieribus* in the vernacular. Therefore, in 1506, Vincenzo Bagli appropriated a fourteenth-century translation by Antonio da S. Elpidio which had been rendered into Tuscan by Niccolò Sassetti. Bagli published this as his own in printed form.[8] Albanzani's late medieval translation was thus replaced by a 'newer' version which appeared more consonant with contemporary tastes in the vernacular. The appearance of a translation at this date would suggest a renewed interest not only in the *De mulieribus claris*, but in Boccaccio's works as a whole (Bembo's *Asolani* had been published in 1505). More particularly, there was a potential audience for a contemporary translation of the *De mulieribus*, due to the cultural expansion of the courts and the increasing success of a more militant vernacular literary 'movement'.

In the preface to his translation, Bagli creates a fantasy in which the long dead Boccaccio appears to him in a vision and instructs him to translate his Latin work. Equally, if not more importantly, the spectre tells him to whom the translation should be dedicated: "I desire that the work *Famous Women*, composed by me, be dedicated to madam Giovanna [Baglioni]."[9] Boccaccio's 'instructions' were taken up with alacrity, as can be seen from the result. The medieval writer's authority is reduced to that of a fictitious courtier-cum-adulator whose sole concern is the promotion of his translator's patron. The focus has decisively shifted from Boccaccio's historical research; history has been transformed into metaphor and ornamentation. The translator's message is clear: the translation of Boccaccio's Latin text can best serve as a repertoire of flattering parallels for a contemporary woman of note; the strategy also serves to foreclose more substantial and 'uneasy' interpretations of the text. Vincenzo Bagli's preface represents one of the more seductive readings (for Renaissance men) of the Boccaccian archetype; that is, the text is taken up as the supreme guidebook of courtly flattery directed in the first instance towards women. The preface to the early sixteenth-century translation paid exaggerated attention to only one element of a complex text, trying to ensure that the reader perceived Boccaccio's work as part of a strategy designed to institute a woman at the centre of a literary system.

Bagli's printed translation of *the De mulieribus claris* was current for the early sixteenth century. It was eventually replaced in 1545 by Giuseppe Betussi's translation.[10] In his dedication, Betussi explains that the new translation stemmed from his concern about the neglect of the work: "and I have put his work into the vernacular for no other reason than compassion for it, seeing it almost destroyed and completely dispersed without anyone bringing it together again."[11] Betussi was certainly referring to Bagli's early sixteenth-century version, which undoubtedly would have seemed linguistically old-fashioned in the wake of Bembo's linguistic revolution. Throughout the Renaissance, printed editions of Boccaccio's work had always been available in Latin, but Latin was predominantly the language of men. In his dedication, Betussi is at pains to point out that his ideal public consists of women.[12] This could be dismissed as a marketing ploy[13] directed towards expanding a female readership, rather than a new ideological position vis-à-vis women. Yet it does mark a significant change from the Boccaccian archetype within which the humanistic elements of the work were an important element of its appeal to male readers. Betussi's "addizione" [continuation] constitutes a large-scale addition to the core of Boccaccian women, which once again emphasizes the encomiastic possibilities of the archetype.[14]

The ethos of Bagli's 1506 preface and Betussi's dedication of 1545 was one very much in vogue in Renaissance society. It constitutes a normalization of the female subject in the context of the court where opportunity for the highest-born women was potentially greater than elsewhere in society. One of the advantages of rewriting the *De mulieribus claris* was that women were extremely visible in court society. The encomiastic element which was not accentuated in the original was transformed into one of the central aspects of the genre. It would be too easy to dismiss such manipulations as invalidating and ignoring the Latin text. Rather, these subsequent and altered emphases reveal the various mechanisms available for talking about women in the Renaissance, also highlighting the often precarious nature of this discourse.

The translations which also incorporated the lives of additional women in the versions of Betussi and later compilers such as Serdonati indicate that the pioneering work of Boccaccio in collecting female biographies from disparate sources was of less interest to the Reniassance reader than the possibilities for social advancement afforded by the *De mulieribus*. But, translations were not the only means by which the *De mulieribus* entered into dialogue with Italian Renaissance culture.

Collections of Biographies of Famous Women
as a Distinctive Genre

In the wake of Boccaccio's *De mulieribus claris*, the fascination of illustrious women for male writers reached its acme between the appearance of Antonio Cornazzano's poem *De mulieribus admirandis* of 1467 and the publication of Henricus Cornelius Agrippa's *De nobilitate et praecellentia foeminei sexus* [*On the Nobility and Superiority of the Female Sex*], published for the first time in 1529, but actually written twenty years previously. The choice of beginning and end, although to a degree arbitrary, illustrates the development of the collection of biographies of famous women, from predominantly narrative to increasingly discursive. It also highlights a geographical shift from local beginnings to European dissemination. Cornazzano's poem was never printed; its circulation was probably limited to those courts in which he was active, particularly Ferrara and Milan.

A similar story can be told for other texts in this genre: Bartolommeo Goggio *De laudibus mulierum* (1487); Sabadino degli Arienti, *Trattato della pudicizia* (1487), *Gynevera de le clare donne* (1489–90/92), *Elogio di Isabella* (1490s); Vespasiano da Bisticci, *Il libro delle lode e commendazione delle donne* (early 1490s); Jacobo Filippo Foresti, *De plurimis claris selectisque mulieribus* (1497); Agostino Strozzi, *Defensio mulierum* (composed in about 1500); Mario Equicola, *De mulieribus* (1501); Bernardino Cacciante,

Libro apologetico delle donne (1503–4); Galeazzo Flavio Capra, *Della eccellenza e dignità delle donne* (1525); Baldassar Castiglione, Book III of *Il libro del cortegiano* (published in 1528, but begun about 25 years earlier); Pompeo Colonna, *Apologia mulierum* (c. 1529). Foresti's collection of female biographies had a new lease of life when it was included in an anthology put together by Ravisius Textor, *De memorabilibus et claris mulieribus aliquot diversorum scriptorum opera*, published in Paris in 1521.

It is not the place here to trace the dissemination of the *De mulieribus claris* into European culture. It provided an increasingly distant model which was not exactly imitated, but reshaped sometimes almost beyond recognition. Chaucer's *Legend of Good Women*, for example, abandons the Latin prose of the *De mulieribus* for vernacular poetry and, in Italy, Antonio Cornazzano also experimented with a poetic version of the original.

The absence of women writers from the list is an obvious omission. But, the most systematic response to the *De mulieribus* was the work of Christine de Pizan who programmatically challenged the ambiguities and uncertainties of the earlier work for the purpose of creating a more coherent and more persuasively 'feminist' text. There is also at least one example of an Italian woman humanist engaged in re-thinking and re-using Boccaccio's illustrious women: Laura Cereta, a fifteenth-century Brescian humanist writer whose output is principally in the form of letters written expressly, it would seem, for publication. A letter entitled "Defence of the Liberal Instruction of Women" (January 13, 1488) represents a careful re-reading of the *De mulieribus*. The listing of mainly classical women assumes a position that is perhaps even more polemical than Christine de Pizan's.

Christine de Pizan had rewritten the basic structure of the *De mulieribus*, in common with every other Renaissance compiler of female biographies and treatises on women. In fact, no later biographer accepted the chronological structure Boccaccio imposed on his selection of famous women. Numerous systems were adopted to engage with the problem of 'ordering' the women, particularly according to criteria of moral themes or the special virtues of women. The open-endedness of the *De mulieribus* found no favour with Christine de Pizan who invented a structure so tight and controlled that it was at the opposite end of the spectrum from Boccaccio's work.

There is another noticeable feature that most writers adopt, the reduction in the number of biographies. Christine de Pizan was one of the few writers who produced a text that might be called substantial in the manner of the *De mulieribus*. The diminution in the number of women reflects in part a more focused interest in a specific number or category of women in order to advance a more tightly argued case.

Clearly this contrasts with Boccaccio's encyclopedic spread within which moral comments were scattered in a seemingly haphazard and unconnected manner. Even those writers who chose to include more *exempla* than Boccaccio did, for example, Foresti in his *De plurimis claris selectisque mulieribus*, ensure that there is a clear meta-narrative to the collection.

In the early sixteenth-century, one can note that increasing space was devoted to theoretical (philosophical, biological and social) issues in texts that could now be properly called treatises. We are dealing with hybrid texts that combined female biographies and discursive material bringing together arguments from a variety of sources in order to present a seemingly coherent revision of standard thought on women. Texts by Capra, Equicola, and Goggio are examples of this development. The *exempla* themselves were often abbreviated with respect to Boccaccio. They may have been well enough known to avoid a complete and detailed account. Further, the narrative thrust of the *exempla* in some cases conflicted with the discursive nature of the new organic treatise on woman so that to avoid a massive breakdown in the argument short *précis* of the narrative were employed. Thus, in the course of time, Italian treatises openly discussed more general issues, transforming the genre into a more discursive form which clarified or obfuscated the main issues to be drawn from the exemplary biographies.

Neither the originality of Boccaccio's project nor its difficulties should be underestimated. It placed humanism on the cutting edge of culture, putting itself forward as a tool for social analysis and at times implicitly contradicting the traditional teachings of the Church on women. Such audacity will not be repeated by many of the subsequent writers engaging with the genre, most of whom will re-introduce Christian figures to retain a sense of balance in a compromise with traditional authority. The greater or lesser presence of 'religious' women is often a sign of the extent of the text's adhesion to newer values emphasized in particular by those texts composed towards the end of the fifteenth century. Thus Bisticci's *Il libro delle lode e commendaztione delle donne* is monopolized by female martyrs, and is much closer to traditional hagiographical collections. On the other hand, Mario Equicola's *De mulieribus* hardly mentions martyrs or other Christian women. Indeed, these two works represent the two extremes of this literature on famous women: Equicola's *De mulieribus* is court-centred, and makes a weak excuse for not treating Christian women in more detail—possibly an indication that the work remained unfinished, but more likely a sign of the author's lack of interest in this material.

The biographers all have as their basic point of reference Boccaccio's *De mulieribus*. It is not viewed as a sacred text, but one that can be dismembered, vivisected and added to when necessary. As a starting point, it contained the material on to which other elements could be grafted according to the perspective of subsequent writers. In the later fifteenth century this other material included Plutarch's *Mulierum virtutes*, a major humanistic find of the period which had been unknown to Boccaccio. Although the number of women contracted in such works, the 'data base' was expanded and improved. A number of writers corrected Boccaccio's mistakes in the narration or added details of which he was not aware.

The post-Boccaccian writers were in a literal sense subversive: they often undermine the authority of Boccaccio by refiguring the personages treated by him placing divergent emphases on the same figures. They undermine some of the basic ideological structures of their society, through a process of rewriting its archetypal females. To take an extreme example, Bernardino Cacciante utterly rewrites Boccaccio's Cleopatra in his *Libretto apologetico delle donne*. Against the grain, he transforms her into an astute female politician who dies regretting her people's loss of liberty. This forms a powerful contrast to Boccaccio's Cleopatra who was exclusively defined by her lust both sexual and political.[15] Cacciante and others like him counter the prevailing attitudes and patterns that under-lie the representation of some of Boccaccio's illustrious women.[16] Cacciante may have been playing with the traditional view of Cleopatra, but by so doing he constructed an alternative model which challenged the prevailing stereotype. By presenting an alternative image of Cleopatra he laid bare the ideological mechanisms that create a stereo-type; he brought to the surface the arbitrary nature of its signification disrupting its apparent seamlessness and authority. Cacciante demon-strated that there was not one single inalienable view of historical events. History is subject to point of view, subjective reading of sources, empha-sis and de-emphasis. In short, it is an ideological exercise.

The re-elaboration and reappropriation of stereotypes is a crucial process in the long debate on women in the early modern period. If stereotypes offer a crude and negative picture of women, then part of the process of the 'discursive rehabilitation' of women must necessarily consist in replacing older stereotypes with newer more appropriate ones or bringing out the positive aspects of the more entrenched images of women. This will be a very long process and will concern writers for many centuries. It is notable that at the very end of the sixteenth cen-tury, Moderata Fonte in her *Il merito delle donne* subjects some of those *exempla* which had been circulating since Boccaccio's *De mulieribus* to a rigorous logical analysis in order to demonstrate the flimsiness of their ideology.[17] By the end of the sixteenth century numerous *exempla* had been used and re-used so often that they were able to be taken for granted. In the period with which I am concerned here the increasing emphasis on classical *exempla* , frequently cross-referenced to Boccaccio, provided these writers with the opportunity to re-tell a story and hence urge upon the reader a different ideological message, a different image of women. The classical *exempla* in particular allowed the writer to re-evaluate the Christian versions of exemplary women. The more radical writers with whom we are concerned achieved on occasion some displacement in meaning which served to produce a narrative shock, as in the case of Cacciante's Cleopatra, where the reader's expectations about her as a character are demolished and replaced with a positive revision, based on a re-reading of the same sources.

Boccaccio's Achievement in the *De mulieribus*

Boccaccio's *De mulieribus* is devised as a monument to developing humanist practice. It is both a tribute to Petrarch and a sign of the writer's own individuality. One of Boccaccio's undoubted sources for some of the women is the *Divina commedia*, a text venerated by Boccaccio, but less so by Petrarch. Extremely brief references in the poem are expanded into full biographies on the basis of Boccaccio's researches into the classical sources. In a sense, some of these biographies can be read as glosses and a number of them will be translated and find a place in the *Esposizioni*.

The *De mulieribus* bears witness to Boccaccio's hybrid interests, in particular to those achievements that he wishes to display in public—his knowledge of Greek culture or hitherto little used classical texts. It is a statement of his seriousness of a scholar *in fieri*. The *Genealogie* represents the culmination of a process that sees the literariness of the Latin works steadily give way to analytical procedures that valorize the recovery of the classical past using a systematic, 'historicist' methodology. If the *De casibus* still overtly displays itself as a literary construct with strong sermonizing tendencies, the *De mulieribus* marks the half-way point on the road to a 'scientific' evaluation of the past. It does not entirely give up a fondness for narrative, but it is increasingly based on some sort of analysis of the available documents, albeit at times quite primitive. There is some attempt to integrate in the one chapter historical analysis and moral teachings. The structure of the *De mulieribus* does not grant greater importance to the moral messages of the text than to historical reconstructions of female lives. The lack of a *cornice* perhaps suggests that it was as a historian that Boccaccio wanted to be judged. The *Genealogie* represents a more scholarly approach to its materials than the *De mulieribus*. It cites its sources more accurately, reduces the amount of narration, offers sophisticated reading strategies of the sources. The interest of the *De mulieribus*, in this respect, lies in its hybrid nature, in its effort to reconcile diverse tendencies in Boccaccio's writing without entirely relinquishing any of them: narrative, historical, and moral.

The representation of women in the *De muleribus* is enigmatic. The subjects of the individual biographies are under siege from the commentaries which either contradict the sense of the historical narrative or focus only on one particular aspect of the life story. The insistence on sexual purity together with the penchant for narrative suggests that the *De muleribus* was an attempt to over-write the *Decameron*, to eradicate natural sexuality and to demonize it. The biographies seem to open the horizons of their female and male readers to distant possibilities of public roles for women, only to shut them off. However, the text is far from systematic and allows loopholes to appear, fissures in its arguments. The elite audience to which the *De mulieribus* is addressed receives contradictory messages, but messages that can potentially subvert the Aristotelian assumptions on which the work is partially built. The very openness of the *De mulierbus* encouraged later writers to rethink women in a more focussed way either more radically or more conservatively. The *De mulieribus* claris is the foundation work in a genre that will be used to further the debate on women in early modern Europe.

·   ·   ·   ·   ·

𝔑otes

Introduction

1 The term 'biography' is used throughout the text in the knowledge that it is not wholly satisfactory. In English, it only came into use in the eighteenth century. The other term that has found favour with scholars, 'life-writing', is, in my view, even less satisfactory for the purposes of this book because it includes different sub-genres, such as autobiography. Perhaps the term 'life' could have been used but, there would have been some loss of the notion that these lives had been reconstructed by a male writer for ideological purposes. Therefore, to avoid cumbersome circumlocutions and awkward terminology, 'biography' will generally be utilized. The *De mulieribus claris*, as we shall see, can be regarded as a series of *exemplary* biographies which further complicates the issue. See Mayer and Woolf, *The Rhetorics of Life-Writing*, pp.1–26.

2 Müller suggests that the Christian martyr or the holy woman is replaced by the virginal artist/intellectual in the *De mulieribus* (*Ein Frauenbuch*, pp.137–38). However, it also means that Christian humanism, as proposed by Boccaccio, has replaced the ideal of passive suffering. The classical past is a source of knowledge no less valid than Christian writing although it has to be often hedged or modified by specific moralizing interventions in the text.

3 Jamieson defines the double bind as follows: "A double bind is a rhetorical construct that posits two and only two alternatives, one or both penalizing the person being offered them. In the history of humans, such choices have been constructed to deny women access to power and, where individuals manage to slip past their constraints, to undermine their exercise of whatever power they achieve" (pp.13–14).

4 *Writing a Woman's Life*, p.81. This view is shared to a large degree by Sommerville who states that "exceptional women were just exceptions to the normal rule" (*Sex and Subjection*, p.42), but she notes that female inferiority did not extend to all areas ("Virtually no early-modern theorist ever attempted to argue that all women were inferior to all males in every respect," p.40). These sentiments are also shared by Klapisch-Zuber: "*A contrario*, ces femmes exceptionnelles en droit et en fait rejettent d'autant plus lestement du côté de l'histoire immobile, ou plutôt de la non-histoire, leurs compagnes qui n'ont pas eu

la chance d'être sélectionnées par ce type d'hagiographie" ("Le médiéviste, la femme et le sériel," p.40). Koelsch is even more decisive: "the 'exceptional' woman is shown either to be not so exceptional...or really not to be a woman after all" ("Public and private," p.24). Gerda Lerner puts us on our guard concerning the category of outstanding women "because the bias of patriarchally framed selection has tended to make only those women 'notable' and 'worthy' who did what men did and what men recognize as important" (*The Creation of Feminist Consciousness*, p.16). Montagu argues against this position believing that in the mid-twentieth century, there were more women entering the public arena to make the exceptional woman redundant (*The Natural Superiority of Women*, p.20).

5 "Women on top," p.133. Davis acknowledges that such representations were unlikely to stir the "masses of people to resistance." She hypothesizes that "the exceptional woman-out-of-her-place enriched the fantasy of a few real women and might have emboldened them to exceptional action" (p.144). In the *De mulieribus claris*, Bocccaccio's concept of social rank means that the exceptional woman as a sociological construct was generally restricted to the nobility.

6 Cf. Maclean, *The Renaissance Notion of Woman*, p.63.

7 Jordan in her *Renaissance Feminism* remarks that the *De mulieribus claris* offers "an ambiguity that goes deeper than mere contradiction" (p.37). Bullough is more measured: "Ambivalence, however, was better than hostility, and Boccaccio represented a step forward over most of his contemporaries" (*The Subordinate Sex*, p.193).

8 Although Jordan states that "it would be a mistake to write it off merely as a cunning vilification of women, a sophisticated version of the misogynist side of the *querelle des femmes*" ("Boccaccio's in-famous women," p.26), this is precisely what Jordan does!

9 Meale, "Legends of good women in the European Middle Ages," p.60.

10 "Woman, space, and Renaissance discourse," p.168.

11 Cf. Glenn, who argues that "silence is more than the negative of not being permitted to speak, of being afraid to speak; it can be a deliberate, positive choice" (*Rhetoric Retold*, p.176).

12 Wayne, "Zenobia in medieval and Renaissance literature," p.61; "Woman, space, and Renaissance discourse," p.168.

13 "Il *Liber de claris mulieribus* di Giovanni Boccaccio. Parte prima," p.260.

14 "Il *Liber de claris mulieribus* di Giovanni Boccaccio. Parte prima," p.268. More recently, King, *Women of the Renaissance*, puts forward a rather backhanded defence of the *De mulieribus claris*: "He should not be blamed, *perhaps*, for the harm he unintentionally inflicted upon women with this set of portraits laden with misogynist elements" (p.182; my emphasis). She concludes that these biographies "could also serve the cause of female oppression" (p.183).

15 "Il *Liber de claris mulieribus* di Giovanni Boccaccio. Parte prima," p.268.

16 *Boccaccio*, pp.249, 251. A similar, but more understated, approach is to be found in McLeod, *Virtue and Venom*, who states that "*De claris mulieribus* is very much a mixed bag" (p.6). This point is later expanded with the suggestion that although there is a strong "misogynistic pattern" to the book, there are "some interesting deviations" (p.78); "it is one of the first catalogs of women since antiquity to posit feminine fame based on women's deeds" (p.79).

17 Buettner also employs the term "ambivalent" in connection with the *De mulieribus claris*' stance on the position of women in society (*Boccaccio's Des cleres et nobles femmes*, p.18).

18 See, for example, Hortis, *Studj sulle opere latine del Boccaccio*, pp.69–116; Hauvette, *Boccace*, pp.396–413; De Nolhac, "Boccace et Tacite"; Coulter, "Boccaccio's acquaintance with Homer."

19 Ricci, "Studi sulle opere latine e volgari del Boccaccio", pp.3–21.

20 See, for example, his "Boccaccio e Tacito."

21 Typical from this point of view is Bruni, *Boccaccio. L'invenzione della letteratura mezzana*, who claims that there is a "mancanza di interesse politico" on the part of the writer (p.461), whether sexual or institutional politics. Aurigemma argues against this view, suggesting that the *De mulieribus claris* hosts "una civile conversazione" ("Boccaccio e la storia," p.85). The same scholar attempts a survey of the text's attitude towards women and concludes that Boccaccio's contradictory attitude towards women is constituted by his belief in natural principles and the potential women have of overcoming their nature ("Boccaccio e la storia," pp.90–91).

22 Cerbo, "Il *De mulieribus claris* di Giovanni Boccaccio," pp.55–56, 62, 65 and *Ideologia e retorica*, p.51. In Cerbo's interpretation the religious tendencies of the text are exemplified in the figure of the poet Proba. Again we see the dangers of summarizing the work through a single biography.

23 *Reading Dido*, p.68, Delany expresses a divergent view of the *De mulieribus claris*: "Boccaccio too undertook to rewrite woman better, if not entirely good, and to redress the imbalance produced by misogynistic literature" ("Rewriting woman good," p.88).

24 The critical material is now abundant. For the purposes of this study the following have been found useful: Groag Bell, "Christine de Pizan (1364–1430): Humanism and the problem of a studious woman," pp.173–84; Gottlieb, "The problem of feminism in the fifteenth century," pp.337–64. Gottlieb argues that ventures into the *querelle des femmes* by men were little more than a "literary game" connected with their hopes for patronage from powerful women (p.357).

25 See Jeanroy, "Boccace, Christine de Pizan.," pp.93–105; Bozzolo, "Il *Decameron* come fonte del *Livre de la cité des dames*," pp.3–24; Phillippy, "Establishing authority: Boccaccio's *De claris mulieribus* and Christine de Pizan's *Le livre de la cité des dames* ," pp.167–194; Quilligan, "Translating dismemberment: Boccaccio and Christine de Pizan," pp.253–66; Stecopoulos, "Christine de Pizan's *Livre de la cité des dames*: The Reconstruction of myth" in *Reinterpreting Christine de Pizan*, pp.48–62.

26 See, for example, Stecopoulos, who maintains the view that "Boccaccio is subverted [by Christine]: his peculiar illustriousness of women—of certain women which, somewhat ambiguously, he presents as exemplary (but to what end?), is reinterpreted as something not at all peculiar, but rather necessary and true. Christine's women are real actors in the drama of human history" (p. 51). See also the comments of Brown-Grant, "Bien loin de célébrer les femmes, Boccace en fait une critique, subtile mais acérée" ("Des hommes et des femmes illustres," pp.473, 475) and Barricelli, "Satire of satire," p.103. Even stronger is the reaction of Meale who claims that the *De mulieribus claris* "is a deeply misogynistic work" ("Legends of good women," p.61). Robin goes even further, calling the work "exaggeratedly misogynistic" ("Woman, space, and Renaissance dis-

course," p.167). One begins to wonder about the use of "misogynistic" which seems to be employed as a blanket term to convey a sense of moral condemnation of Boccaccio's textual strategy. Cf. Arjava, "Jerome and women" p.5. Quilligan states the case with startling clarity: "the variations between Christine's and Boccaccio's versions of these stories is due not so much to historical period as more specifically to gender" ("Translating dismemberment," p.256). Gender, therefore, is considered a transcendent, ahistorical entity which ensures that the male is labelled as negative.

27 Stecopoulos refers to Boccaccio's "'authorial' misogyny" (p. 49). Kellogg outlines the basic difference in the treatment of mythological figures in both works to the detriment of the male writer ("Christine de Pizan and Boccaccio," p.127). A slightly more nuanced view of Boccaccio's work is expressed by Slerca, "Dante, Boccace, et le *Livre de la cité des dames*," p.223.

28 See Blamires, *The Case for Women*, pp.234–40. Blamires' comparison of Boccaccio and de Pizan sees the latter transcending "the grudgingness of Boccaccio's presentation of 'famous 'women'" (p.182). His statement is qualified by the recognition of the ideological obstacles to a feminist position for *both* writers. Although Blamires maintains the contrastive approach, he does delineate in general terms in his conclusion the limits of medieval feminism and the strengths of an approach which was adopted by, amongst others, Boccaccio.

29 See Newman, "On the ethics of feminist historiography," p.705.

30 See Blanchard, "Compilation and legitimation in the fifteenth century," p.240. Blanchard gives this biography as an example of "reduction" (p.240), allowing Christine de Pizan to concentrate on Semiramis as a ruler. Reduction has a political aspect that Blanchard alludes to only indirectly; it silences those elements of the Boccaccian discourse that make the women less than perfect. It is a methodical process, so in this sense we can talk about a program which proposes a positive image for women, opposing the flawed picture of Semiramis in the *De mulieribus*. Christine de Pizan represses sexuality in the Assyrian queen to free her from the traditional construct of a woman prey to her sexual desire.

31 Cf. Ames, "The feminist connections of Chaucer's *Legend of Good Women*," pp.69–70 and Delany, "Rewriting woman good," pp.86–88. While Christine de Pizan and Chaucer abbreviate and omit details in their female biographies, Boccaccio expands and amplifies, providing divergent accounts of the same events.

32 See, for example, Blanchard, "Compilation and legitimation," pp.237–40.

33 Cf. Brownlee, "Martyrdom and the female voice," pp.115–35.

34 Leaena in the *De mulieribus claris* bit off her tongue too, but did not spit it back in the tyrant's face ("she bit down sharply on her tongue, severed it, and spat it out" [*FW* 207]). Although a pagan, Leaena's story resembles many tales of martyrdom. Boccaccio's choice of Leaena illustrates the limitations of pagan female virtue and courage. The fact that she was a courtesan lends a certain ambiguity to her actions. Indeed she goes against the grain of most of Boccaccio's heroines in that she is not of noble birth ("in order to show that a noble spirit is not always connected to grand titles only, and that virtue does not scorn anyone who desires it" [*FW* 205]). Her promiscuity is a sign of her paganism to be implicitly contrasted with the virginal purity of a Christian martyr. That Leaena remains silent is again ambiguous. She breaks with the stereotype of the garrulous woman, defining herself as in control of the situation. To speak would have

meant betrayal of her co-conspirators. The emphasis on silence shows a positive side to female behaviour, but does not move into a more active role similar to the one performed by Saint Christine who significantly turns back her oppression against the oppressor. Cf. Benson, *The Invention of the Renaissance Woman*, p.26. Christine Reno notes that the narrative of Saint Christine is the longest because of the author's additions to the account found in the *Golden Legend*. The added material emphasizes the confrontation of the saint with the forces of patriarchy ("Christine de Pisan's use of the *Golden Legend*," pp.93–94).

35 See Anson, "The female transvestite in early monasticism," pp.1–32; Warner, *Joan of Arc. The Image of Female Heroism*, pp.145–55.

36 Cf. Willard, "The manuscript tradition of the *Livre des trois vertus*," pp.440–41.

37 See Blanchard, "Compilation and legitimation," pp.228–249. Blanchard's interpretation is one of the few that question the work's 'feminist' credentials: he views it as an "alibi to speak more freely of something else: the book as such" (p.230).

38 *The Invention of the Renaissance Woman*, p.18. At times, Benson seems to withdraw from a such a forceful, positive reading: "the moral independence of the individual women does not upset the conventional hierarchy of society, and, thus, the *De mulieribus* can be said to be conservative although not antifeminist" (p.21). Smarr also recognizes that Boccaccio is capable of "radical exhortations" even if equality between the sexes is not a given in the text ("Boccaccio and Renaissance women," p.281).

I. Shaping the Text: Formation of the *De mulieribus claris*

1 See Ricci, "Un autografo del *De mulieribus claris*" in his *Studi sulla vita e le opere del Boccaccio*, pp.115–24, and in the same volume, "Le fasi redazionali del *De mulieribus claris*," pp.125–35. For necessary clarifications and corrections to Ricci's hypotheses, see Zaccaria, "Le fasi redazionali del *De mulieribus*," pp.293–95, 323–32, and Zappacosta-Zacccaria, "Per il testo del *De mulieribus claris*," pp.239–70.

2 Ricci, "Le fasi," pp.132–34 and Zaccaria, "Le fasi," p.293. See Müller for a comparison of the two positions (*Ein Frauenbuch*, pp.18–21).

3 Zaccaria, "Le fasi," p.293. For a listing of the women in Group (i) see Ricci, "Studi sulle opere latine e volgari del Boccaccio," pp.3–32; p.13n; Group (ii) consists of the following biographies in the order they appeared in the first redaction: Opis, Juno, Venus, Medusa, Niobe, Pocris, Argia, Manto, Hypsipyle, Gaia Cyrilla, Megulia, Claudia, Busa, Tertia Emilia, Curia, Sulpicia, Epicharis, Pompeia Paulina, Triaria, Proba, Constantia; Group (iii) Sabina Poppaea, Rhea Ilia, "Romana iuvencula," wife of Orgiago, Hypermestra, Thisbe.

4 Ricci, "Le fasi," pp.130–32, and Zaccaria, "Le fasi," 293–94. On Acciaiuoli consult Léonard, 'Acciaiuoli, Niccolò' in *DBI*, vol.1, pp.87–90, with an extensive bibliography. See also Ugurgieri della Berardenga, *Gli Acciaioli di Firenze nella luce dei loro tempi (1160–1834)*, vol.1, pp.203–317.

5 See Zaccaria, "Le fasi redazionali," pp.254, 293–95. The new commentaries are in chapters XXVI, XXVII, LI, and LXXVII.

6 The probable source for Boccaccio's biography is the Eusebius-Jerome *Chronicon*: "Huius [Cornificius] soror Cornificia, cuius insignia extant epigrammata" (241 F; p.159). The extreme brevity of the entry did not prevent Boccaccio from transforming it into a paean to the female poet.

7 Ricci does not distinguish between the various additions, having them all belong to the same phase ("Le fasi," p.127); Zaccaria, on the other hand, introduces a subdivision into Ricci's chronology, separating them into stages 5 and 6 according to his classification ("Le fasi," pp.323–24).

8 See also Ricci, "Studi," p.14n. Ricci refers to the elimination of doubles, the removal of unsuitable material, for example, Circe's love for Glaucus.

9 The women are "Martia Catonis, Cornelia Pompei, Calpurnia Cesaris dictatoris" (*DMC* 557).

10 Bibl. Laurenziana, Florence , Ms. 90 sup. 98. See Ricci, "Un autografo del *De mulieribus claris*," pp.3–12 and Zaccaria, "Le fasi," p.253.

11 "Non enim est animus michi hoc claritatis nomen adeo strictim summere, ut semper in virtutem videatur exire" (*DMC* 24).

12 The occasional Christian woman may be mentioned in support of a point as in chapter CIV where Elizabeth, the mother of John the Baptist, is praised for having given birth to her son at an advanced age.

13 *DMC* 38 and *Genealogie*, I, viii; pp.110–113.

14 *Genealogie*, I, viii; p.110 ("non nulli volunt").

15 *Genealogie*, IV, i; pp.366–369.

16 "fraus et decipula demonum," "et apud inferos alligata" (*DMC* 40). The cult of Juno (IV) spread "through the persuasion of the Enemy of humankind" [*FW* 29]. In Isis' biography, a similar sentiment is expressed: "fallente ignaros dyabolo" (*DMC* 58).

17 Zaccaria believes that the texts have two distinct methodologies: "narrativo-moraleggiante nel *De mulieribus*, erudito-mitografica nelle *Genealogie*" (*Gen.*, VII, p.17). As my discussion will make clear, the distinction is not so well-defined or adhered to in all cases.

18 "quod plurimi arbitrantur imitari mens est" (*DMC* 56). Cf. "Et sic de patre et matre huius inter se discrepant autore; ego autem vulgatiorem secutus" (*Genealogie*, II, xix; p.222).

19 *FW* 49.

20 The analysis takes the form of "qui...alii....et qui..." (*DMC* 60).

21 See Romano, "Invenzione e fonti nella *Genealogia* del Boccaccio," p.165.

22 To these goddesses can be added Europa (IX) and Lybia (X) whose names were given to geographical areas as an expression of the human power to conquer and civilize.

23 "Sane huius discordantie ego non curo, dum modo constet Floran meretricem et divitem extitisse" (*DMC* 258). Boccaccio devotes most space to a "lepidam et ridiculam..hystoriam" (*DMC* 256–58) which recounts how Flora became so rich. The account is peppered with phrases like "nam alii dicunt," "alii vero" (*DMC* 256), "verum sunt qui dicant" (*DMC* 258). The purpose of the alternative versions is to stress how unlike a goddess was Flora's behaviour, especially as recounted by Ovid.

24 *FW* 443 ("imperandi avida"; *DMC* 418). The Empress gained control through "femineo quodam astu" (*DMC* 418), a key element in a number of biographies (e.g. Semiramis) where it forms the vital link between women and power since

the normal outlets have been denied them. It has negative resonances (under-hand cunning associated with the feminine) and contrasts with the more male-oriented *ingenium* which appears to win the approval of the writer.

25 *FW*443; *DMC* 420). The use of the adjective "clara" to describe the ruler is sig-nificant here (she is also referred to as "clara mulier" [*DMC* 422]). It underlines the success of her reign and seems to suggest that it was faultless and is judged by one of the basic Roman political and humanistic values. Yet, by reference to the title of the book in which the biography appears, it takes on more ambigu-ous hues. Her fame also includes the fierce struggle with her son, something that could not add to her reputation as a good ruler.

26 *FW* 443 ("per decennium egregie imperio presedit"; *DMC* 418).

27 *FW* 445 ("nepharius homo"; *DMC* 422).

28 Arachne is briefly mentioned in the biography of Minerva (VI) with regard to the "famous contest that she had with Arachne of Colophon" (*FW* 37). It is noticeable that Boccaccio does not make any reference to the chapter on Arachne at this point, something he would have done in the *Genealogie*.

29 "seu quesita studiis, seu Dei dono, seu potius dyabolica fraude" (*DMC* 142). The pagan spirit of divination in Cassandra and Manto marks a contrast with the two Sibyls.

30 On three occasions Boccaccio refers to her worth: "meritum" (*DMC* 94), "meruerit" (*DMC* 94), "quibus meritis" (*DMC* 96).

31 See the *Natural History*, XXV, 147–48, where the briefest details are provided. Under the rubric "pinxere et mulieres" Pliny the Elder lists six female painters of whom Boccaccio mentions Timarete [LVI], Yrene [LIX], and Iaia [LXVI] (whom Boccaccio calls, perhaps because of a misunderstanding, "Martia Varronis"). The latter receives the most extensive treatment in Pliny from whom Boccaccio takes some of his details. See also *Textes grecs et latins à l'his-toire de la peinture ancienne*, p.168 n.161, p.172, n.170.

32 In the chapter on Circe in the *Genealogie* Boccaccio states: "Homerus autem in Odyssea dicit...." (Liber IV, XIV, p.400).

33 Boccaccio puts the position succinctly in the *Genealogie*: "after he had van-quished other monsters, he succumbed to the love of a woman" ("nam cum cetera superasset monstra, amori muliebri succubuit" [Liber XIII, I, p.1276]). Hercules exemplifies the position concisely described by Phyllis Rackin; "a man effeminated by passion for a woman suffered a double degradation, the enslavement of his higher reason by his base, bodily appetites, and the subjec-tion of the superior sex to the inferior one" ("Historical difference/Sexual dif-ference," p.41).

34 On the Thisbe episode see Vecchiolino, "Due modi di narrare," pp.655–77. Boccaccio may also have known the anonymous *lai* of Pyramus and Thisbe inserted in the *Ovide moralisé* (Delany, "The naked text," pp.276–77, 291).

35 "'invide' dicebant 'paries, quid amantibus obstas?'" (*Metamorphoses*, IV, 73; p.182).

36 "Her prayers touched the gods and touched the parents; for the colour of the mulberry fruit is dark red when it is ripe, and all that remained from both funeral pyres rests in a common urn" ("vota tamen tetigere deos, tetigere par-entes;/nam color in pomo est, ubi permaturuit, ater,/quodque rogis superest, una requiescit in urna." (*Metamorphoses*, IV, 164–66; p.190)

37　For this biography's relationship to the narrative of the *Decameron* see Vecchiolino, "Due modi di narrare," pp.668–74.

38　*FW* 55 ("infelicis amoris exitu"; *DMC* 66).

39　*Decameron*, tr. McWilliam, p.331 ("e loro, li quali Amor vivi non aveva potuti congiugnere, la morte congiunse con inseparabile compagnia"; *Decameron*, p.417).

40　"In time love grew, and they would have been joined in marriage, too, but their parents forbade" ("tempore crevit amor; taedae quoque iure coissent,/sed vetuere patres...," *Metamorphoses*, IV, 60–61). Boccaccio makes very little of this theme in his version.

41　*FW* 61 ("Immoderati vigoris est cupidinis passio et adolescentium fere pestis et comune flagitium, in quibus edepol patienti animo tolleranda est"; *DMC* 70). The use of the term "pestilence" is interesting here since it indirectly forges a link with the *Decameron*. Passion creates social chaos in the *DMC*, and hence the need to see it usefully channelled. See Levenstein, "Out of bounds," pp.314, 317. In the *Decameron* (II, vi) Currado defends his behaviour by asking that his youthfulness be excused: "Se i vecchi si volessero ricordare d'essere stati giovani e gli altrui difetti con li lor misurare e li lor con gli altrui..." (*Decameron*, p.152).

42　At the end of the chapter on Cephalus in the *Genealogie*, Boccaccio refers to the opinion of Hyginus that the goddess in the story was in fact a woman: "Quod et Theodontius arbitratur, et sic erit hystoria et non fictio quod narratur" (XIII, LXV; p.1342). This could partially explain why Boccaccio included the account in a predominantly historical work.

43　..."ego Procrin amabam;/pectore Procris erat, Procris mihi semper in ore" (*Metamorphoses*, VII, 707–708). Pocris is mentioned by Virgil as one of Dido's companions in the nether world (see Perret, "Les compagnes de Didon," p.249 and Gera, *Warrior Women*, pp.49–53).

44　*FW* 113. The compassion expressed by Cephalus for Pocris in the Ovidian version is absent in Boccaccio. There is no admission by the husband that he would have sinned in the same way ("I too might have yielded in the same way under the temptation of gifts, if so great gifts were offered to me [*Metam.* VII, 748–49]). In the Ovidian version the couple live "sweet years together in harmony" (*Metam.*, VII, 752) after the incident. This does not happen in the *De mulieribus* where guilt destroys the marriage.

II. Boccaccio the Humanist

1　For an analysis of Boccaccio's Greek sources see Müller, *Ein Frauenbuch des Frühen Humanismus*, pp.62–65.

2　See Zaccaria, "Presenze del Petrarca," pp.251–52.

3　Cf. Miglio, "Boccaccio biografo," p.151.

4　The biography of Semiramis may be read in de Nolhac, "Le *De viris illustribus* de Pétrarque," pp.119–21. Petrarch's biography offers numerous similarities to Boccaccio's in the *De mulieribus claris*. Both have a bi-partite structure in which Semiramis' military achievements are balanced against her sexual depravity, described in greater detail by Boccaccio who employs a wider range of sources, whereas Petrarch concentrates on the incestuous relationship with her son, Ninyas. Similar language is used to describe Semiramis' great deception, "mentito sexu," "astu mirabili." Indeed, both biographies include the same material except that Boccaccio investigates Semiramis' ancestors in accordance with the schema of the *De mulieribus*. Petrarch includes a final paragraph which attempts to justify her inclusion in the *De viris*. See Martellotti, "Storiografia del Petrarca," pp.179–87. For the 'final' version of the *De viris*, see Petrarca, *Prose*, pp.217–267 for extracts and for the critical edition see *De viris illustribus*, vol.1, edizione critica per cura di Guido Martellotti. See also Petrarca, *La vita di Scipione l'Africano*, p.18. It is to be noted that Petrarch does occasionally include a non-Roman in the final version, but usually someone who struggled against Rome, such as Hannibal. See also Aurigemma, "La concezione storica del Petrarca," pp.368–69.

5 "Illustres itaque viros, quos excellenti quadam gloria floruisse doctissimorum hominum ingenia memorie tradiderunt, eorumque laudes, quas in diversis libris tanquam sparsas ac disseminatas inveni, colligere locum in unum et quasi quodammodo constipare arbitratus sum" (*Prose*, p.218). On the fundamental characteristics of Petrarch's historical writing see Donato, "Gli eroi romani," pp.114–115.

6 Petrarch is specific about the type of narrative history he is writing, emphasizing its closure to elements that might disturb its smooth surface: ..."temerariam et inutilem diligentiam eorum fugiendam putavi, qui omnium historicorum verba relegentes, nequid omnino pretermisisse videantur, dum unus alteri adversatur, omnem historie sue textum nubilosis ambagibus et inenodabilibus laqueis involverunt" (*Prose*, p.220).

7 On the ideological problems of the text see Jordan, *Renaissance Feminism*, pp.35–40, and Kolsky, "La costituzione di una nuova figura femminile letteraria," pp.43–44. Benson, *The Invention of the Renaissance Woman*, also notes these contradictions, pinpointing their source in the notion that Boccaccio wrote "a profeminist text without political consequences" (p.9). It is debatable whether any text is without "political consequences." Benson argues that Boccaccio "never directly advocates social change" (p.9). This is certainly a negative from a post-feminist perspective. However, what kind of change could the writer have advocated? Perhaps the change we should be seeking is not so much in a social program, rather in questioning and extending the range of female stereotypes to include learned women, politicians, and so on.

8 Hic enim, nisi fallor, fructuosus historici finis est, illa prosequi que vel sectanda legentibus vel fugienda sunt, ut in utranque partem copia suppetat illustrium exemplorum (Petrarca, *Prose*, p.224). Cf. Aurigemma, "La concezione storica del Petrarca," p.366. *Rerum familiarum*, 6.4, is a defence of the exemplary method. See Morse, "The exemplary Griselda," pp.59–60

9 Petrarch states clearly that his reason for including particular people in the collection is based on whether the subject has performed noteworthy acts: "Illos inquam viros describere pollicitus sum quos *illustres* vocamus, quorum pleraque *magnifica* atque *illustria* memorantur, quanquam aliqua obscura sint" (*Prose*, p.222; my emphases). This theoretical model is partially followed in the *De mulieribus* in that Boccaccio generally focuses on a particular moment, or sometimes a series of events, which will characterize the woman's achievement—except that noteworthy can also possess negative connotations for the

women included in the collection. Petrarch employs a term, "illustre," to describe the achievements of his heroes that has nothing ambiguous about it. Boccaccio's emphasis is different: "clarus" emphasizes the archeological act of discovery and re-discovery of women who deserve to be known through some action, whether positive or negative. "Illustre" automatically conveys a sense of glorious achievement in male-dominated, public activities. Therefore, the adjective implies ideological presuppositions about what constitutes valid actions by men (the defence of the state, military valour, and the like), relegating women to near invisibility.

10 "veram et excelsam gloriam" (*Prose*, p.238). On another occasion in his life of Scipio, Petrarch further elucidates the concept of glory: "cuius quidem glorie solius cupidum fuisse reperio, eiusque non aliter quam ut mala cessaret ambitio" (*Prose*, p.244).

11 Petrarch describes Scipio's physical appearance as follows: "forma illi rara et excellens, neque femineus sed virilis cultus atque habitus militaris" (*Prose*, p.248). Part of Petrarch's programme is to offer a positive example of Roman *gloria* in order to contrast it with contemporary male behaviour. For a full discussion of Scipio and the implications for Petrarch's thought see Bernardo, *Petrarch, Scipio and the 'Africa,'* pp.11–46.

12 Cf. Boccaccio's remarks in the preface that the "illustrious men" (*FW* 11; "viros illustres") can also be negative exemplars, but unlike the women he mentions their vices are not primarily sexual resulting from personal relationships. The 'good' women are identified solely by their sexual purity and the 'bad' by the lack of restraint. The 'bad' men are bad in a variety of ways as can be seen from the adjectives to describe their misdeeds: "turbulent," "sly," "treacherous," and so on (*FW* 11). The writer's usage of "clarus" and "illustre" underscores the key role gender differences play in the definition of fame. The preface does not do justice to the complexities of the text which expands the rigid definition of female reputation. The writer may have been concerned to present a traditional version of female heroism in order to reassure the male reader. Boccaccio seems to be referring specifically to the *De viris* as a model for his own text (*FW* 11; para. 6).

13 Constance Jordan's statement that "the principal text that served as Boccaccio's model [was] Plutarch's *Mulierum virtutes*" (*Renaissance Feminism*, p.37 n.43) is totally without foundation. There is no evidence from a comparative analysis of both texts that Boccaccio knew Plutarch's work on women. The Latin translation had considerable impact on *later* writers on women, expanding their supply of exemplary material.

14 The text of the letter [*Familiarum rerum* XXI 8] is in Petrarca, *Le familiari*, vol.IV, Liber vicesimus primus, 8, pp.61–68 and Petrarca, *Opere*, pp.1098–1104. For the dating of the letter consult Wilkins, *The Prose Letters of Petrarch*, p.84 and *Idem*, *Petrarch's Eight Years in Milan*, p.166. See also Müller, *Ein Frauenbuch*, pp.27–28; Kolsky, "La costituzione di una nuova figura femminile letteraria," pp.36–41.

15 Petrarch is absolutely clear about the relative failure of the Empress: "Neque vero tuum hoc et meum et comune gaudium imminuat, quod primus tibi femineus partus est, nam ut sapientibus placet; sepe principium debile melior fortuna prosequitur" (*Opere*, p.1099).

16 "Ad Annam imperatricem, responsio congratulatoria super eius femineo licet partu et ob id ipsum multa de laudibus feminarum" (*Opere*, p.1098).

17 Another of Petrarch's works, the *Rerum memorandum libri*, is a conscious imitation of Valerius Maximus. See also Casella, *Tra Boccaccio e Petrarca*, pp.67–88.

18 The women that appear in both works are as follows in the order of the Petrarchan epistle (the chapter number in brackets refers to the *De mulieribus claris*): Minerva [VI], Isis [VIII], Carmenta/Nicostrata [XXVII], Sappho [XLVII], Proba [XCVII], the Sibyls [Erythraea, XXI; Almathea, XXVI], Orithya [XIX–XX], Penthesilea [XXXII], Camilla [XXXIX], Hypsicratea [LXXVIII], the women of the Cimbrians [LXXX], Semiramis [II], Tamyris [XLIX], Cleopatra [LXXXVIII], Zenobia [C], 'romana iuvencula' [LXV], the wives of the Minyans [XXXI], Dido [XLII], Europa [IX], Libia [X], Manto [XXX], Lavinia [XLI], Lucretia [XLVIII], Cloelia [LII], Portia [LXXXII]. Of the classical women mentioned by Petrarch, Boccaccio does not devote chapters to Cornelia Martia, daughter of Cato nor to the unknown woman who suckled her father. The other exceptions are the Old Testament figures of Judith, the wives and concubines of Abraham, and the early medieval Matilde of Canossa.

19 Proba recounted in Virgilian and Homeric verses "mundi originem et fortunas patrum et Cristi adventum historiamque" (*Opere*, p.1099). The Sibyls, none of whom is mentioned by name, are described as "divinas feminas et prescias futurorum et divini consilii conscias" (p.1099) because they foretold the coming of Christ.

20 "cuius facti testis statua eodem illo festinantis regine habitu multis seculis in ea urbe permansit" (*Opere*, p.1100).

21 "Quid vero nunc romanas eloquar matronas, quibus nichil honestius habuit, nichil candidius orbis terre?" (*Opere*, p.1102).

22 Hypsicratea is an example of wifely loyalty rather than of a woman who takes up arms and goes to war with her husband. Tamyris defeated Cyrus, driven on by the thought of revenge for her son "inque filii vindictam et solamen" (*Opere*, p.1100). On occasion, the identification of such women in the text emphasizes their function in the patriarchal system: Carmenta is immediately defined as 'Evandri regis mater' (p.1099) and Proba as 'Adelphi uxor' (p.1099). Cornelia is described both as 'Africani filiam' and Gracchorum matrem' (p.1103).

23 "[Zenobia] mulier fidutie ingentis clarissimeque virtutis, inter cetera—quod Cleopatre defuit—castitatis eximie"(*Opere*, p.1101).

24 "viriles quoque animos concussuram" (*Opere*, p.1103).

25 "Nam cuius, oro, animum spectacula illa non flecterent, iuvenis nate ubera famelica mater anus, sed multo maxime inedia confectus et senio sugens pater?" (*Opere*, p.1101).

26 "Multas sciens volensque pretereo precipue tibi notissimas e virginibus nostris, que non pro terrenis affectibus sed pro pietate pro veritate pro castitate pro fide pro eterne vite desiderio, teneris corporibus fortibus animis dura tulere supplicia, duras mortes" (*Opere*, p.1103).

27 The two sets of *exempla* follow one another and are considered one unit: "Quis non legit israeliticum populum et duarum unius viri coniugum totidemque sponsalium ancillarum fecunditate progenitum, et unius vidue constantia liberatum, ducis hostium caput in gremio referentis?" (*Opere*, p.1102). The first example fits into the thematic grouping of female founders of Empires, countries and cities; the second slightly less easily since it deals not with the foundation of a culture or of a political entity, but its salvation. It is an indication of the

attraction of the Judith story that Petrarch includes it in his list. On Judith see Ciletti, "Patriarchal ideology in the Renaissance iconography of Judith," p.60.

28 This example may not have seemed a terribly apt one to address to the wife of the Holy Roman Emperor since Matilde was involved in a long struggle against Henry IV on behalf of the papacy, but may have carried a suggestion to her husband about his future politics.

29 "virili animo" (*Opere*, p.1101).

30 "profusam et plusquam femineam largitatem" (p.1101).

31 On the importance of Valerius Maximus for the medieval *exemplum* see Battaglia, *La coscienza letteraria*, pp.463–67; Le Goff, "L'*exemplum*," p.4.

32 The *exempla* taken from Valerius Maximus are: Semiramis, the wives of the Minyans, the wives of the Cimbrians, Tamyris, Cloelia, Harmonia, Berenice, Busa, the wife of Orgiago, Tertia Aemilia, Dripetine, Sempronia, Hypsicratea, Hippo, Megullia Dotata, Veturia, Artemisia, Claudia, the "romana iuvencula," Lucretia, Virginia, Julia, Portia, Curia, Hortensia, Sulpicia [wife of Fulvius Flaccus], Sulpicia [wife of Lentulus Truscellio], Antonia.
The nine books each have a general theme with various sub-categories related to the principal subject. For example, the first book deals with religion and associated phenomena, such as prodigies and prognostications.

33 For example, in VI, 3, Pontius Aufidianus kills not only the tutor who deflowered his unnamed daughter, but the daughter as well. The anecdote, perhaps a poor copy of the Virginia episode, is not corroborated in Livy, and lacks any telling details. Some of the *exempla* in Valerius Maximus descend into the absurd and would have served Boccaccio's purpose well had his intention been to openly and viciously denigrate women. For example, the unnamed wife of Egnatius Mecenius was whipped by him until she died because he had seen her drinking! [VI, 3, 9]

34 The Roman *exempla* are Lucretia [VI, 1, 1], Virginia [VI, 1, 2]; the foreign women are Hippo [VI, 1, ext. 1], the wife of Orgiago [VI, 1, ext. 2], the wives of the Teutons [VI, 1, ext. 3].

35 The chapter on conjugal love ["De amore coniugali"] displays a similar pattern: two out of five Roman examples are taken up in the *De mulieribus* (Julia [IV, 6, 4], Portia [IV, 6, 5]) and all three of the 'foreign' wives (Artemisia, Hypsicratea, the women of the Minyans [IV, 6, ext. 1–3]).

36 Valerius Maximus provides the case of Antonia [IV, 3, 3] as the example *par excellence* of the virtuous widow who, although in the flower of youth, never remarried. In this he is followed by Boccaccio.

37 "Quid feminae cum contione? Si patrius mos servetur, nihil" (III, 8, 6). Valerius Maximus regards Sempronia as very much the exception to the general rule of non-interference by women in men's (public) affairs. For the writer, she is indicative of a crisis in Roman society that can only be resolved by a return to traditional values.

38 "cuius si virilis sexus posteri vim sequi voluissent, Hortensianae eloquentiae tanta hereditas una feminae actione abscissa non esset" (VIII, 3, 3; p.556). In his own chapter on Hortensia, Boccaccio chose to follow Valerius Maximus' final remarks to stress the lack of virility of later men. See Hallett, "Women as *same* and *other*," pp.62, 66 and Jamieson, *Beyond the Double Bind*, p.92.

39 Valerius Maximus uses a similar strategy in treating Busa [IV, 8, 2] who aided the Roman survivors after the battle of Cannae. She is contrasted unfavourably

with Fabius Maximus [IV, 8, 1] who sold his only property for the good of the state, whereas Busa used only a fraction of her wealth. Boccaccio does not follow this line of argument, but does compare her action with that of a man (Alexander), probably at Valerius Maximus' suggestion. Boccaccio's male point of reference is ambiguously to Busa's advantage as it brings out the special quality of her generosity—the fact that she was able to overcome the perceived shortcomings of female nature: "Alexander was a man; Busa, a woman, and stinginess is as habitual, or rather innate, to women as is their lack of boldness" [*FW* 287]. Indeed, Boccaccio indirectly criticizes Valerius Maximus' judgement of Busa by stating: "in my opinion Busa made the best use of her wealth" [*FW* 287]. In the case of Busa, Boccaccio opted for Livy's interpretation of events which he follows reasonably closely. Thus Boccaccio can show his critical independence from his sources, even if in other respects he closely adheres to their ideological positions. The exceptional woman does not invalidate the basic rules of female nature, but demonstrates that they can be overcome.

40 *FW* 319 ("sunt preterea qui"; *DMC* 306).

41 The following women are common to both Livy and Boccaccio: Opis, Minerva, Lavinia, Rhea Ilia, Carmenta [Nicostrata], Virginia, Lucretia, Cloelia, Veturia, Virginia [wife of Lucius Volumnius], Harmonia, Busa, Sophonisba, Theoxena, the wife of Orgiago, Claudia Quinta. Often the same *exemplum* appears in both Livy and Valerius Maximus. In these cases, it is clear from the *De mulieribus* that Boccaccio has frequently taken into account both sources, extracting those details which best suited his purposes. Often Valerius Maximus provides less detail and a less interesting narrative account than Livy. See also Casella, *Tra Boccaccio e Petrarca*, pp.67–88. For Livy's treatment of women see Saxonhouse, *Women in the History of Political Thought*, pp.107–12.

42 "from these [lessons of every kind of experience] you may choose for yourself and for your own state what to imitate, from these mark for avoidance what is shameful in the conception and shameful in the result" (quoted in Saxonhouse, *Women in the History of Political Thought*, p.108). Boccaccio refers to the women of the *De mulieribus claris* in similar terms.

43 The wife of king Orgiago is in Livy, XXXVIII, 12–14, 24 and Theoxena in XL, 3–4.

44 "Huius atrocitas facinoris novam velut flammam regis invidiae adiecit, ut vulgo ipsum liberosque execrarentur" (XL, 4, 1).

45 "Quam ubi filius aspexit, 'Expugnasti' inquit 'et vicisti iram meam'" (V, 4, 1).

46 "Non inviderunt laude sua mulieribus viri Romani—adeo sine obtrectione gloriae alienae viebatur,—monumentoque quod esset, templum Fortunae muliebri aedificatum dedicatumque est" (Livy, II, XL, 5–9; p.350). Valerius Maximus divided his account into two parts. The later consequences of Veturia's act are analysed in the chapter on gratitude (V, 2, 1). They are also not seen as in any way negative.

47 *FW* 231. The passage refers to the conspicuous consumption of valuable ornamentation, which was supposedly regulated by sumptuary laws, and to the other consequences of Veturia's action.

48 See Coulter, "Boccaccio's acquaintance with Homer," pp.47–48, 51–53; Pertusi, *Leonzio Pilato fra Petrarca e Boccaccio*, pp.16–23, 371–72, 379. Boccaccio defends his citation of Greek poetry in the *Genealogie* from the charge of ostentation, noting "I owned Homer's works, and do yet, and drew from them much that

was of great use to my work" (Osgood, *Boccaccio on Poetry*, p.118). In spite of his acknowledged lack of mastery of ancient Greek, Boccaccio was proud of his achievement: "it is my peculiar boast and glory to cultivate Greek poetry among the Tuscans" (Osgood, *Boccaccio on Poetry*, p.120). These comments have some relevance for the *De mulieribus claris*.

49 See de Nolhac, "Boccace et Tacite," pp.127–29, 131–48; Zaccaria, "Boccaccio e Tacito," pp.225–29. On Tacitus' treatment of women see Saxonhouse, *Women in the History of Political Thought*, pp.112–18.

50 *FW* 399. The commentary here fully reveals its masculinist bias through the use of the pronoun "we" which excludes women and the strengthening of the stereotyped view of women as the weaker sex. In this case, the exceptional woman serves to wind in the possibility of social change. The chapter is a call to arms for degenerate men who seem to form the greater part of the population!

51 It should be noted that Paolino da Venezia (d. 1344) was the author of a *Satirica ystoria* on which see Heullant-Donat, "Entrer dans l'histoire," pp.382, 414–19. Boccaccio had an extremely low opinion of Paolo da Venezia ("Iste Venetus bestia," cited by Heullant-Donat, p.385). It seems likely that the reference here is intended to distance Boccaccio from the type of historical compilation associated with the bishop of Pozzuoli. Although one of Paolino's stated aims was to reconcile narrative history with chronology, he draws on the tabular representation of the Eusebius-Jerome *Chronicon*. The adjective *satirica* refers to the mixture of texts that constitute the work (Latin: *satura*). Boccaccio is perhaps more indebted to Paolino than he would have us believe. However, he applies a humanist broom to the methodology of the *Satirica ystoria*.

52 I do not think it is possible to share Zaccaria's view (p.544, n.8) that Boccaccio's sole interest here is narrative. It is true that Boccaccio is in many ways following a different tack from the *De casibus* where the sermon prevailed, but his statement contains a large dose of irony because it is all the same perfectly plain from the narrative what kind of women Sabina Poppaea was and what conclusions should be drawn.

53 Tacitus describes her as " violent beyond her sex" ("ultra feminam ferox"; *The Histories*, II, lxiii; pp.260, 261). Boccaccio's account moves from such a presupposition by embroidering Tacitus' account which is quite spare: "Some accused Triaria, wife of Lucius Vitellius, with girding on a soldier's sword and behaving haughtily and cruelly in the horrible massacre that followed the capture of Tarracina" (*Histories*, III, lxxvii; p.463). The medieval writer provides a full narrative context unlike the Roman historian.

III. Constructing Discourses: Medieval Patterns and Christian Models

1 See Miller, "The wounded heart," pp.340–41; Delhaye, "Le dossier anti-matrimonial de l'*Adversus Jovinianum*," pp.66–70; McLeod, *Virtue and Venom*, pp.35–47.

2 It is interesting to note that Boccaccio does not include Pliny's annotations on marriage ritual: "Hence arose the practice that maidens at their marriage were accompanied by a decorated distaff and a spindle with thread" (*Natural History*,

VIII, lxxiv, 194). In the *De mulieribus* exceptional behaviour is characterized by a rejection of these domestic symbols. Therefore, it would seem that the origins of marriage are ambiguously celebrated as 'heroic'. Boccaccio's source for Roman ritual is the anonymous *De praenominibus*: "et ideo institutum ut novae nuptae, ante ianuam mariti interrogatae quaenam vocarentur, Gaias esse se dicerent" (7; p.799).

3 "I will quickly run through Greek and Roman and Foreign History, and will show that virginity ever took the lead of chastity" (*Against Jovinianus*, I, 41; p.379). One can also note his divisions of history follow the model of Valerius Maximus.

4 See Kinter and Keller, *The Sibyl*, pp.30–31.

5 Jerome reports Seneca's criticism of Claudia Quinta's action: "Yet, as the uncle of Lucan the poet says, it would have been better if this circumstance had decorated a chastity tried and proved, and had not pleaded in defence of a chastity equivocal" (I, 41; p.379). Boccaccio also criticizes Claudia Quinta, but for different reasons: she engaged in an arrogant act that underlined her concern for worldly values.

The major source for the episode is Ovid's *Fasti* (IV, 255–348) which Boccaccio follows along its general lines. He omits the extended descriptions of the religious rites as they would have detracted from the main point of the story and made its setting overly pagan. Claudia Quinta's prayer takes up six lines of verse in Ovid whereas Boccaccio curtly reports the supplication in a sentence.

6 Jerome talks about "heathen error" (I, 41; p.379) when discussing Minerva. Boccaccio will take up this concept and expand it in the *De mulieribus*. See Barr, "The influence of Saint Jerome," p.99.

7 "I will proceed to married women who were reluctant to survive the decease or violent death of their husbands for fear they might be forced into a second marriage, and who entertained a marvellous affection for the only husbands they had. This may teach us that second marriage was repudiated among the heathens" (I, 43: p.381). See Atkinson, *The Oldest Vocation*, pp.66–68. For the development of this theme in canon law, see Metz, "La femme en droit canonique médiéval," pp.91–92.

8 Even women from Jerome's text who are not mentioned specifically by Boccaccio may have suggested to him certain ideas about the usage of classical *exempla*. Alcibiades' concubine buried his body in spite of an interdiction. Boccaccio will make use of perhaps a more suitable *exemplum* that of Argia who buried her husband in similar circumstances. The act of Alcibiades' concubine produces the following comment from Jerome: "Let matrons, Christian matrons at all events, imitate the fidelity of concubines, and exhibit in their freedom what she in captivity preserved" (I, 44; pp.381–82). Classical *exempla* have contemporary relevance in so far as both Jerome and Boccaccio believe they serve the purpose of 'shaming' Christian women. Jerome's deployment of female *exempla* can be seen as a precedent for Boccaccio's own use of pagan women for Christian ends, and hence a defence of the humanistic method.

9 Helen is not even referred to by name in Jerome's satirical jibe against her: "and on account of the rape of one wretched woman Europe and Asia are involved in a ten year's war" (*Against Jovinianus*, I, 48; p.385). In the *De casibus*, Boccaccio takes up Jerome's remarks on the way in which women generally aggravate dangerous political situations. According to Jerome, "In all the bom-

bast of tragedy and the overthrow of houses, cities, and kingdoms, it is the wives and concubines who stir up strife" (p.385 [48]). Boccaccio has generally eschewed Jerome's negative examples perhaps because they are too one-dimensional and too overtly satirical(I, 48; p.384–85), or depict comic scenes of the reversal of authority of husband and wife as is the case with Socrates and Xantippe.

10 The identical *exemplum* is still being proposed in the same terms by Agrippa, *Of the Vanitie*, pp.203–204. The information that Boccaccio found in the sources was extremely concise, lacking in detail—half a sentence in Pliny (*Natural History*, VII, xxiii, 87) and similarly in the Eusebius-Jerome *Chronicon* ("< H > armodius et Aristogiton Hipparchum tyrannum interfecerunt et L < e > aena meretrix amica eorum, cum tormentis coegeretur ut socios proderet, linguam suam mordicus amputavit" [188 F; p.106]). These few lines are transformed into a chapter of some two pages (six paragraphs). Most of the biography is in the form of a moral commentary contrasting loose sexual *mores* with Leaena's steadfastness in the face of torture.

11 "Who will deny that fortune was to blame for Leaena's life in the brothels?" [*FW* 207]. Apart from "fortune crimine," Boccaccio hypothesizes that a lack of parental control contributed to her becoming a prostitute.

12 "this dissolute woman reflected with gratitude on the value of the holy and venerable name of friendship" [*FW* 207].

13 "we must condemn those practices but in such a manner that we do not lessen the praise of virtue. In such instances, virtue is more worthy of admiration since the person in question was thought incapable of it" [*FW* 205]. This ambiguous annotation can be read two ways: (i) in most instances women are incapable of heroism (ii) the exceptional can aspire to that condition against all expectations. It leaves undecided the basic question of whether all women can defy conventional wisdom. However, the text seems to suggest that only the rare exceptional woman is capable of such defiance. Woman's script is written in advance and only allows the occasional improvisation.

14 The following women are common to the *Divina Commedia* and the *De mulieribus claris*: Eve, Semiramis, Opis, Juno, Ceres, Minerva, Venus, Europa, Thisbe, Niobe, Hypsipyle, Medea, Arachne, Medusa, Iole, Deianira, Jocasta, Argia, Manto, Penthesilea, Polyxena, Hecuba, Helen, Circe, Camilla, Penelope, Lavinia, Dido, Lucretia, Tamyris, Julia, Cleopatra, Gualdrada, Constance. For the female figures in Dante's poem see Delmay, *I personaggi della "Divina commedia," Ad vocem*.
Cloelia (and references to Dido and Semiramis) appears in the *De monarchia*.
A little more than a decade later Boccaccio took up Dante again in the *Esposizioni sopra "La comedia" di Dante*. Although he deals only with the first sixteen cantos of the *Inferno*, some of the women whom he had previously discussed in his Latin work are treated to extensive biographies, suggestive of the way he may have thought about glossing the Dantesque references to produce the readings of the *De mulieribus*.

15 For a list of the *De mulieribus* women used in the *Esposizioni* consult Padoan, *L'ultima opera*, p.95. On the treatment of Helen in the *Esposizioni* see *L'ultima opera*, pp.29–30 and for other female figures, pp.27–28.

16 See Tescari, "Per una vecchia querela a Virgilio e a Dante," pp.116–30. The most recent discussion on the efforts of Petrarch and Boccaccio to revive a chaste

Dido is Kallendorf's "Boccaccio's two Didos," pp.58–76. See also Cerbo, "Didone in Boccaccio," pp.177–219. Cerbo interprets the episode as an example of how Boccaccio uses pre-Christian history to demonstrate "la presenza e l'annunzio del messaggio cristiano" (p.199). Later writers (such as Sabadino degli Arienti) would see a problem in Dido and similar pagan figures who committed suicide since for them this constituted an un-Christian act. Cerbo's insistence on Dido as a Christian figure (she has "il valore paradigmatico del protagonismo cristiano," p.207) seems exaggerated and ignores other aspects that are perhaps even more crucial. As we have already seen, Boccaccio's authorial commentary engages with the question of virtuous widowhood to the exclusion of other matters.

17 See Mazza, "L'inventario della 'parva libraria'," p.3; Edmunds, "A note on Boccaccio's sources," p.248.

18 For example, in the preface to the *Chronicon*, it is asserted that "Semiramin autem et Abraham contemporales fuisse manifestum" (p.5).

19 Semiramis, Isis, Niobe, Europa, Hypsipyle, Medea, Helen, Amazon queens, Dido, Rhea Ilia, Sappho, Lucretia, Tamyris, Leaena, Veturia, Virginia, Olympias, Cleopatra, Cornificia, Agrippina mother of Nero, Zenobia are the principal women who when excerpted from the *Chronicon* create the outline of a chronological shape for the *De mulieribus*. The chronological ordering of the *Chronicon* is followed by Boccaccio (the women are listed here in the order they appear in the Eusebius-Jerome text). Boccaccio found a number of details which he would use in the *De mulieribus*: the district in Rome where Zenobia spent her captivity became known by her name (*Chronicon*, p.185). Boccaccio will add further clarification as to the precise identification of the area. Cornificia's brother is reported to have used an expression ("Cornificius potea a militibus desertus interuit quos saepe fugientes *galeatos lepores* appellarat" [*Chronicon*, p.139; my emphasis]) that Boccaccio will adapt in his chapter on Penthesilea. The entries in the *Chronicon* are generally of the utmost brevity. Their structural arrangement is more important than the reduced content of the individual 'biographies'.

20 See Constantini, "La presenza di Martino Polono," pp. 363–70.

21 Vincentius Bellovacensis, *Speculum Historiale*, vol.4. Boccaccio was certainly aware of the *Speculum* since in the *Genealogie* he refers to "Vincentius Gallicus hystoriographus" (VI, xxiv; p.658).

22 On Athaliah, *Sp. Hist.*, Lib. II, Cap.LXXXIX [p.76]; on Harmonia, Lib. II, Cap.XXXV [p.98]; and on Olympias, Lib. IV, Cap.XIII [p.121]. Vincent also notes Europa (Lib. I, Cap.LXXI [p.27]: "et partem tertiam orbis ex eius nomine appellavit" and the Sibyls for whom his principal source of information is Isidor (*Sp. Hist.*, Lib. II, Cap. C, CI, CII [p.79]).

23 "virgines reservant, quas non lanificio, sed armis, et equis et venationibus assuefaciunt" (*Sp. Hist.*, Lib. I, Cap.XCVI [p.36]).

24 *Sp. Hist.*, Liber I, cap.CIII [p.38].

25 "Archemidora autem vel sicut alibi legitur Artemisia regina Alicarnasi" (*Sp. Hist.*, Lib. II, cap.XXXVIII [p.99]).

26 "mortem avidam sanguinis" (I,14; p.10).

27 "tanto atrocius miseros quanto longius a remedio verae religionis alienos" (I, 14; p.10).

28 "amore saevo sauciae" (I, xii, 10; p.72).

29 "non muliebriter increpitans" (II, vii; p.116).

30 *FW* 257. In chapter LXXVI Boccaccio is referring to Orosius when he states that
    some historians believe that Sempronia killed her husband Scipio Aemilianus.
    Although mentioned, it is not granted any particular status in Boccaccio's text—
    but all the same, it serves to destabilize Sempronia's achievements. Orosius also
    mentions Cleopatra. His description of the manner of her death provided
    Boccaccio with some details for his account.

31 In the latter case, Boccaccio's most likely source that contains the particulars
    reported by the *De mulieribus* is Florus, *Epitome* (I, xxxviii, 16–18). The episode
    assumes sharper ideological dimensions because of its connection with the
    anti-remarriage theme as well as the motif of female chastity, so prominent in
    the text. In letter CXXIII. Ad Gervchiam, St. Jerome places the case of the
    Cimbrian women in a list that includes Dido, Lucretia, and a reference to
    Against Jovinianus for more *exempla*.

32 "Ex omnibus colligamus unde unum fiat, sicut unus numerus fit ex singulis"
    (Macrobius, *I Saturnali*, I, 8; p.102).

33 A particularly pertinent example is the chapter on Semiramis [II] where
    Boccaccio offers a series of possible motives for Ninyas' murder of his mother,
    but they are not ordered according to any systematic examination of probabili-
    ties. Needless to say, the historians are not mentioned by name.

34 Kohl, "Petrarch's prefaces," p.139.

35 Boccaccio places the falsity of pagan attributions of divinity under the spotlight.
    Minerva's genealogy (VI) is recounted in such a way as to bring out its absurd-
    ity, and to ridicule those who believed in it (thus indirectly raising the status of
    knowledge in the Christian era). Boccaccio does not bother to subject the
    claims of the ancients about Minerva's birth to rational analysis: it is enough for
    him to state that the Greeks believed she was born from Jove's brain and had no
    mother.

36 *FW* 39; similarly see chap. XLI [Lavinia], LVI [Tamyris], LXIV [Flora].

37 *FW* 281. Boccaccio simply registers the diversity of opinion without discussing
    the sources any further: "Some sources say that she died a virgin; others report
    that she was the wife of a certain Themistius" [*FW* 281].

38 See also IX (Europa), XVIII (Arachne), XXV (Jocasta), XXX (Manto), XXXII
    (Penthesilea), XXXVII (Helen), LXXXVIII (Cleopatra).

39 "What else is there left to say? Nothing: we know nothing about Tamyris except
    this deed" [*FW* 203]. Similar acknowledgements occur in other biographies,
    such as the closing statement in chap.XI–XII (Marpesia and Lampedo), XVI
    (Hypsipyle), XVII (Medea), XIX–XX (Orithya and Antiope), XXI (Erythraea),
    XXXVII (Helen), XXXVIII (Circe), XCVI (Triaria). The last-mentioned biogra-
    phy appears to use this absence of documentation in an ironical mode to under-
    line the morally dubious actions of the biographical subject.

40 Quintilian briefly mentions the use of female exemplars that fits in with
    Boccaccio's notion of exceptional women: "Arguments from unlikes are most
    useful in exhortation. Courage is more remarkable in a woman than in a man"
    ("Ad exhortationem vero praecipue valent imparia. Admirabilior in femina
    quam in viro virtus" [*Institutio oratoria*, V, xi, 10; pp. 276, 277]).

41 Le Goff, "L'*exemplum* et la rhétorique de la prédication," pp.3–29. See also
    Racconti esemplari di predicatori del Due e Trecento, in particular, vol. 2, Giordano
    da Pisa, *Esempi*, pp.39–464, is an edition of the *exempla* used by this medieval

preacher, unfortunately separated from the original context of the sermons in which they are found.

42 The *Rhetorica ad Herennium* compares an *exemplum* to a *testimonium* that is used to prove a point. Its principal use is to clarify: "First and foremost, examples are set forth, not to confirm or to bear witness, but to clarify" (Cicero, *De ratione dicendi (Rhetorica ad Herennium)*, IV, III, 5. Cicero defines his position as follows: "Exemplification is the citing of something done or said in the past, along with the definite naming of the doer or author. It is used with the same motive as a Comparison" (IV, XLIX.62.). See also Mulas, "Funzione degli esempi," pp.97–99.

43 For fuller bibliographical details consult Bremond, Le Goff, Schmitt, *L"Exemplum,"* pp.17–26. See Battaglia, *La coscienza letteraria del medioevo*, pp.447–85; Delcorno, "L'exemplum nella predicazione volgare di Giordano da Pisa," pp.3–121; Idem, *Exemplum e letteratura. Tra medioevo e Rinascimento*; Haug and Wachinger, *Exempel und Esempelsammlungen*; Hampton, *Writing from History. The Rhetoric of Exemplarity in Renaissance Literature*, pp.1–30; Lord, "Dido as an example of chastity," pp.22–28; Stierle, "L'histoire comme exemple, l'exemple comme histoire," pp.176–98; Lyons, *The Rhetoric of Example in Early Modern France and Italy*, pp.3–34.

44 See Phillippy, "Establishing authority," p.169.

IV. Fallen Women, Fallen Texts: From the *De casibus* to the *De mulieribus*

1 Samson is first described in terms which consolidate the view that his story is in reality the story of his relationship with Delilah: 'perfidiam dilecte mulieris Sanson exclamitans adest' (*De casibus*, I,xvi; p.84). The text does not spare Delilah, describing her as "a woman truly devoted to evil" (*The Fates*, p.40).

2 *The Fates*, p.39; "Nec defuerunt qui leonem a se occisum Nemeum dicerent, et Herculem arbitrarentur Sansonem: quod etsi non affirmem, contradixisse nescio quid resultet" (*De casibus*, I, xvii; p.86).

3 The theme is also present in a more complex form in the biography of Mariamme (LXXXVII) in the *De mulieribus claris*. The effect of her beauty on her husband, king Herod, is the focus of the chapter: "Herod took enormous pride in the fact that he alone in the whole world was the owner of such divine beauty" (*FW* 357). That beauty is the cause of his "insania." Boccaccio does not accept Josephus' interpretation of Mariamme as stepping over the boundaries of wifely behaviour ("but she wanted moderation, and had too much of contention in her nature" [*The Antiquities of the Jews*, 15, 7; p.412]). Indeed, Boccaccio balances the baleful effects of her beauty with her "great nobility of spirit" (*FW* 361), which enables her to face death with equanimity.

4 "But wait a moment. As exalted as all this was, so their lives suddenly fell into almost extreme misery" (*The Fates*, p.4).

5 "et ideo preter nos nemo decentius quod queris dabit principium" (*De casbus*, I, i; p.12).

6 "ei non ad sollicitudinem, ut hodierne sunt coniuges, verum ad solatium iuncta est" (*De casibus*, I, i; p.12).

7 *FW* 17. The indirect ironic allusions to the Fall are also reinforced by overt comments on Eve's behaviour that are an integral part of the misogynist tradition.
There are references to her levity ("levitas feminea"; *DMC* 30), her stupidity
("stolide," *DMC* 30) and her overweening ambition to go beyond imposed limits,
as well as to her seductive powers.

8 Cutting chronologically across the *De casibus* and *De mulieribus* is the *Lettera
consolatoria a Pino de' Rossi* (the text of the letter is in Boccaccio, *Opere in versi*,
pp.1112–1141 and in *Tutte le opere di Giovanni Boccaccio*, vol.V, tomo secondo,
pp.629–51 from which all references are taken . For the dating and composition
see Ricci, "Studi sulle opere latine," pp.21–32 and Chiecchi, "La lettera a Pino
de' Rossi," pp.296–99), which takes up the political themes of the rise and fall of
an individual's fortunes, here applied to contemporary Florence from where
Pino de' Rossi, member of a powerful Florentine family, found himself in exile
(Cf. Miglio, "Boccaccio biografo," p.158). Boccaccio makes free use of the exemplary male figures employed in the *De casibus*. He utilizes as well some of the
female figures who will appear in the *De mulieribus,* mainly to support the basic
assertion of the text that a wife who is "good, chaste and courageous" ("buona e
pudica e valorosa," p.641) is man's greatest comfort in adversity. The
Consolatoria provides a historical periodization and contextualization of
Boccaccio's interest in a wife who stays by her husband's side in adversity.
However, rather than immediately citing such exemplary women, Boccaccio
first of all recounts, with apparent relish, stories of unfaithful wives; including
Helen (who provoked "almost eternal destruction" ("quasi etterna distruzione,"
p.641), and Cleopatra, who, "after a thousand adulterous affairs" ("dopo mille
adulteri," p.1129) received her just punishment. These are *exempla* of improper
behaviour—anti-models. Most of them are mentioned in the *De mulieribus* and
provide examples of the consequences to themselves (not to mention to men
and society as a whole) when women attain the "grande stato" [p.642] ("control
of the state") and nourish political ambitions of their own. Boccaccio mentions
Jezabel briefly in the *De mulieribus* in the chapter on her daughter Athaliah
who is depicted as being even more bloodthirsty than her mother. Whilst he
does not directly refer to Jezabel's misdeeds, he calls her "regine nequissime"
(*DMC* 206). Boccaccio spares no detail in the description of her death (*FW* 211).
Tullia Servilia, who rode her chariot over her father's body, is mentioned at
some length in the *De casibus*. Given that there was no pressing need to mention such 'evil women' in a consolatory epistle, their inclusion indicates
Boccaccio's fascination with the potential of women to exert power. He highlights their excesses by placing them in juxtaposition to the more 'correct'
examples of wives who know their place ... next to their husbands: "I do not
believe that there can be any greater consolation to an unhappy man" ("niuna
consolazione credo che essere possa maggiore allo infelice," p.641). The examples he then cites of wives either following their husbands into exile, or dying
because of their husbands' misadventures are all to be found in the *De
mulieribus*. These *exempla*, directed towards Giovanna, through the arbiter of
her conduct, her husband Pino, attempt to label her by circumscribing her
range of possibilities as a woman. She must be viewed either as a Helen, the
anti-model of the good wife, or "your wife can be another Hypsicratea or any of
the others I've mentioned that *you desire* ("la vostra monna Giovanna essere
un'altra Isicratea o quale altra delle predette *volete*"; p.642, my emphasis).

Hence, Boccaccio is manipulating female *exempla* in such a way that the rhetoric serves a contemporary political purpose. Exile, both a reality and a literary theme, is described as a possibly ennobling experience, but one that should, in spite of the political turmoil, maintain the basic family structure—the one bond that could maintain stability in a parlous situation. Thus, there appears to be a dialectical relationship between the collapse of the state (in its microcosmic form, exile, faction fighting and so on) and the need to affirm traditional roles for a woman. However, the polarization of female behaviour (so obvious in the *Consolatoria*) is not so neatly replicated in the *De mulieribus claris*, where some of the most notorious examples of misogynist literature are played down or omitted altogether: for example, Jezabel, Tullia, and Messalina (the latter also appears in the *De casibus*). They are mentioned only in passing if at all in the *De mulieribus*—thus rendering its anti-female slant less obvious and less vicious.

9 Eve [I,i], Jocasta [I, viii], Hecuba [I, xiii], Athaliah [II, vii], Dido [II, x], Olympias [IV, xii], Arsinoe, Queen of Macedonia [IV, xv], Arsinoe, Queen of Cyrene [IV, xviii], the three Cleopatras [Vi, iv], Cleopatra, Queen of Egypt [VI, xv], Valeria Messalina [VII, iii], Zenobia [VIII, vi], Rosmunda [VIII, xxii], Brunichilda [IX, i], Romulda [IX, iii], Philippa [IX, xxvi].

10 Out of 18 women so named only eight form the subject of chapters in the *De mulieribus* (the surviving eight are: Eve, Jocasta, Hecuba, Athaliah, Dido, Olympias, Cleopatra VII, Zenobia). Of the eight two have biblical origins, while the rest derive from classical sources.

11 See *De casibus*, pp.XXV–XXVI, XLVIII and the comments of Pastore Stocchi, "Il Boccaccio del *De casibus*," pp.421–30, who disagrees with Zaccaria on the extent of the *Amorosa visione*'s influence on the *De casibus* (p.428). Pastore Stocchi suggests that the model of the *Divina commedia* dominates Boccaccio's earlier poem. I do not think it necessary to posit that one or other of the two texts in question has priority in the elaboration of the *De casibus*. The concept of amassing a huge number of characters in a serious Latin text was perhaps suggested contemporaneously by the two poems as part of its process of composition. Certainly, the Dantesque frame of characters pleading with the narrator to be heard is an effective mechanism borrowed from the *Commedia*. Boccaccio had already experimented with the Dantesque form in the *Amorosa visione*. Now with the reversion to prose he was anxious to offer a general moral message to the reader instead of a moral dilemma, the resolution of which was unsure in the *Amorosa visione*. Thus, the intercalation of 'sermon' material is intended to ensure that the biographical episodes are read correctly and that their universal significance is explicated.

12 The following women are mentioned in *De casibus* and have chapters in *De mulieribus*: Agrippina [Germanici uxor], Agrippina [Neronis mater], Arachne, Arthemidora [called Artemisia in the *De mulieribus*], Athaliah, Cassandra, Ceres, Circe, Cleopatra, Clytemnestra, the women of the Cimbrians, Deianira, Dido, Europa, Eve, Hecuba, Helen, Hypsicratea, Jocasta, Isis, Lucretia, Lybia, Mariamme, Marpesia, Medea, Minerva, Olympias, wife of Orgiago, Orythya, Polyxena, Sabina Poppaea, Rhea Ilia, Semiramis, Sophonisba, Sulpicia, Tamyris, Venus, Virginia, Iole, Irene, Zenobia.

In the *De casibus* they are often dealt with extremely briefly and it is only in *De mulieribus* that they receive extensive treatment. Some of the references are brief indeed. Boccaccio provides the names of a couple of exemplary women, noted for their adhesion to the ideals of chastity, in order to highlight Valeria Messalina's choice of sexual licence: "Sulpicia, spouse of Fulvius Flaccus or the wife of Orgiago" ("Sulpitiam Fulvii Flacci coniugem seu Orgiagontis uxorem," VII, iii; p.588).

13 When her family is wiped out, Rosmunda is forced to marry the conqueror, Alboinus, king of the Longbards. At a banquet, she is forced to drink to her husband's health from a cup made out of her father's skull. Small wonder that she plots to kill the king!

14 "omissis mortis Gisulphi lacrimis et publice salutis vigiliantia, mentem omnem in austerum hostis aspectum converteret, nil magis cupiens quam ut eius potiretur amplexibus" (p.762).

15 Juvenal calls Messalina "that whore-empress" (VI, 118). Her night visits to the brothel are graphcally described by the Latin poet: "she took on all comers, for cash, without a break" (VI, 127). There is nothing else in Juvenal's description, only her insatiable sexuality.

Boccaccio may have also included other negative women under the influence of Juvenal, in particular, Niobe, who is noted in the sixth satire for her "fatuous pride" (1.176). The mention of the Floral festival in the same satire may have, by virtue of its position, encouraged Boccaccio to include Flora in the *De mulieribus*, after carrying out more detailed researches, probably in Macrobius. Agrippina is briefly mentioned as a poisoner. Juvenal does mention evil women of mythology (Medea and Clytemnestra are to be found in the *De mulieribus*), but they are in a different class to the women of contemporary Rome: "Such women were monsters of daring/In their own day—but not from the lust for cash" (1.645). Juvenal sees something almost heroic in their evildoing, absent from the base motives of the women of imperial Rome.

16 Carraro, "Tradizioni culturali e storiche nel *De casibus*," emphasizes the moral aspects of the work which, in her opinion, far outweigh anything else including the elaboration of a historiographical methodology (see, for example, pp.198, 209, 222, 233, 252, 260). By contrast, Chiecchi, "Sollecitazioni narrative nel *De casibus virorum illustrium*," stresses the importance of the rhetorical structures of the text, relating them to the *Decameron* and other works. In the episode under examination the latter critic suggests that the *contesa* marks "il trionfo dell'eloquenza anche sugli schemi etici e ideologici" (p.117) and that the subsequent surfacing of the truth has been achieved by the use of narrative.

17 "At illa firmiori vultu et oratione integriori, quam putes illecebri fuisse mulieri, adversus exasperantes hos inquit..." (p.586).

The attribute of intelligent discourse is present in the 'heroines' of the *Decameron* with whom Messalina is thus placed in a problematic continuum. Her sexuality is roundly condemned, but this does not prevent her from being morally superior to the two emperors.

18 See Aurigemma, "Boccaccio e la storia: osservazioni sul *De casibus virorum illustrium*," pp.73–78.

19 "Etsi erubescam, non inficiar: lasciva luxuriosa adultera et concubitu plurimo semper avida fui" (p.586). She then goes on to state that women are defined by their sexuality, which is feminine for destiny: "under the influence of this sky I was born to this compulsion" ("Celo igitur urgente in hoc [amore] nata sum," p.586). This statement claims the inalterability of female sexuality; her behav-

iour is thus beyond human control and is therefore to be discounted. When Messalina compares herself to Hercules to demonstrate that both of them have been conquered by the same force of love (p.588) the comparison cuts both ways: Messalina transforms herself metaphorically into the role of a great champion and secondly sympathizes with him when the hero has lost his manhood and sits spinning with the women. For Hercules, this is a betrayal of his gender but, for Messalina, this is her 'natural' state. She further elucidates her position by referring to three other exemplary female figures, who will each be given chapters in the *De mulieribus* (Sulpicia, the wife of Orgiago, Lucretia), contrasting 'good' and 'bad' sex. The former can be defined as adhesion to the law of chastity in spite of violation, which is in any case avenged by either the woman herself or the menfolk.

20 The scale of the emperors' political irresponsibility is emphasized by Messalina: "ut in mortem humanum genus omne dissolveres" (p.588).

21 Messalina refers most unflatteringly to Tiberius as "that filthy old man" ("spurcissimum istum senem"). Her anger reflected in the phrase "toto affectu" (p.590) presents her as a woman who really cares about the decadence of ancient Rome brought about, in her view, by its leaders.

22 Using details from Sallust, Messalina can refer to Tiberius' depravity: "Pudet me scelestam feminam referre quod te, princeps inclite, pisciculis adhibitis tuis, commisisse non puduit" (p.590). The antithesis of "pudet" and "non puduit" renders the hierarchical distinction between the two sets of sinning behaviour. In her speech, Messalina refers explicitly to the double standard used to measure women against men. The reference to *pudicitia* "honestarum matronarum unicum esse thesaurum" (p.590) is intended to suggest that the term be applied rigorously to men as well—if not, criticism of women by men is invalid. Such an 'extreme' position will not be reiterated in the *De mulieribus* where *pudicitia* will take on increasing significance in the definition of female behaviour.

23 Harvey argues "the male poet's transvestism of voice is... at once a strategy for confronting the narrowness of the imprisoning bounds of gender definitions, and also (paradoxically) a way of coping with the anxiety generated by the radical instability of gender difference within a particular cultural context" (*Ventriloquized Voices*, p.17). Boccaccio's Messalina does not exactly fit into this category because of 'her' ambiguous attitude towards her own sexuality which moves to an acceptance of traditional male norms.

24 "te noverim, quia tue animi iniquitates sint, mee corporis; tue excogitate, mee coacte; tue humano generi toto damnose mee ignominia pudoris feminei sublata, nemini" (p.596).

25 "Hec cum illa infracta quadam vivacitate narrasset et ego, non solum absque tedio, sed summa cum delectatione elevatis audissem auribus, truces homines confusi et illius victoriam taciturnitate pandentes..." (p.600).

26 "magis ad suam gloriam extollendam quam imperium augendum" (XLIX; p.198). Boccaccio adds that Cyrus was "hac ergo tractus aviditate" (p.198) as if drawn to Tamyris by an ineluctable destiny, though not of the same dimensions as the fate of *De casibus*.

V. Vulgar Women: Boccaccio's Vernacular Writing and the *De mulieribus*

1 "I intend to provide succour and diversion for the ladies, but only for those who are in love, since the others can make do with their needles, their reels and their spindles" (*The Decameron*, p.47); "in soccorso e rifugio di quelle che amano, per ciò che all'altre è assai l'ago e 'l fuso e l'arcolaio" (*Decameron*, ed. Branca, p.5). In contrast to *De mulieribus*, the exceptional women are *lovers* who are separated from the domestic sphere, symbolized by spinning. Yet, the same basic division exists in the *De mulieribus* between the generality of women and the exceptional ones. The Latin work only rarely privileges the female lover. See Bruni, *Boccaccio. L'invenzione della letteratura mezzana*, pp.461–64.

2 *The Decameron*, p.726 ("Questa novella dalla reina detta diede un poco da mormorare alle donne e ridere a' giovani"; *Decameron*, ed. Branca, p.838).

3 *The Decameron*, p.325 ("che alla mia età non sta bene l'andare omai dietro a queste cose, cioè a ragionar di donne o a compiacer loro"; *Decameron*, ed. Branca, p.345).

4 See Levenstein, "Out of bounds," p.317.

5 For quotation and discussion see Olson, "Petrarch's view of the *Decameron*," pp.69–79; Idem, *Literature as Recreation*, pp.217–22; Middleton, "The clerk and his tale," pp.125–35; Morse, "The exemplary Griselda," p.58; Bliss, "The Renaissance Griselda," pp.303; Kolsky, "La costituzione di una nuova figura femminile letteraria," p.52; Kirkpatrick, "The Griselda story," pp.233–38; Bronfman, *Chaucer's 'Clerk's Tale'*, pp.7–9, 16.

6 Cf. Pastore Stocchi, "Prospettiva del Boccaccio minore," p.36 and Marti, "Per una metalettura del *Corbaccio*," p.86.

7 Billanovich, *Restauri boccacceschi*, pp.138–39.

8 *The Decameron*, p.209 ("saper cavalcare un cavallo, tenere uno uccello, leggere e scrivere e fare una ragione che se un mercatante fosse"; *Decameron*, ed. Branca, p.205).

9 "né alcuna cosa era che a donna appartenesse, sì come di lavorare lavorii di seta e simili cose, che ella non facesse meglio che alcuna altra" (*Decameron*, ed. Branca, p.205). Zinevra is praised as specifically skilled in silk work.

10 "niuna altra più onesta né più casta potersene trovar di lei" (*Decameron*, ed. Branca, p.206).

11 *The Decameron*, p.208 ("avere una donna per moglie la più compiuta di tutte quelle virtù che donna o ancora cavaliere in gran parte o donzello dee avere" (*Decameron*, ed. Branca, p.205).

12 See Cerbo, "Tecniche narrative" and Ganio Vecchiolino, "Due modi di narrare." Cerbo carries out a detailed analysis of the Paulina chapter in "Una novella in latino del Boccaccio." In "Tecniche narrative" she uses Thisbe as one of her main examples (pp.322–25, 333–35). Ganio Vecchiolino, seemingly unaware of Cerbo's work, covers some of the same ground, perhaps more convincingly using Paulina as her primary example, but providing an interesting analysis of Thisbe.

13 Ganio Vecchiolino notes "questo discorso [on narrative in the *De mulieribus*] in verità non riguarda tutta la produzione senile, ma alcuni capitoli del *De mulieribus* (oltre a quello su Paolina, quelli su Tisbe, Flora, Cleopatra e sulla papessa Giovanna) sono indubbiamente esempi di vive narrazioni" (p.666).

Some scholars have noted the use of narrative in the *De casibus* (See Chiecchi, "Sollecitazioni narrative nel *De casibus virorum illustrium*"). Boccaccio's interest in the story is evinced by its presence in the *Zibaldone magliabechiano* (See Constantini, "Studi," p.36).

14 *The Decameron*, p.47 ("delle quali le già dette donne, che queste leggeranno, parimente diletto delle sollazzevoli cose in quelle mostrate e utile consiglio potranno pigliare, in quanto potranno cognoscere quello che sia da fuggire e che sia similmente da seguitare"; *Decameron*, ed. Branca, p.5).

15 Boccaccio goes on to add that he has lengthened some of the biographies with respect to his sources, that is, strengthened the narrative in order to make the work more palatable to women: "It is my belief that the accomplishments of these ladies will please women no less than men. Moreover, since women are generally unacquainted with history, they require and enjoy a more extended account" (*FW* 11, 13). However, his historical discourse normally attempts to limit the 'outbreaks' of narrative. Stylistic variations of this kind can be explained partially in terms of the multiple and contradictory reactions of the writer-turned-critic of his own vernacular *novelle*.

16 The problem of the dating of the *Triumphi* is of considerable complexity, and scholars are hotly divided on the issue. For the belief that Boccaccio was completely responsible for Petrarch's decision to begin composing the *Triumphi* see Billanovich, "Dalla *Commedia* e dall'*Amorosa visione* ai *Trionfi*'," pp.1–52. The other view expresses the conviction that Petrarch had adumbrated the idea of the *Triumphi* well before he had read the *Amorosa visione* and hence is independent of its inspiration. For such an interpretation see Wilkins, "On the chronology of the *Triumphs*," pp.254–72. Raimondi, "Review" (pp.223–26), also discounts any major Boccaccian influence on the *Triumphi*, but admits the possibility of 'reverse influence' on the B-redaction of the *Amorosa visione*.

17 See Billanovich, "Dalla *Commedia*," p.8 and Vittore Branca's introductory essay to the English translation of the *Amorosa visione* ("Introduction" in Boccaccio, *Amorosa visione. Bilingual Edition*, pp.ix–xxviii). Branca argues for the poem's influence on the *Triumphi* in strong terms: "The *Amorosa Visione* is the most important instance of the literary influence exerted on Petrarch by Boccaccio" (p.xxiii; see also Branca, "Petrarch and Boccaccio," pp.198–210). Branca's arguments in favour of the writer's revision of the poem in the period 1355–60 are to be found in Boccaccio, *Amorosa visione, edizione critica*, pp.LXVII–CLVII.

18 See Billanovich on the relatively small-scale 'reforming' of the text ("Dalla *Commedia*," pp.8–9).

19 The women common to both works are: Semiramis, Europa, Arachne, Juno, Venus, Thisbe, Tamyris, Niobe, Elissa (Dido), Helen, Clytemnestra, Penthesilea, Lavinia, Iole, Deianira, Jocasta, Hecuba, Polyxena, Medea, Penelope, Camilla, Rhea Ilia, Cloelia, Veturia, Cleopatra, Julia, Pocris, Giovanna I, Queen of Naples.

Andrea Acciaiuoli appears in both works but is seen in two contrasting lights, negative vs. postive (in the later text she is the dedicatee). See Kolsky, "La costituzione di una nuova figura femminile," pp.42–43.

20 Boccaccio included the following goddesses in this group: Opis (III), Juno (IV), Ceres (V), Minerva (VI), Venus (VII), Isis (VIII), Europa (IX).

21   Boccaccio, *Amorosa visione. Bilingual Edition*, p.75; "Ornata come vecchia e di dolore/piena era quivi Giuno invidiosa" (*Amorosa visione*, B, c.XVIII, ll. 4–5; p.192).

22   Boccaccio, *Amorosa visione. Bilingual Edition*, p.75; "con falso aspetto" (*Amorosa visione*, III, B, c.XVIII, l. 14; p.192).

23   The female guide of the *Amorosa visione* (introduced immediately after Fiammetta) is described in signficant terms, especially given the reactions of the later Boccaccio to Juno: "Just like Juno in her sidereal choir/did she step." The influence of genre (in the case of the *Amorosa visione*, narrative poetry tending towards the epic) required mythological symbolism in order to lend the poem a 'high' tone, consonant with the literary ambitions of the poet. Thus, the comparison could be justified through its literary context and range of reference. However, with the *De mulieribus* and the subsequent change in genre, such a comparison was no longer acceptable; poetic grandeur having been replaced by other values. Mythology in Boccaccio's later works is analysed and made the subject of commentary.

24   See Cooke, "Euhemerism: A mediaeval interpretation of classical paganism," pp.396–410. It is interesting to note that when Boccaccio mentions the cult of Io in the *Amorosa visione* there is no hint of the sarcasm against such devotion that we find in his Latin work on women: "e così fatta dea, lì celebrata/ da quella gente fu, e con voti assai/ e molti incensi la vedea onorata" (*Amorosa visione*, B, c.XVII, ll. 40–42; pp.190–91).

25   Boccaccio, *Amorosa visione. Bilingual Edition*, p.7; "Move nuovo disio l'audace mente,/donna leggiadra, per voler cantare/narrando quel ch'Amor mi fé presente" (*Amorosa visione*, III, B, c.I, ll. 1–3; p.151).

26   For this line of interpretation of the *Amorosa visione* see Huot, "Poetic ambiguity and reader response in Boccaccio's *Amorosa visione*," pp.109–22; and Smarr, *Boccaccio and Fiammetta. The Narrator as Lover*, pp.101–128.

27   The presentation of the narrator in this fashion is not so far distant from the rebuke that Boccaccio delivered to himself in the *De casibus virorum illustrium* through the intermediary of Petrarch. Boccaccio imagines Petrarch reproving him for not proceeding with the work in hand and allowing himself to fall into "the most complete laziness" (*The Fates*, p.202; "amplissimum ocium" [*De casibus*, p.650]). However, the change is significant: no longer is it a woman who is attempting to direct the energies of Boccaccio-narrator, but a definite mortal man—Petrarch—who validates the rightness of Boccaccio's change of language and genre, acting as guarantor of the quality of the writer's humanistic research. Boccaccio-narrator stresses the intellectual relationship with Petrarch as a way of lending respectability to his own work, leaving aside differences between their approaches: "my great and venerable teacher, whose counsels always spurred me toward virtue, and whom I had admired above all others from my earliest youth" (*The Fates*, p.203; "optimum venerandumque preceptorem meum, cuius monitus michi semper ad virtutem calcar extiterant et quem ego ab ineunte iuventute mea pre ceteris colueram" [*De casibus*, VIII, i, p.652]). In his speech to the narrator, Petrarch upholds the value of such elitistic study and writing "so that he [the intellectual] will be separated from the common herd" (*The Fates*, p.206; "ut a vulgari segregemur grege" [*De casibus*, VIII, i; p.660]) since through learning one acquires *gloria*. Cf. Chiecchi, "Sollecitazioni narrative," pp.106–108.

28 Cf. Bergin, *Boccaccio*, p.254.

29 *Amorosa visione*, III, A, c.X, ll. 76–88; pp.50–51 and B, c.X, ll. 76–88; pp.174–75.

30 *Amorosa visione*, III, notes to c.X, ll. 76–88; p.623. On Dante's choice of women see Kirkham, "A canon of women in Dante's *Commedia*'," pp.21–22.

31 See Lucan, *The Civil War*, II, 326–391. Marcia pleads with Cato: "Grant me to renew the faithful compact of my first marriage; grant me only the name of wife: suffer men to write on my tomb, 'Marcia, wife of Cato'" (II, 341–344). In spite of such eloquent entreaties, Boccaccio was not moved to include her so as not to validate remarriage in any way in the body of the text.

32 *Amorosa visione*, B, c.XII, ll. 41–42; p.178.

33   See *Amorosa visione*, B, c.XI, ll. 16–27; pp.175–76 and B, c.XXIX, ll. 37–39; p.219.

34 B, c.XXIX, ll.1–3, 28–30; pp.218, 219. See Tescari, "Per una vecchia querela," pp.120–22. Aeneas makes a walk-on appearance in the chapter on Dido in the *De mulieribus*, not even meeting her! The reason for Aeneas' presence is not at all clear ("come c'entri qui Enea Troiano non si capisce bene," writes Tescari). It is all the more puzzling since in the *Esposizioni* Boccaccio could not be clearer about the non-coincidence of Dido and Aeneas (canto V, Esposizione litterale, paras. 82–83; p.300). The trace of Aeneas that remains in Dido's biography could be read as the thinest of threads that still connnects the writer to his earlier works, such as the *Amorosa visione*, and insubstantial as it may be, Boccaccio was unwilling to cut it off altogether at that stage. By the time he came to write the *Esposizioni*, Boccaccio exhibited no such hestitation.

35 For some discussion consult *Il Corbaccio*, ed. Natali, pp. vii–xii. My interest here is not so much in the exact dating of the *Corbaccio*, rather in its relationship with the Latin text. See the persuasive arguments of Padoan, "Sulla datazione del *Corbaccio*" in his *Il Boccaccio le muse il Parnaso e l'Arno*, pp.199–228 and his "Il *Corbaccio* tra spunti autobiografici," pp.23–24; and Marti, "Per una metalettura del *Corbaccio*," pp.63–69.

36 See *Il Corbaccio*, ed. Natali, pp. ix–xi.

37 *The Corbaccio*, p.16; "...in sul ragionare delle valorose donne venimmo; e prima avendo molte cose dette delle antiche, quale in castità, quale in magnanimità, quale in corporal fortezza lodando, condiscendemmo alle moderne. Fra le quali il numero trovandone piccolissimo da commendare, pure esso, che in questa parte il ragionare prese, alcune ne nominò della nostra città" (*Il Corbaccio*, ed. Natali, paras. 134–35; p.34).

The areas of 'expertise' listed in the *Corbaccio* only partially corresponds to the chronologically arranged women of the *De mulieribus claris*. The Boccaccio of the *Corbaccio* has re-produced a more straightforward version of the Latin work, purged of questionable women and arranged according to categories as some Renaissance compilers would do. The allusion in the *Corbaccio* omits all reference to women of power, intellectuals, and writers; Boccaccio's inclusion of women who display exceptional "corporal fortezza" may be a reference to the Amazonian and related women whose biographies are to be found in the *De mulieribus claris*.

38 *The Corbaccio*, p.46; "le valorose antiche" (*Il Corbaccio*, ed. Natali, para.344; p.95).

39 *The Corbaccio*, p.16; "e oltre alla natura delle femmine, lei s'ingegnava di mostrare essere uno Alessandro, alcuna delle sue liberalità raccontando, le

quali per non consumare il tempo in novelle, non curo di raccontare" (para.136; p.35). The comparison with Alexander is made a second time in the text (*The Corbaccio*, p.46; *Il Corbaccio*, ed. Natali, para.345; p.95) in order to underline the widow's squalid nature.

It is possible that to the reader of the *De mulieribus*, the reference to Alexander brings to mind the general's mother Olympias, tainted with adultery, and also Semiramis who, like Alexander, penetrated into India but whose reputation is sullied by her sexual exploits.

40 *The Corbaccio*, p.34; "e le nostre femmine di grado hanno il cammino smarrito, né vorrebbero già che il cammino fosse loro rinsegnato" (*Il Corbaccio*, ed. Natali, para.269; p.72).

41 *The Corbaccio*, p.32; "quasi ciascuna di loro debba essere l'undecima" (*Il Corbaccio*, ed. Natali, para.257; p.68). There were ten Sybils, as Boccaccio states in the *De mulieribus*.

42 *The Corbaccio*, p.33; "L'altre poche che a questa reverendissima e veramente donna s'ingegnarono con tutta lor forza di somigliare...In luogo d'ira e di superbia ebbero mansuetudine e umiltà; e la rabbiosa furia della carnale concupiscenzia con astinenzia mirabile domarono e vinsono, prestando maravigliosa pazienzia alle temporali adversità e a' martiri" (*Il Corbaccio*, ed. Natali, para.264; p.70).

43 In the *Corbaccio* Boccaccio appears intent on reaffirming distances and re-establishing hierarchies that do not degenerate into impure mixtures. Thus the saints have no connection with the "porcile delle femmine moderne" (*Il Corbaccio*, ed. Natali, para.261; p.69), otherwise referred to as "questa vil turba" (*Il Corbaccio*, ed. Natali, para.262; p.69). In a similar fashion, Boccaccio wants to stress his own hierarchical position, as a scholar in relation to the "meccanica turba" (*Il Corbaccio*, ed. Natali, para.279; p.75).

44 *The Corbaccio*, pp.33–34; "io direi che essa [la natura] fieramente avesse in così fatte donne [le sante] peccato, sottoponendo e nascondendo così grandi animi, così *virili* e così costanti e forti, sotto così *vili* membra e sotto così *vile* sesso come è il femminile, perché bene riguardando chi quelle furono e chi queste sono che nel numero di quelle si vogliono mescolare e in quello essere onorate e reverite, assai bene si vedrà mal confarsi l'una con l'altra, anzi essere del tutto l'une all'altre contrarie" (*Il Corbaccio*, ed. Natali, para.267; p.71 [my emphasis]).

45 Hollander, *Boccaccio's Last Fiction*, p.42.

46 *The Corbaccio*, pp.11–12. ("la sconvenevole pazienzia colla quale io comportai le scellerate e disoneste maniere di colei la quale tu vorresti d'aver veduta esser digiuno" [*Il Corbaccio*, ed. Natali, para.106; p.26).

47 *The Corbaccio*, p.20; "'il secondo Absalone'" (*Il Corbaccio*, ed. Natali, para.170; p.42).

48 See Padoan, *Il Boccaccio*, pp.213–14, 219.

49 *The Corbaccio*, p.32; "Mirabile cosa, in tante migliaia d'anni quante trascorse sono poiché 'l mondo fu fatto, intra tanta moltetudine quanta è stata quella del femmineo sesso, essersene dieci solennissime e savie trovate; e a ciascuna femmina pare essere o una di quelle o degna d'essere tra quelle annoverata" (*Il Corbaccio*, ed. Natali, para.258; p.68).

VI. The Dangers of Dedication: *De mulieribus claris* and Contemporary Politics

1 *Consolatoria*, p.634.
2 *Consolatoria*, p.634.
3 For the dating of the *Consolatoria* see *Tutte le opere di Giovanni Boccaccio*, V, ii, p.617.
4 "germanica..barbarie" (*DMC* 424). See Benson, "Transformations of the 'buona Gualdrada' legend," pp.404–406.
5 Gualdrada's 'outspoken' words correct her father's fawning attitude towards the Emperor and exhibit the desire that her position as a woman and daughter be respected: "lowering her eyes to the ground said in a firm but respectful voice..." [*FW* 449]. Cf. Benson, "Transformations of the 'buona Gualdrada' legend," p.405. Boccaccio re-uses the biography in the *Esposizioni sopra "la Comedia"* (ed. Padoan, pp.690–692). It remains basically the same but the vernacular version includes certain factual details (for example, the name of Boccaccio's informant, the exact name of Gualdrada's father, and more details of territories granted to Guido). These particulars are more suited to the Dante commentary than to Gualdrada's biography which is principally concerned with the presentation of a modest girl transformed into a productive wife.
6 "Frederick, who later turned out to be the monster and scourge not only of Sicily but of all Italy" [*FW* 453].
7 Lactantius provided the key for Boccaccio's 'historical' analysis of the mythicization of Flora in Ovid's *Fasti* (V, 193–212): "Those things [Ovid's account of Flora] are said honestly, but they are dishonestly and disgracefully believed; coverings of poetic language ought not to deceive us when truth is being sought" (*The Divine Institutes*, I, 20; p.76).
8 "Et in quello luogo e campi intorno ove fu la città edificata, sempre nascea fiori et gigli; et però la maggior parte degli abitatori furono consenzienti di chiamarla Flora, e sì che fosse in fiori edificata, cioè con molte delizie" [Cited in Fallani ed., *Inferno*, 1965, commentary on Canto XV, v. 62].
9 See Benson, "Transformations of the 'buona Gualdrada' legend," pp.411, 413. There are later Medicean propagandistic uses of Ovid's version of the Flora myth. See Harness, "La Flora," pp.456–62.
10 *Consolatoria*, p.634. At the end of the *Consolatoria* Boccaccio refers to the natural joys of Certaldo including the "verdi frondi" and "vari fiori" in contrast to the city "dove i cittadini sono tutti atti fittizi" (p.650).
11 Becker makes it clear that the Florentine magnates, given the chance to govern in the aftermath of the expulsion of Walter of Brienne, showed themsleves to be self-serving and failing to work for the general well-being of the city (*Florence in Transition*, II, pp.108–111).
12 "essendo buoni uomini riputati dagl'ingannati, al timone di sì gran legno, in tante tempeste faticato, sono posti" (*Consolatoria*, p.634).
13 *Consolatoria*, p.630.
14 *Consolatoria*, p.642.
15 Brucker, *Florentine Politics*, p.147.
16 When one considers that Boccaccio's *Genealogie* was commissioned by no less a personage than Hugo IV, King of Cyprus (to whom it was dedicated), the wording of the text seems to suggest a hierarchy of humanistically acceptable sub-

jects. See *Genealogie*, I, Prohemium 1, p.44. For the circumstances surrounding the commission of the *Genealogie* see Romano, "Invenzione e fonti," p.156.

17 *FW* xiv–xv. The dedication reveals Boccaccio's intentions in going to Naples, where 'real' power resides in Andrea's brother. It can be read as a rather convoluted declaration of his 'alliance' with Acciaiuoli as virtual ruler of the Kingdom. Boccaccio's invitation had been issued by Acciaiuoli and so it would seem more appropriate for the book to be dedicated to Andrea as a belated tool to further his patronage relations with the family.

18 *FW* xv.

19 I am indebted to Carolyn James for this translation. *Amorosa visione,* vol. III, XLII, ll.28–33, pp.127, 251 ("....con sembianza umile/venia colei che nacque di coloro/li qual, tal fiata con materia vile/aguzzando l'ingegno al lor lavoro./ fer nobile colore ad uopo altrui,/moltiplicando con famiglia in oro").

20 Cf. *FW* xvii–xviii. Virginia Brown attributes this oversight either to "haste or maladroitness" (p.xv) on Boccaccio's part.

21 Boccaccio emphasizes Andrea's exceptionality by referring to her nobility of soul and intelligence "far surpassing the endowments of womankind" [*FW* 3, 5], and stating that God infused her with those virtues which "nature has denied the weaker sex" [*FW* 5]. For a fascinating discussion of the dedication see Benson, *The Invention of the Renaissance Woman*, pp.10–14. Benson argues that by virtue of having a female patron the text is somehow 'feminized', threatening gender roles and relations, "rewriting gender" (p.11). However, because of her public function, Andrea fulfils a 'masculine' role. Thus Benson emphasizes the contradictory nature of the undertaking; that is, the discrepancy between the interests of women and those of the male writer. The choice of Andrea rather than Giovanna, Benson argues, prevents the text from being radically feminist because it shifts the emphasis from the political to the ethical, preventing the possibility of a woman considering taking political power. Thus matriarchy, apparently indicated in the choice of Giovanna, has no real consequences for the ideological position of the text. Benson's argument would have gained more weight, I think, if she had viewed the dedication and the life of Giovanna as a later addition. Up to this point, Boccaccio had included no contemporary female figures in his text and, while the additions do create a new layer of meaning, I do not believe they are irreconcilable with the previous redactions. In other words, Benson's assertion of the text's pro-feminism is perhaps over-stated, and the depth of the contradictions is not fully examined.

22 *FW* 5. A similar statement is to be found in the chapter on Dido: "That pagan woman, for the sake of empty glory, was able to master her ardour and subject herself to a principle; but a Christian woman cannot practise such control in order to acquire eternal glory!" [*FW* 179].

23 Quilligan asserts that the *De mulieribus claris* "is aimed at shaming contemporary male readers into greater humanistic effort" ("Translating dismemberment," p.253).

24 "I think it will be useful and appropriate to deal with the stories at somewhat greater length" [*FW* 11].

25 "I have decided to insert at various places in these stories some pleasant exhortations to virtue and to add incentives for avoiding and detesting wickedness" [*FW* 11]. Boccaccio is insisting here that the commentaries form an essential part of the textual pattern. What is perhaps more noticeable is that the com-

mentaries themselves are considered to be pleasurable as well. The "blandimenta" are described as "lepida." The use of the adjective "lepida" is of further interest because Boccaccio also uses the noun "lepiditas" in the dedication to Andrea Acciaiuoli to refer to the stories themselves. Thus, one might talk about Boccaccio trying to achieve a light, playful touch in the *De mulieribus* in order to insinuate the moral messages into the reader's consciousness, also to make history entertaining as well as informative—in a sense one might regard the 'stories' as pleasant narratives which have a point in the same way as Castiglione would describe (a hundred and fifty years later) the extended joke in the *Cortegiano.* There is, however, a more serious side to the text which comes in the form of "incentives"; that is, the stories themselves together with their moral re-readings are considered overall to militate for a moralistic interpretation.

26 *FW* 11, 13. Margaret Miles notes that "figures of woman can effectively incite both women and men to adopt certain self-images, attitudes and behavior, even when the texts in which representations of woman appear are not addressed to women at all, but rather to men" (*Carnal Knowing,* p.168).

27 See Benson, *The Invention,* pp.22–23. She notes that Penthesilea's history is not explicitly related to the experiences of contemporary women, but does propose that such an avenue is not completely closed off because Boccaccio "leaves it to the reader to apply the knowledge to the modern world" (p.23). However, Boccaccio does not encourage the reader to move far along this path because of the way he structures the final paragraph, guiding it towards a critique of contemporary virility. In fact, the interest of the episode in social terms is removed from the women to how men behave in contemporary society.
The relationship between practice and nature is not as clear as Benson indicates. Boccaccio explains that Penthesilea's extraordinary actions result from the fact that "practical experience can change natural dispositions" [*FW* 131; "usus in naturam vertatur alteram"]. The key word here is "altera" which can be translated as a second nature; that is, not completely transforming 'female' nature, but covering it over or existing alongside the first one. This can be seen in Penthesilea's case in that the major incident of her biography is that she falls in love with Hector, thus forcing the reader's attention back on a more typical female mode of behaviour. The ideological stand represented by *usus* is somewhat contradicted by the life of Penthesilea who conforms more than the other Amazon queens to a more acceptable female role.

28 *FW* 131 ["lepores galeatos"]. The source of this phrase may be found in the Eusebius-Jerome *Chronicon:* "Cornificius [brother of Cornifica (LXXXVI)] poeta a militibus desertus interiit, quos saepe fugientes galeatos lepores appellarat" (241 F; p.159; my emphasis). Cf. Smarr, "Boccaccio and Renaissance women," p.280.

29 "divino quidem munere nobis animus insitus est, cui ignea vis et origo celestis et glorie inexplebilis" (*De casibus,* p.258).

30 "The two groups [pagan and biblical/Christian] do not harmonize very well with each other, and they appear to proceed in different ways: "Following the commands and example of their holy Teacher, Hebrew and Christian women commonly steeled themselves for the sake of true and everlasting glory to an endurance often at odds with human nature" [*FW* 13].

31 "Pagan women, however, reached their goal, admittedly with remarkable strength of character, either through some natural gift or instinct or, as seems more likely, through a keen desire for the fleeting glory of this world; sometimes they endured grievous troubles in the face of Fortune's assaults" [FW 13].

VII. Creating Lives: The Forms of Female Biography

1 In nearly all cases the most obvious signs of narrative pleasure have been eliminated; direct speech is rarely found, often in the form of a concluding statement (single examples of the use of direct speech are in the biographies of Niobe [XV], Pocris [XXVIII], Lucretia [XLVIII], Tamyris [XLIX], and Virginia [LVIII], Cleopatra [LXXXVIII], Paulina [XCI], and Gualdrada [CIII]). The exception that proves the rule is the commentary in the chapter on Dido [XLII] where the text ventriloquizes the standard justifications for remarriage using direct female voices for the purpose of discrediting them. Occasionally, women make long set-piece speeches to persuade others of their point of view: Veturia [LV], Sophonisba [LXX], Camiola [CV]. Flashbacks and flashforwards, magical or improbable details have no place in the De mulieribus. Cf. Müller, pp.43-45.

2 See Aurigemma, "La concezione storica del Petrarca," pp.365-88 and Idem, "Boccaccio e la storia: Osservazioni sul De casibus virorum illustrium ," pp.69-92.

3 The comments of Vittorio Zaccaria are pertinent here: "L'intento moralistico non è dunque superiore a quello letterario; anzi il propositio della edificazione è inferiore a quella della divulgazione culturale (DMC 6). The editor has pinpointed the change in emphasis; in particular, that the effort to push home the moral message of each life treated has become less evident in contrast to De casibus. The question is whether or not the moral discourse takes on new, more subtle forms in recognition of the complexity of the subject-matter.

4 See McLeod, Virtue and Venom, pp.60-63, 76-80.

5 "Hypermnestra, famous [clara] for her lineage and merit, was the daughter of Danaus, king of the Argives, and the wife of Lynceus" [FW 61]. The use of the adjective "clara" is interesting here in light of the work's title because Hypermnestra's fame is due to two elements, one to her birth and the other to her worth. This pairing would appear to be exemplary in the De mulieribus with its strong emphasis on inherited nobility in order to be included in the gallery in the first place and the addition of a noteworthy action which complements the first.

6 The narrative is a good example of how the exceptional woman relates to other women. Hypermnestra is the only one of fifty sisters who spares her husband. This point does not go unnoticed by the commentary on the execrable plan formulated by their father: "Danaus did not notice what an unfortunate example of audacity, deceit, and detestable excess he would bequeath to evil women in the future" [FW 65]. The other unnamed sisters form a counter-exemplum embedded in the same discourse that singles out Hypermnestra. Boccaccio reiterates the point in the last sentence of the chapter. This procedure makes visible, in quasi statistical terms, the rarity of a heroic woman and emphasizes the importance of trust in marriage [FW 65].

7 *FW* 39. Boccaccio then goes on to cite various attributions à la *Genealogie*. In some cases, he attempts to explain why they may have been made (some considered Venus the daughter of Jove in order to create divine origins for her exceptional beauty).

8 Similar details are described in the *Genealogie*; see Bergin, *Boccaccio*, pp.235-36 where the section on Venus is translated.

9 *FW* 129. The case of Gaia Cyrilla [XLVI] is not without interest in this context. Even though the name of her husband is known to Boccaccio, no details of her original family have come down to him: "Although I do not find any record of her origin, I think that Gaia Cyrilla was a Roman or an Etruscan woman" [*FW* 191]. This is the best Boccaccio can do here; he takes care to inform the reader that he has hunted for information, but has come up with a blank. He does, however, make a deduction as to her nationality based on the information he has uncovered in the historical texts available to him. In this way, Boccaccio, draws attention to the fact that he is attempting a historical reading of his information, not an allegorical or a poetical one. The opening statements are his credentials. His 'deduction' also betrays a desire on his part to ensure that 'good' women get a good lineage. This position is partially confirmed in the biography of Sempronia romana [LXXIX] where the writer claims amnesia concerning the family origins of his subject leaving him free to discuss those actions or qualitites that can be considered praiseworthy: "Since I do not recall who they are [her ancestors], let us come to those things that ought to occupy the first place in our discussion because they make a woman worthy of praise or render her name illustrious" [*FW* 329]. The problem is that in this particular biography Boccaccio is more concerned with pointing out Sempronia's negative points (her aberrant sexuality) than praising her positive qualities. Therefore, what could have been viewed as a theoretical realignment (supported by other biographies) is more likely to be an ironical jibe in the context of Sempronia's life story. If the story conformed to Boccaccio's version of positive female qualities, then, the statement could have greater potential in the text. Boccaccio follows his source Sallust particularly closely (*Bellum Catilinarium* [*The War with Catiline*]; XXV). Almost as long as the biography itself is the commentary which explores more general points concerning Sempronia romana's behaviour. This woman, who was a gifted poet in Latin and Greek, seems to be a parody of Cornificia [LXXXVI], also a poet, but chaste and modest. Sempronia's sexuality makes her a danger to men, her poetry challenges male power just as Catiline's conspiracy challenged the Roman state.

10 "[Nobility] arises from a certain habit of the will in the soul that is known by its effects and its strong achievements in rejecting vice and imitating virtue" ("[nobilitas] surgens ex alicius habituata animi voluntate pro viribus executioni mandata spernendi vitia imitandeque virtutis" (*De casibus*, VI, iii, p.488).

11 "plebeiam degeneremque feminam" (*De casibus*, p.854).

12 Ovid concentrates on describing the works of art produced by the two rivals in an extensive *ekphrasis* (*Metam.* VI, 70-128). This is completely eliminated in Boccaccio who is more concerned with drawing out the eheumeristic elements in the account.

13 *FW* 251. Boccaccio's source is Cicero who refers to Leontium as a "little prostitute" ["meretricula"]. Both writers focus on her sexuality rather than her philosophical skills. See Snyder, *The Woman and the Lyre*, pp.103-105.

14 *FW* 193. The use of "clarus" here is interesting since it appears to combine nobility and fame, perhaps with more emphasis on the former.

15 *FW* 217 ("generositas animi"; *DMC* 212). Boccaccio does not emphasize Cloelia's heroism to the same degree as Valerius Maximus (III, 2, 2) or Livy (II, xiii, 6-11). Livy goes so far as to propose that "her feat was a greater one than those of Cocles and Mucius" (II, xiii, 8; p.263). Valerius Maximus suggests that Cloelia showed the way for male valour. Livy concludes his account by remarking that the Roman maiden displayed "new valour in a woman" ("novam in femina virtutem"; II, xiii, 11; p.263) and for this she was given a new honour, an equestrian statue. Boccaccio does not draw out any implications for women and their ability to participate in patriotic heroism; that statue is solely a mark of gratitude. The medieval writer seems more interested in revealing its site in ancient Rome rather than its potential significance in re-gendering heroism. Closer to Dante (*De monarchia*, III, iv, 10), Boccaccio insists on the detail of crossing the Tiber as a piece of exciting narrative and indulges in some speculation about whether Cloelia had ever ridden a horse before! Boccaccio does not view Cloelia as setting a new trend in female valour—it is fundamentally exceptional, and thus the writer does not make any comparisons with heroic actions by men.

16 *FW* 217. The younger Seneca regarded Cloelia as a legendary Roman hero; see Hallett, "Women as *same* and *other*," pp.63-64 and Saxonhouse, *Women in the History of Political Thought*, pp.104-105.

17 "Hecuba, the most famous queen of the Trojans, provides a notable illustration of fleeting glory as well as a sure example [documentum] of human misery" [*FW* 135]. The structure of this sentence nicely reflects the origins of this *exemplum*, re-used from the *De casibus*. The division into two reflects the duality of the earlier text: the culmination of earthly power and splendour followed by catastrophe.

18 Curia's story [LXXXIII] is expressed in the following terms: "she was a splendid example [specimen] in the ancient world of extraordinary constancy and absolute fidelity" [*FW* 345]; and Argia [XXIX] who is similarly praised for her devotion to her husband: "she left to posterity a flawless, splendid, and eternal record of conjugal love" [*FW* 117].

19 *FW* 67. The phrase deliberately contrasts knowledge and false pride, which will be one of the main threads of Boccaccio's re-telling of the myth. Boccaccio separates Niobe and Arachne whose misadventures follow one another in the *Metamorphoses* (VI, 150-51), breaking up the rhythm of good women with the regular intrusion of 'bad'. The deaths of Niobe's children are attributed to a plague by Boccaccio whereas Ovid graphically portrays their end through the direct intervention of the gods—another instance of his euhemeristic approach which lends greater realism to the prose account and makes it more acceptable as a morality tale for a Christian public.

20 "For the most part, Nature has made men high-spirited, while she has given a meek and submissive character to women, who are more suited to luxury than to power" [*FW* 69]. This analysis of difference brought to the surface in this relatively early chapter of the *De mulieribus*, acts as a break on the exceptional women displayed in the text. It reminds the reader that there is a price to pay for breaking the code. The concept of the exceptional woman is so tenuous that it risks becoming part of the oppressive arsenal used against women. The

famous woman is transgressive since "they go beyond the boundaries of their weakness" (*FW* 69).

21 *FW* 361. For a discussion of Boccaccio's Cleopatra see Godman, "Chaucer and Boccaccio's Latin works," pp.282-85.

22 *FW* 361. The mention of Cleopatra's beauty in this context serves to underline the irony of the preface to the *De mulieribus*. The connection that is made between *claritas* and *formositas* undermines the former at the expense of saying anything positive about female beauty; it is seen as a trap not only for men, but for women themselves who define themselves or are defined solely by their sexuality.

23 From the very beginning of the account Triaria is presented as an anti-model. Boccaccio provides a general statement of her 'qualities', emphasizing harmful excess and a lack of control over her passions and sentiments. Triaria's love for her husband is described as "fervidus" (*DMC* 390), and her behaviour more generally is characterized as barbaric and ferocious ("atrocitas" and "ferocitas" [*DMC* 390] are the nouns ascribed to her). Triaria was probably included because she joined her husband in attacking the enemy camp by night and showed herself to be more bloodthirsty and ruthless than most men. In the context of the *De mulieribus* the comment on Triaria, taken up from Tacitus, is significant: "Such was her ferocity...that she seems worthy of mention precisely for this non-feminine characteristic" [*FW* 409]. The implication is that Boccaccio accepted the 'standard' view of a woman as soft and gentle and that the numerous exceptions recorded in the *De mulieribus* demonstrate female possibilities of overcoming their nature, though this is not necessarily considered positive. Triaria is part of the tradition of the *virago*, but represents its decadent face; an example of what happens when pure brutality substitutes for epic bravery.

24 In the biography of Semiramis [II] Boccaccio's methodology is made explicit: "Of Semiramis' many deeds we shall single out the one most worthy of remembrance" [*FW* 21].

25 An example is provided by Claudia [LXII] whose origins are unknown to the writer: "Considering the remarkable devotion she had for her father, I am inclined to believe that Claudia, a Vestal virgin, was a worthy descendant of noble Roman stock" [*FW* 259].

26 This is particularly clear in the commentary on Dido where the contrast between wrongful Christian behaviour and virtuous pagan example is forcefully made, as it was in the dedication to Andrea Acciaiuoli: "let them [women of today] bow their heads in sorrow that Christian women are surpassed in chastity by a woman who was a limb of Satan" [*FW* 179]. Cf. Padoan, "Il *Corbaccio* tra spunti autobiografici e filtri letterari," pp.23-24.

27 The commentary to the biography of Camilla [XXXIX] asks the female reader to concentrate her attention on her chastity. There is no correlative for the freedoms associated with Camilla's break from male-dominated society. Instead, the imaginings of the female reader are all redirected towards her sexual purity.

28 "Indeed, for a woman to be considered completely chaste, she must first curb her wanton and wandering eyes, keeping them lowered and fixed on the hem of her dress" [*FW* 279].

29 Boccaccio follows Pauline tradition by insisting on women's need to curb their speech: "Her words must be not only respectable but brief and uttered at the

right moment" [*FW* 279]. Because of the closed nature of each chapter, possible contradictions are held in suspension, warded off by the sententiousness of some of the commentaries.

30 "She must take care of her house, close her ears to shameful conversation, and avoid gadding about" [*FW* 279].

31 "I decided to write this account as a reproach to the girls of our own day who are so giddy and of such loose morals that, at the wink of an eye or any gesture, they rush into the arms of whoever looks at them" [*FW* 449].

32 Argia's actions bring together all those elements which constitute a heroic version of marriage bonds: "Such were the deeds taught her by true love, total devotion, the sanctity of marriage, and an unshaken chastity" [*FW* 121].

33 Pliny's *Natural History* (VII, xxxv, 120) and Valerius Maximus (VIII, 15, 12) provide basic accounts on to which Boccaccio grafts a commentary concerning chastity constituting about half the chapter.

34 See Müller, pp.123-26.

35 The numerous exclamations of the commentary indicate a firmness of purpose and clarity of judgement about contemporary female behaviour on the part of the commentator. Comments such as "What an insane desire!" [*FW* 177] or "How well spoken!" [*FW* 179] are common in this part of the text. Boccaccio may have been aware of Jerome's letter to Geruchia in which the saint bemoans the decadence of contemporary matrons who might even contemplate marrying "a fourth or even fifth time" (CXXIII.8; p.82). See Desmond, *Reading Dido*, pp. 51-64.

36 It is for this reason that Boccaccio prefers Valerius Maximus to Livy's account as an exemplary source for the wife of Orgiago. Livy introduces a number of details (for example, the complicated machinations required to obtain the gold needed for her release) which are not used by Boccaccio since they only serve to distract from the main point of the story, that is, the dramatic revenge of Orgiago's wife. Indeed, Boccaccio is more interested in providing a substantial commentary on chastity.

37 This section of the Dido chapter also mentions other exemplary figures to make its points: Susanna (in the rare use of a biblical figure), and the negative figure of Valeria Messalina who is now solely characterized by her sexual drive.

38 "Certainly the impulses of the young should be curbed, but this should be done gradually lest we drive them to ruin in their despair by setting up sudden obstacles in their path" [*FW* 61].

39 The choice of Rhea Ilia's punishment is not that recorded by the classical sources, but is found in Polonus, *Chronicon*, p.399 and Eusebius-Jerome, *Chronicon*, p.85a.

40 Boccaccio also discusses other matters such as pride in women at the end of the chapter on Niobe [XV]; foolish ambition, which is connected logically to the story of Arachne [XVIII]; men's and women's respective intellectual gifts (Almathea, XXVI); the importance of the Latin heritage (Nicostrata, XXVII); the relative degrees of guilt of Aegistus and Clytemnestra [XXXVI]; the wrongful acquisition of power and the eventual retribution of divine justice, already discussed in *De casibus* (Athaliah, LI); painting as a superior form of female activity in contrast to the traditional ones (Tamaris [LVI] and chapter on Irene [LIX]; similarly for writing, Cornificia [LXXXVI], Proba [XCVII]); corrupt men of power (Virginia, LVIII); Claudia's love for her father idealized and generalized

[LXII]; "pietas" [LXV] and in the conclusion to the chapter on Harmonia [LXVIII]. The chapter on Busa has a double conclusion: it makes a comparison between Busa and Alexander, and comments positively on the way in which Busa used her wealth; Sophonisba confronts death more bravely than a man [LXX]; the narrator attacks Claudia Quinta's pagan attitude towards the gods contrasting it unfavourably with a Christian one [LXXVII].

41 Christine de Pizan adopts the opposite view, emphasizing the positive role women took in establishing civilization. See Brown-Grant, "Décadence ou prgrès?," pp.295-303.

42 See the commentaries on Medusa [XXII], Pocris [XXVIII] and, Sempronia romana [LXXIX]. Boccaccio claims in the chapter on Pocris that "nothing on earth is more powerful than gold" [FW 115].

43 See the brief discussion in Aurigemma, "Boccaccio e la storia. Osservazioni sul De claris mulieribus," p.100.

44 "If Rome's liberty had not been saved by her pleas, I would curse Veturia for the haughtiness that women have assumed as a result of her actions" [FW 231].

VIII. In the Family/Out the House: Women in Public

1 The chapter on the "Romana iuvencula" [LXV] reverses the normal situation of mother nurturing child with child nurturing mother.

2 FW 305 ("sexus oblita"; DMC 292). It is not the first or only time that Boccaccio used this or a similar expression ("mentita sexum"; FW 19; DMC 32).

3 McLeod, Virtue and Venom, espouses this view (p.67). She considers that good wives are "not very numerous," about 17% of the total. However, McLeod sees the "numerous wicked heroines" (p.68) as more important to the interpretation of the text and concentrates more fully on that category. Yet, the presence of both types would seem to present an opening to analysis.
    I am including under this category the following women: Hypermnestra [XIV], Argia [XXIX], the wives of the Minyans [XXXI], Penelope [XL], Lucretia [XLVIII], Virginia, wife of L. Volumnius [LXIII], Sulpicia [LXVII], wife of Orgiago [LXXIII], Tertia Emilia [LXXIV], Hypsicratea [LXXVIII], wives of the Cimbrians [LXXX], Julia [LXXXI], Portia [LXXXII], Curia [LXXXIII], Sulpicia [LXXXV], Pompeia Paulina [XCIV], Zenobia [C]. Triaria [XCVI] and Sophonisba [LXX] provide ambiguous examples of marital fedelity. This list does not take into account those wives who lose their husbands and still remain faithful to their memory: Dido [XLII], Artemisia [LVII], Antonia [LXXXIX].

4 FW 207 ("virilis femina"; DMC 204). Quilligan argues that "female taciturnity of a such violently self-silencing stripe is the equal of male eloquence in virtue" ("Translating dismemberment," p.261).

5 The wife of Orgiago [LXXIII] offers a forceful variation on the Lucretia theme. She revenges her lost chastity in a memorable way by killing the centurion who had violated her and bringing his head to her husband: "Shouldn't we say that this woman was no barbarian, but a Roman—indeed, a Roman woman who ranks with Lucretia?" [FW309].

6 Boccaccio does not lose this occasion to draw attention to his knowledge of the original sources, here principally Homer's Iliad, to show that he has direct expe-

rience of them ("Every ancient source, first Greek and then Latin, reports that Helen's beauty was so extraordinary as easily to surpass that of other women" [*FW* 143]). This statement tends to support the view that Boccaccio still depended on the Latin sources for his depiction of Helen, but was prepared to complement them with his own experiments in Greek.

7 The text talks of her as "yearning for admiration" [*FW* 147]. And although Helen is not considered the innocent victim of Paris' passion, nonetheless the initial impulse came from the Trojan: "and so, his eyes sparkling with passion, Paris took advantage of every opportunity to instil secretly in her unchaste breast a desire for his love" [*FW* 147].

8 Polyxena's biography bears a certain resemblance to Sophonisba's [LXX], especially in the commentary which focuses on her bravery when confronted with certain death. Her death fills the greater part of the biography (three paragraphs out of four). Only a brief mention is made of her seduction of Achilles leading to his death through her great beauty. Although the commentary highlights the exceptional bravery of Polyxena, it almost lets pass unnoticed the misuse of her beauty. Nevertheless, if the reader takes the women of Troy as a group with Helen as the reference point, then a pattern begins to emerge of beauty bringing about the death and destruction of all those who are seduced by it.

9 In the case of Hecuba, connections are made with Helen's story, but they are not pursued. She sees Deiphobus (Helen's third husband) slaughtered before her eyes, as well as Cassandra and Polyxena who each have a biography in the *De mulieribus*.

10 Harmonia [LXVIII], Sophonisba [LXX]. Boccaccio insists, as he had done, for example, in Argia's biography, that Polyxena's courage depended on the suppression, amongst other things, of "her tender age, female sex, royal delicacy, and altered fortune" [*FW* 133].

11 *FW* 243. Cf. Joshel, "The body female," pp.121–28.

12 As I have already noted, although the *De casibus* includes stories of several of the women who will appear in the *De mulieribus*, the perspective is quite different. For example, in the *De casibus* the female figures are not listed under their own names; rather, it is the man as the carrier of political significance from whom the chapter titles are derived. In general terms, the *exempla* are related to the wider experience of the political world. In contrast, whilst not ignoring the political implications of an historical episode, the *De mulieribus* tends to reduce them to a bare minimum, emphasizing instead values associated with women (such as virginity/chastity). Thus, in spite of many of the *exempla* sharing common elements they are interpreted in a vastly different manner. In the *De casibus* the narrative of Appius Claudius and Virginia provided the author with a forum for an impassioned diatribe against corruption in public office—a diatribe that, in the later work, is reduced to an authorial commentary on the tragic events surrounding the violation and death of Virginia. Moreover, it can be considered almost irrelevant to the narrative thrust of the story; being, rather, the result of the irruption of civic concerns into a work which (given the ambiguous status of women in the *De mulieribus* who are often depicted as active in the social and political world) does not easily accommodate them.

13 Minerva [VI] is declared a virgin, but whether or not this was the source of her
   inspired intellect is not addressed by the biographer; Thisbe [XIII] is a virgin,
   yet the fact is of little or no relevance to the unfolding of her love story; the
   same discourse holds for Penthesilea [XXXII], Polyxena [XXXIII], and Harmonia
   [LXVIII]. In the case of the last-mentioned woman the narrator does not at all
   push the point of her virginity being the inspiration of her action [FW 281]. If
   the narrator's belief in virginity had been such that it was essential for all good
   actions, then his remarks would certainly have been of a different temper.

14 Manto's virginity is only discussed in the last paragraph [7], as it is for
   Erythraea. The assertion of Manto's virginity contradicts the main narrative in
   which her son was the founder of Mantua. In contrast to Erythraea, Manto's
   virginity does not receive unqualified praise. In fact, the commentary ends on
   a negative note because of Manto's association with "nephastis artibus" and her
   pagan beliefs.

15 Apart from Tamaris, they are Irene [LIX] and Marcia [LXVI].

16 Pliny contains very little information on the ancient women painters. The
   longest account is of Martia. Pliny's skeletal biography (Nat. Hist., XXXV,
   147–48) allows Boccaccio to re-focus it and stress the relationship between
   female chastity and art.

17 Boccaccio does not waste this opportunity to castigate men who cannot do the
   same as Marcia: "I believe it was through purity of mind alone that she conquered the sting of the flesh, which occasionally overcomes even the most
   illustrious men, and she kept her body unblemished by any relations with men
   until her death" [FW 275]. By implying that Marcia is superior to some excellent
   men, the text is urging sexual abstinence on both sexes in order to enhance
   their achievements.

18 "Knowledgeable in both Latin and Greek, she did not hesitate to compose
   verses when she wished, and these she wrote, not in the way women usually
   do, but with such discernment as to elicit the admiration of all her readers—a
   feat that would have been notable and praiseworthy for a man of learning" [FW
   329]. It is worth noting that Boccaccio refers to Sempronia's knowledge of Greek
   as part of his program to extend the range of humanistic studies. She displays
   her difference from other women by developing a style of her own, but one
   that is explicitly regarded as masculine wherein, according to Boccaccio, lies
   her achievement.

19 "Then her lover died. Joan, realizing that she had a good mind and drawn by
   the charms of learning, retained her masculine dress and refused to attach herself to anyone else or admit that she was a woman. She persisted diligently in
   her studies and made such progress in liberal and sacred letters that she was
   deemed to excel everyone" [FW 439].
      For a discussion of this chapter and of Boccaccio's manipulation of his
   source for Joan, Martinus Polonus, see Boureau, pp.226–34 and for an
   overview see Patrides, "A palpable hieroglyphick," pp.152–81. Cf. Bullough,
   "Transvestites in the Middle Ages," pp.1388–89; Delcourt, Hermaphrodite,
   pp.89–90 and Atkinson, The Oldest Vocation, pp.1–3. Davis, "Women on top,"
   calls Boccaccio's Joan "a hybrid of the transvestite saint and the cruelly tamed
   shrew" (p.134).

20 See Phillippy, "Establishing authority," p.183; Taylor, "Martin Le Franc's rehabilitation of notorious women," pp.270–71. Boccaccio's probable source,

Martinus Polonus, *Chronicon*, takes a similar negative attitude towards the female Pope: "Nec ponitur in cathalogo sanctorum pontificum propter mulieris sexus quantum ad hoc deformitatem" (p.428).

21 Clarissa Atkinson sees the story as being about "disorder" and Joan "brought down by her own body" (*The Oldest Vocation*, p.3).

22 Boccaccio criticizes men's lack of knowledge of the Bible and unfavourably compares men's attempts at similar, though less difficult enterprises: "From her efforts we can draw another conclusion no less praiseworthy, namely, that Proba had a complete or at least a very full knowledge of the Bible. How rarely this is true of even the men of our own day we know to our regret" [*FW* 413].

By the same account, as he had done for certain of the woman painters, the commentator distances Proba's literary achievement from the domestic tasks of most women. He grants no consideration to social factors that might impinge on women's ability to become writers. Instead, it is put down to female inertia.

23 If we take as our example Chapter XIV, the fact that Hypermnestra was queen of the Argives has no direct bearing on the unfolding of her story.

24 "Their concerns, however, were different from our own vis-à-vis the upbringing of girls. The distaff, workbaskets, and other womanly tasks were set aside" [*FW* 53]. The result of these activities was the acquisition of "virile robur" (*DMC* 64), manly strength that marks their difference from the feminine stereotype. The rejection of domestic activities brings the Amazons close to those other women, such as painters, who are considered to have made a similar choice.

25 *DMC* 62.

26 Interestingly enough, Boccaccio eliminates all those references in the *Aeneid* that make Camilla an Amazon. Virgil is explicit in this regard: "Amid the carnage, like an Amazon,/Camilla rode exultant, one breast bared/For fighting ease, her quiver at her back" (XI, 881–883). Further, Virgil locates the cause of Camilla's downfall "In a girl's love of finery" (XI, 1066). Boccaccio renders the Virgilian sense in more knightly terms as desire for the armour of the man she was pursuing. He also reduces to a bare minimum references to her exploits on the field of battle which show her as a fearsome warrior ("Then to her full height risen drove her axe/Repeatedly through helmet and through bone/As the man begged and begged her to show mercy./Warm brains from his head-wound wetted his face" [XI, 945–948]). It would appear that Boccaccio is trying to attain a fine balance between writing an accurate paraphrase of the Virgilian episode and ignoring those elements that make Camilla too alien, too Amazonian and hence detract from her potential as a model for sexual purity.

27 Boccaccio appears to purposely misread his sources for the queen of Judah by not making explicit the fact that her son had been murdered. He simply states that "Ahaziah died of an arrow wound" (*FW* 209). The sources are clear on this point: "and then they went in search of Ahaziah. the latter was captured while trying to hide in Samaria, and taken to Jehu who put him to death. But they gave him burial" (2 Chronicles 22:8–9). This failure to acknowledge that Athaliah was responding to the political assassination of her family places her future acts in a different light, altogether more bloodthirsty, placing her in yet more stark opposition to the following biography of Cloelia (LII). In Boccaccio's interpretation Athaliah is placed alongside "Atreus, Dionysius, and Jugurtha" (*FW* 211) so that the writer can expatiate on power politics and its ills (perhaps

with an eye to contemporary developments?). Athaliah becomes the material by which Boccaccio expresses his profound disdain of wrongful government.

28 Boccaccio always follows the tradition of Hercules' love for Iole and not Omphale. See *Amorosa visione* (1944), p.XC.

29 In the *De mulieribus* woman's intelligence is generally downgraded to *astutia*, and here is no exception. Iole is the archetypal seductress who manges to 'conquer' Hercules through the manipulation of amorous sentiment, exposing the man's weakness for all to see. The crucial intertext for the effeminate Hercules is Lactantius, *Institutiones divinae*, which defines his actions as "detestabilis turpitudo" (I, IX, 7).

30 *FW* 93. For an interpretation of the Deianira-Hercules relationship see Hallissy, *Venomous Woman*, pp.18–19.

31 Boccaccio's conclusion to the narrative part of the chapter is significant: "In fact, his conqueror Iole triumphed as much and in a more glorious fashion than did Hercules in his victorious struggle, at Eurystheus' behest, with the monsters" [*FW* 93].

32 *DMC* 32. "It was almost as if she wanted to show that spirit, not sex, was needed to govern" [*FW* 19]. The radical possibilities of this statement are substantially undermined by the second part of the biography which shows a Semiramis in the thrall of her sexuality.

33 Cf. Christine de Pizan's treatment of Semiramis discussed by Dulac, "Un mythe didactique chez Christine de Pizan," pp.315–26.

34 See Hamer, *Signs of Cleopatra*, pp.xix, 29–34. This perceptive analysis of Boccaccio's Cleopatra has to be tempered by the fact that Hamer takes the Egyptian queen as representative of the writer's general attitude towards female power. My argument is that Cleopatra is a particular type of queen to be found in the *De mulieribus*—but not the only type. And although sexuality is not neglected by Boccaccio in all his depictions of queens it has varying degrees of explanation for the behaviour of the women.

35 *DMC* 350. Boccaccio purposely fuses the language of sexual desire and that of imperial conquest: "desiderium" refers to both sexual appetite and territorial expansion. The verb "complector" describes Cleopatra's great imperial ambitions and refers indirectly to the means she used to obtain them.

36 *FW* 241. Interestingly enough, Boccaccio was more 'historical' in the *De casibus* in that he accepted the existence of a woman called Artemidora who fought alongside Xerxes, and recognized her historical separation from Artemisia.

37 *FW* 429. In common with other 'positive' figures in the text: "she scorned all womanly occupations" [*FW* 429], thus giving her the space for public action outside the domestic hearth. On Zenobia see Godman, "Chaucer and Boccaccio's Latin works," pp.272–75; Wayne, "Zenobia in medieval and Renaissance literature," pp.51–52, 54–56; O'Brien, "Warrior queen," pp.53–63.

38 Boccaccio alludes to the fact that his account is based on his readings of sources: "legimus" (*DMC* 410) indicates that his work is factually grounded in authoritative writings.

39 It is interesting to note that Christine omits the physical description of Zenobia which is found in the *De mulieribus*. The description forcibly brings to the fore Zenobia's otherness. It emphasizes her dark complexion, suggestive of an innate barbarism. The omission increases Zenobia's standing as a model for readers, while slightly diminishing her 'strangeness'.

40 It may not be coincidental that Cleopatra is mentioned in passing in Zenobia's biography. Cleopatra is seen as the model for convivial, perhaps excessive behaviour: "[She] gave banquets like those of the Roman emperors, using jewelled and golden vessels which she believed had once been used by Cleopatra" [FW 433]. Thus even with such a 'positive' figure as Zenobia one can detect the excess which is generally so heavily punished in the De mulieribus. In fact, just like Cleopatra, she is tending to usurp Roman power by superior emulation and in this one respect she claims adherence to Oriental pleasures.

41 The Emperor and his son are no better than slaves (literally and figuratively) [FW 429].

42 The wording is precise and contrasts strongly with Boccaccio's historical queens: "Soldiers were then dispatched under the command of a courageous leader" [FW 471].

Conclusion

1 For biographical information consult Martellotti, "Albanzani, Donato," pp.611–613. See also Bertoni, Guarino da Verona, pp. 5–7, Scarpati, "Note sulla fortuna editoriale del Boccaccio," pp.211–12 and Zaccaria, "I volgarizzamenti," pp.132–37.

2 Albanzani also translated Petrarch's De viris illustribus, thereby lending credence to the notion that the two works formed a pair. It is difficult to date the translation of De mulieribus claris, but it was certainly written after 1382 (the year of the death of queen Giovanna whose biography is completed in the translation) and most probably around 1395, two years before the Petrarch translation was finished (See Delle donne famose, p.396 where one of the manuscripts of the translation bears the date of its transcription as 8 April 1395, but cf. Martellotti, "Albanzani, Donato," p.612). For the original Latin version of the additional material see Hortis, Studj sulle opere latine del Boccaccio, pp.114–116.

3 The translation is dedicated to the "magnifico Marchese Nicolò da Este principe e signore di Ferrara" (Delle donne famose, p.1). The continuation of the chapter on queen Giovanna allows Albanzani a degree of freedom not provided by the rest of the translation. Thus, before he begins to treat the new material he makes a few remarks about his own patronage relations with Niccolò d'Este: "I, Donato of Casentino, considered the addition necessary by order of the illustrious prince Niccolò, second marquis of Este, who takes more pleasure in books and in famous stories than did Philadelphus. As I was a trusted employee of his family, he instructed me, like another Demetrius, to find books for him" ("E questo giudicai essere a me Donato del Casentino necessario per il comandamento dell'illustre principe Nicolò secondo marchese da Este, il quale ha tanto diletto de' libri, e tanto piacere delle famose storie, che Filadelfo non l'avanzò, essendo io domestico suo famiglio, e da quello essendomi imposto di trovar libri come ad un altro Demetrio"; Delle donne famose, p.391). Demetrius was librarian at Alexandria under Philadelphus. Albanzani is therefore championing the cultural patronage of Niccolò III (and his own position) by making such a comparison.

4 Bartolommeo Goggio, the author of *De laudibus mulierum* composed around 1487) was a Ferrarese notary. Mario Equicola [*De mulieribus*, c.1501] and Agostino Strozzi [*Defensio mulierum*, c.1500] both had close relations with the Ferrarese court. Sabadino degli Arienti [*Gynevera de le clare donne*, 1489–1490; with some material added in 1492] assiduously cultivated his relationship with the duke of Ferrara Ercole d'Este. Jacobo Foresti's, *De plurimis claris selectisque mulieribus* (1497) was probably inspired by a visit to Ferrara which provided him with the opportunity to read Arienti's *Gynevera*.

5 "...studiosamente adornò quest'ultima di maravigliose lodi, perchè quest'opera pervenisse alle sue mani" (*Delle donne famose*, p.390).

6 "And for this reason he was silent, and by remaining quiet he hid many details which might be called true and attempted with marvellous eloquence to magnify that which belonged to her praise" ("E per questo avvenne che egli tace, e tacendo nasconde più cose, le quali si potevano dire vere, e forzossi con maravigliosa eloquenza magnificare quelle che appartenevano a sua lode"; *Delle donne famose*, p.390).

7 "but all-powerful Fortune against which resistence is impossible, as Virgil says, controls everything" ("Ma la fortuna onnipotente, alla quale non si puote resistere, secondo che dice Virgilio, conduce ogni cosa"; *Delle donne famose*, p.393).

8 See Torretta, "Il *Liber de claris mulieribus*," pp.35–36 and Scarpati, "Note sulla fortuna editoriale del Boccaccio," p.212.

9 "Voglio che quella opera *De claris mulieribus*, da me composta, è intitulata a madona Giovanna" (f.A3r). There is another, good example of the translation being used for local encomiastic purposes. In the early sixteenth century, Pietro Summonte, added the life of Eleonora Sanseverino as the last biography of the *De mulieribus claris* (see Mercati, "L'elogio di Eleonora Sanseverino," pp.113–19).

10 *Libro di M. Gio. Boccaccio delle donne illustri, tradotto per Messer Giuseppe Betussi con una addizione fatta dal medesimo delle donne famose dal tempo di M. Giovanni fino a i giorni nostri, e alcune altre state per inanzi con la vita del Boccaccio, et la tavola di tutte l'historie e cose principali, che nell'opra si contengono. All'Illustriss. S. Camilla Pallavicina, marchesa di Corte Maggiore.* [In Venetia per Comin da Trino di Monferrato a instanza di M. Andrea Arrivabene al segno del pozzo. Con grazia et privilegio MDXLV]. For Betussi's biography see Zonta, "Note betussiane," pp.32–66; Mutini, "Betussi, Giuseppe," pp.779–781. See also Kolsky, "Donne gonzaghesche nella *Additione al libro delle donne illustri* di Giuseppe Betussi (1545)," pp.71–88; Nadin Bassani, *Il poligrafo veneto Giuseppe Betussi*, pp.47–54 for some useful comments on the nature of the "Additione"; Mendelsohn, "Boccaccio, Betussi e Michelangelo," pp.329–30; Scarpati, "Note sulla fortuna editoriale del Boccaccio," pp.214–16; Zaccaria, "I volgarizzamenti," pp.137–44.

11 "et il suo ho ridotto in volgare non ad altro fine che per compassione dell'opra, veggendola quasi andata male et per tutto dispersa senza essere da nessuno raccolta" ([f.*iiv).

12 "I have also translated it for the greater pleasure and benefit not of erudite and learned men, but of those noble and virtuous women" (fs.*iiv–*iiir; "L'ho ancho fatto volgare per maggior ornamento et beneficio non degli uomini studiosi et leterati, ma quelle donne nobili et virtuose"). The Latin text was continuously

available from the end of the fifteenth century and throughout the sixteenth. In the fifteenth century, editions were printed in 1473, 1474/5, 1487, and in the sixteenth in 1531, 1539—an indication that the text was still an attractive proposition in spite of shortcomings in terms of its humanistic research, and would enjoy, perhaps partly because of the fame of its author, continued popularity throughout the Renaissance. It was never printed in Italy. In the sixteenth century the number of Latin editions was overtaken by the vernacular translations of which there are five (1506, 1545, 1547, 1558, 1595–96). with the exception of the 1506 edition all the others are the translation of Giuseppe Betussi.

13 Betussi further notes in the dedication "the work has up to now been known to few, but henceforth it will be read by many" (f.*iiir; "che essendo stato fin'ora in cognizione di poche, da qui inanzi andrà per le mani sarà letto da molte"). The adjectives "poche" and "molte" are both in their feminine plural forms.

14 "Benché l'animo mio sia di seguir solamente l'opra del Boccaccio et ripigliandola far memoria non di tutte, ma d'alcune donne le più illustri che siano dopo Giovanna, regina di Gierusalem et di Sicilia fino a giorni nostri" (f.150v).

15 *Libretto apologetico*, p.106. Cacciante stresses Cleopatra's heroic qualities, including in his account only the defeat at the battle of Actium and its consequences. Her suicide 'per grandezza d'animo' has one reason only: the loss of Egypt to the Romans ("non possendo el iugo de la insueta servitù per pacto alcuno patire, essendo stata sì nobile et grande regina, volse più presto morire che vivere serva" [p.106]).

16 One can also recall Equicola's brief treatment of Pope Joan which has no negative overtones unlike the almost entirely negative account found in the *De mulieribus*.

17 See Kolsky, "Wells of knowledge: Moderata Fonte's *Il merito delle donne*," pp. 78–79.

· · · · ·

Bibliography

Primary Sources

Manuscripts

Arienti, Sabadino degli, Giovanni, *Trattato della pudicizia*
    Oxford, Bodleian Library, Ms. Broxbourne 85.7
    ———, *Elogio*
    Dresden, Sächsische Landesbibliothek, F. 134
Boccaccio, Giovanni, *De mulieribus claris*
    Florence, Biblioteca Laurenziana, Ms. go sup. 98
Cornazzano, Antonio, *De mulieribus admirandis*
    Biblioteca Estense e Universitaria, Mss It. Alpha, J. 6, 21.
da Bisticci, Vespasiano, *Libro delle lodi e commendazione delle donne*
    Florence, Biblioteca Riccardiana, Cod. Riccardiano 2293.
Goggio, Bartolommeo, *De laudibus mulierum*
    London, British Library, Add. Ms. 17415.
Strozzi, Agostino, *Defensione delle donne*
    Florence, Biblioteca Nazional Centrale, Ms Palat. 726

Printed Books

Alighieri, Dante. *Opere minori di Dante Alighieri*. Vol. 2 (*Monarchia* e *Questio de aqua et terra*). ed. Pio Gaia. (Turin: UTET, 1986).
———. *Inferno*. ed. Giovanni Fallani (Florence: Messina, 1965).
Bellovacensis, Vincentius. *Speculum historiale*. Vol. 4. (Graz: Akademische Druck—u. Verlagsanstalt, 1965).
Boccaccio, Giovanni. *Johannis Bocacii de Certaldo viri doctissimi Epistola ad Andream de Acciarolis de florentia Alte Ville Comitissam feliciter incipit. Explicit compendium Johannis Boccacij de Certaldo i[d?] quod de precalris mulieribus ac famam perpet-*

uam edidit felictier. (Impressum Rouanii per me Egidium van der Heerstraten. Anno domini MCCCCLXXXVII).

———. *Liber Johannis Boccacij de Certaldo de mulieribus claris summa cum diligentia amplius solito correctus ac per Johannem Ezeiner de Reutlingen.* (Ulme impressus finit filiciter anno domini Mcccclxxiii).

———. *L'opera de misser Giovanni Boccaccio de mulieribus claris.* (Venetia: per Zuanne de Trino 4to, 1506).

———. *Delle donne famose.* Translated by M. Donato degli Albanzani di Casentino detto l'Apenninigena. ed. Giacomo Manzoni. (Bologna: Gaetano Romagnoli editore della R. Commissione pei testi di lingua, 1881).

———. *Amorosa visione.* ed. Vittore Branca. (Florence: Sansoni, 1944).

———. *Concerning Famous Women.* Translated with an introduction and notes, by Guido A. Guarino. (London: George Allen and Unwin, 1964).

———. *Esposizioni sopra la comedia di Dante.* Vol. VI. *Tutte le opere di Giovanni Boccaccio,* ed. Giorgio Padoan (Milan: Mondadori, 1965).

———. *The Decameron.* Translated by G. H. McWilliam. (Harmondsworth: Penguin, 1972).

———. *Amorosa visione.* Vol. III. *Tutte le opere di Giovanni Boccaccio,* ed. Vittore Branca. (Milan: Mondadori, 1974).

———. *The Corbaccio.* Translated by Anthony K. Cassell. (Urbana: University of Illinois Press, 1975).

———. *Decameron.* Vol. 4. *Tutte le opere di Giovanni Boccaccio,* ed. Vittore Branca. (Milan: Mondadori, 1976).

———. *Amorosa visione. Bilingual Edition.* Translated by Robert Hollander, Timothy Hampton, Margherita Frankel, with an introduction by Vittore Branca. (Hanover and London: University Press of New England, 1986).

———. "Consolatoria a Pino de' Rossi." In Vol. V, ii. *Tutte le opere di Giovanni Boccaccio,* ed. Giuseppe Chiecchi. 617-681. (Milan: Mondadori, 1992).

———. *Il Corbaccio.* ed. Giulia Natali. (Milan: Mursia, 1992).

———. *Genealogie deorum gentilium.* Vol. VII-VIII, i. *Tutte le opere di Giovanni Boccaccio,* ed. Vittorio Zaccaria. (Milan: Mondadori, 1998).

———. *Genealogie deorum gentilium; De montibus, silvis, fontibus, lacubus, fluminibus, stagnis seu paludibus, de diversis nominibus maris.* Vol. VII-VIII, ii. *Tutte le opere di Giovanni Boccaccio,* ed. Vittorio Zaccaria and Manlio Pastore Stocchi. (Milan: Mondadori, 1998).

———. *Ioannis Boccatii de certaldo insigne opus de claris mulieribus.* (Bernae Helvetiorum [Bern]: Excudebat Matthias Apiarius, [1539]). Fol.

Chaucer, Geoffrey. *The Legend of Good Women.* Translated by Ann McMillan. (Houston: Rice University Press, 1987).

[Cicero]. *De ratione dicendi (Rhetorica ad Herennium).* Translated by Harry Caplan. (Cambridge, Mass. and London: Harvard University Press and Heinemann, 1968).

de Pizan, Christine. *The Book of the City of Ladies.* ed. Earl Jeffrey Richards. (New York: Persea, 1982).

Diaconus, Paulus. *Historia Romana.* ed. Amadeo Crivellucci. (Rome: Tipografia del Senato, 1914).

Historia d'Egesippo.Tra i christiani scrittori antichissimo de le valorose imprese fatte da Giudei ne l'assedio di Gierusaleme e come fu abbattuta quella città, e molte altre del paese. Breve somma del medesimo di quanto è compreso ne l'opera. Tradotta di latino in italiano per Pietro Lauro modonese. (In Venetia: per Michel Tramezino, MDXLIIII).

Florus, Lucius Annaeus. *Epitome of Roman History. Cornelius Nepos.* Translated by Edward Seymour Forster. (London and New York: William Heinemann and G.P. Putnam's Sons, 1929).

Fulgentius the Mythographer. Translated from the Latin, with introductions by Leslie George Whitbread. (Columbus: Ohio State University Press, 1971).

Jerome, St. *St. Jerome: Letters and Select Works.* Vol. 6. A Select *Library of Nicene and Post-Nicene Fathers of the Christian Church,* ed. Philip Wace Henry Schaff. (New York, Oxford and London: The Christian Literature Company, Parker & Company, 1893).

Jerome, St. *Saint Jérôme. Lettres.* Vol. VII. ed. Jérome Labourt. (Paris: Société d'Edition "Les belles lettres," 1961).

The Works of Josephus. Translated by William Whiston, A.M. (Peabody, Mass.: Hendrickson, 1987).

Justin. *Delle istorie di Giustino, abbreviatore di Trogo Pompejo. Volgarizzamento del buon secolo tratto dai codici riccardiano e laurenziano e migliorato nella lezione colla scorta del testo latino.* ed. Luigi Calori. [Ristampa fotomeccanica eseguita dalla editrice Forni di Bologna sulla edizione di Gaetano Romagnoli, Bologna, 1880]. (Bologna: Commissione per i testi di lingua, 1968).

Justin. *Epitome of the Philippic History of Pompeius Trogus.* Translated by J.C. Yardley, with introduction and explanatory notes by R. Develin. (Atlanta, GA: Scholars Press, 1994).

Juvenal. *The Sixteen Satires.* ed. with an introduction and notes by Peter Green. (Harmondsworth: Penguin, 1967; repr. 1985).

Kohl, Benjamin G. "Petrarch's prefaces to *De viris illustribus.*" *History and Theory* 13 (1974): 132-144.

Lactance. *Institutions divines, livre 1.* Texte critique Introduction traductions et notes par Pierre Monat. (Paris: Les éditions du cerf, 1986).

Lactantius. *The Divine Institutes.* Translated by Sister Mary Francis McDonald, O.P. (Washington, D.C.: The Catholic University of America Press, 1964).

Livy. Vol. 1. Translated by B.O. Forster. (London and New York: Heinemann and Putnam's Sons, 1919).

Lucan. *The Civil War (Pharsalia).* Translated by J.D. Duff. (Cambridge, Mass. and London: Harvard University Press and William Heinemann, 1977).

Macrobius. *The Saturnalia.* Translated with an introduction and notes by Percival Vaughan Davies. (New York and London: Columbia University Press, 1969).

Massimo, Valerio. *Detti e fatti memorabili.* ed. Rino Faranda. (Milan: TEA, 1988).

Maximi, Valeri. *Facta et dicta memorabilia. Libri VII-IX. Ivli Paridis Epitoma. Fragmentvm de praenominibvs. Ianvari nepotiani Epitoma.* Vol. 2. ed. John Briscoe. (Stuttgart and Leipzig: B.G. Teubner, 1998).

Orosio. *Le storie contro i pagani.* Vol. 1 (Libri I-IV). Translated by Aldo Bartalucci, ed. Adolf Lippold. (Milan: Fondazione Lorenzo Valla, 1976).

Osgood, Charles G. *Boccaccio on Poetry.* (New York: The Liberal Arts Press, 1956; repr. of 1st ed. [Princeton University Press, 1930]).

Ovid. *Heroides and Amores.* Translated by Grant Showerman. (London and New York: Heinemann and MacMillan, 1914).

———. *Metamorphoses.* Vol. 2. Translated by Frank Justus Miller. (London and New York: Heinemann and G.P. Putnam's Sons, 1916).

————. *Fasti*. Translated by Sir James George Frazer. (London and New York: Heinemann and G.P. Putnam's Sons, 1931).

Petrarca, Francesco. *Rerum memorandum libri*. ed. Giuseppe Billanovich. (Florence: Sansoni, 1943).

————. *La vita di Scipione l'Africano*. ed. Guido Martellotti. (Milan-Naples: Ricciardi, 1954).

————. *Prose*. ed. P.G. Ricci, G. Martellotti, E. Carrara, E. Bianchi. (Milan-Naples: Ricciardi, 1955).

————. *Le familiari*. ed. Umberto Bosco. [Ristampa anastatica della prima edizione del 1942] (Florence: Sansoni, 1968).

————. *Le familiari [Libri I-XI]*. Vol. 1/1, 1/2. ed. Ugo Dotti. (Urbino: Argalìa, 1974).

————. *Opere [Canzoniere, Trionfi, Familiarum Rerum Libri]* (Florence: Sansoni, 1975).

————. *Opere latine*. Vol. 2. ed. Antonietta Bufano. Reprint of 1975 ed. (Turin: UTET, 1987).

————. *Triumphi*. ed. Marco Ariani. (Milan: Mursia, 1988).

Petrarch's 'Africa'. Translated and annotated by Thomas G. Bergin and Alice S. Wilson. (New Haven and London: Yale University Press, 1977).

Pliny. *Natural History*. Vol. II (Libri III-VII). Translated by H. Rackham. (London and Cambridge, Mass.: Heinemann and Harvard University Press, 1942).

————. *Natural History*. Vol. III (Libri VIII-XI). Translated by H. Rackham. (London and Cambridge, Mass.: William Heinemann and Harvard University Press, 1947).

[Polonus, Martinus]. *Martini Oppaviensis Chronicon pontificum et imperatorum*. Vol. XXII. *Monumenta Germaniae Historica Scriptorum*, ed. Ludewicus Weiland. (Hanover: Bibliopolii Aulici Halniani, 1872).

Sallust. Translated by J.C. Rolfe. (London and Cambridge, Mass.: William Heinemann and Harvard University Press, 1965).

Strabo. *The Geography of Strabo*. Vol. III. Translated by Horace Leonard Jones. (Cambridge, Mass. and London: Harvard University Press and William Heinemann, 1967; [First published 1924]).

Tacitus. *The Histories*. Vol. 2. Translated by Clifford H Moore. (Cambridge, Mass. and London: Harvard University Press and William Heinemann, 1968).

Teodosio, Macrobio. *I saturnali*. 1st ed. 1967; 2nd ed. revised 1977, ed. Nino Marinone. (Turin: UTET, 1977).

Textes grecs et latins relatifs à l'histoire de la peinture ancienne. Vol. 1. Traduits et commentés par Adolphe Reinach. (Paris: Klincksieck, 1921).

Varanini, Giorgio and Baldassarri, Guido, ed. *Racconti esemplari di predicatori del Due e Trecento*. Vol. 2. (Rome: Salerno, 1993).

Secondary Sources

VI Centenario della morte di Giovanni Boccaccio. Mostra di manoscritti, documenti e edizioni. Firenze—Biblioteca medicea laurenziana 22 maggio—31 agosto 1975. Vol. I, *manoscritti e documenti*. (Certaldo: 1975).

Allen, Don Cameron. "Marlowe's *Dido* and the tradition." In *Essays on Shakespeare and Elizabethan Drama in Honour of Hardin Craig*, ed. Richard Hosley. 55–68. (London: Routledge & Kegan Paul, 1963).

Allen, Prudence. *The Concept of Woman: The Aristotelian Revolution 750BC–AD1250.* (Montreal and London: Eden Press, 1985).

Ames, Ruth M. "The feminist connections of Chaucer's *Legend of Good Women.*" In *Chaucer in the Eighties,* ed. Robert J. Wasserman and Julian N. Blanch. 57–74. (Syracuse, N.Y.: Syracuse University Press, 1986).

Anderson, Bonnie S. and Zinsser, Judith P. *A History of Their Own. Women in Europe from Prehistory to the Present.* Vol. 2. (New York: Harper & Row, 1988).

Anson, John. "The female transvestite in early monasticism: the origin and development of a motif." *Viator* 5 (1974): 1–32.

Appleton, Ch. "Trois épisodes de l'histoire ancienne de Rome: Les Sabines, Lucrèce, Virginie." *Revue historique de droit français et étranger* 3 (1924): 193–271, 592–670.

Arjava, Antti. "Jerome and women." *Arctos. Acta philologica pennica* 24 (1990): 5–18.

Atkinson, Clarissa W. *The Oldest Vocation: Christian Motherhood in the Middle Ages.* (Ithaca and London: Cornell University Press, 1991).

Aurigemma, Marcello. "La concezione storica del Petrarca nel primo nucleo del *De viris illustribus.*" In *Miscellanea di studi in onore di Vittore Branca,* 365–88. Vol. 1, *Dal medioevo al Petrarca.* (Florence: Olschki, 1983).

———. "Boccaccio e la storia: osservazioni sul *De casibus virorum illustrium.*" *Studi latini e italiani* 1 (1987): 69–92.

———. "Boccaccio e la storia. Osservazioni sul *De claris mulieribus.*" In *Humanitas e poesia. Studi in onore di Gioacchino Paparelli,* ed. L. Reina. 85–102. (Salerno: Laveglia, 1988–1990).

Bacchi della Lega, Alberto. *Serie delle edizioni delle opere di Giovanni Boccaccio latine volgari, tradotte e trasformate.* [Ristampa anastatica della ed. di Bologna, Romagnoli, 1875] (Bologna: Forni, 1967).

Barański, Zygmunt G. "The constraints of form: towards a provisional definition of Petrarch's *Triumphi.*" In *Petrarch's 'Triumphs! Allegory and Spectacle,* ed. Konrad Eisenbichler and Amilcare A. Iannucci. 63–83. (Ottawa: Dovehouse, 1990).

Barr, Jane. "The influence of saint Jerome on medieval attitudes to women." In *After Eve,* ed. Janet Martin Soskice. 89–102. (London: Collins Marshall Pickering, 1990).

———. "The Vulgate Genesis and St. Jerome's attitudes to women." In *Equally in God's Image. Women in the Middle Ages,* ed. Constance S. Wright, Julia Bolton Holloway and Joan Bechtold. 122–28. (New York: Peter Lang, 1990).

Barricelli, Gian Piero. "Satire of satire: Boccaccio's *Corbaccio.*" *Italian Quarterly* 18 (1975): 95–111.

Baskins, Cristelle L. *Cassone Painting, Humanism, and Gender in Early Modern Italy.* (Cambridge: Cambridge University Press, 1998).

Battaglia, Salvatore. *La coscienza letteraria del medioevo.* (Naples: Liguori, 1965).

Becher, Ilse. *Das bild der Kleopatra in der Griechischen und Lateinischen literatur.* (Berlin: Akademie–Verlag, 1966).

Becker, Marvin B. *Florence in Transition.* Vol. II, *Studies in the Rise of the Territorial State.* (Baltimore: The Johns Hopkins Univerity Press, 1968).

Benson, Pamela Joseph. *The Invention of the Renaissance Woman. The Challenge of Female Independence in the Literature and Thought of Italy and England.* (University Park, Pennsylvania: The Pennsylvania State University Press, 1992).

———. "Transformations of the 'buona Gualdrada' legend from Boccaccio to Vasari: A study in the politics of Florentine narrative." In *Women in Italian Renaissance Culture and Society,* ed. Letizia Panizza. 401–20. (Oxford: Legenda, 2000).

Bergin, Thomas G. *Boccaccio*. (New York: Viking, 1981).

———. "Boccaccio and the family." *Rivista di studi italiani* 1 (1983): 15–30.

Berlioz, Jacques. "*Exempla* as a source for the history of women." In *Medieval Women and the Sources of Medieval History*, ed. Joel T. Rosenthal. 37–50. (Athens and London: The University of Georgia Press, 1990).

Berlioz, Jacques and Polo de Beaulieu, Marie Anne, ed. *Les Exempla médiévaux. Introduction à la recherche, suivie des tables critiques de l'Index exemplorum' de Federic C. Tubach*. (Carcassone: Gavae/Hesiode, 1992).

———. "Les recueils d'*Exempla* et la diffusion de l'encyclopédisme médiéval." In *L'enciclopedismo medievale*, ed. Michelangelo Picone. 179–212. (Ravenna: Longo, 1992).

Bernardo, Aldo S. *Petrarch, Scipio and the 'Africa'. The Birth of Humanism's Dream*. (Westport, Connecticut: Greenwood Press, 1962)

———. *Petrarch, Laura, and the 'Triumphs'*. (Albany: State University of New York Press, 1974).

———. "Triumphal poetry: Dante, Petrarch, and Boccaccio." In *Petrarch's 'Triumphs'. Allegory and Spectacle*, ed. Konrad Eisenbichler and Amilcare A. Iannucci 33–45. (Ottawa: Dovehouse, 1990).

Berriot-Salvadore, Evelyne. *Un corps, un destin. La femme dans la médecine de la Renaissance*. (Paris: Champion, 1993).

———. "The discourse of medicine and science." In *Renaissance and Enlightenment Paradoxes*, ed. Natalie Zemon Davis and Arlette Farge. 348–388. Vol. 3 of *A History of Women in the West*. (Cambridge, Mass. and London: Belknap Press of Harvard University Press, 1994).

Bertoni, Giulio. *La biblioteca estense e la coltura ferrarese ai tempi del Duca Ercole I (1471–1505)*. (Turin: Loescher, 1903).

Billanovich, Giuseppe. "Dalla *Commedia* e dall'*Amorosa visione* ai *Trionfi*." *Giornale storico della letteratura italiana* 123 (1946): 1–52.

———. *Petrarca letterato*. Vol. I, *Lo scrittoio del Petrarca*. (Rome: Edizioni di storia e letteratura, 1947).

———. *Restauri boccacceschi*. (Rome: Edizioni di storia e letteratura, 1947).

———. "Il Boccaccio, il Petrarca e le più antiche traduzioni in italiano delle *Decadi* di Tito Livio." *Giornale storico della letteratura italiana* 130 (1953): 311–337.

Bird, Phyllis. "Images of women in the Old Testament." In *Religion and Sexism. Images of Woman in the Jewish and Christian Traditions*, ed. Rosemary Radford Ruether. 41–88. (New York: Simon and Schuster, 1974).

Biscoglio, Frances M. "'Unspun heroes': iconography of the spinning woman in the Middle Ages." *Journal of Medieval and Renaissance Studies* 25 (1995): 163–176.

Blamires, Alcuin. *The Case for Women in Medieval Culture*. (Oxford: Clarendon Press, 1997).

Blanchard, Joël. "Compilation and legitimation in the fifteenth century: *Le Livre de la Cité des Dames*." In *Reinterpreting Christine de Pizan*, ed. Earl Jeffrey Richards with Joan Williamson, Nadia Margolis, and Christine Reno. 228–249. (Athens and London: The University of Georgia Press, 1992).

Bliss, Lee. "The Renaissance Griselda: a woman for all seasons." *Viator* 23 (1992): 301–343.

Bloch, R. Howard. "Medieval misogyny." *Representations* 20 (1987): 1–24.

Blumenfeld-Kosinski, Renate. "Christine de Pizan and the misogynistic tradition." *Romanic Review* 81 (1990): 279–292.

Bock, Gisela. "Women's history and gender history: aspects of an international debate." *Gender & history* 1 (1989): 7–30.

Boureau, Alain. *La papesse Jeanne*. (Paris: Aubier, 1988).

Bozzolo, Carla. "Il *Decameron* come fonte del *Livre de la cité des dames* di Christine de Pizan." In *Miscellanea di studi e ricerche sul Quattrocento francese*, ed. Franco Simone. 3–24. (Turin: Giappichelli, 1967).

Branca, Vittore. "L'*Amorosa visione* (tradizione, significati, fortuna)." *Annali della R. Scuola Normale Superiore di Pisa* serie II, 11 (1942): 20–47.

———. *Tradizione delle opere di Giovanni Boccaccio. I. Un primo elenco dei codici e tre studi*. Vol. 1. (Rome: Edizioni di storia e letteratura, 1958).

———. *Giovanni Boccaccio. Profilo biografico*. (Florence: Sansoni, 1977).

———. "Petrarch and Boccaccio." In *Francesco Petrarca Citizen of the World. Proceedings of the World Petrarch Congress Washington, D.C., April 6–13 1974*, ed. Aldo S. Bernardo. 193–221. (Padua and Albany: Antenore and State University of New York Press, 1980).

———. *Tradizione delle opere di Giovanni Boccaccio. II. Un secondo elenco di manoscritti e studi sul testo del 'Decameron' con due appendici*. Vol. 2. (Rome: Edizioni di storia e letteratura, 1991).

———. *Boccaccio medievale e nuovi studi sul 'Decameron'*. Nuova ed. riveduta e corretta (Florence: Sansoni, 1996).

Bremond, Claude, Jacques Le Goff, and Jean-Claude Schmitt. *L'Exemplum*. (Turnhout: Brepols, 1982).

Bronfman, Judith. *Chaucer's 'Clerk's Tale'. The Griselda Story Received, Rewritten, Illustrated*. (New York & London: Garland, 1994).

Brown Jr., Emerson. "Biblical women in the *Merchant's Tale*: feminism, antifeminism and beyond." *Viator* 5 (1974): 387–412.

Brown-Grant, Rosalind. "Décadence ou progrès? Christine de Pizan, Boccace et la question de l'âge d'or." *Revue des langues romanes* 92 (1988): 295–303.

———. "Des hommes et des femmes illustres: modalités narratives et transformations génériques chez Pétrarque, Boccace et Christine de Pizan." In *Une femme de lettres au Moyen Age. Etudes autour de Christine de Pizan*, ed. Liliane Dulac and Bernard Ribémont. 469–480. (Orléans: Paradigme, 1995).

Brownlee, Kevin. "Martyrdom and the female voice: saint Christine in the *Cité des dames*." In *Images of Sainthood in Medieval Europe*, ed. Renate Blumenfeld-Kosinski and Timea Szell. 115–35. (Ithaca and London: Cornell University Press, 1991).

———. "Il *Decameron* di Boccaccio e *La Cité des Dames* di Christine de Pizan." *Studi sul Boccaccio* 20 (1991–92): 233–51.

———. "Discourses of the self: Christine de Pizan and the *Romance of the Rose*." In *Rethinking the 'Romance of the Rose'. Text, Image, Reception*, ed. Kevin Brownlee and Sylvia Huot. 234–61. (Philadelphia: University of Pennsylvania Press, 1992).

Brucker, Gene A. *Florentine Politics and Society, 1343–1378*. (Princeton, New Jersey: Princeton University Press, 1962).

Bruni, Francesco. *Boccaccio. L'invenzione della letteratura mezzana*. (Bologna: Il Mulino, 1990).

Bryce, Judith. "Women's experience in Renaissance Florence: some recent research." *Journal of the Association of Teachers of Italian* 55 (1989): 3–16.

Buettner, Brigitte. *Boccaccio's 'Des cleres et nobles femmes'. Systems of Signification in an Illuminated Manuscript.* (Seattle and London: College Art Association in association with University of Washington Press, 1996).

Buford, Albert H. "History and biography: the Renaissance distinction." In *A Tribute to George Coffin Taylor*, ed. A. Williams. 100–112. (Chapel Hill, N.C.: University of North Carolina Press, 1953).

Bullough, Vern L. "Medieval medical and scientific views of women." *Viator* 4 (1973): 485–501.

———. *The Subordinate Sex: A History of Attitudes Towards Women.* (Urbana, Chicago, London: University of Illinois Press, 1973).

———. "Transvestites in the Middle Ages." *American Journal of Sociology* 79 (1974): 1381–94.

Cadden, Joan. *Meanings of Sex Difference in the Middle Ages. Medicine, Science, and Culture.* (Cambridge: Cambridge University Press, 1993).

Cadogan Rothery, Guy. *The Amazon in Antiquity and Modern Times.* (London: 1910).

Callu, Florence and Avril, François. *Boccace en France. De l'humanisme à l'érotisme.* (Paris: Bibliothèque Nationale, 1975).

Capomacchia, Anna Maria G. *Semiramis. Una femminilità ribaltata.* (Rome: "L'Erma" di Bretschneider, 1986).

Carraro, Analisa. "Tradizioni culturali e storiche nel *De casibus*." *Studi sul Boccaccio* 12 (1980): 197–262.

Casali, Sergio. "Tragic irony in Ovid, *Heroides* 9 and 11." *Classical Quarterly* 45 (1995): 505–511.

Casella, Maria Teresa. *Tra Boccaccio e Petrarca. I volgarizzamenti di Tito Livio e di Valerio Massimo.* (Padua: Antenore, 1982).

Castelli, Elizabeth. "Virginity and its meaning for women's sexuality in early Christianity." *Journal of Feminist Studies in Religion* 2 (1986): 61–88.

Cerbo, Anna. "Il *De mulieribus claris* di Giovanni Boccaccio." *Arcadia. Accademia letteraria italiana. Atti e Memorie*, Serie 3a, 6 (1974): 51–75.

———. "Didone in Boccaccio." *Annali dell'Istituto Universitario Orientale di Napoli, Sezione Romanza* 21 (1979): 177–219.

———. "Tecniche narrative del Boccaccio latino." *Annali dell'Istituto Universitario Orientale di Napoli, Sezione Romanza* 22 (1980): 317–57.

———. "Una novella in latino del Boccaccio: 'De Paulina romana femina'." *Annali dell'Istituto Universitario Orientale di Napoli, Sezione Romanza* 23 (1981): 561–606.

———. *Ideologia e retorica nel Boccaccio latino.* (Naples: Ferraro, 1984).

Chabot, Isabelle. "'Sola, donna, non gir mai'. Le solitudini femminili nel Tre-Quattrocento." *Memoria* 18 (1986): 7–24.

———. "Widowhood and poverty in late medieval Florence." *Continuity and Change* 3 (1988): 291–311.

Chiari, Alberto. *Indagini e letture. Terza serie.* (Florence: Le Monnier, 1961).

Chiecchi, Giuseppe. "La lettera a Pino de' Rossi. Appunti cronologici, osservazioni e fonti." *Studi sul Boccaccio* 11 (1979): 295–331.

———. "Sollecitazioni narrative nel *De casibus virorum illustrium*." *Studi sul Boccaccio* 19 (1990): 103–49.

Chojnacki, Stanley. "Daughters and oligarchs: gender and the early Renaissance state." In *Gender and Sex in Renaissance Italy*, ed. J.C. Brown and R.C. Davis. 63–86. (New York: Longman, 1998).

Ciletti, Elena. "Patriarchal ideology in the Renaissance iconography of Judith." In *Refiguring Woman. Perspectives on Gender and the Italian Renaissance,* ed. Marilyn Migiel and Juliana Schiesari. 35–70. (Ithaca and London: Cornell University Press, 1991).

Cohn Jr., Samuel K. "Donne in piazza e donne in tribunale a Firenze nel Rinascimento." *Studi storici* 22 (1981): 515–33.

———. "The social history of women in the Renaissance." In *Women in the Streets. Essays on Sex and Power in Renaissance Italy,* ed. Samuel K. Cohn Jr. 1–15. (Baltimore and London: The Johns Hopkins University Press, 1996).

Collina, Beatrice. "L'esemplarità delle donne illustri fra umanesimo e controriforma." In *Donna, disciplina, creanza cristiana dal XV al XVII secolo. Studi e testi a stampa,* ed. Gabriella Zarri. (Rome: Edizioni di storia e letteratura, 1996).

Consoli, Joseph P. *Giovanni Boccaccio: An Annotated Bibliography.* (New York: Garland, 1991).

Constantini, Aldo Maria. "Studi sullo zibaldone magliabechiano." *Studi sul Boccaccio* 7 (1973): 21–58.

———. "La presenza di Martino Polono nello zibaldone magliabechiano del Boccaccio." In *Italia Venezia e Polonia tra medio evo e età moderna,* ed. Vittore Branca and Sante Craciotti. 363–70. (Florence: Olschki, 1980).

Cooke, John Daniel. "Euhemerism: A mediaeval interpretation of classical paganism." *Speculum* 2 (1927): 396–410.

Cortese, Albertina. "Un documento sulla condanna di Pino de' Rossi." *Studi sul Boccaccio* 2 (1964): 15–24.

Coulter, Cornelia C. "Boccaccio's acquaintance with Homer." *Philological Quarterly* 5 (1926): 44–53.

———. "Boccaccio's knowledge of Quintilian." *Speculum* 33 (1958): 490–96.

———. "The manuscripts of Tacitus and Livy in the 'parva libreria'." *Italia medioevale e umanistica* 3 (1960): 281–85.

Cox, Patricia. *Biography in Late Antiquity. A Quest for the Holy Man.* (Berkeley, Los Angeles, London: University of California Press, 1983).

d'Alverny, Marie-Thérèse. "Comment les théologiens et les philosophes voient la femme." *Cahiers de civilisation médiévale. Xe-XIIe siècles* 20 (1977): 105–129.

D'Ancona, Paola. "Gli affreschi del castello di Manto nel Saluzzese." *L'arte* 8 (1905): 94–106, 183–98.

D'Onofrio, Cesare. *La Papessa Giovanna: Roma e papato tra storia e leggenda.* (Rome: Romana società editrice, 1979).

Daenens, Francine. "Eva, mulier, femina: étymologies ou discours véritables sur la femme dans quelques traités italiens du XVIe siècle." *Les lettres romanes* 41 (1987): 5–28.

Davies, Stevie. *The Idea of Woman in Renaissance Literature. The Feminine Reclaimed.* (Brighton: The Harvester Press, 1986).

Davis, Natalie Zemon. "Women on top." In *Society and Culture in Early Modern France,* 124–51. (Stanford, California: Stanford University Press, 1975).

De La Mare, Albinia C. and Reynolds, Catherine. "Boccaccio visualizzato VI. 4. Illustrated Boccaccio manuscripts in Oxford libraries." *Studi sul Boccaccio* 20 (1991–92): 55–60.

De Maio, Romeo. *Donna e Rinascimento.* (Milan: Mondadori, 1987).

De Matteis, M.C., ed. *Idee sulla donna nel medievo. Fonti e aspetti giuridici, antropologici, religiosi, sociali e letterari della condizione femminile.* (Bologna: Pàtron, 1981).

de Nolhac, M. Pierre. "Le *De viris illustribus* de Pétrarque. Notice sur les manuscrits originaux, suivie de fragments inédits." *Notices et extraits des manuscrits de la Bibliothèque nationale et autres bibliothèques* 34 (1891): 61–148.

———. "Boccace et Tacite." *Mélanges d'archéologie et d'histoire* 12 (1892): 125–148.

Dean-Jones, Lesley. "The cultural construct of the female body in classical Greek science." In *Women's History and Ancient History*, ed. Sarah B. Pomeroy. 111–37. (Chapel Hill and London: The University of North Carolina Press, 1991).

Degani, Chiara. "Riflessi quasi sconosciuti di *exempla* nel *Decameron*." *Studi sul Boccaccio* 14 (1983–84): 189–208.

Delany, Sheila. "Rewriting woman good. Gender and the anxiety of influence in two late-medieval texts." In *Chaucer in the Eighties*, ed. Julian N. Wasserman and Robert J. Blanch. 75–92. (Syracuse, New York: Syracuse University Press, 1986).

———. "The naked text: Chaucer's 'Thisbe', the *Ovide moralisé*, and the problem of *translatio studii* in *The Legend of Good Women*." *Mediaevalia* 13 (1987): 275–94.

Delcorno, Carlo. "L'exemplum nella predicazione volgare di Giordano da Pisa." *Istituto veneto di scienze, lettere ed arti. Memorie. Classe di scienze morali, lettere ed arti* 36 (1972): 3–121.

———. *Exemplum e letteratura. Tra medioevo e Rinascimento*. (Bologna: Il Mulino, 1989).

———. "Nuovi studi sull'exemplum'. Rassegna." *Lettere Italiane* 46 (1994): 459–97.

Delcourt, Marie. *Hermaphrodite. Myths and Rites of the Bisexual Figure in Classical Antiquity*. Translated by Jennifer Nicholson. (London: Studio Books, 1961).

Delhaye, Ph. "Le dossier anti-matrimonial de l'*Adversus Jovinianum* et son influence sur quelques écrits latins du XIIe siècle." *Mediaeval Studies* 13 (1951): 65–86.

Delmay, Bernard. *I personaggi della "Divina commedia." Classificazione e regesto*. (Florence: Oschki, 1986).

Desmond, Marilynn. *Reading Dido. Gender, Textuality, and the Medieval 'Aeneid'*. (Minneapolis and London: University of Minnesota Press, 1994).

Donaldson, Ian. *The Rapes of Lucretia. A Myth and its Transformations*. (Oxford: Clarendon, 1982).

Donato, Maria Monica. "Gli eroi romani tra storia ed 'exemplum'. I primi cicli umanistici di Uomini Famosi." In *Memoria dell'antico nell'arte italiana*. Vol. 2, *I generi e i temi ritrovati*. ed. Salvatore Settis. 97–125. (Turin: Einaudi, 1985).

Doran, Madeleine. "Pyramus and Thisbe once more." In *Essays on Shakespeare and Elizabethan Drama in Honour of Hardin Craig*, ed. Richard Hosley. 149–61. (London: Routledge & Kegan Paul, 1963).

Dronke, Peter. "*Semiramis*. The recreation of myth." In *Poetic Individuality in the Middle Ages. New Departures in Poetry 1000–1150*. 66–113. (Oxford: Clarendon, 1970).

DuBois, Page. *Centaurs and Amazons: Women in the Pre-History of the Great Chain of Being*. (Ann Arbor: University of Michigan Press, 1982).

Dulac, Liliane. "Un mythe didactique chez Christine de Pizan: Sémiramis ou la veuve héroique (Du *De mulieribus claris de Boccace à la Cité des dames*)." In *Mélanges de philologie romane offerts à Charles Camproux*, 315–43. Vol. 1. (Montpellier: 1978).

Edmunds, Lowell. "A note on Boccaccio's sources for the story of Oedipus in *De casibus illustrium virorum* and in the *Genealogie*." *Aevum* 56 (1982): 248–252.

Elshtain, Jean Bethke. *Public Man, Private Woman. Women in Social and Political Thought*. (Oxford: Princeton University Press, 1981).

Fietze, Katharina. *Spiegel der vernunft. Theorien zum menschsein der frau in der anthropologie des 15. Jahrhunderts.* (Paderborn, Munich, Vienna, Zurich: Schöningh, 1991).

Foresti, Arnaldo. "Il Boccaccio a Ravenna nell'inverno 1361–62." *Giornale storico della letteratura italiana* 98 (1932): 73–83.

Fraioli, Deborah. "The literary image of Joan of Arc: prior influences." *Speculum* 56 (1981): 811–30.

Freccero, Carla. "Economy, Woman, and Renaissance discourse." In *Refiguring Woman. Perspectives on Gender and the Italian Renaissance,* ed. Marilyn Migiel and Juliana Schiesari. 192–208. (Ithaca and London: Cornell University Press, 1991).

Gaeta, Franco. "L'avventura di Ercole." *Rinascimento* 5 (1954): 227–60.

Galinsky, G. Karl. *The Herakles Theme. The Adaptations of the Hero in Literature from Homer to the Twentieth Century.* (Oxford: Blackwell, 1972).

Galinsky, Hans. *Der Lucretia-stoff in der weltliteratur.* (Breslau: Priebatsch, 1932).

Ganio Vecchiolino, Paola. "Due modi di narrare: il Boccaccio latino e il *Decameron.*" *Critica letteraria* 77 (1992): 655–77.

Garraty, J.A. *The Nature of Biography.* (Oxford: Alden Press, 1957).

Gera, Deborah. *Warrior Women. The Anonymous "Tractatus de mulieribus."* (Leiden: E.J. Brill, 1997).

Gilman, Donald. "Petrarch's Sophonisba: seduction, sacrifice, and patriarchal politics." In *Sex and Gender in Medieval and Renaissance Texts. The Latin Tradition,* ed. Barbara K. Gold, Paul Allen Miller, and Charles Platter. 111–138. (Albany: State University of New York Press, 1997).

Ginsberg, Warren. *The Cast of Character: The Representation of Personality in Ancient and Medieval Literature.* (Toronto, Buffalo, London: University of Toronto Press, 1983).

Glenn, Cheryl. *Rhetoric Retold. Regendering the Tradition from Antiquity Through the Renaissance.* (Carbondale & Evansville: Southern Illinois University Press, 1997).

Godman, Peter. "Chaucer and Boccaccio's Latin works." In *Chaucer and the Italian Trecento,* ed. Piero Boitani. 269–295. (Cambridge: Cambridge University Press, 1983).

Gottlieb, Beatrice. "The problem of feminism in the fifteenth century." In *Women of the Medieval World. Essays in Honor of John H. Mundy,* ed. Julius Kirshner and Suzanne F. Wemple. 337–64. (Oxford: Blackwell, 1985).

Hacker, Barton C. "Women and military institutions in early modern Europe: A reconnaissance." *Signs: Journal of Women in Culture and Society* 6 (1981): 643–671.

Haley, Shelley P. "Livy's Sophoniba." *Classica et Mediaevalia* 40 (1989): 171–181.

Hallett, Judith P. "Women as *same* and *other* in classical Roman elite." *Helios* 16 (1989): 59–78.

Hallissy, Margaret. *Venomous Woman. Fear of the Female in Literature.* (New York, Westport, Connecticut, London: Greenwood Press, 1987).

Hamer, Mary. *Signs of Cleopatra. History, Politics, Representation.* (London and New York: Routledge, 1993).

Hampton, Timothy. *Writing from History. The Rhetoric of Exemplarity in Renaissance Literature.* (Ithaca and London: Cornell University Press, 1990).

Hansen, Elaine Tuttle. "The feminization of men in Chaucer's *Legend of Good Women*." In *Seeking the Woman in Late Medieval and Renaissance Writings. Essays in Feminist Contextual Criticism*, ed. Sheila Fisher and Janet E. Halley. 51–70. (Knoxville: The University of Tennessee Press, 1989).

Hardwick, Lorna. "Ancient Amazons—heroes, outsiders or women?" *Greece & Rome* 37 (1990): 14–36.

Harness, Kelley. "*La Flora* and the end of female rule in Tuscany." *Journal of the American Musicological Society* 51 (1998): 439–476.

Harvey, Elizabeth. *Ventriloquized Voices. Feminist Theory and English Renaissance Texts.* (London and New York: Routledge, 1992).

Haug, Walter and Wachinger, Burghart, ed. *Exempel und Esempelsammlungen.* (Tübingen: Niemeyer, 1991).

Hauvette, Henri. *Boccace. Etude biographique et littéraire.* (Paris: Armand Colin, 1914).

Heilbrun, Carolyn G. *Toward a Recognition of Androgyny.* (New York: Knopf, 1973).

——. *Writing a Woman's Life.* (New York: Ballantine, 1988).

Herlihy, David. "Women and the sources of medieval history. The towns of northern Italy." In *Medieval Women and the Sources of Medieval History*, ed. Joel T. Rosenthal. 133–154. (Athens and London: The University of Georgia Press, 1990).

Heullant-Donat, Isabelle. "Entrer dans l'histoire. Paolino da Venezia et les prologues de ses chroniques universelles." *Mélanges de l'Ecole Française de Rome. Moyen Age* 105 (1993): 381–442.

Hollander, Robert. *Boccaccio's Last Fiction 'Il Corbaccio'.* (Philadelphia: University of Pennsylvania Press, 1988).

Horowitz, Maryanne Cline. "Aristotle and woman." *Journal of the History of Biology* 9 (1976): 183–213.

——. "The woman question in Renaissance texts." *History of European Ideas* 8 (1987): 587–595.

Hortis, Attilio. *Studj sulle opere latine del Boccaccio con particolare riguardo alla storia della erudizione nel medio evo e alle letterature straniere. Aggiuntavi la bibliografia delle edizioni.* (Trieste: Libreria Julius Dase, 1879).

Hotchkiss, Valerie R. "Gender transgression and the abandoned wife in medieval literature." In *Gender Rhetorics. Postures of Dominance and Submission in History*, ed. Richard C. Trexler. 209–218. (Binghamton, New York: Center for Medieval & Early Renaissance Studies, 1994).

Hufton, Olwen. *The Prospect Before Her. A History of Women in Western Europe.* Vol. 1, 1500–1800. (London: HarperCollins, 1995).

Huot, Sylvia. "Poetic ambiguity and reader response in Boccaccio's *Amorosa visione*." *Modern Philology* 83 (1985–86): 109–22.

Hyde, Thomas. "Boccaccio: the genealogies of myth." *PMLA* 100 (1985): 737–45.

Imray, Linda and Middleton, Audrey. "Public and private: marking the boundaries." In *The Public and the Private*, ed. Eva Gamarnikow, David H.J. Morgan, June Purvis, and Daphne Taylorson. 12–27. (Hampshire: Gower, 1986).

Jamieson, Kathleen Hall. *Beyond the Double Bind. Women and Leadership* (New York: Oxford University Press, 1995).

Jeanroy, A. "Boccace, Christine de Pizan, le *De claris mulieribus*, principale source du *Livre de la cité des dames*." *Romania* 48 (1922): 93–105.

Joost-Gaugier, Christiane L. "Giotto's hero cycle in Naples: A prototype of 'Donne illustri' and a possible literary connection." *Zeitschrift fur kunstgeschichte* 43 (1980): 311–318.

———. "The early beginnings of the notion of 'uomini famosi' and the 'De viris illustribus' in Greco-Roman literary tradition." *Artibus et Historiae* 6 (1982): 97–115.

Jordan, Constance. "Feminism and the humanists: the case of Sir Thomas Elyot's *Defence of Good Women.*" In *Rewriting the Renaissance. The Discourses of Sexual Difference in Early Modern Europe,* ed. M.W. Ferguson *et. al.* (Chicago: Chicago University Press, 1986).

———. "Boccaccio's in-famous women: gender and civic virtue in the *De mulieribus claris.*" In *Ambiguous Realities. Women in the Middle Ages and Renaissance,* ed. Carole Levin and Jeanie Watson. 25–47. (Detroit: Wayne State University Press, 1987).

———. *Renaissance Feminism: Literary Texts and Political Models.* (Ithaca and London: Cornell University Press, 1990).

Joshel, Sandra R. "The body female and the body politic: Livy's Lucretia and Verginia." In *Pornography and Representation in Greece and Rome,* ed. Amy Richlin. 112–130. (New York: Oxford University Press, 1992).

Kallendorf, Craig. "Boccaccio's two Dido's." In *In Praise of Aeneas. Virgil and Epideictic Rhetoric in the Early Renaissance,* ed. Craig Kallendorf. 58–76. (Hanover and London: University Press of New England, 1989).

Kaufman, Michael W. "Spare ribs: The conception of woman in the Middle Ages and the Renaissance." *Soundings* 56 (1973): 139–63.

Kellogg, Judith L. "Christine de Pizan and Boccaccio: rewriting classical mythic tradition." In *Comparative Literature East and West: Traditions and Trends,* ed. Cornelia Moore and Raymond A. Moody. 124–131. (Honolulu: University of Hawaii Press, 1989).

Kelly, Joan. "Did women have a Renaissance?" In *Women, History & Theory. The Essays of Joan Kelly,* 19–50. (Chicago and London: Chicago University Press, 1984).

Kelso, Ruth. *Doctrine for the Lady of the Renaissance.* (Urbana: Illinois University Press, 1956).

Kennedy, Angus J. *Christine de Pizan: A Bibliographical Guide.* (London: Grant and Cutler, 1984).

Kieckhefer, Richard. *Unquiet Souls: Fourteenth-Century Saints and Their Religious Milieu.* (Chicago and London: The University of Chicago Press, 1984).

King, Margaret L. *Women of the Renaissance.* (Chicago and London: The University of Chicago Press, 1991).

Kinter, W., and Keller, J. *The Sibyl Prophetess of Antiquity and Medieval Fay.* (Philadelphia: Dorrance & Company, 1967).

Kirkham, Victoria. "A canon of women in Dante's *Commedia.*" *Annali d'Italianistica* 7 (1989): 16–41.

———. "The last tale in the *Decameron.*" *Mediaevalia* 12 (1989 [for 1986]): 205–223.

Kirkpatrick, Robin. "The Griselda story in Boccaccio, Petrarch and Chaucer." In *Chaucer and the Italian Trecento,* ed. Piero Boitani. 231–40. (Cambridge: Cambridge University Press, 1983)

Klapisch-Zuber, Christiane. "Le médiéviste, la femme et le sériel." In *Une histoire des femmes est-elle possible?* sous la direction de Michelle Perrot et à l'initiative d'Alain Paire. 38–47. (Marseilles: Rivages, 1984).

Klindienst Joplin, Patricia. "Ritual work on human flesh: Livy's Lucretia and the rape of the body politic." *Helios* 17 (1990): 51–70.

Koelsch, Patrice Clark. "Public and private: some implications for feminist literature and criticism." In *Gender, Ideology, and Action. Historical Perspectives on Women's Public Lives*, ed. Janet Sharistanian. 11–39. (Connecticut: Greenwood Press, 1986).

Kohl, Benjamin G. "Petrarch's prefaces to *De viris illustribus*." *History and Theory* 13 (1974): 132–44.

Kolsky, Stephen. "Wells of knowledge: Moderata Fonte's *Il merito delle donne*." *The Italianist* 13 (1993): 57–96.

———. "La costituzione di una nuova figura letteraria. Intorno al *De mulieribus claris* di Giovanni Boccaccio." *Testo* 25 (1993): 36–52.

———. "Donne gonzaghesche nella *Additione al libro delle donne illustri di Giuseppe Betussi* (1545)." *Civiltà mantovana* 33 (1998): 71–88.

Kristeller, Paul Oskar. "Learned women of early modern Italy: humanists and university scholars." In *Beyond Their Sex. Learned Women of the European Past*, ed. Patricia H. Labalme. 91–116. (New York and London: New York University Press, 1980).

Kuehn, Thomas. *Law, Family, & Women. Toward a Legal Anthropology of Renaissance Italy*. (Chicago and London: The University of Chicago Press, 1994).

La Courreye Blecki, Catherine. "An intertextual study of Volumnia: From legend to character in Shakespeare's *Coriolanus*." In *Privileging Gender in Early Modern England*, ed. J.R. Brink. 81–91. (Kirksville, Missouri: 16th Century Journal Publishers, 1993).

Laird, Judith. "Good women and *bonnes dames*: virtuous females in Chaucer and Christine de Pizan." *The Chaucer Review* 30 (1995): 58–70.

Le Goff, Jacques. "L'*exemplum* et la rhétorique de la prédication aux XIIIè et XIVè siècles." In *Retorica e poetica tra i secoli XII e XIV. Atti del secondo convegno internazionale di studi dell'Associazione per il Medioevo e l'Umanesimo Latini (AMUL) in onore e memoria di Ezio Franceschini*, ed. Claudio Menestò and Enrico Leonardi. 3–29. (Florence: La Nuova Italia, 1988).

Lecourt, Marcel. "Notice sur l'histoire des neuf preux et des neuf preues de Sébastien Mamerot." *Romania* 37 (1908): 529–37.

Leo, Friedrich. *Die griechisch-römische Biographie nach ihrer litterarischen Form*. (Leipzig: Teubner, 1901).

Léonard, E. G. "Acciaiuoli, Niccolò," *Dizionario biografico degli italiani*, vol. 1 (Rome: Istituto della Enciclopedia Italiana, 1960): 87–90.

Lerner, Gerda. *The Creation of Feminist Consciousness: From the Middle Ages to Eighteen-Seventy*. (Oxford: Oxford University Press, 1993).

Levenstein, Jessica. "Out of bounds: passion and the plague in Boccaccio's *Decameron*." *Italica* 73 (1996): 313–35.

Lindheim, Sara H. "Hercules cross-dressed, Hercules undressed: unmasking the construction of the Propertian *Amator* in Elegy 4.9." *American Journal of Philology* 119 (1998): 43–66.

Lipking, Lawrence. *Abandoned Women and Poetic Tradition*. (Chicago: University of Chicago Press, 1988).

Litchfield, Henry Wheatland. "National *exempla virtvtis* in Roman literature." *Harvard Studies in Classical Philology* 25 (1914): 1–53.

Lord, Mary Louise. "Dido as an example of chastity: The influence of example literature." *Harvard Library Bulletin* 17 (1969): 22–44, 216–32.

Lyons, John D. *The Rhetoric of Example in Early Modern France and Italy.* (Princeton, N.J.: Princeton University Press, 1989).

Maclean, Ian. *Woman Triumphant. Feminism in French Literature 1610–1652.* (Oxford: Clarendon, 1977).

———. *The Renaissance Notion of Woman. A Study in the Fortunes of Scholasticism and Medical Science in European Intellectual Life.* (Cambridge: Cambridge University Press, 1980).

Macrì-Leone, Francesco. "Il zibaldone boccaccesco della Magliabechiana." *Giornale storico della letteratura italiana* 10 (1887): 1–41.

Martellotti, Guido. "Momenti narrativi del Petrarca." *Studi petrarcheschi* 4 (1951): 7–33.

———. "Albanzani, Donato." In *Dizionario biografico degli Italiani*, 611–13. Vol. I. (Rome: Istituto della Enciclopedia Italiana, 1960).

———. "Storiografia del Petrarca." In *Convegno internazionale Francesco Petrarca*, 179–87. (Rome: Accademia Nazionale dei Lincei, 1976).

Marti, Mario. "Per una metalettura del *Corbaccio*: il ripudio di Fiammetta." *Giornale storico della letteratura italiana* 153 (1976): 60–86.

Matthews Grieco, Sara F. "Corpo, aspetto e sessualità." In *Storia delle donne in occidente dal Rinascimento all'età moderna*, ed. Arlette Farge & Natalie Zemon Davis. 53–99. Vol. 3. (Rome-Bari: Laterza, 1991).

Mayer, Thomas F. and D.R. Woolf, ed. *The Rhetorics of Life-Writing in Early Modern Europe. Forms of Biography From Cassandra Fedele to Louis XIV.* (Ann Arbor: The University of Michigan Press, 1995).

Mazza, Antonia. "L'inventario della 'parva libraria' di Santo Spirito e la biblioteca del Boccaccio." *Italia medioevale e umanistica* 9 (1966): 1–74.

McGinn, Bernard. "*Teste David cum Sibylla*: The significance of the Sibylline tradition in the Middle Ages." In *Women of the Medieval World: Essays in Honor of John F. Mundy*, ed. Julius Kirshner and Suzanne F. Wemple. 7–35. (Oxford: Blackwell, 1985).

McLaughlin, E.C. "Equality of souls, inequality of sexes: women in medieval theology." In *Religion and Sexism: Women in the Jewish and Christian Traditions*, ed. R.R. Reuther. 213–266. (New York: Simon and Schuster, 1974).

McLaughlin, Megan. "The woman warrior: gender, warfare and society in medieval Europe." *Women's Studies* 17 (1990): 193–209.

McLeod, Glenda. *Virtue and Venom. Catalogs of Women From Antiquity to the Renaissance.* (Ann Arbor: The University of Michigan Press, 1991).

———. "Poetics and antimisogynist polemics in Christine de Pizan's *Le livre de la Cité des Dames*." In *Reinterpreting Christine de Pizan*, ed. Earl Jeffrey Richards et. al. 37-47. (Athens and London: The University of Georgia Press, 1992).

McLeod, Glenda and Katharina Wilson. "A clerk in name only—A clerk in all but name. The misogamous tradition and *La cité des dames*." In *The City of Scholars. New Approaches to Christine de Pizan*, ed. Margarete Zimmermann and Dina De Rentiis. (Berlin and New York: Walter de Gruyter, 1994).

McLucas, John. "Amazon, sorceress, and queen: women and war in the aristocratic literature of sixteenth century Italy." *The Italianist* 8 (1988): 33–55.

McMillan, Ann. "Men's weapons, women's war: The nine female worthies, 1400–1640." *Mediaevalia* 5 (1979): 113–139.

McNamara, J.A. "Sexual equality and the cult of the Virgin in early Christian thought." *Feminist Studies* 3 (1976): 145–158.

Meale, Carol M. "Legends of good women in the European Middle Ages." *Archiv für das Studium der neueren Sprachen und Literaturen* 229 (1992): 55–70.

Mendelsohn, Leatrice. "Boccaccio, Betussi e Michelangelo: ritratti delle donne illustri come *Vite parallele*." In *Letteratura italiana e arti figurative. Atti del XII convegno dell'Associazione internazionale per gli studi di lingua e letteratura italiana (Toronto, Hamilton, Montreal, 6–10 maggio 1985)*, ed. Antonio Franceschetti, 323–34, (Florence: Olschki, 1985).

Mercati, Giovanni. "L'elogio di Eleonora Sanseverino principessa di Bisignano di Pietro Summonte." In *Ultimi contributi alla storia degli umanisti*, 110–19. Fascicolo II. (Città del Vaticano: Biblioteca Apostolica Vaticana, 1939).

Metz, René. "Le statut de la femme en droit canonique médiéval." In *La femme. Deuxième partie*, 59–113. (Brussels: Editions de la librairie encyclopédique, 1962).

Middleton, Anne. "The clerk and his tale: some literary contexts." *Studies in the Age of Chaucer* 2 (1980): 121–50.

Miglio, Massimo. "Biografia e raccolte biografiche nel Quattrocento italiano." *Atti della Accademia delle scienze dell'Istituto di Bologna classe di scienze morali. Rendiconti* 63 (1974–1975): 166–99.

———. "Boccaccio biografo." In *Boccaccio in Europe. Proceedings of the Boccaccio Conference, Louvain, December 1975*, ed. Gilbert Tournoy. 149-63. (Louvain: Leuven University Press, 1977).

———. "Biografia e raccolte biografiche nel Quattrocento italiano." In *Acta conventus neo-Latini amstelodamensis. Proceedings of the Second International Congress of Neo-Latin Studies, Amsterdam 19-24 August 1973*, ed. P. Tuynman, G.C. Kuiper, and E. Kessler. 775–85. (Munich: Wilhelm Fink, 1979).

Miles, Margaret R. *Carnal Knowing.* (Boston: Beacon Press, 1989).

Miller, Robert P. "The wounded heart: courtly love and the medieval antifeminist tradition." *Women's Studies* 2 (1974): 335–50.

Mingazzini, P. "Due pretese figure mitiche: Acca Larenzia e Flora." *Athenaeum* 25 (1947): 140–65.

Miola, Alfonso. "Le scritture in volgare dei primi tre secoli della lingua ricercate nei codici della Biblioteca nazionale di Napoli." *Il Propugnatore*, nuova serie, vol. 1 (1888): 131–133.

Momigliano, A. *The Development of Greek Biography.* (Cambridge, Mass.: Harvard University Press, 1993).

Monat, Pierre. "La polémique de Lactance contre Hercule. Tradition orientale et culture occidentale." *Annales littéraires de l'université de Besançon* (1984): 575–583.

Montagu, Ashley. *The Natural Superiority of Women.* (New York: Macmillan, 1953).

Monti, Carla Maria. "Testi ignoti di Donato Albanzani." *Studi petrarcheschi*, nuova serie, 2 (1985): 231–61.

Morse, Charlotte C. "The exemplary Griselda." *Studies in the Age of Chaucer* 7 (1985): 51–86.

Morse, Ruth. "Medieval biography: history as a branch of literature." *Modern Language Review* 80 (1985): 257–268.

Mulas, Luisa. "Funzioni degli esempi, funzione del *Cortegiano*." In *La corte e il "Cortegiano,"* vol. 1, *La scena del testo*, ed. Carlo Ossola. 97–117. (Rome: Bulzoni, 1980).

Müller, Ricarda. *Ein Frauenbuch des Frühen Humanismus Unterschungen Zu Boccaccios 'De mulieribus claris'.* (Stuttgart: Franz Steiner Verlag, 1992).

Mutini, C. "Betussi, Giuseppe." In *Dizionario biografico degli Italiani*, 779–781. Vol. IX. (Rome: Istituto della Enciclopedia Italiana, 1967).

Nadin Bassani, Lucia, *Il poligrafo veneto Giuseppe Betussi* (Padua: Antenore, 1992).

Newman, Barbara. "On the ethics of feminist historiography." *Exemplaria* 2 (1990): 702–706.

Novati, Francesco. "Donato degli Albanzani alla corte estense." *Archivio storico italiano*, serie V, 6 (1890): 365–85.

———. "Un cassone nuziale senese e le raffigurazioni delle donne illustri nell'arte italiana dei secoli XIV e XV." *Rassegna d'arte* 11 (1911): 61–67.

O'Brien, Dennis J. "Warrior queen: The character of Zenobia according to Giovanni Boccaccio, Christine de Pizan, and Sir Thomas Elyot." *Medieval Perspectives* 8 (1993): 53–68.

O'Faolain, Julia and Martines, Lauro. *Not in God's Image: Women in History from the Greeks to the Victorians.* (New York: Harper, 1973).

Olson, Glending. "Petrarch's view of the *Decameron*." *MLN* 91 (1976): 69–79.

———. *Literature as Recreation in the Later Middle Ages.* (Ithaca and London: Cornell University Press, 1982).

Ortner, Sherry B. "Is female to male as nature is to culture?" In *Woman, Culture and Society*, ed. Michelle Zimbalist Rosaldo and Louise Lamphere. 67–87. (Stanford, California: Stanford University Press, 1974).

Osgood, Charles G. *Boccaccio on Poetry* (Indianapolis: Bobbs, 1956; 1st ed. 1930)

Padoan, Giorgio. *L'ultima opera di Giovanni Boccaccio. Le 'Esposizioni sopra la "Comedia" di Dante'.* (Florence: Olschki, 1959).

———. *Il Boccaccio le muse il Parnaso e l'Arno.* (Florence: Olschki, 1978).

———. "Il *Corbaccio* tra spunti autobiografici e filtri letterari." *Revue des Etudes Italiennes* 37 (1991): 21–37.

Pagels, Elaine. *Adam, Eve, and the Serpent.* (New York: Random House, 1988).

Pastore Stocchi, Manlio. "Prospettiva del Boccaccio minore." *Cultura e scuola* 9 (1964): 29–38.

———. "Review of Giovanni Boccaccio, *De mulieribus claris*, a cura di Vittorio Zaccaria." *Studi sul Boccaccio* 6 (1971): 249–56.

———. "Il Boccaccio del *De casibus*." *Giornale storico della letteratura italiana* 161 (1984): 421–30.

Patrides, C.A. "'A palpable hieroglyphick': the fable of Pope Joan." In *Premises and Motifs in Renaissance Thought and Literature*, 152–81. (Princeton, New Jersey: Princeton University Press, 1982).

Paulmier, Monique. "Les *Flores* d'auteurs antiques et médiévaux dans le *Speculum historiale*." *'Spicae'. Cahiers de l'atelier Vincent de Beauvais* 1 (1978): 31–70.

———. "Les *flores* d'auteurs antiques et médiévaux dans le *Speculum historiale*—suite 1." *'Spicae'. Cahiers de l'atelier Vincent de Beauvais* 2 (1980): 9–16.

Paulmier-Foucart, Monique and Lusignan, Serge. "Vincent de Beauvais et l'histoire du *Speculum maius*." *Journal des savants* (1990): 97–124.

Pease, Arthur Stanley. "Things without honor." *Classical Philology* 21 (1926): 27–42.

Pereira, M. ed. *Né Eva né Maria. Condizione femminile e immagine della donna nel Medioevo.* (Bologna: Zanichelli, 1981).

Perret, Jaques. "Les compagnes de Didon aux enfers (*Aen.* 6. 445–449)." *Revue des études latines* 42 (1964): 247–261.

Pertusi, Agostino. *Leonzio Pilato fra Petrarca e Boccaccio. Le sue versioni omeriche negli autografi di Venezia e la cultura greca del primo umanesimo.* (Venice-Rome: Istituto per la collaborazione culturale, 1964).

Phillippy, Patricia A. "Establishing authority: Boccaccio's *De claris mulieribus* and Christine de Pizan's *Le livre de la cité des dames.*" *Romanic Review* 77 (1986): 167–93.

Piéjus, Marie-Françoise. "Index chronologique des ouvrages sur la femme publiés en Italie de 1471 à 1560." In *Images de la femme dans la littérature italienne de la Renaissance. Préjugés misogynes et aspirations nouvelles,* ed. Marie-Françoise Piéjus, José Guidi, Adelin-Charles Fiorato. 157–165. (Paris: Université de la Sorbonne Nouvelle, 1980).

Quaglio, Antonio Enzo. "Tra fonti e testo del *Filocolo.*" *Giornale storico della letteratura italiana* 140 (1963): 321–63, 489–551.

Quilligan, Maureen. *The Allegory of Female Authority. Christine de Pizan's 'Cité des dames'.* (Ithaca and London: Cornell University Press, 1991).

———. "Translating dismemberment: Boccaccio and Christine de Pizan." *Studi sul Boccaccio* 20 (1991-92): 253–66.

Rackin, Phyllis. "Historical difference/sexual difference." In *Privileging Gender in Early Modern England,* ed. Jean R. Brink. 37–63. (Kirksville, Missouri: Sixteenth Century Journal Publishers, 1993).

Raimondi, Ezio. "Review of *Un inedito petrarchesco. La redazione sconosciuta di un capitolo del 'Trionfo della Fama',* a cura di R. Weiss (Rome: Edizioni di storia e letteratura, 1950)." *Studi petrarcheschi* 3 (1950): 215–29.

Reno, Christine M. "Christine de Pisan's use of the *Golden Legend* in the *Cité des dames.*" *Les bonnes feuilles* 3 (1974): 89–98.

Ricci, Pier Giorgio. "Studi sulle opere latine e volgari del Boccaccio." *Rinascimento* 10 (1959): 3–32.

———. *Studi sulla vita e le opere del Boccaccio.* (Milan-Naples: Ricciardi, 1985).

Richards, Earl Jeffrey with Joan Williamson, Nadia Margolis, and Christine Reno, eds. *Reinterpreting Christine de Pizan.* (Athens and London: The University of Georgia Press, 1992).

Rinaldi Dufresne, Laura. "Women warriors: a special case from the fifteenth century: *The City of Ladies.*" *Women's Studies* 23 (1994): 111–31.

Robin, Diana. "Space, woman, and Renaissance discourse." In *Sex and Gender in Medieval and Renaissance Texts: The Latin Tradition,* ed. Barbara K. Gold, Paul Allen Miller and Charles Platter. 165–87. (Albany: The State University of New York Press, 1997).

Romano, Vincenzo. "Invenzione e fonti nella *Genealogia* del Boccaccio." *Studi e problemi di critica testuale* 2 (1971): 153–71.

Rosenthal, Elaine G. "The position of women in Renaissance Florence: neither autonomy nor subjection." In *Florence and Italy: Renaissance Studies in Honour of Nicolai Rubinstein,* ed. Peter Denley and Caroline Elam. 369–81. (London: Westfield College, University of London, 1988).

Rossi, Guido. "Statut juridique de la femme dans l'histoire." In *La femme. Deuxième partie,* 115–34. (Brussels: Editions de la librairie encyclopédique, 1962).

Sabatini, Francesco. *Napoli angioina. Cultura e società.* (Naples: Edizioni scientifiche italiane, 1975).

Salisbury, Joyce E. *Medieval Sexuality. A Research Guide.* (New York and London: Garland, 1990).

Samuel, Irene. "Semiramis in the Middle Ages: the history of a legend." *Medievalia et Humanistica* 2 (1944): 32–44.

Saxonhouse, A.W. *Women in the History of Political Thought*. (New York: Praeger, 1985).

Scarpati, Claudio. "Note sulla fortuna editoriale del Boccaccio. I volgarizzamenti cinquecenteschi delle opere latine." In *Boccaccio in Europe. Proceedings of the Boccaccio Conference, Louvain, December 1975*, ed. Gilbert Tournoy. 209–220. (Louvain: Leuven University Press, 1977).

Schibanoff, Susan. "Botticelli's *Madonna del Magnificat*: constructing the woman writer in early humanist Italy." *PMLA* 109 (1994): 190–206.

Schmidt, Paul Gerhard. "Hercules indutus vestibus Ioles." In *From Wolfram and Petrarch to Goethe and Grass. Studies in Literature in Honour of Leonard Forster*, ed. L.P. Johnson D.H. Green Dieter Wuttke. 103–107. (Baden-Baden: Valentin Koerner, 1982).

Schmidt, R. "'Aetates mundi'. Die weltalter als gliederungsprinzip der geschichte." *Zeitschrift für Kirchengeschichte* 67 (1955–1956), 306–308.

Schroeder, Horst. *Der Topos der 'Nine Worthies' in Literatur und Bildender Kunst*. (Gottingen: Vandenhoeck & Ruprecht, 1971).

Shemek, Deanna. "Of women, knights, arms, and love: The *Querelle des Femmes* in Ariosto's poem." *MLN* 104 (1989): 68–97.

Slerca, Anna. "Dante, Boccace, et le *Livre de la cité des dames* de Christine de Pizan." In *Une femme de lettres au moyen age. Etudes autour de Christine de Pizan*, ed. Liliane Dulac and Bernard Ribémont. 221–230. (Orléans: Paradigme, 1995).

Smarr, Janet Levarie. "Boccaccio and the choice of Hercules." *MLN* 92 (1977): 146–52.

———. *Boccaccio and Fiammetta. The Narrator as Lover*. (Urbana and Chicago: University of Illinois Press, 1986).

———. "Boccaccio and Renaissance women." *Studi sul Boccaccio* 20 (1991–92): 279–97.

Smith, Nicholas D. "Plato and Aristotle on the nature of women." *Journal of the History of Philosophy* 21 (1983): 467–478.

Smits, E.R. "Vincent of Beauvais: a note on the background of the *Speculum*." In *Vincent of Beauvais and Alexander the Great. Studies on the "Speculum maius" and its Translations*, 1–9. (Groningen: Egbert Forsten, 1986).

Snyder, Jane McIntosh. *The Woman and the Lyre. Women Writers in Classical Greece and Rome*. (Carbondale and Edwardsville: Southern Illinois University Press, 1989).

Sommerville, Margaret R. *Sex and Subjection. Attitudes to Women in Early Modern Society*. (London: Arnold, 1995).

Spisak, James W. "Chaucer's Pyramus and Thisbe." *The Chaucer Review* 18 (1984): 204–210.

Stecopoulos, Eleni with Uitti, Karl D. "Christine de Pizan's *Livre de la Cité des Dames*: the reconstruction of myth." In *Reinterpreting Christine de Pizan*, ed. Earl Jeffrey Richards with Joan Williamson Nadia Margolis, and Christine Reno. 48–62. (Athens and London: The University of Georgia Press, 1992).

Stella, A. "Le fonti del Boccaccio nella biografia di Irene." *Roma e l'Oriente* 9 (1915): 76–82.

Stierle, Karlheinz. "L'histoire comme exemple, l'exemple comme histoire. Contribution à la pragmatique et à la poétique des textes narratifs." *Poétique* 10 (1972): 176–98.

Taylor, Beverly. "The medieval Cleopatra: the classical and medieval tradition of Chaucer's 'Legend of Cleopatra'." *Journal of Medieval and Renaissance Studies* 7 (1977): 249–269.

Taylor, Steven M. "Martin Le Franc's rehabilitation of notorious women: the case of Pope Joan." *Fifteenth Century Studies* 19 (1992): 261–77.

Tescari, Onorato. "Per una vecchia querela a Virgilio e a Dante." *Convivium* 16 (1947): 116–30.

Tomas, Natalie. "Woman as helpmeet: The husband-wife relationship in Renaissance Florence." *Lilith: A Woman's History Journal* 3 (1986): 61–78.

Torretta, Laura. "Il *Liber de claris mulieribus* di Giovanni Boccaccio. Parte III. I traduttori del *Liber de claris mulieribus*." *Giornale storico della letteratura italiana* 40 (1902): 35–65, 57–60.

Tramontana, Salvatore. "Una fonte trecentesca nel 'De rebus siculis' di Tommaso Fazello e la battaglia di Lipari del 1339." *Bullettino dell'Istituto storico italiano per il medio evo e Archivio muratoriano* 74 (1962): 227–55.

Tuana, Nancy. *The Less Noble Sex. Scientific, Religious, and Philosophical Conceptions of Woman's Nature.* (Bloomington and Indianapolis: Indiana University Press, 1993).

Tyrrell, William Blake. *Amazons. A Study in Athenian Mythmaking.* (Baltimore and London: The Johns Hopkins University Press, 1984).

Ugurgieri della Berardenga, Curzio. *Gli Acciaioli di Firenze nella luce dei loro tempi (1160–1834)*, 2 vols. (Florence: Olschki, 1962).

———. *Avventurieri alla conquista di feudi e di corone (1356–1429)*. (Florence: Olschki, 1963).

Verdicchio, Massimo. "The rhetoric of enumeration in Petrarch's *Trionfi*." In *Petrarch's 'Triumphs'. Allegory and Spectacle*, ed. Konrad Eisenbichler and Amilcare A. Iannucci. 135–46. (Toronto: Dovehouse, 1990).

Warner, Marina. *Joan of Arc. The Image of Female Heroism.* (New York: Knopf, 1981).

Wayne, Valerie. "Zenobia in medieval and Renaissance literature." In *Ambiguous Realities: Women in the Middle Ages and Renaissance*, ed. Carole Levin and Jeanie Watson. 48–65. (Detroit: Wayne State University Press, 1987).

Westphal, Sarah. "Camilla: the Amazon body in medieval German literature." *Exemplaria* 8 (1996): 231–58.

Wiesner, Merry E. "Women's defense of their public roles." In *Women in the Middle Ages and Renaissance*, ed. Mary Beth Rose. 1–27. (New York: Syracuse University Press, 1986).

———. *Women and Gender in Early Modern Europe.* (Cambridge: Cambridge University Press, 1993; repr. 1995).

Wilkins, Ernest Hatch. "On the chronology of the *Triumphs*." In *Studies in the Life and Works of Petrarch*, 254–72. (Cambridge, Mass.: The Mediaeval Academy of America, 1955).

———. "Boccaccio's early tributes to Petrarch." *Speculum* 38 (1963): 79–87.

———. "A survey of the correspondence between Petrarch and Boccaccio." *Italia medioevale e umanistica* 6 (1963): 179–84.

———. *The Prose Letters of Petrarch.* (New York: S.F. Vanni, n.d.)

Willard, Charity Cannon. "The manuscript tradition of the *Livre des trois vertus* and Christine de Pizan's audience." *Journal of the History of Ideas* 27 (1966): 433–44.

Zaccaria, Vittorio. "Le fasi redazionali del *De mulieribus claris*." *Studi sul Boccaccio* 1 (1963): 253–332.

———. "Boccaccio e Tacito." In *Boccaccio in Europe. Proceedings of the Boccaccio Conference, Louvain, December 1975*, ed. Gilbert Tournoy. 221–37. (Louvain: Leuven University Press, 1977).

———. "La fortuna del *De mulieribus claris* del Boccaccio nel secolo XV: Giovanni Sabbadino degli Arienti, Iacopo Filippo Foresti e le loro biografie femminili (1490–1497)." In *Il Boccaccio nelle culture e letterature nazionali*, ed. Francesco Mazzoni. 519–45. (Florence: Olschki, 1978).

———. "I volgarizzamenti del Boccaccio latino a Venezia." In *Boccaccio Venezia e il Veneto*, ed. Vittore Branca e Giorgio Padoan. 131–52. (Florence: Olschki, 1979).

———. "Presenze del Petrarca nel Boccaccio latino." *Atti e memorie dell'Accademia patavina di scienze lettere ed arti. Memorie della classe di scienze morali lettere ed arti* 99 (1986–87): 245–66.

———. "Il genio narrativo nelle opere latine del Boccaccio." *Italianistica* Anno XXI (1992): 581–95.

Zancan, Marina. "La donna." In *Letteratura italiana*, ed. Alberto Asor Rosa. 765–827. Vol. 5. (Turin: Einaudi, 1986).

Zappacosta, Guglielmo—Zaccaria, Vittorio. "Per il testo del *De mulieribus claris*." *Studi sul Boccaccio* 7 (1973): 239–70.

Zonta, Giuseppe, "Note betussiane," *Giornale storico della letteratura italiana*, 52 (1908): 32–66.

.   .   .   .   .   .

Index

Studies in the Humanities

Edited by Guy Mermier

The Studies in the Humanities series welcomes manuscripts discussing various aspects of the humanities. The series' emphasis is on medieval and Renaissance literatures with a focus on Western civilizations and cultures. Submissions dealing with linguistics, history, politics, or sociology within the same time frame and geographical bounds are also encouraged. Manuscripts may be submitted in English, French, or Italian. The preferred style manual is the MLA Handbook (1995).

For additional information about this series or for the submission of manuscripts, please contact:

Dr. Heidi Burns
Peter Lang Publishing, Inc.
P.O. Box 1246
Bel Air, MD 21014-1246

To order other books in this series, please contact our Customer Service Department:

(800) 770-LANG (within the U.S.)
(212) 647-7706 (outside the U.S.)
(212) 647-7707 FAX

or browse online by series:

WWW.PETERLANGUSA.COM